SIR HALLEY STEWART TRUST: PUBLICATIONS

Volume 7

THE UNMARRIED MOTHER AND HER CHILD

THE UNMARRIED MOTHER AND HER CHILD

VIRGINIA WIMPERIS

Edited by
CLIFFORD WITTING

LONDON AND NEW YORK

First published in 1960 by George Allen & Unwin, Ltd.

This edition first published in 2025
by Routledge
4 Park Square, Milton Park, Abingdon, Oxon OX14 4RN

and by Routledge
605 Third Avenue, New York, NY 10158

Routledge is an imprint of the Taylor & Francis Group, an informa business

© 1960 George Allen & Unwin Ltd.

All rights reserved. No part of this book may be reprinted or reproduced or utilised in any form or by any electronic, mechanical, or other means, now known or hereafter invented, including photocopying and recording, or in any information storage or retrieval system, without permission in writing from the publishers.

Trademark notice: Product or corporate names may be trademarks or registered trademarks, and are used only for identification and explanation without intent to infringe.

British Library Cataloguing in Publication Data
A catalogue record for this book is available from the British Library

ISBN: 978-1-032-88962-7 (Set)
ISBN: 978-1-032-80660-0 (Volume 7) (hbk)
ISBN: 978-1-032-80701-0 (Volume 7) (pbk)
ISBN: 978-1-003-49817-9 (Volume 7) (ebk)

DOI: 10.4324/9781003498179

Publisher's Note
The publisher has gone to great lengths to ensure the quality of this reprint but points out that some imperfections in the original copies may be apparent.

Disclaimer
The publisher has made every effort to trace copyright holders and would welcome correspondence from those they have been unable to trace.

This book is a re-issue originally published in 1960. The language used and views portrayed are a reflection of its era and no offence is meant by the Publishers to any reader by this re-publication.

The Unmarried Mother and Her Child

VIRGINIA WIMPERIS
M.A. (CANTAB.)

Edited by Clifford Witting

PUBLISHED FOR
THE SIR HALLEY STEWART TRUST

GEORGE ALLEN & UNWIN LTD
LONDON

FIRST PUBLISHED IN 1960

This book is copyright under the Berne Convention. Apart from any fair dealing for the purpose of private study, research, criticism or review, as permitted under the Copyright Act, 1956, no portion may be reproduced by any process without written permission. Enquiries should be addressed to the Publishers

© *George Allen & Unwin Ltd.*, 1960

*Printed in Great Britain
in 11 on 12 pt. Imprint type
by East Midland Printing Company Limited
Bury St. Edmunds, Peterborough, Kettering
and elsewhere*

AUTHOR'S NOTE

The English studies of which this book is mainly composed were made at a variety of dates from 1950 to 1958. Most of the chapters were rechecked by experts between 1958 and 1960. Where practicable, information has been brought up to date to 1960, but the reader will understand that, covering so large a scope, it was impossible to keep every aspect fully up to date. The coming into operation of the Legitimacy Act, 1959, when the book was already in the press, gave rise to considerable emendation.

Material relating to other countries was last checked and brought up to date in the summer of 1958. That final check included Eastern Germany and the U.S.S.R., but not references to the other People's Republics in Europe. Information about the latter, collected between 1951 and 1953, was at best fragmentary and, in the absence of information as to how their laws are administered in practice, its value limited.

In writing of the services for unmarried mothers and their children in overseas or foreign countries, I have deliberately concentrated upon aspects of their work that throw a useful light upon contemporary English problems and have, of course, nowhere attempted to give a complete picture of any other country's services in this field.

I was able, to my regret, to include very little about either the United States or countries of the Commonwealth overseas, except to a small extent Canada, since this would have required a knowledge of the legal and administrative background of individual States and Provinces that I do not possess. Scotland too is only touched upon lightly: it is very competent to write its own book!

I shall be happy if these limitations provoke research workers, here or in other countries, to write their own deeper and more complete studies of any attempts that have been made to solve this complex human problem.

Cambridge   VIRGINIA WIMPERIS
May 1960

ACKNOWLEDGMENTS

This book, that took ten years in the making, appears under my name but represents the work of many people. I hope that all who gave their help will think of it as partly their book. I can name only a few. Parents and children who have helped must remain anonymous and so, for their sake—and to my regret—must most of the social workers. Help from Government departments, local authorities, voluntary organizations and social workers all over the world was, in any case, so extensive that I can name only a few of those to whom I am most indebted.

The chief person who made this book possible is Miss Valerie Hughes, who made it a most generous gift of her own research studies. As a student of the London School of Economics and Political Science, she designed and carried out, with the encouragement of Professor Glass, the first sociological study in this country of the parents of illegitimate children. It forms the core of chapter 2 and is a keystone of this book. She later began a study of the psychology of unmarried mothers by means of a survey of women entering Mother and Baby Homes. Many mothers, and matrons of Homes and other social workers, responded generously, but the sample proved too incomplete to fulfil its original purpose. It has instead proved to be a gold-mine regarding the attitudes, experiences and economic position of a group mainly of younger mothers, and as such I have gratefully drawn upon it. She and I would like to take this opportunity of thanking all those who made these studies possible. We both received much help and kindness from those at 'Midboro', from Miss Steel of the Church of England Moral Welfare Council and—as one always does—from the National Council for the Unmarried Mother and Her Child.

A welcome gift of research material came from the Rev. Egerton Ryerson, who handed on to me his collection of the bastardy laws of other countries and so saved months of preliminary work.

The book had at moments several co-authors. Two mothers record their own views and experiences in chapter 9. My sister, Barbara Watson, who acted as midwife to much of the book, helped to write several of the key chapters. For a while we worked together and later, with sisterly equanimity, she would take over a chapter when I felt stuck and hand it back partly or wholly rewritten when I felt able to tackle it again. The pleasant result was, of course, that she tended to write the difficult bits: such as the early pages of chapter 4. She has contributed to the book an eloquent presentation of one Christian vision of personal relationships; I do not share her faith, or her gift for writing, but because of the outstanding value of those pages, I risk appearing inconsistent—to use no stronger word—and welcome their inclusion. The reader will find other passages in the book in a maturer style than my own.

The editor, Mr Clifford Witting, next brought male logic to bear on the book and rearranged much of the material. The book owes a great deal to his skilled and meticulous work, and I am especially grateful to him for his help with the introduction, his careful internal check of the figures, and for the completion and simplifying of certain chapters. He also improved the tables, made the index and—with much kind help from Mrs Witting—saw the book through the press.

A disconcerting number of changes took place in the English law while the book was in the press. With very great kindness, Mr G. S. Wilkinson, Clerk to the Justices at Cambridge and expert in this field, has rewritten a number of pages in chapter 6 to bring them up to date. I was unwell at the time and am especially grateful to him.

I would like to thank those who first sponsored my research and those who gave it their financial backing. Professor W. J. M. Mackenzie of the then Department of Government and Social Administration of the University of Manchester, in which I was an assistant from 1950 to 1952, gave me the opportunity to begin the work, and I owe much to him and to Mrs Rodgers of that Department for their encouragement and advice. Professor Titmuss, Professor Mackenzie and the National Council for the Unmarried Mother and Her Child then most kindly acted as my sponsors with the Sir Halley Stewart Trust, who made me a generous grant to continue this work on a full-time basis for several years. I am grateful to the Trustees for the freedom and support they gave me, and also for their patience and generosity when my work was delayed by several spells of ill-health.

I have at all stages had—and valued—the encouragement and help of the National Council for the Unmarried Mother and Her

Child, and want especially to thank Dr Winner, Miss Puxley, Dr Letitia Fairfield, Mr Schapiro and Miss Granger.

Two Moral Welfare Committees gave me the valued opportunity of short periods of work among unmarried mothers; many Mother and Baby Homes and Hostels kindly let me visit them; Devon County Children's Committee allowed me to make the study described in chapter 12; and for access to other materials of various kinds I should like to thank Mr George Mitchell, Dr E. K. Macdonald and Miss M. Walters.

In 1954 I made brief visits to Norway, Sweden and Denmark, and have happy memories of the kindness and generous help given by officials and social workers in those countries. They will be quick to appreciate that on the basis of such short visits I could do no more in this book than pick out elements in their services of particular interest to us here. Among many who generously helped me both then and later I must mention Mrs Elsa Wollmer of the Swedish Royal Social Board; Mr Jørgen Dahl, Bailiff of Alimony in Oslo, and the members of the International Division of the Ministry of Social Affairs in Copenhagen.

My grateful thanks are due to all those who have supplied me with facts and figures, or who have allowed me to quote from their works, published and unpublished. Wherever possible, sources are mentioned in the text or footnotes, while in the bibliography all books and other writings referred to or quoted in the body of the book are marked by asterisks.

Among those who have already published studies in this field, I am particularly grateful to Mr Cyril Greenland. Too little mention of his work is made in this book, since most of it was drafted before I had read his work, but it has been encouraging to discover how very closely our findings bear one another out.

I am indebted to those who read the book or sections of it in manuscript and made suggestions and emendations, especially to Dr D. H. Stott, Dr Letitia Fairfield, Mr Kenneth Brill, Mr L. Schapiro, Dr E. K. Macdonald, Miss Margaret Kornitzer, Professor Hans Binder, Mrs Elsa Wollmer, Mr Jørgen Dahl, the Danish Ministry of Social Affairs, Dr Rudolf Schlesinger and the editor of *Neue Justiz*. Neither they nor anyone else I have mentioned here is, of course, responsible for anything I have said in this book.

Finally I would like to thank several personal friends who did much in different ways to make the writing of the book possible;

ACKNOWLEDGMENTS

Rosemary Smith, Rosaleen Cooper, my brother-in-law John Watson, and the two to whom this book is affectionately dedicated.

V.W.

*for a ten-year-old
and his mother*

PREFACE

This has been described as the 'children's century', but will the social historian of A.D. 2000 substantiate that claim? Looking back to 1950, when half the century had run its course, what sort of picture will he build up?

He will find that the culture of the non-Communist countries of Europe was nominally Christian, both Church and State standing for the courageous principle of faithful lifelong monogamous marriage, with a fairly complex structure of laws and moral and social sanctions to maintain it. None the less, he will find that, of the 5,000,000 children born in those countries during that year, close on 318,000 were recorded as illegitimate. He will find that in England and Wales, with a total of 35,250 illegitimate births, every twentieth child was born illegitimate, every eighth was conceived outside marriage, every fourth mother conceived her first-born before her wedding-day; that among the children below school-leaving age over half a million were illegitimate; that there were tens of thousands of 'unofficial families', children growing up with parents cohabiting without marriage, and tens of thousands too of women whose pregnancies were illegally terminated, many of the unmarried ones resorting to abortion for fear that if they had their child they would be ostracized and treated with contempt.

He will find—and may well ponder on the fact—that although in the previous fifty years immense changes had taken place in the attitude to the rights of children, and although social legislation had benefited all children, whether legitimate or not, the laws governing the status, custody and maintenance of the natural child had remained unaltered in fundamentals since the Bastardy Laws Amendment Act of 1872, 'drawn up in an entirely different mental climate from our own'.[1] Certainly there was nothing to prevent a gifted natural child from rising to the highest position in the land (Ramsay MacDonald was the illegitimate son of a Scottish crofter's daughter), yet the laws of affiliation and bastardy left a rankling sense of injustice with many children and showed, like straws in the wind, the severe spirit that still underlay those enactments.

[1] Dr Ivy Pinchbeck makes these points in *Social Attitudes to the Problem of Illegitimacy* (*British Journal of Sociology*, December 1954).

He will find too that, despite the great advances in child care, the average health of illegitimate children was still below normal and large numbers of them were dying in infancy (1,400 in 1950, most of them before they were a month old, a third of them on the day of their birth). A proportion of those who survived passed from hand to hand unwanted, and ended in public care, thereby facing the Children's Departments with the largest single problem with which they had to deal.

Many of these children were growing up disturbed; they crowded the juvenile courts and Child Guidance Clinics. Others, less obviously maladjusted, were growing up with an unsatisfied need for stable and affectionate relationships, for the wise love of parents, for the reasonably secure and thoroughly happy childhood that a good parent wishes to provide, for the affectionate, intelligent support of society and friends, from day to day and in times of special strain—a need so little met that they were not able to make satisfactory friendships or become in their turn good husbands, wives or parents. In spirit, as in law, society seemed to be disinheriting them. They were *filii nullius*—nobody's children.

Although it was widely admitted that their need was acute, there was in 1950 extremely little curiosity about their position as a whole. Practically nothing was known about their fate and development as a group. Precise information of any kind was hard to come by. Social workers were too busy to undertake research, and the general public was relatively indifferent to the problem— except that it had very strong moral feelings, which perhaps inhibited both its desire to know and its will to help. That the children's—and parents'—existence faced the nation with a great and urgent challenge to generosity was little understood.

The large number of illegitimate children born during World War II had, indeed, begun to force this problem into the daylight. It threw a formidable burden of practical problems on social workers and public servants, and many of them were eager for reforms. But it was very difficult to see how to redesign the present services in the absence of precise knowledge about what was happening to the children—or even about the parents; nor, while the public remained indifferent, was it at all easy to see how reforms could be pressed through.

This was broadly the position in 1950. The social historian of A.D. 2000 might note that, as 1960 approached, things had improved a little: that is to say, many more persons in responsible positions were growing uneasy about their own ignorance, and there was a real, if limited, movement to discover the facts. Several local authorities and other bodies and individuals were undertaking research into the early years at least of the children's lives. The change may have been due partly to a natural growth of interest in so large a problem, but it also owed something to a skilful challenge to research thrown out in 1952 by Dr John Bowlby in a report for the World Health Organization.[1] The position he took up on several issues in his book was by no means welcomed by social workers, but it left them admirably uneasy at their own ignorance, since they were unable to confute his contentions without undertaking research themselves. He therefore won without difficulty the case for research.

One impediment to research and constructive thought over recent years has been the absence of any book in which is assembled and discussed the little that is so far known about who have illegitimate children, what happens to the children as they grow up, or the measures taken to help them in this and other countries. Many of the facts have lain hidden in the records of Moral Welfare workers, the courts and Children's Departments, or other unpublished or unpublishable sources. A few have been set out in a handful of articles in learned periodicals here and abroad, or in books perhaps written in other languages.

This book is therefore a first attempt to set together some of this material. We hope that it will be of help to the public and to research workers, and also even to social workers whose knowledge, within their own fields, is so much greater than our own. Thus it may open the way to further research, discussion and action.

[1] John Bowlby, *Maternal Care and Mental Health* (1952).

CONTENTS

PREFACE   *page* 11

PART I
THE SCOPE OF THE PROBLEM

1. THE INCIDENCE OF ILLEGITIMACY
   Numbers and Rates in Europe, 1957—A Rising Rate in a Changing or Unstable Society—No Simple Pattern—Comparison of the Rates in Different Parts of the World—Attempts to Explain Variations in Rates   21

2. WHO HAVE ILLEGITIMATE CHILDREN?
   The Midboro Survey—Age of Parents—Length of Relationship—Social Level—Mental Level—Home Environment—Marital Status of Parents—Those Who Were Free to Marry but Did Not—Unofficial Families—The Child's Place in the Family—The Deeper Question   51

3. THE PREGNANT BRIDE
   Pre-Marital Conceptions—Ages of the Mothers—'Forced' Marriages—The Incidence of Pre-Marital Conceptions   76

4. THE HUMAN BACKGROUND
   Western and Christian Marriage—The Social Group—The Family—Difficulties of Psychological Study—The Emotionally Disturbed—A Swiss Study—Studies of the Fathers   85

PART II
HELP FOR THE MOTHER AND CHILD

5. THE MOTHER'S STRUGGLE
   The Unwelcome Lodger—Earning Capacity—Danish and Canadian Studies—Prostitution   113

6. THE FATHER'S CONTRIBUTION
   His Responsibilities Towards the Child—The Mother's Only Claim upon Him—Why Do So Few Women Apply for Affiliation Orders?—The Case for Special Courts and Private Agreements—Applying for an Order—The Hearing—Proof of Paternity—Payment under Affiliation Orders—The Problem of Arrears   122

7. THE STATE'S CONTRIBUTION
   National Insurance—National Assistance   157

CONTENTS

8. **THE LOCAL AUTHORITIES' AND VOLUNTARY SOCIETIES' CONTRIBUTION**
Arousing Public Interest—Statutory Duties of Local Authorities—The Voluntary Societies—Case-Work Among Unmarried Mothers—Institutions and Homes Run by Local Authorities—Mother and Baby Homes Run by Voluntary Societies—Statutory and Voluntary Homes Compared—When the Mother Leaves the Home—The Provision of Hostels—Flatlets for Unmarried Mothers—Vocational Training—Foster Grants—Help Given by Other Voluntary Societies—After-Care Among Unmarried Mothers   176

9. **TWO MOTHERS TELL THEIR STORIES**
Sandra's Mother—Ian's Mother   211

PART III
CITIZENS OF THE FUTURE

10. **THE INFLUENCE OF SOCIAL POLICIES ON THE CHILDREN'S FATE**
The Old-Fashioned Punitive Attitude—The Policy of Helping Mother and Child to Remain Together—Effect of the Divorce Laws—Possibility of Adoption   233

11. **WHAT HAPPENS TO THE CHILDREN AS THEY GROW UP?**
Follow-Up Surveys—Death in Infancy—Children Whose Mothers Marry After Their Birth—Children of Unofficial Families—When the Father Seeks Custody—Children Brought up in the Grandparents' Home—Children Living with Solitary Mothers—Children Placed with Foster-Parents—Children in the Care of the Voluntary Societies—Children Who Are Adopted—Coloured Children—Children of Mentally Defective Mothers   243

12. **CHILDREN IN PUBLIC CARE**
A General Survey—Reasons Why Children Come into Care   277

13. **THE CHILDREN'S DEVELOPMENT**
The Home Background—Illegitimacy as a Cause of Juvenile Delinquency—Effects on Child of Mother's Disturbed Pregnancy—Some Clinical Studies—A Canadian Study of Teen-Age Children—A Challenge to Research   295

CONTENTS 17

PART IV
THE DEVELOPMENT OF A NEW APPROACH

14. LEGISLATIVE REFORMS IN OTHER COUNTRIES
    The French Inheritance Law and Its Aftermath—A New Philosophy in Scandinavia: The Castberg Laws—The Place of a Natural Child in a Communist Society   313

15. THE STATE AS GUARDIAN
    The German Scheme—Scandinavian Schemes   333

PART V
THE SUMMING UP

16. SOME QUESTIONS AND CONCLUSIONS
    Why Is the Illegitimacy Rate So High?—How Can the Rate Be Reduced?—Wise Treatment of Mother and Child   343

BIBLIOGRAPHY   353

PRINCIPAL TABLES IN TEXT
    Countries of Europe: numbers and percentage of all live births as registered, 1957   21
    Certain Counties and Boroughs of England and Wales: natural children in public care, 1953   280

TABLES IN APPENDIX
   1. *Countries of the World:* illegitimate percentage of all live births as registered, 1876-1950
   2a. *Countries of Europe:* illegitimate percentage of all live births as registered, 1900, 1938-57
    b. *Countries outside Europe:* illegitimate percentage of all live births as registered, 1900, 1933, 1938-57
   3. *Towns of the World:* illegitimate percentage of all live births as registered, 1880, 1900, 1950
   4. *England and Wales:* illegitimate percentage of all live births as registered, 1842-1958
   5. *England and Wales:* numbers of illegitimate births, 1851-1958
   6. *Counties of England and Wales:* illegitimate percentage of all live births as registered, 1842, 1850, 1900, 1938, 1945, 1950, 1957
   7. *Towns of England and Wales:* illegitimate percentage of all live births as registered, 1950, 1957
   8a. *London:* illegitimate percentage of all live births as registered, 1842, 1900
    b. *London:* illegitimate percentage of all live births as registered, 1938, 1950, 1957
   9a. *England and Wales:* ages of mothers of illegitimate and legitimate children, 1950

b. *England and Wales:* ages of mothers at illegitimate and legitimate maternities, 1957
10. *England and Wales:* illegitimate and pre-maritally conceived legitimate maternities, 1938-56
11. *England and Wales:* the first-born child of marriage, 1938-57
12. *England and Wales:* percentage of maternities irregularly conceived among mothers of different ages, 1950
13. *England and Wales:* age distribution of mothers, 1950
14. *Standard Regions of England and Wales:* children conceived out of marriage, 1950
15. *England and Wales:* ages of illegitimate children at adoption and who adopted them, 1950, 1957

Map of England and Wales showing the illegitimate percentage of live births, 1900	25
Map of England and Wales showing the illegitimate percentage of live births, 1945	26
Map of England and Wales showing the illegitimate percentage of live births, 1950	27
Graph showing the effect of World War II on the illegitimacy rates in belligerent and neutral countries	28
Map of Europe showing the illegitimate percentage of live births, 1938	32
Map of Europe showing the illegitimate percentage of live births, 1950	33

INDEX 389

PART I
THE SCOPE OF THE PROBLEM

CHAPTER I

THE INCIDENCE OF ILLEGITIMACY

NUMBERS AND RATES IN EUROPE, 1957

Every year more than a quarter of a million children in Western Europe are born illegitimate.

In 1957, 270,473 among more than five million children born in the non-Communist countries were recorded as illegitimate, or five out of every hundred; nearly 40,000 of them in the British Isles and over 230,000 on the Continent.

These are the figures officially quoted by each country:

	ILLEGITIMATE LIVE BIRTHS 1957	% OF ALL LIVE BIRTHS 1957
Western Germany	61,339	7.7
France	50,142	6.2
England and Wales	34,562	4.8
Italy	24,711	2.8
Portugal	22,297	10.5
Spain	20,919	3.8
Austria	15,785	13.3
Sweden	10,850	10.1
Denmark	5,229	6.9
Scotland	4,017	4.1
Finland	3,749	4.3
Switzerland	3,475	3.8
Belgium	3,047	2.0
Netherlands	2,911	1.2
Greece	2,360	1.5
Norway	2,225	3.5
Iceland[1]	1,192	24.9
Eire	1,032	1.7
Northern Ireland	731	2.4

[1] Still births included.

These figures are small compared with the vast tide of illegitimate births that accompanied the Second World War, but they are disquieting enough and contain one most disturbing feature: for ten years after the war, the numbers were dropping over Europe but now, in many of the northern countries, they are rising again—in Scandinavia, Switzerland, Western Germany, England and Wales. A parallel rise is taking place in the United States, Australia, New Zealand, South Africa and Canada.

The change is most marked in our own country. In 1955, there were 31,145 recorded illegitimate births in England and Wales. The tide turned in the following year, and in 1958, the latest year for which figures are available, there were 36,174 illegitimate births—a figure higher by some 10,000 than in 1938.

What, then, lies ahead? Are we to expect a continuing increase in this, one of the most intractable of post-war problems?

A RISING RATE IN A CHANGING OR UNSTABLE SOCIETY

Nation-wide figures of illegitimate births were not kept in England until 1842, but a study of parish registers suggests that between the years 1600 and 1800 they increased something like sevenfold. The figures for *Letheringham* in Suffolk can be taken as fairly typical of the trend all over the country.[1]

	REGISTERED AS ILLEGITIMATE	%
1600-1650	1 birth in 144	0.7
1650-1700	1 birth in 74	1.4
1700-1750	1 birth in 33	3.0
1750-1800	1 birth in 21	4.8

In 1842, when the national rate (that is, the rate expressed in terms of the relationship between illegitimate and total live births) was calculated for the first time in England and Wales, it was 6.7 per cent; in 1845 it stood at 7 per cent—one child in every fourteen. Whether this was the highest figure England and Wales had ever experienced one cannot say, but this rising rate certainly showed some correspondence with the change from an agricultural population, living in scattered groups, cut off from each other by

---

[1] Mary Hopkirk, *Nobody Wanted Sam*, p. 83. (1949), a brilliant account of the mishandling of illegitimate children down the ages.

THE INCIDENCE OF ILLEGITIMACY

difficulties of transport, to an industrial population living largely in the towns and with the increased means of communication provided by new roads and canals. With labourers pouring into the new centres of employment and young women thronging to the mills, the balance of population was upset in both town and country, the moral sanctions of the little rural communities were weakened, and the births of 'bastard children' were recorded in increasing numbers.

'In most countries', writes Professor Crew, 'a rising illegitimacy rate is one of the most significant indices of the social changes associated with industrialization.'[1]

Alva Myrdal writes in her study of the problem in *Sweden:* 'In the course of social development, industrialization set in. Its effect did not come primarily through a shift in mores, but through increased mobility ... The migrant labourers, and foremost among them the navvies, the industrial workers and the commercial travellers, did not have the same respect for the girls as the local men, implying either abstinence from sexual intercourse or birth control through *coitus interruptus* or finally marriage. And the girls did not have at their disposal the impact of the whole society to force the men into marriage, if relations resulted in issue ... Migration itself thus led to the virtue of daughters becoming a social problem. Illegitimacy, not resulting in subsequent marriage, rose.'[2]

From 1845 the rate fell steadily (see Table 4) until early in the present century. The lowest recorded point, 3.9 per cent, was reached in 1901 and again in 1902, 1903 and 1907. In 1914 it was 4.2 per cent, 2.8 per cent less than in 1845, and it might have fallen still farther had not World War I interrupted the downward trend by again creating conditions favouring illegitimacy: a highly mobile population, with lovers separated and women in touch, to a much greater extent than usual, with men not members of their own social circle. The rate rose in 1915 to 4.4 per cent, comparable with 1890, and by 1918 had reached a new peak of 6.3 per cent, the highest since 1864. After 1919 (6 per cent) the wave quickly subsided and by 1925 the proportion of ex-nuptial births—4.1 per cent—was less than in 1914 and only 0.2 per cent above the lowest rate ever recorded.

[1] F. A. E. Crew, *Measurements of the Public Health*, p. 66 (1948).
[2] Alva Myrdal, *Nation and Family*, p. 44 (1945).

From 1920 to 1938 the average rate was below 4.4 per cent. In 1938 and 1939 it was 4.2; in 1940 it was 4.3; then, with the beginning of active operations, it rose far more rapidly than in World War I, in a vast tidal wave—5.4 in 1941, 5.6 in 1942, 6.4 in 1943, 7.3 in 1944, reaching its peak in 1945 with the record-breaking figure of 9.3 per cent. In that year every eleventh mother in England and Wales gave birth to her child outside marriage, a result of 'the general loosening of social restraints and compulsions in time of war, the easier avoidance of responsibility brought about by a slackening in conventional ties formerly imposed by the families concerned, by friends and by neighbours'.[1] Since then we have been slowly recovering from the effects of war, and in the mid-1950's the illegitimacy rate stood at 4.8 per cent as in the 1880's. Now it is again rising.

That there is a very close association between illegitimacy and the movements of population that takes place in war-time is clear from the maps on the following pages. In the nineteenth century and the early part of the twentieth, illegitimacy had been but a small problem in the counties south of the Thames; its centre lay in the north of England. But the troop movements in World Wars I and II created a wholly new situation. Where there had been stable communities, there was now a constant flux. For the time being illegitimacy moved south. In a rather similar way the graph on page 28 shows the rates during World War II rising in the belligerent countries and remaining unchanged, or falling, in neutral countries.[2] Possibly if a similar graph could be made of the rates in *Greece* and *Spain* during the civil wars, one might find the same increase had taken place, but no statistics could be kept in those disturbed times, nor are there any for *Israel* showing the rates during the recent great influx of population.

In *Western Germany*, however, one can see a striking proof of the devastating consequences of large-scale movements of population. Under Hitler the illegitimacy rate was about 7.8 per cent;[3] in 1946, after the displaced persons poured in, it soared to 16.5 per cent, the highest rate Germany has ever recorded. With a partial solution of the D.P. problem it fell to 9.6 per cent by 1950, but even in that

---

[1] Hilde Fitzgerald, *Illegitimacy and War*, chapters 3 and 4, p. 92. *History of the Second World War: Studies in the Social Services* (1954).
[2] Tables 1 and 2 also apply.
[3] Average for 1936-40.

ENGLAND AND WALES

Illegitimate Percentage of Live Births, 1900
National Rate: 4.0 per cent

ENGLAND AND WALES

Illegitimate Percentage of Live Births, 1945
National rate: 9.3 per cent

ENGLAND AND WALES

Illegitimate Percentage of Live Births, 1950
National rate: 5.1 per cent

THE EFFECT OF WAR UPON THE ILLEGITIMACY RATE

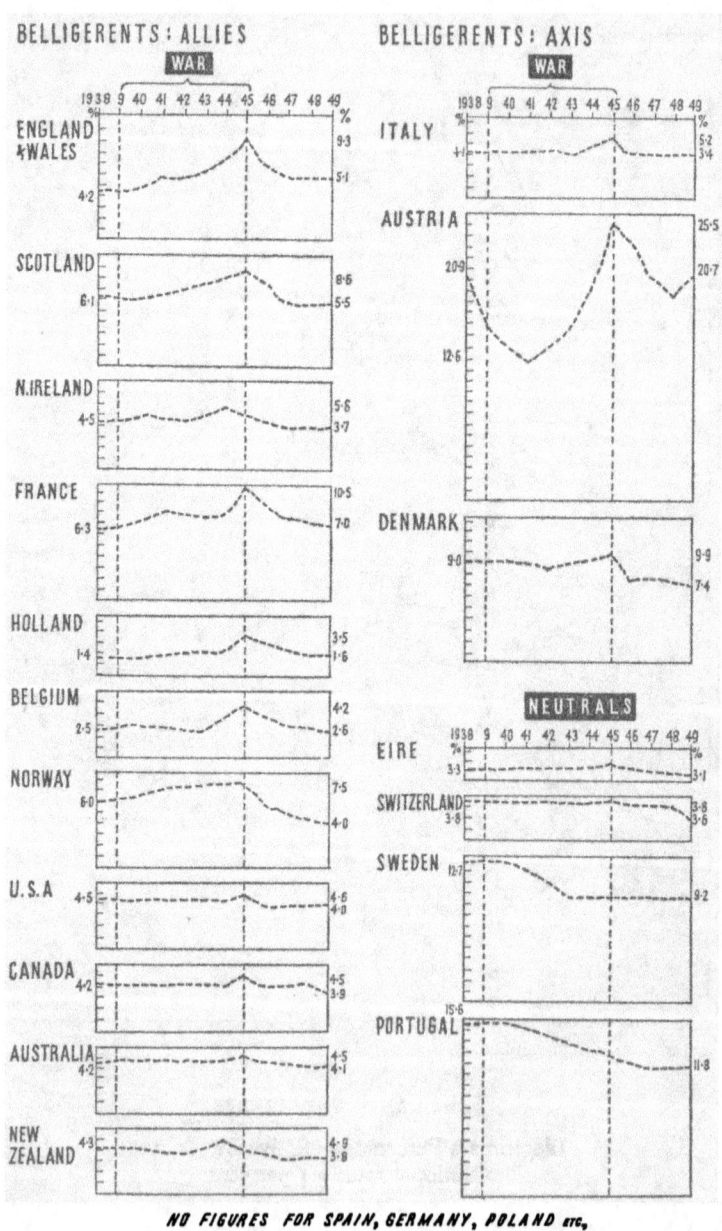

NO FIGURES FOR SPAIN, GERMANY, POLAND etc.,

year 75,000 children were born outside marriage in Western Germany.

On 15th March 1958 it was noted in the *Manchester Guardian* that a German medical journal had reported that British, French and American servicemen had left in Western Germany 67,753 illegitimate children, born between 1945 and 1955, of whom 53 per cent had American fathers, 15 per cent French and 12.6 British; over 4,500 were children of coloured men.

According to figures quoted by Mrs Frances P. Bolton in the U.S. House of Representatives on 6th July 1954, American servicemen are said to have fathered 70,000 illegitimate children in *Great Britain* and 100,000 in *Japan*; and the Russians are reported to have 'called home' from Germany to Russia 29,000 illegitimate children of Red Army soldiers.

These figures take no account of the tens of thousands of children fathered by Germans and other nationals of the Axis Powers during the occupation of various European States.

NO SIMPLE PATTERN

The pattern for *England and Wales*—a rising figure from about 1600 to the mid-nineteenth century, dropping to its lowest point at about the turn of the century, rising in a small wave during World War I and in a much greater wave during World War II, and since then slowly subsiding until it began to rise once more in 1956—is not as simple as it seems.

After 1870 birth control began to have its effect upon the size of the average family. The change in the legitimacy rate was very marked. By 1925 the average woman had only half as many children as her grandmother of 1870. One might have expected this to be reflected in an increased percentage of illegitimate births, yet this rate also dropped steeply in the latter half of the nineteenth century. This means that the proportion of unmarried women who bore children must have decreased greatly over those years, either as the effect of birth control, or perhaps due to what the Registrar-General had referred to in 1854 as 'improved manners'.

During the first half of the twentieth century, other changes have had a reverse effect. Large numbers of illegitimate children (perhaps a third of the total) are now conceived by divorced women or those living apart from their husbands. In the Victorian era divorce was almost unknown; women had smaller earning power and few property rights, and could rarely afford even to live apart from their husbands. Today the greater number of separations greatly increases the risk of illegitimate births, and the rate is consequently rather higher than at the turn of the century. That it should be still as high as it is is probably due both to this factor and to an increase in extra-marital relations.

Since the illegitimacy rate rose from 4.2 per cent in 1938 to 9.3 per cent in 1945, it would seem natural enough to assume that there was a great increase in 'immorality'—that is, in extra-marital relations—during the war period. But there do not seem to be any secure grounds for believing this. There was no increase in the number of unmarried women who became pregnant, and no increase (a slight decrease, in fact) in the number of children born of irregular conceptions; instead there was a sharp drop in the number of couples who, having conceived a child, were able in war conditions to keep in touch and marry before its birth. Added to which, many of the women could bring no social pressure to bear on their lovers to marry them.

Table 10 applies to the following observations of the Registrar-General in his *Statistical Review of England and Wales*, 1940-5:

'From the point of view of sexual irregularity, it is not with these columns separately that interest is concerned but with their combined numbers in column 4 which shows the total number of maternities[1] conceived out of wedlock. The annual changes here are far more moderate [than the relative increases in the illegitimacy rate]; in fact the numbers declined materially during the first two years of the war and though they rose toward the end, the average for the six war years 1940-45 was lower at 86,059 than either of the two pre-war years for which we have record [1938, 94,381; 1939, 86,915] . . . Instead of the irregularly conceived being one-seventh of all the children born as before the war, the proportion for the war years was little more than an eighth, not a startling change perhaps, but one of improvement rather than deterioration.

'The significant feature . . . is the decline in the proportion of parents who regularized their actions by marriage before birth took place . . . In the last year, 1945, it was only 37%, or little more than half its peace-time level.

[1] See footnote, Table 10.

'The explanation is almost unquestionably to be found in the enforced degree of physical separation of the sexes imposed by the progressive recruitment of young males into the Armed Forces and their transfers to war stations at home and abroad, rendering immediate marriage with their home brides increasingly difficult—and, in the case of many, quite impossible . . . If, for example, the normal proportion of parents expected to marry before the birth of the extra-maritally conceived child can be taken as 70%—the proportion recorded prior to the war—then about 361 thousands of 516,355 maternities conceived out of wedlock in the years 1940-45 should have been so regularized as compared with the 254 thousands which were in fact regularized, leaving the difference, viz. 107,000 as a general indication of the magnitude of the illegitimate births, which, but for the exigencies of the war, would otherwise have been included in the legitimate class . . .

'To the extent to which this is the explanation, the lapse will often have been of a temporary character only, since it is to be presumed that in many, probably a large proportion, of the cases where the parents were reunited after the war they will have married and thereby legitimated many of the children registered as illegitimate and secured to them the normality of home life and upbringing of which they might otherwise have been deprived. In such circumstances it will usually be in the future interest of the child to complete the rectification process as far as possible by re-registering the birth under the arrangements authorized by the Legitimacy Act of 1926. The record of re-registrations to date shows that this has not so far been done to any great extent . . .'[1]

In 1930 and 1935 re-registration had amounted to 3,989 and 2,956 respectively, as compared with 4,354 in 1940 (when there was a certain rush to qualify previously illegitimate children for services allowances) and 3,741 in 1945.

Comparing the numbers of irregularly conceived maternities with the number of unmarried women of child-bearing age, the wartime figure was about 7 per cent above that of 1938.

'Taking the six war years as a whole the average increase of 6% in the total number of irregularly conceived births will hardly be regarded as inordinate, having regard to the wholesale disturbance to customary habits and living conditions in conjunction with the temporary accession to the population of large numbers

[1] *Statistical Review*, Text, Civil, p. 144.

EUROPE
Illegitimate Percentage of Live Births, 1938

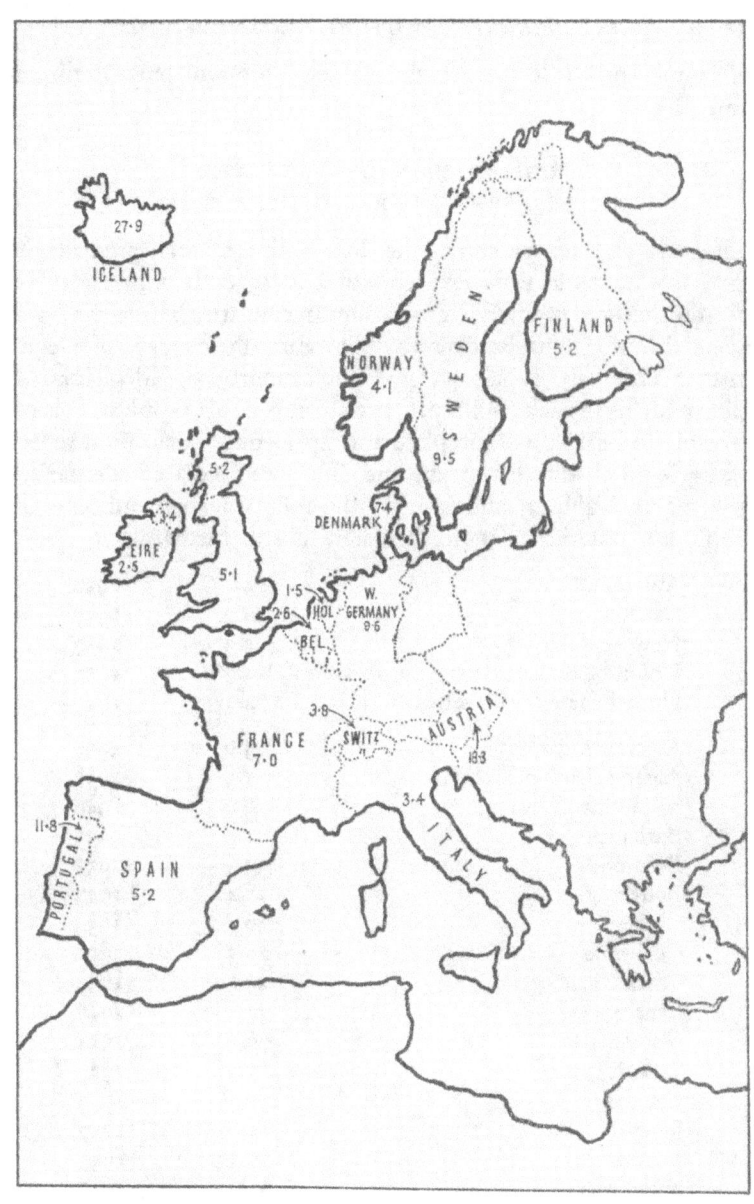

EUROPE

Illegitimate Percentage of Live Births, 1950

COMPARISON OF THE RATES IN DIFFERENT PARTS OF THE WORLD

The map on page 32 shows the distribution of registered illegitimate live births in European countries in 1938. It shows also the position in some of the Eastern European countries before they were affected by Communist decrees obliterating the concept of illegitimacy.[1] The map on page 33 gives the proportion of illegitimate to all live births in each country in 1950. Table 2a also applies. It is not possible to build up a complete and up-to-date world picture as a background to this European one, but some basis of comparison is given in Table 1, and also by the following percentages from Table 2b. Asterisks denote inclusion of still births.

Australia	4.2	1957
Canada	4.0	1957
New Zealand	4.9	1957
Union of South Africa (European only)	1.7*	1957
United States of America	4.7	1957
Algeria, European	5.6	1952
Algeria, Mohammedan	1.5	1952
Argentina	26.6	1948
Barbados	61.5	1955
Bermuda	30.6	1952
Bolivia	28.4	1947
Chile	26.5	1952
Colombia	26.5	1952
Costa Rica	24.2	1952
Ecuador	34.8	1947
Guatemala	76.1	1944
Hawaii	7.5	1945
Jamaica	70.9	1953
Japan	1.5	1957
Mexico	27.3	1945
Nicaragua	63.9	1945

[1] See EASTERN EUROPE, page 329. The only recent figures obtainable from official sources in countries on the other side of the Iron Curtain are those for Hungary in 1946 (8.1), Rumania in 1947 (11.9) and for Czechoslovakia in 1949, when 18,437 (6.6) Czech children were recorded as born out of wedlock.

THE INCIDENCE OF ILLEGITIMACY

Panama	66.3	1943
Paraguay	56.6	1946
Peru	25.8	1951
Salvador	55.6	1949
Trinidad and Tobago	50.3	1954
Venezuela	58.2	1951
Windward Is. (St. Vincent)	76.6*	1954

Before any study is made of these maps and tables, it is vital to understand their limitations. First, the figures, although taken from official sources, must be viewed with caution and not accepted as fully reliable or comparable. They are not valueless. It is unlikely, for instance, that the illegitimacy rate of any country is *lower* than the official rate given, and it is quite possible that some of the countries quote a figure within 1 per cent of the truth. But many babies certainly escape the official net. There is inevitable under-registration, impossible to measure and varying in degree from country to country and from year to year.

It is only human nature that a woman who has given birth to an illegitimate child should want to register it as legitimate if she can find a way to do so. And there are many ways. A married woman who has had a child that is not her husband's (extra-marital in physical fact, but in law not illegitimate unless later proved so) does not necessarily tell her husband or the registrar. Again, a girl may adopt her lover's surname and register the child jointly with him as though they were married. The registrar does not normally ask to see the wedding lines. Should he ask for the date of the marriage, he may be given a fictitious one. Again, although this is rare in England, the mother may omit to register the child at all. In some countries there are penalties for non-registration, but she may well not know of these. Again, she may abandon, murder or expose the child soon after its birth.

Then in some countries the registrars may be less thorough in compiling their records, or less conscientious in making their returns. An apparent increase in the illegitimacy rate—as shown, for instance, in *Canada* and *Jugoslavia* between 1927 and 1934— may simply indicate more accurate registration. It must be remembered that compulsory registration of births is a comparatively new conception, and that trained officials may be few and natural difficulties great—remote and scattered settlements, or many people on the move. The registrar may or may not include still-born children—this fact is not always indicated in the final returns—and some countries appear to define still births more narrowly than others.

A second limitation that must be remembered in studying these figures is what they purport to show. They include only ex-nuptial births, and generally only live-born children. The proportion of ex-nuptial still births to living children varies greatly from country to country. They give no picture of the comparative incidence of extra-marital conceptions. Thousands of these never issue in a living child, but end with miscarriage or abortion, and many hundreds of thousands of pregnant women marry before the child is born. In *Sweden* in the 1930's one child in three was conceived outside marriage, but less than half of these were born illegitimate.

Still less, of course, can the figures be used as an index of the prevalence of extra-marital relationships in any country. Whether these will lead to conception depends on too many factors—among them the girl's fertility, how careful she is not to have an unwanted child (this in turn will depend on whether the stigma in her country is grave or slight) and what methods of birth control are available. In countries where efficient contraceptives are widely used, pre-marital relations may be common, and yet the illegitimate birth rate low. Any fluctuation in these figures, then, does not necessarily imply a change in sexual behaviour.

Nor do the illegitimacy figures reflect at all closely the size of the social problem for the country concerned. The tables include many children who are illegitimate for only a few days or months. The Statistical Bureau of *Iceland* states that a quarter of the natural children born in the republic are legitimated by their parents' marriage within a year of their birth. In some countries many are quickly adopted. In any event the word 'illegitimate' covers a variety of situations. In some parts of Europe the legal disabilities incurred through illegitimacy are severe, in others very slight. The figures for every country include situations as non-comparable as that of the child brought up in a stable home by both parents who, although unmarried, live together in a lifelong union and are socially accepted by their neighbours, and that of the child who grows up separated from his mother and never learning his father's identity.

The figures on the maps and tables, then, are not strictly comparable, and any simple attempt to explain the wide differences between them is doomed to failure. Yet one cannot but ask why the differences are so extreme. In *England and Wales* one child in twenty is born illegitimate; in *Eire* one in thirty; in the *Netherlands* one in sixty; but in *Austria* one in five. Outside Europe the differences are still more striking. Mohammedan *Algeria* showed a rate of 0.7 per cent when it was 66.5 in *Paraguay*. Varying degrees of under-registration cannot account for this.

ATTEMPTS TO EXPLAIN VARIATIONS IN RATES

Several attempts have been made to explain these great variations: to look for a direct association with such factors as poverty, custom, climate, religion, literacy or environment. Although this book is written neither by nor for statisticians, it may be interesting to test these theses simply and superficially, in order to clear one's mind of wrong assumptions.

Poverty and Custom
Other things being equal, one might expect to find a higher illegitimacy rate in the poorest sections of many populations. The cost of contraceptive appliances of a good standard of reliability puts them beyond the reach of the very poor; and the 'natural' methods that cost nothing are far from reliable. Yet poverty and illegitimacy show no constant correlations, presumably because other social factors often outweigh poverty in importance. The rates in the East End of London have been consistently lower than those in the West End (see Table 8). Rich *Sweden's* rate is consistently about three times that of poor *Italy*. On the other hand, poverty is certainly a factor in the *West Indies* and in parts of *Central and South America* —for example, in *Peru* and parts of the *Argentine*, where the illegitimacy rates are as high as 60 to 70 per cent and the exceptional fate is to be born legitimate.

In some of these poorer and less-developed countries the cost of a civil or religious wedding, even if it be only the equivalent of a few shillings, may be prohibitive to those who live on what they grow or gather, whose cash income is tiny or non-existent, or to those whose wages are very low. Above all, among a large section of the *Caribbean* working-class population, for example in *Jamaica*, marriage is a comparatively new custom, since so many of their ancestors were slaves and not allowed to marry; and it is still regarded as almost a luxury. So, though the population is deeply religious, children are born outside marriage without the mother feeling any sense of guilt. It is not the custom to marry and there is little social pressure for it. If it is also expensive, that is enough to decide a couple against it. Even the cost of a wedding ring may be put forward as a difficulty.

Climate
It is often taken for granted that illegitimacy is more widespread in the so-called 'hot-blooded' countries. The map of Europe in 1938 shows that this is not so. The illegitimacy rate in *Iceland* was seventeen times as high as in *Greece*; in *Sweden* it was three times as high as in *Italy*. On the other hand, the rates in *Scotland* and *Spain* were almost identical. There was no common tendency in the north: three countries—*Iceland, Sweden* and *Denmark*—showed particularly high rates, but in *Holland* it was only 1.4 per cent. Nor was the south more consistent: in *Greece* the rate was 1.4 per cent, in *Austria* 20.9 per cent.

Religion
Nor can the differences be explained in terms of religious affiliation. The map for 1938 shows that some of the Roman Catholic countries had low rates—*Eire* 3.3 per cent, *Italy* 4.1 per cent, *Belgium* 2.5 per cent—while others—*Austria* 20.9 per cent and *Portugal* 15.6 per cent—were exceptionally high. The same is true of the Protestant countries; the figures seem to be scattered with a complete disregard for religious affiliation. Listed in order, the highest rates in Europe during that year were in Lutheran *Iceland* (23.7 per cent), Catholic *Austria* (20.9 per cent) and *Portugal* (15.6 per cent), and Lutheran *Sweden* (12.7 per cent). The lowest were in Orthodox *Greece* (1.4 per cent), mixed Lutheran and Catholic *Holland* (1.4 per cent), Catholic *Belgium* (2.5 per cent) and mixed Orthodox and Moslem *Bulgaria* (2.9 per cent).

Eire, whose rate is consistently low, is sometimes quoted as 'proof' that the rate in Catholic countries is low; *Austria* and *Bavaria* just as often as 'proof' that it is high. But even in *Eire* there is no assurance that the low incidence of illegitimacy is due to religious factors, since the low rate (2.5 per cent in 1953) is matched by an almost equally low one in *Northern Ireland* (2.8 per cent at the same date). Only about 34 per cent of the population of Northern Ireland is Roman Catholic as compared with over 90 per cent in Eire, and the birth rate in both countries is about the same.[1]

One must not, however, draw an invalid corollary. Whether or not there is a connexion between *active* religious belief and sexual behaviour is quite another question. Professor Kinsey's study[2] showed that in America the active members of religious groups had fewer extra-marital relationships than the inactive members. But not very much is known about this matter, and the illegitimacy rate bears no fixed relation to the incidence of extra-marital relationships.

It might be enlightening to know what the official policy, if any, of the different Churches has been in different countries—whether to persuade every pregnant unmarried girl into a 'cover-up' marriage for the sake of giving the child a father and a home, or whether to do so only if there seems a reasonable chance of the marriage proving a good, lifelong and happy one. That there are two schools of Christian thought among clergy is widely known.

It is argued that the rate in Catholic countries is affected by the fact that they are forbidden the use of contraceptives. But far too little is known about the practice of birth control by the unmarried, in either Catholic or Protestant countries, for any very firm conclusion to be drawn. According to a sample taken in England by the Population Investigation Committee in connexion with their report on Family Limitation, probably as many as 40 to 46 per cent of the younger married Catholics in this country practise birth control, and about half of these use contraceptive appliances.[3] This figure was about 20 per cent lower than among the married Protestants, but it is still high enough to dispose of the idea that Catholics automatically obey the Papal ruling.

It is generally believed, although we have no evidence on this point, that the illegitimacy rate among Catholic girls in *London* and *Liverpool* is high, but this is not necessarily a matter of religion, since in London many Catholic girls are Irish or Continental, separated from their homes and home traditions and so more liable to get themselves into trouble; while in Liverpool it might also be

---

[1] Cyril Greenland, *Some Ecological Aspects of Unmarried Parenthood* (Lancet, 19th January 1957).
[2] A. C. Kinsey, *Sexual Behaviour in the Human Male* (1948).
[3] H.M.S.O., 1949. Table 60.

a reflection of poor living standards; so many poor immigrants settled there from Ireland during the famine years towards the end of the last century.

Dr Halliday Sutherland mentions that many unmarried girls come over from Eire to England when they are pregnant, because they are frightened of harsh treatment in their own country or want to have their babies quickly adopted.[1] Not all of them wish to get into touch with their own Church authorities over here, so it is difficult to compile figures, but it is known that many come to London and one Catholic organization, the Crusade of Rescue in the Diocese of Westminster, had, between 1950 and 1953, from eighty to a hundred and twenty applications from girls of this kind—and four times as many from Irish girls who had become pregnant in this country.

Education

The Registrar-General has made many attempts to account for the differing rates in various parts of England and Wales. His interest was aroused in 1854, when the illegitimacy rate for the nation dropped by 0.1 per cent.

'The proportions', he commented, 'show a gratifying diminution. This may be the result of improved manners . . . Even Norfolk, Herefordshire, Shropshire, Nottingham, Cumberland and Westmorland, which have hitherto enjoyed an unhappy pre-eminence, show symptoms of improvement.'[2]

He sought first for an explanation in terms of the different levels of education, hoping to find a connexion between illegitimacy and illiteracy, since 'ignorance on the part of women would make them fall easy victims of seduction'; but *Westmorland*, 'a well-educated county where men and women write their names', proved 'disappointingly' to have one of the highest rates in England, whereas in *Monmouthshire*, in Wales, where education was low, illegitimacy was not high.[3]

His conviction that education and morality were somehow associated was not, however, easily shaken. In 1879 he returned to it again from an improved angle:

'It is quite possible that a wider diffusion of elementary education

---

[1] Halliday Sutherland, *Irish Journey*, pp. 84 ff. (1956).
[2] *Annual Report of Births, Deaths and Marriages*, England and Wales, 1854.
[3] *Ibid.* 1861.

among men may lead to the same result as the ignorance of women, for education leads to prudence, and prudent men marry later than imprudent men; and late marriage is often preceded by illicit connexions.'

But the rates in counties where men could sign their names with the cunning of serpents and women made crosses with the simplicity of doves, proved no higher than anywhere else. 'The curious geographical distribution of illegitimacy . . . seems hardly capable of explanation simply on this basis.'

Illegitimacy does not seem to be particularly associated with lack of education. In *Ireland* and *Brittany* there has been a high percentage of illiteracy when the illegitimacy rate has been exceptionally low.[1] And in *Paris* in 1900 the rate was 26.8 per cent, while in *Cardiff* it was 2.5 per cent. Should one claim that the people of Cardiff were ten times better educated than the people of Paris?

Education, of course, plays some part in birth control, a certain degree of it being needed for any form except *coitus interruptus*, the least safe and the least humanly satisfying. Even the counting of strings of coloured beads to determine the 'safe days' demands thought, remembrance of instructions, and self-discipline; the birth-control appliances still more so.

Age at Marriage

'It might be supposed', the Registrar-General pondered in 1870, 'that the prevalence of early marriage would tend to diminish the number of illegitimate births', but 'it does not appear to have any such influence . . . For example . . . although Cumberland and Shropshire show a high rate of illegitimacy combined with a low proportion of persons married under 21 years of age, yet in Norfolk, where the proportion of illegitimate children is also high, the proportion of minors married is above the average . . . London and the extra-metropolitan parts of Surrey, Kent and Middlesex show a combination of low proportions of illegitimate children and of persons married under age.'[2]

It has been claimed that illegitimacy increases during periods of depression, when marriage has to be postponed, but that where early marriage is the rule the illegitimate birth rate is low. This

---

[1] *Illegitimacy* (*Encyclopaedia Britannica*, 11th ed.)
[2] *Annual Report.*

is commonly the case, but not always. For instance, in *Sweden* marriage takes place late, after a long engagement. Before the last war, women married at an average age of twenty-seven and men twenty-nine, and at least 20 per cent of Swedish women reaching fifty years of age never married,[1] while the corresponding figure for *Denmark* was about 15 per cent and for *France* about 10 per cent. So it is not surprising to find the illegitimacy rate was very high in Sweden (12.7 in 1938), lower in Denmark (9 per cent) and barely half as great in France (6.3 per cent). On the other hand, in *Eire* the average age at marriage is very high and two thirds of the women of child-bearing age are unmarried,[2] but the illegitimacy rate is exceptionally low in 1938, only 3.3 per cent.

Re-expression of the Statistics
'Why', asked the frustrated Registrar-General in 1857, 'do 25 in Norfolk and 11 in Devon bear children annually out of the same numbers of unmarried women?'

Of all varying suggestions the most fruitful consisted simply in a re-expression of the statistics. The illegitimacy rate had always been calculated simply as a proportion of all live births, but this gave rather a misleading picture, for in some districts there were higher numbers of unmarried women of child-bearing age. When, however, the rate was re-expressed as a percentage of the number of 'unmarried women and widows aged 15 to 45', some of the differences between one county and another disappeared. In 1876 the number of single women was very high in *Shropshire, Norfolk, Cumberland, Hereford, Westmorland, North Wales, Bedfordshire* and *Cornwall*—all counties with exceptionally high illegitimacy rates. In *Co. Durham*, as in *Staffordshire*, there were few spinsters and very few illegitimate children.

This way of re-expressing the rate is still quite often used in the belief that it gives a more accurate picture; but it no longer applies, since nowadays large numbers of divorced and separated women also bear illegitimate children.

Some of the differences between international rates diminish if the rates are re-expressed. Differences in the English and American rates, for instance, almost disappear. The percentages given below relate to (*a*) the illegitimacy rate per hundred live

[1] Alva Myrdal, *Nation and Family*, p. 35.
[2] T. W. Freeman, *Ireland*, p. 151 (1950).

THE INCIDENCE OF ILLEGITIMACY 43

births, and (b) the illegitimacy rate per hundred single women and widows aged fifteen to forty-four in the United States and fifteen to forty-five in England and Wales:

		(a)	(b)
1940	United States	3.8	0.7
	England and Wales	4.3	0.6
1948	United States	3.7	1.3
	England and Wales	5.3	1.2

On the other hand, ex-nuptial births per hundred unmarried women aged fifteen to forty-nine have been found to vary from 3.8 per cent in *Hungary* (1906-15) to 0.4 per cent in *Ireland* (1909-12) and 0.4 per cent in *Bulgaria* (1910-11).[1] The illegitimacy rates in these countries per hundred live births stood in the same relationship.

Town and Country
Is there any correspondence between illegitimacy and the extent to which the people of a country live in cities or villages? There seems to be some correspondence, but it favours sometimes the urban, sometimes the rural society. In the 1920's, for example, in *Finland* the town rate of illegitimacy was double that of the rural areas; on the *Scottish* mainland the rural rate was well above that of the towns; and in the *Netherlands* it was lowest in the countryside and highest in the cities.[2]

At the beginning of this century the highest rates in England were in the six farming counties lying isolated in the far north, the east and the west: *Cumberland, Westmorland, Norfolk, Suffolk, Shropshire* and *Herefordshire*. Mining areas such as *Durham*, manufacturing counties such as *Lancashire*, and even the remote agricultural areas of the south—*Devon* and *Cornwall*—had much lower rates, as will be seen from the map on page 25. Half a century earlier the situation was much the same; half a century later there was a rather different picture.

---
[1] *Annuaire International de Statistique* (Vols. II and V), quoted in *Australian Vital Statistics*, 1947.
[2] *Illegitimacy* (*Encyclopaedia Britannica*).

	1850	1900	1950
National rate	6.8	4.0	5.1
Cumberland	10.1	6.0	4.2
Westmorland	9.0	6.7	5.1
Norfolk	10.7	6.1	5.7
Suffolk	8.4	5.6	
West			5.6
East			5.2
Shropshire	9.5	6.2	5.8
Herefordshire	11.0	6.0	6.7
Durham	6.6	3.3	3.8
Lancashire	7.5	3.8	5.2
Devon	5.3	3.6	5.8
Cornwall	6.0	5.1	5.2

By 1950 the only one of the six counties listed by the Registrar-General in 1854 that still 'enjoyed an unhappy pre-eminence' was *Herefordshire*. The highest rate was in the soke of *Peterborough* (7.1 per cent), the second highest in *East Sussex* (7.0 per cent, equal to London), and *Herefordshire* and *Huntingdonshire* (6.7 per cent) tied for third place. In Wales the highest was in *Merioneth* (10.2 per cent) and the second *Anglesey* (7.0 per cent).

Illegitimacy was not a serious problem in large towns until as late as the 1930's. In *London* the rate remained well below the average for the country as a whole, though this might have been due in part to false registration. Below are the 1880 and 1900 figures for London and other large towns in relation to the national figures.

	1880	1900
National rate	4.8	4.0
London	3.9	3.6
Birmingham	4.3	4.0
Liverpool	4.7	6.0
Manchester	3.3	3.4
Cardiff	2.7	2.5

The only one above the national rate was *Liverpool* in 1900.

These low rates, however, left the Registrar-General feeling rather sceptical. 'It is impossible to resist the conclusion', he observed in his report for 1879, 'that such large towns as London, Birmingham, Liverpool, Manchester, exercise some influence by which illegitimacy is kept down, as such towns can hardly be assumed to be seats of exceptionally high morality. It is probable that the explanation lies in the fact that the unrestrained passions which in other districts result in illegitimate offspring are in these large towns diverted into the channel of barren prostitution.' Whether that was in fact an important contributory reason, one can hardly tell at this late date. It was certainly not the only explanation, for the cities in Great Britain stand in strong contrast to those on the Continent. In most of the major cities of Europe around the turn of the century, illegitimacy rates were very high indeed. In *Vienna* almost every third child was illegitimate. Here are some figures for 1900, based on Table 3:

Stockholm	31.2	Sweden	11.4
Budapest	27.5	Hungary	9.4
Moscow	27.3	Russia	2.5 (1902)
Paris	26.8	France	8.8
Brussels	25.3	Belgium	7.4
Copenhagen	24.5	Denmark	9.6
Rome	17.8	Italy	5.9

These compare with:

Edinburgh	7.9	Scotland	6.5
London	3.6	England	4.0
Dublin	3.0	Ireland	2.7
Cardiff	2.5	Wales	3.8

The figures for 1950 (excluding Hungary and the U.S.S.R., for which no statistics are available) were as follows:

Paris	16.6	France	7.0
Vienna	15.5	Austria	18.3
Brussels	12.0	Belgium	2.6
Copenhagen	11.4	Denmark	7.4
Stockholm	10.5	Sweden	9.5
Rome	7.0	Italy	3.4
London	7.0	England	5.1
Edinburgh	5.3	Scotland	5.2
Cardiff	4.8	Wales	4.1
Dublin	1.8	Eire	2.5

Sporadically during the growth of English towns a few high rates appeared. In 1842 *Wigan* had the highest rate in England, 18.2

per cent; in 1950, the lowest, 2.6 per cent; in 1957 it stood at 1.9 per cent. *Liverpool*, more typically, had in 1842 a rate of only 3 per cent, less than half the rate in the country as a whole, though by 1900 it had doubled; in 1950 it still stood at 6 per cent, and in 1957 it was down to 5.3 per cent.

The largest *numbers* of illegitimate births have, of course, for many years been in the cities, the greatest centres of population. In 1949[1] the numerical distribution for England and Wales was as follows:

	ILLEGITIMATE BIRTHS
Greater London	6,983
County boroughs	13,092
Urban districts	10,333
Rural districts	6,500

Gradually the rates themselves have shifted from countryside to city, thus:

	RURAL DISTRICTS	URBAN DISTRICTS	COUNTY BOROUGHS
1912	4.9	4.1	4.3
1920	5.5	4.6	4.6
1930	5.0	4.2	4.5
1935	4.3	3.8	4.3
1938	4.2	3.7	4.4
1945	9.6	8.9	10.0
1949	4.8	4.5	5.6

Nowadays the high rates are overwhelmingly in the towns. The highest of all are in the pleasure resorts—the large and small seaside and inland towns invaded every summer by visitors, and girls taking seasonal work; towns where lovers meet and lose touch quickly, creating again the problem of a shifting population. Their mild climate, good health services and holiday associations may also lead to the deliberate choice of these towns by mothers who leave home to have their babies. A study of the tables below will show that the districts with the highest rates in 1950 were all seaside or inland pleasure resorts; that most but not all of the large cities have high rates; that the ports and manufacturing centres vary considerably; that the rates in the mining towns are on the whole

---

[1] Chosen because in later years these figures were expressed in density aggregates by conurbations, a form less comprehensible to the general reader.

THE INCIDENCE OF ILLEGITIMACY 47

very low, as are, in most cases, the rates in the London suburbs and dormitories. In 1949 the lowest rate in the country was *Bexley*, Kent, eleven miles from the capital, with 2.4 per cent.

PLEASURE RESORTS, 1950

	%
New Windsor (35)[1]	9.1
Brighton	8.9
Hastings	8.2
Margate (44)	8.1
Hove	8.0
Penzance (23)	8.0
Bournemouth	8.0
Eastbourne	7.9
Leamington Spa (45)	7.8
Bognor Regis (24)	7.8
Maidenhead (35)	7.7

LARGEST CITIES IN ORDER OF SIZE, 1950

London	7.0
Birmingham	5.5
Liverpool	6.0
Manchester	7.3
Sheffield	3.8
Leeds	6.8

PORTS, 1950

Plymouth	7.6
Grimsby	7.3
Manchester	7.3
Dover (44)	7.2
London	7.0
Southampton	6.9
Portsmouth	6.6
Folkestone (43)	6.1
Liverpool	6.0
Hull	5.8
Cardiff	4.8
Newcastle-upon-Tyne	4.5
Bristol	4.3

[1] Number of illegitimate births, if less than 50, shown in brackets.

MANUFACTURING CENTRES, 1950

	%
Salford	7.2
Halifax	7.2
Middlesbrough	7.2
Nottingham	7.2
Bradford	6.9
Coventry	6.3
Oxford	6.0
Northampton	5.9
Leicester	5.9
Wolverhampton	5.2
Oldham	5.1
Croydon	5.1
Stoke-on-Trent	4.5
Bolton	4.2

MINING TOWNS, 1950

Darlington	6.0
Newcastle-upon-Tyne	4.5
Tynemouth	4.5
South Shields	4.5
Sunderland	4.2
Stockton-on-Tees	4.0
Jarrow (24)	4.0
Rhondda	3.6
Gateshead	3.5
Merthyr Tydfil (36)	3.4
Swansea	3.1
Newport, Mon.	2.9
Durham (9)	2.5

LONDON SUBURBS AND DORMITORIES, 1950

Hendon	7.0
Richmond	6.5
Willesden	6.0
Brentford and Chiswick (47)	5.2
Hornsey	4.8
Ealing	4.8
Surbiton (39)	4.6
Romford	4.5
Edmonton	4.4
Dagenham	4.2

		%
Ruislip-Northwood (38)		4.1
Uxbridge (32)		4.0
Thurrock		3.9
Enfield		3.8
Walthamstow		3.8
Finchley		3.7
Leyton		3.5
Hornchurch		3.4
Harrow		3.3
Ilford		3.0
Wembley		2.8
Beckenham (26)		2.8
Barking		2.5

Low rates in the areas around London may be due in part to the large number of black-coated workers, the most consciously 'respectable' element of the community, and perhaps to the tendency of unmarried girls from these neighbourhoods to leave their homes if they become pregnant and move in to swell the Central London illegitimacy rate. Both the rates and numbers of applications for affiliation orders are particularly high in areas near the big London railway stations where cheap boarding-houses are found. Or the explanation may be that the new housing estates and new towns around London attract young married couples with young children. In these areas the proportion of adolescents or unmarried women may be low at present, but in a few years the position may be reversed, for some of these towns have a birth rate double the national rate. Already these districts foresee the risk of a serious problem of juvenile delinquency, unless steps are taken now to build up healthy and happy communities. Is it not also possible that the illegitimacy rates and proportion of pre-marital conceptions might rise seriously in these areas?

London itself shows a curious phenomenon: consistently lower rates in the poor districts than in the well-to-do. Unfortunately the comparative incidence of pre-marital conceptions in these districts is not known.

The failure of the Registrar-General to account for the differences in rate between one part of the country and another may serve as a warning. So many factors contribute—the comparative numbers of men and women of marriageable age, local customs, the flux of population—that only detailed sociological studies in each area could explain them.

CHAPTER 2

WHO HAVE ILLEGITIMATE CHILDREN?

Who are the parents of illegitimate children? Are they in fact unmarried? Do they belong predominantly to any one age group or social class? Is there a large proportion among them of the mentally sub-normal, the neurotic, the promiscuous, or of those who themselves have had a disturbed childhood?

Most of these questions cannot be answered on a national basis. The only nation-wide statistics about illegitimate children and their parents are those of the Registrar-General, which do not go deep enough, and the very few deeper studies are not wide enough; any picture tends to be either superficial or unrepresentative. A really representative study at sufficient depth may indeed never be possible, but several local authorities and certain voluntary bodies are now conducting large-scale research into the health and history of illegitimate children in their areas during their early years, and this will probably bring much to light about their parentage.

Up to the present only a handful of detailed surveys bearing upon these questions have been made. The first was made by the *Manchester* Health Department in 1938. Its primary concern was to follow up the fate of all the illegitimate children born in Manchester in 1933 (we shall return to it in that connexion in Part III of this book), but incidental facts emerged about their parentage. In 1950 Miss Valerie Hughes, of the London School of Economics and Political Science, made a sociological study of the mothers in one midland city—here known as *Midboro*—who gave birth to children in 1949. With great generosity she has placed her first analysis at our disposal, and this chapter, which draws extensively—and often verbally—upon her work, owes much to her pioneering enterprise.

Since the figures that follow are based largely on the records of one city in one year, though supplemented by any available records from other cities and occasional national statistics, they are given with full consciousness of their limitations. How far the Midboro figures may be typical of the rest of the country is not known. Their chief value lies in the fact that Midboro's standard of record-keeping is exceptionally high and the relationship between the social workers and those they are trying to help a happy and therefore relatively intimate one.

THE MIDBORO SURVEY

Midboro has rather over a quarter of a million inhabitants. Its illegitimacy rate in 1949 was 5.6 per cent, an average figure for a city of this size and not far from the national average of 5.1 per cent for that year. According to the Registrar-General, two hundred and eighty-four Midboro women gave birth to illegitimate children in 1949; according to Midboro's social welfare workers (the local authority Maternity and Child Welfare Department and the Church of England Moral Welfare Association), the number was two hundred and seventy-eight—eighteen of them in diocesan Homes just outside the city boundary.

That these figures do not tally precisely is to be expected. The Registrar-General's total includes not only those women whose home was at Midboro and who had their children there, but also the women who gave birth to children elsewhere, but gave Midboro as their home address. In the same way, a child born to, say, a Plymouth woman who came to Midboro for the birth, would be transferred back to Plymouth if she gave that as her home address. As distinct from this, the social welfare workers' case-histories were all of births that took place locally—case-histories that were of necessity incomplete. They might be asked to visit a home where there was a new-born baby, to find that mother and child had left, 'address not known'; or an unmarried pregnant girl, helped by the agencies and entered in their records, might marry a few days before the child's birth and disappear a few days afterwards. Again, what is recorded cannot in this field invariably be taken as the truth; a single woman living under her lover's name can register her child as legitimate by describing herself as a married woman. Further, the law assumes that a married woman's child is born in wedlock unless her husband takes steps to prove non-access. Such children, only biologically 'illegitimate', would not be recorded

WHO HAVE ILLEGITIMATE CHILDREN? 53

by the Registrar-General, yet might come within the purview of the social welfare workers.

With the generous and valuable help of the Moral Welfare Association, whose records were unusually detailed, and the Maternity and Child Welfare Department, who filled in special questionnaires, Miss Hughes was able to follow up over 95 per cent of the cases recorded by these two bodies, in total:

Moral Welfare worker's records	109
Health visitors' forms	169
TOTAL	278

Five years later an important study of the same group was made by the Midboro Health Department (the survey being carried out jointly by the Child Welfare Department and the Moral Welfare Association) in connexion with a follow-up of the children's progress.[1] That study covered two hundred and sixty-five of the women and consequently certain of the facts given here differ a little from it in detail. However, in no respect do the conclusions drawn in the official study differ from those in Miss Hughes's. Indeed they confirm one another so closely that it has seemed best here to ignore the small discrepancies entirely. Where there are any differences, the Health Department's study, needless to say, remains the official one.

From these Midboro parents and other sources we can learn something about those who have illegitimate children—and get some picture of the kinds of people they are.

AGE OF PARENTS

Age of Mothers
The mothers of illegitimate children tend to be younger than those who have legitimate children. From Table 13, which applies to the year 1950, it will be seen that the peak age for illegitimate births was twenty, as compared with twenty-four for all legitimate maternities and twenty-two for legitimate first births.

---

[1] The fate of the two hundred and sixty-eight children in the study is followed up in Part III of this book.

The comparative ages of the Midboro mothers of illegitimate children were as follows:

AGE	NUMBER	%
15-19	45	16.2
20-24	73	26.3
25-29	57	20.5
30-34	47	16.9
35-39	37	13.3
40-44	17	6.1
45	2	0.7
TOTAL	278	100.0

From Table 9a it will be seen that over 15 per cent of illegitimate children are born to girls in their teens. Of the unmarried mothers included in the Midboro total, over 25 per cent had their first child at eighteen or under, while of the women who gave birth to legitimate children over the same period, only 4 per cent were eighteen or under. The problem is still greater in the United States where, in 1947, as many as 42 per cent of the mothers of illegitimate children were in their teens.[1]

Some of these mothers are very young. In 1950 two hundred and eighteen children (automatically illegitimate) were born in England and Wales to girls under the age of sixteen. It is mentioned in the report for 1952-3 of the National Council for the Unmarried Mother and Her Child that in the five years from 1946 to 1950 alone, over two hundred girls aged twelve, thirteen and fourteen gave birth to babies.

In 1957 (see Table 9b) there were two mothers aged twelve, nine aged thirteen, forty-five aged fourteen and two hundred and forty-one fifteen-year-olds: in all, two hundred and ninety-seven babies born to girls still under the age of consent, quite apart from the many more conceived below the age of consent but born when the mother was sixteen years old.

In a survey of seven thousand and fifty-seven mothers who were helped by Moral Welfare workers in 1952, over half (52.5 per cent) were twenty-two or younger, the peak age being nineteen. Three of these mothers were thirteen, twenty-six were fourteen, one

---

[1] Sam Shapiro, *Illegitimate Births, 1938-47* (American Office of Vital Statistics, 1950).

hundred and two were fifteen, and two hundred and fifty-six were only sixteen years of age.[1]

Age of Fathers
The comparative ages of the Midboro fathers of illegitimate children were as follows:

AGE	NUMBER	%
Under 20	6	2.7
20-24	44	20.0
25-29	47	21.2
30-34	50	22.6
35-39	29	13.1
40-49	38	17.2
50-59	6	2.7
60	1	0.5
Age not given	57	
TOTAL	278	100.0

Teen-age fathers were far rarer than teen-age mothers,[2] but few men were many years older than the girls. Three-quarters of the women under thirty had their children by men within five years of their own age, and none of the teen-agers bore a child to a man over thirty. If two fathers were twenty-five years senior to the mothers, extreme differences were as common in the other direction: a middle-aged woman, mentally unstable, had a child by a boy of nineteen, and five women in their thirties or forties were seven to fifteen years older than the fathers. But normally the men and women were, as in marriage, near together in age.

LENGTH OF RELATIONSHIP

The Midboro survey shows that the large majority of the children's fathers were at conception either the fiancé or a friend of the mother's. In only some twenty cases was he a casual acquaintance. This information is based on the women's own statements, which are not necessarily to be trusted in every instance. There is, how-

---

[1] Celia M. Joy, *Illegitimate Children and Their Parents—A Survey of Case Work for 1952 (Moral Welfare,* January 1954).
[2] In the Moral Welfare survey of 1952 seven of the fathers were aged fourteen or fifteen.

ever, no obvious reason why such large numbers should state that they had known the father for many years if this were not true. They claim to have known the men for the following lengths of time:

PERIOD	NUMBER		%	
10 years or more	11		4.0	
5 years or more	33		11.9	
2 years or more	81		29.2	
'Years' or 'some years'	20		7.2	
	145	145	52.3	52.3
1 year or more	19		6.8	
3 months to one year	24		8.6	
'Some time'	8		2.9	
For some time, as shown by other evidence	21		7.5	
	72	72	25.8	25.8
No information		40	14.4	
Probably brief or casual		21	7.5	
TOTAL		278	100.0	

Fewer than 20 per cent had known the man less than a year—or, allowing for all unknown cases, at the most a third. Only six claimed that they had never met the man before. Even in some of these cases it may not be true.

Professor Binder's *Swiss* study, *Uneheliche Mutterschaft* ('Unmarried Motherhood'), which is described in more detail in chapter 4, gives a very different impression. Of three hundred and fifty unmarried mothers, 35 per cent had had frequent sexual relations in one or more love affairs, and 17 per cent were entirely promiscuous (see table on page 102). Although one should, of course, be careful not to confuse a study of length of acquaintance with a study of sexual experience, these two groups of women do seem to have been of rather different kinds. It is surely of significance that in Midboro only three of the women (2.8 per cent) were prostitutes, and only three (including one of the prostitutes) were found to be suffering from V.D

SOCIAL LEVEL

It is difficult nowadays—perhaps impossible—to give anything but the most general indication of anyone's social level. The phrase has no precise modern meaning. It is highly subjective: where the lines are drawn depends very much on where the speaker stands—or thinks he stands. It is fluid: the social status of the hospital nurse, the industrial chemist and the miner have all changed greatly in this century. And it is a blend of so many elements: education, ancestry, occupation, amount and form of capital and of income, personal habits, and attitudes to social conventions. Where, for instance, would one place today a window-cleaner's daughter who became a college-trained secondary school-teacher and married a raw but capable locomotive engineer? or a gentle old lady who came down in the world and eked out a small unearned income by doing alterations for a busy dressmaker?

In this study only two criteria of social level are considered: education and occupation.

Educational Level of Mothers

The table below shows that less than 10 per cent of Midboro's unmarried mothers are believed to have had a secondary education, and nearly 90 per cent an elementary education only.

	NUMBER	%
Elementary (or little schooling)	218	78.4
Probably elementary	30	10.8
Secondary	16	5.8
Probably secondary	11	4.0
Not known	3	1.0
TOTAL	278	100.0

It is not possible to relate these figures to the educational level of the Midboro mothers as a whole, since some had had a pre-war and some a wartime education; but in England and Wales in 1938, around 20 per cent of children aged fourteen to seventeen were in process of having a secondary education.

Occupation of Mothers

Ninety-five of the Midboro women gave their occupation as 'housewife', ninety-one were factory workers, and the remainder were as set out in the following table:

	NUMBER	%
'Housewives'	95[1]	34.2
Factory workers	91	32.8
Workers in cafés, hotels or canteens	14 }	8.6
Domestic servants (two resident)	10	
Shop assistants	17	6.1
Clerks or typists	12	4.3
Hospital nurses	7	2.5
Land workers	3	1.1
Sundry occupations (one in each), including usherette, social worker, variety artist, prostitute and schoolgirl	29	10.4
TOTAL	278	100.0

Midboro is a town in which about 40 per cent of the occupied women, as distinct from housewives and the retired, work in factories. They account, however, for 50 per cent of the occupied women, as distinct from 'housewives', who had illegitimate babies. With the women in domestic and institutional work the position was reversed: 14 per cent of the occupied women were so employed, as compared with 13 per cent of the occupied women who had illegitimate babies—twenty-four out of one hundred and eighty-three.

In *Manchester* in 1933, a quarter of the women who had illegitimate children were resident domestic servants: in Midboro in 1949—sixteen years later—only two in all. The traditional association of the illegitimate baby with the seduced servant girl is out of date. Girls in their teens and twenties, with the wide range of occupations now open to them, prefer work with free evenings, higher cash wages and more contemporary company. It is probable that there are not only fewer domestic servants but also that such as there are are older.

The only figure here that at first sight seems surprising is that of the seven nurses. It seems surprising for two reasons: first, that they were the only professional women in the survey. There was not one teacher, though the teaching profession in England and Wales numbered 90,000 women of child-bearing age, as compared with 140,000 nurses. Moreover, though the figures are, of course, very small, at a diocesan Home outside Midboro for middle-

[1] Two of these were also prostitutes.

class girls, 30 per cent of the unmarried mothers were nurses. Secondly, one would have expected nurses to be familiar with contraceptive techniques, and to have a high standard of self-discipline. It is unexpected that they should conceive unwanted children.

But on further study both points seem less surprising. Of the seven—all state registered nurses, and all but one employed in hospital work—four were Roman Catholic and so quite possibly Irish or Continental, far from home and averse to birth control. Girls who go in for nursing are often strongly maternal, and an unconscious desire for motherhood may well play a part. Resident hospital nurses form a large proportion, too, of the young middle-class girls who work away from home. To be away from home is a factor that encourages emotional adventures. A girl feels freer and more independent, less influenced by the outlook of older generations, less restrained by the solidarity of a family circle or neighbourhood, where all take an intense interest in what the rest are doing. She longs for affection, either missing the natural warmth of family life or seeking what she has missed there. In addition, some girls react strongly against the conditions of a nurse's life, as they are at least in some hospitals: the highly disciplined existence, lack of privacy, and irregular hours of duty, which make social life difficult.

It is worth noting that the fathers of these seven nurses' children were in no known case either doctors or patients in the hospitals where the girls worked, nor were they significantly above or below them socially.

Although there is no evidence to prove or disprove it, it is possible that other Midboro professional or upper- and middle-class women besides the nurses had natural children. If a woman leaves her home town to have a child and refuses to give her real address to the registrar in the town of its birth, the registrar has no option but to register it in his own town. As we have noted, some districts of London and many attractive coastal towns have illegitimate birth rates well above the average. This may be one of the contributory reasons, for women of these classes are more mobile—have more money, more education, more experience of the world and perhaps a more widely scattered set of friends and relatives to turn to in time of need. A hospital nurse is probably already away from home, but other professional women are not, and if one of these is expecting an illegitimate child she is much more likely than, say, a factory worker to want to escape and have her child quietly in some locality where she is unknown; she is also much more likely to be able to arrange this. The same is true of the young daughter of a professional or middle-class father. Midboro has registered none of these women, but it is well-known to social and medical workers that there are illegitimate children of such parentage.

Social Level and Occupation of Fathers

There is no indication in the Midboro survey of any significant difference in social level between the mothers and the fathers. No local Cophetuas attached themselves to beggar-maids. Employers may have affairs with their secretaries, but no children from such unions appear in this survey, and the only girl who had a child by an American was herself American.

The following table shows the occupation of the fathers, the Registrar-General's classification—'Social Classes I to V'— being used:

	SOCIAL CLASS	NUMBER	%
I	Professional etc. occupations	2	0.9
II	Intermediate (salaried workers etc.)	15	6.9
III	Skilled workers (including black-coated wage-earners)	123	56.4
IV	Semi-skilled workers	25	11.5
V	Unskilled labourers	26	11.9
III-V	Other manual workers of unspecified skill	27	12.4
	TOTAL	218	100.0
	Class not known	60	
	TOTAL	278	

The 1951 census shows that 2.1 per cent of Midboro men over eighteen belonged to Class I. Of the two men in the survey one was a senior professional man and the other an electrical engineer. The men in Class II (14.5 per cent in the 1951 census) included, a farmer, and several owners or managers of shops. Class III (72.8 per cent in the 1951 census) covers a very wide field of occupations, including both the black-coated wage-earners, the most highly skilled manual workers and all other manual workers whose work involves any degree of skill. The definition of 'skill' is not a high one. By this rule of the Registrar-General, the one hundred and twenty-three fathers belonging to Class III were as follows:

'Black-coated' workers[1]
 4 shop assistants, 2 commercial travellers, 2 civil servants, 1 variety artist, 1 travelling artist — 10

'Manual' workers
 Members of the Forces and Merchant Navy — 26
 Miners — 10
 Engineers (15) and mechanics (5) — 20
 Building and decorative trades — 16
 Drivers of vehicles (10 lorry, 4 bus, 2 taxi, 1 chauffeur) — 17
 Factory and foundry workers — 14
 Others in sundry occupations — 10

TOTAL — 123

It will be noted here that a sizable proportion of these men—forty or so—were either servicemen away from their homes, or those whose employment involved much travelling, such as lorry drivers and commercial travellers. Here again the lack of a stable and affectionate home circle may be a factor. So too may the far wider circle of acquaintances that a traveller acquires over the years. But, here as elsewhere, one must guard against assessing as a cause what may be only an allied factor. A research worker in another field has suggested that many disturbed boys from broken or unhappy homes tend to go in for such jobs as lorry driving: they are perhaps attracted by the change of scene, the restlessness, the variety, the sense of power?

Cyril Greenland, a senior psychiatric social worker, has pointed out that in Scotland as a whole, as shown by Table 28 of the annual report for 1954 of the Registrar-General for Scotland, illegitimacy is rare in Classes I and II and, interestingly enough, in Class V, where most of the 'problem' families would be grouped. It is commonest in Class IV.[2]

---

[1] So far as we can fathom, sociologists do normally describe these as black-coated workers, even though green overalls, hula-hula feathers or travelling coats may more usually be worn.

[2] Cyril Greenland, *Some Ecological Aspects of Unmarried Parenthood* (*Lancet*, 19th January 1957).

A study made by Barbara Thompson of the births that occurred in *Aberdeen* between 1949 and 1952 shows that in that part of Scotland there is a very marked social-class gradient affecting illegitimate births.[1] Seven groups were differentiated:

1. Professional and technical workers
2. Clerical workers
3. Shop assistants etc.
4. Skilled manual workers
5. Unskilled manual workers
6. The fish trade
7. The catering and cleaning trades

Groups 1 to 5 corresponded broadly with the Registrar-General's Classes I to V, while the others—groups with certain distinctive features—were shown separately. The incidence of illegitimacy was found to rise progressively through all seven groups—from 2 per cent in the professional and technical group to 19 per cent among the catering and cleaning workers. 'It is evident', comments Barbara Thompson, 'that illegitimacy tends to be associated with unskilled, unattractive or menial occupations.'

MENTAL LEVEL

There is a natural tendency to associate illegitimacy with low mentality, because those of low mentality form so large a part of the 'problem group' that is more trouble to the authorities than all the rest put together. But however acute the problem, it is nowadays very small in relation to the whole problem of illegitimacy.

As to the illegitimate children of actual mental defectives, some three to four thousand are believed to be in the care of local authorities, but in spite of this, only about half of 1 per cent of all the mothers of illegitimate children are unmarried ascertained defective women, which is rather less than the estimated proportion of mental defectives in the population as a whole.[2]

[1] Barbara Thompson, *Social Study of Illegitimate Maternities* (*British Journal of Social and Preventive Medicine*, April 1956).

[2] See:
  (a) County of Devon Children's Committee. *The Illegitimate Children of Mental Defectives*, 1953. Estimate based on 3 per cent sample.
  (b) Ministry of Health's return for England and Wales, 1950. One hundred and sixty-eight births to unmarried ascertained defective women. A further two hundred and forty-seven had children after marriage, but these are assumed here to have been legitimate.
  (c) Wood Report, 1929. An estimated 0.8 per cent of the population were certified or ascertained mental defectives. This estimate is still believed to hold good.

A wider problem, though not as large as is commonly believed, is that of women who are not defectives but are of generally low mentality. In the Midboro survey, nineteen women were listed by the Moral Welfare worker as of 'poor mentality', and the health visitors stated that three others known to them were 'intellectually defective' and four more of 'low mentality'. The group of very low intelligence thus includes at least twenty-six women, or over 9 per cent of the survey. But there was no suggestion that the other women's intelligence was below average. Some were indeed described by the social workers as of superior intelligence.

A few examples will give an indication of what the social workers assessed as 'low mentality'. Only two were clearly ascertainable or certifiable defectives, but most of the following would generally be considered as border-line cases.

1. Mother 'subnormal mentally', looked after the child 'when she cannot get anyone else to do so'. She had had eight pregnancies, all by different men, and four of the children were dead. Several men helped financially. Child's welfare: bad.

2. Mother 'rather simple'. She lived with her parents and had 'no idea how to care for the child'. It was dirty and ill-kept and at three months old had developed a skin disease. The health visitor was in close touch.

3. Mother, 'mentality poor', could not work and lived on public assistance. This was her second illegitimate child; the father of the first gave her no help. The baby lived with her and her sister, both of whom had had brief terms in prison for petty theft.

4. Mother 'always of poor mentality', had been a backward child, hardly ever at school. She had had six legitimate children and two illegitimate children 'as well as this new baby'. Four were with her husband, one adopted, one dead, and the other three with her and her lover, the father of them, with whom she lived apparently stably. Children's welfare: fair.

5. Mother 'very poor type'. Mentality not described, but apparently the general inheritance was considered low, since no adoption society would take the children. She had three legitimate children, who were with their father, and three illegitimate ones, which she vaguely said she would like to have adopted.

Such assessments are admittedly practical rather than scientific, but the picture built up is fairly clear; around 10 per cent of these Midboro women who had illegitimate children were of too low a mentality to give their children a fair chance of health and happiness without very considerable help from the public authorities. This 10 per cent included quite a number of those who were cohabiting unstably.

One question arises here. Is this inability to cope with life really the by-product of innate low intelligence, or does it flow as much from their whole personality, emotional make-up and personal history, and indeed, from their environment? For instance, much of the feckless, short-sighted behaviour one finds among them might derive from serious inner frustrations or traditional ways of behaviour in the milieu in which they have grown up.

All one can safely say, then, is that about 10 per cent of the Midboro children were born to mothers of apparently poor general mentality, whereas the rest of the mothers appeared to be mentally a fairly normal cross-section of the community.

The question of children with mentally defective parents is taken up in chapter 11.

HOME ENVIRONMENT

Are the women who make unmarried mothers a typical product of broken or unhappy marriages or problem families?

Certainly delinquency, in the formal sense of having run foul of the law, seems to have played only a very small part among the Midboro mothers. The information may not have been complete but, as far as is known, they included only three young delinquents and three ex-prisoners—two petty thieves and a woman who had neglected her children—2 per cent in all.

The question as to whether the women came from happy homes is a far more difficult one, since happiness is not easy to define and also very hard for an outsider to assess. In her study of *Aberdeen*, Barbara Thompson established that in all social groups many more unmarried mothers than married mothers came from *broken* homes. As many as 40 per cent of the unmarried mothers in her study grew up either in homes in which one or other parent was missing, or did not grow up in their parental home at all, whereas among the married women who conceived after marriage, only 18 per cent came from broken homes, and even among those who conceived pre-maritally but were married before the child was born, only 23 per cent were from broken homes. She also noted that homes without a 'father figure' were twice as numerous among unmarried as among married mothers, and that the fathers of illegitimate children, about whom less was known, often came from broken homes themselves, sometimes commenting that they had felt 'smothered' by deserted or widowed mothers.

MARITAL STATUS OF PARENTS

What proportion of parents of illegitimate children are unmarried or, through divorce or the death of a partner, legally free to marry? What proportion are debarred by an existing marriage? The Midboro survey gives us some figures.

Civil Status of Fathers

	NUMBER		%
Married			
Living apart from wife	81		
Living with wife	2		
Not stated	30	113	40.6
Single		96	34.2
Divorced		5	1.8
Widowed		4	1.4
Not stated		61	22.0
TOTAL		278	100.0

Thus at least 37 per cent of the fathers were legally free to marry, and at least 40 per cent not free. It is significant, however, that two men only were certainly living with their wives at the time of the birth. In at least eighty-one cases, or 29 per cent, the marriage had already broken down, whether irreconcilably or not is unknown.

Civil Status of Mothers

	NUMBER	%
Married	73	26.3
Single	167	60.0
Divorced	18	6.5
Widowed	14	5.0
Not known	6	2.2
TOTAL	278	100.0

Between 71 and 74 per cent of these mothers were legally free to marry, and between 26 and 29 per cent were already married to someone other than the child's father. Of the seventy-three married women some sixty to seventy were already living permanently apart from their husbands—though it is not always clear whether they began to do so before or after they took this lover. Over forty of the separations had taken place some years before. A few mothers of natural children were still living with their own husbands but, although the law does not require this of them, registered the child as illegitimate.

Marriage as a Factor	NUMBER	%
He alone married	87	
She alone married	47	
Both married	26	
Bar to marriage	160	57.5[1]
Both single	60	
One single, one divorced, etc.	12	
No bar to marriage	72	26.0[2]
Civil status not known	46	16.5
TOTAL	278	100.0

So at least 26 per cent—possibly as many as 40 per cent—of the couples were free to marry, while at least 57.5 per cent, and perhaps as many as 70 per cent, were debarred.

THOSE WHO WERE FREE TO MARRY BUT DID NOT

Why had not those single in law married before the child was born? These are the women's answers:

	%
She did not wish to	5.0
He did not wish to	4.0
Parents opposed	2.0
Acquaintance too brief	4.0
Man abroad or address not known	2.0
Cohabiting without marriage	3.0
Married after the birth	4.0
Reason not known	2.0
TOTAL	26.0

[1] Or 69 per cent of those whose civil status was known.
[2] Or 32 per cent of those whose civil status was known.

There were only twelve clear cases where the man refused to marry the girl and so himself broke off the relationship. The extent to which illegitimate births result from a man 'letting a girl down'—in this most direct sense—is exaggerated.

It is not clear why some of the couples did not marry until after the child was born. Some, no doubt, were simply slow to make up their minds. But two or three said that they could not afford to marry, evidently meaning that they had not enough money to set up a separate home. Meanwhile they lived together, but in their parents' home, and their parents clearly shared the view that the essence of marriage was a separate household and that the marriage should not take place until they set up independently. One woman, having borne five children to the same man, still argued that they could not afford to marry!

In over half the cases, however, there was a deliberate decision not to marry. To some extent these were the younger ones. Even where parents do not withhold the consent that is necessary in law before those under twenty-one can marry, they often persuade a young girl not to cover up a pregnancy by making what they think would be an unhappy marriage. And many boys and girls in their teens realize for themselves that, though they are biologically mature, they are not yet ready to choose a partner for life, or at least that they have not yet met the right one. Some girls prefer to cut their losses: to bear an illegitimate child rather than to base on this mistake an attempt at a permanent marriage. Some, however, cannot marry because the man is already married. As the tables on page 65 show, while only 26.3 per cent of the Midboro mothers were certainly married (and a possible 2.2 per cent more), as many as 40.6 per cent of the fathers were certainly married (and a possible 22 per cent more). A number of these teen-agers, then, bore children to married men.

Of the 11.5 per cent of the Midboro mothers who were widowed or divorced, many already had legitimate children living with them. Some of these women were cohabiting with the fathers.

UNOFFICIAL FAMILIES

These Midboro parents of illegitimate children fall into three well-marked groups:

1. Those cohabiting stably.

2. Those cohabiting unstably or intermittently.
3. Those not cohabiting, including the many unmarried mothers who were living unsupported by the fathers.

'Stability' of course was impossible to define, but the social workers' opinion was accepted, and is borne out by the fact that 31 per cent of the women having illegitimate children in 1949 had already had one or more children by the same man.

The table below shows the extent of cohabitation in relation to the age groups of the mothers:

AGE	NUMBER	COHABITING STABLY	UNSTABLY	NOT COHABITING	COHABITING STABLY	UNSTABLY	TOTAL
					%	%	%
15-19	45	2	1	42	4.0	3.0	7.0
20-24	73	18	5	50	25.0	7.0	32.0
25-29	57	26	4	27	46.0	7.0	53.0
30-34	47	28	5	14	60.0	10.0	70.0
35-39	37	21	4	12	57.0	11.0	68.0
40-44	17	12	1	4	71.0	5.0	76.0
45	2	2	—	—	100.0	—	100.0
Age not known			1				
All ages	278	109	21	149	39.0	7.0	46.0

Stable Cohabitation

So here emerges the first clear sub-group among illegitimate children. Around 40 per cent of them are born to couples living stably together but debarred from marrying by the still-existing marriage of one or other partner. The study by the Midboro Health Department similarly found that at the actual time of conception about half of the mothers were living with the putative father, and that of those who were married, widowed or divorced, almost three-quarters were cohabiting; five years later the proportion still cohabiting was 44 per cent.

This is the pattern in Midboro. Other cities show a fairly close resemblance. In *Manchester* 35 per cent of the parents who bore illegitimate children in 1933 were cohabiting stably.

'This largest group', wrote the Medical Officer of Health in his annual report for 1938, 'were born into households in which there was an irregular union, and therefore a fairly permanent home in which the children had two parents. In some cases the illegitimacy was not known outside the home. A number of parents had postponed their marriage, others were indifferent to the marriage ceremony, but the largest number were living together in an irregular union because one partner had a husband or wife, and was living apart.'

By the end of five years some of these parents could not be traced. But of those traced, 32 per cent were still cohabiting and had their children with them in an apparently permanent family relationship. A few of these, but only a few, had married one another.

Spence's study, which covered some sixty-seven illegitimate births in *Newcastle-upon-Tyne*, shows that in the first year of their lives not less than twenty-seven (40 per cent) of the children were living with both parents as members of 'unofficial families' and this is apart from some 10 per cent whose parents had since married.[1]

At the 1954 conference of the Scottish Council for the Unmarried Mother and Her Child, Dr Nisbet stated that of two hundred illegitimate births inquired into by the *Kilmarnock* Health Department, sixty (30 per cent) of the mothers were cohabiting.

In a study of the records of the City of *Birmingham's* Maternity and Child Welfare Department for 1955, it emerged that in as many as three hundred cases (54 per cent) out of a total of six hundred and fifty illegitimate births known to the Department, the mother and child were living with the putative father as a complete family unit.

It seems, then, reasonable to assume that, at least in the cities, one in every two or three illegitimate births are to women cohabiting in a more or less permanent relationship. Whether stable cohabitation without marriage is as common in rural areas it is impossible to say. Further research may show these figures to be typical of large towns only, but it is in these that about 55 per cent of all illegitimate births occur. In the country, marriage may be stabler; in small towns it may be harder for lovers to live together without risk of gossip. But this is uncertain.

Stable cohabitation without marriage is common in all classes, though there are class differences. The table below shows that 35 per cent of the seventeen professional and salaried workers in Midboro who had illegitimate children were cohabiting stably with the mothers, as were 40 per cent of the skilled and semi-skilled workers and 69 per cent of the unskilled labourers.

[1] Sir James Spence *et alii*, *A Thousand Families in Newcastle-upon-Tyne* (1954).

SOCIAL CLASS	NUMBER	COHABITING STABLY Number	%	COHABITING UNSTABLY Number	%	COHABITING %
I Professional, etc. occupations	2	1	35.0	—		35.0
II Intermediate (salaried workers etc.)	15	5				
III Skilled Workers (including black-coated wage-earners)	123	49	40.0	11	9.0	49.0
IV Semi-skilled workers	25	10	40.0	4	16.0	56.0
V Unskilled labourers	26	18	69.0	3	12.0	81.0
III-V Other manual workers of unknown skill	27	13				
Class not known	60	13		3		
All classes	278	109	39.0	21	7.5	46.5

The following table, given in order of the proportion cohabiting, shows that behaviour is governed by occupation rather than by class distinctions as defined by the Registrar-General, varying widely both within and across the class barriers:

MAN'S OCCUPATION	NUMBER	COHABITING STABLY	COHABITING UNSTABLY	NOT COHABITING
Commercial traveller	2	2	—	—
Lorry driver	10	8	1	1
Miner	10	5	4	1
Engineer	16	14	—	2
Labourer, dustman, coalman	23	16	3	4
Bus driver or conductor	8	5	—	3
Painter and decorator	5	3	—	2
Builder	2	1	—	1
Factory worker	24	13	3	8
Shop assistant	4	1	—	3
Bricklayer	5	1	—	4
Mechanic	5	—	—	5
Taxi driver	2	—	—	2
Civil servants	2	—	—	2

Occupations force a wide difference in outlook. The civil servants were not cohabiting, the two commercial travellers were. Only a quarter of the shop assistants cohabited, but about 90 per cent of the engineers, miners and lorry drivers. Long-distance lorry drivers, who tend to sleep away from home, perhaps have a more natural opportunity than most workers to set up a household unnoticed and many are well-paid enough to do so. Miners have particularly large wage packets and probably a number come from distant parts. In their home towns in the mining districts high wages and marriage come to them early; there are few surplus women and few illegitimate children. But when they leave home the position may change. As for the 'engineers', the term may cover many grades of workers and it is harder to see an explanation. Wages are high; 'engineers' tend, one supposes, to be self-made men, self-reliant and used to taking their own decisions. No doubt they are sometimes men who married young and then, by individual skill, moved some distance up the social scale, leaving their wives behind them. This is speculative, but it may be significant that an 'engineer' has come to the top of the manual world and arrived at an independent view, whereas a black-coated worker, if he moves up into a new class, is coloured by the caution of someone seeking to find his feet on unfamiliar ground. To him, conformity and respectability are more important than initiative. Or there may be less meaning than this in the above table. It may reflect little more than the fact that well-paid weekly wage-earners feel able to support two families but tend not to save up for a divorce.

By education, nearly half of the women of elementary education were living with the child's father, 40 per cent of them stably, but only 30 per cent of the women of higher educational level cohabited, and nearly all of these were clerks or shop assistants. Only one, a hospital nurse already mentioned, was a professional woman according to the Registrar-General's classification. The explanation is probably simple: weekly wage-earners, and especially the less well-paid, could less easily afford a divorce and possibly, because of this, they had come to attach less importance to it.

As will be seen from the table on page 68, the incidence of stable cohabitation increases fairly steadily with age. This is natural, for as men and women grow older, they tend more strongly to settle to one partner. Steady affection and a home mean more, romantic adventures less. More women have been married; more of them have legitimate children living with them. Eighty-one out of Midboro's married women had other children; of these fifty-six had their children still living with them. The other twenty-five mothers had left their children.[1]

Unstable Cohabitation

There were a few women who lived with men who supported them only intermittently, and a few relationships that had broken down, but there were only twenty-one of these as compared with the one hundred and nine who cohabited stably. They were a curiously well-defined group. All the men were manual workers. The women tended to be of a rather simple type, none with more than an elementary education. Most of them were deserted wives and nearly all had children to support. Possibly they had hoped when they had taken a lover that they had found a wage-earner for their family, and if the relationship broke down it may have been because it was difficult to find anyone who was prepared to take on a family permanently. The entire absence of middle-class couples from this group may mean only that those of better education who have temporary liaisons are more familiar with contraceptive techniques.

Unmarried Women Not Cohabiting

A second large group of illegitimate children now emerges: those born to unmarried women not living in stable cohabitation with a man. They are here distinguished both from those unmarried mothers who have the steady help and support of the child's father in their home, and from those who have had previous experience of marriage and often of childbirth. Sixty per cent of the mothers of illegitimate children in Midboro were single women, the literally unmarried mothers; but over half of these were living stably with a married man. The number here lacks precision because of uncompleted questionnaires and because the Midboro girls did not always know and possibly did not always give correctly the man's marital status. Their own marital status is much more accurately known. The margin of error here is large, but the *minimum* figure of single women living stably with a married man was 31 per cent of the whole, or just over half of the 60 per cent who were single, and a more probable figure is about 35 per cent. So the proportion of illegitimate children born to unmarried women not cohabiting was very roughly 25 per cent.

[1] See also CHILDREN OF UNOFFICIAL FAMILIES, p. 249.

It is a smaller group than that composed of stably cohabiting couples, but it is a group with much greater problems for everyone concerned—the mother, the child, the statutory and voluntary bodies who help, and for society as a whole. The mother, in especial, can hardly avoid acute suffering. She has to face loneliness, shock, financial difficulties, her parents' attitudes, often social ostracism. She has the problems of whether to marry, and whether to keep or give up the child. Her position is in practice very different from that of a cohabiting woman.

If these admittedly rough Midboro figures are representative of the country as a whole, some ten thousand illegitimate children are born each year to unmarried women who are not cohabiting. To put it another way, there may be at present in England and Wales not far short of one hundred and fifty thousand children under school-leaving age who were born to single women without a man's stable support and companionship.

THE CHILD'S PLACE IN THE FAMILY

As for the child's place in the family, information is most complete in the case of the single women. Here are the figures for the one hundred and sixty-seven in the Midboro survey:

BIRTH ORDER	NUMBER	%
1st child	108	64.6
2nd child	34	20.4
3rd child	12	7.2
4th child	4	2.4
5th child	2	1.2
6th child	1	0.6
7th child	2	1.2
8th child	3	1.8
Order not stated but not 1st child	1	0.6
TOTAL	167	100.0

Many of the previous children referred to here had, however, been by the same father.

Of the one hundred and sixty-seven women who had never been married, fifty-nine had more than one child but, as far as is known, at least thirty-six and possibly as many as forty-three of these had each of their children by the same father, as the following table shows:

PROBABLE NUMBER OF FATHERS	NUMBER	%
1	36	21.6
2	12	7.2
2-3	3	1.8
3-4	1	0.6
Not known	7	4.2
TOTAL	59	35.4

A picture of the place of the new-born illegitimate child in his family order bears out the impression that well over a third of the natural children are born to couples living stably together without marriage:

			NUMBER	%
Primiparae			114	41.0
Previous legitimate children only			36	13.0
Previous illegitimate children				
By same man	77	28.0		
By different men	19	7.0		
Uncertain	21	7.0		
	117	42.0	117	42.0
Not known			11	4.0
TOTAL			278	100.0

For 28 per cent of these Midboro women, this baby was a second or later child born in an unofficial family by the same father. So far as is definitely known, only 7 per cent of the women had had illegitimate children by more than one man, and only three of these by more than two. In the five following years about 24 per cent of the mothers from whom information was available (sixty-eight out of two hundred and forty-four) had further illegitimate children, but this is in no way surprising, since so many of the parents were living in stable cohabitation, and in the great majority of cases the father was the same man as before. The idea that a large number of women have illegitimate children by a number of men evidently survives, like so many of the rumours about unmarried mothers, from a small but troublesome minority.

Three out of ten, then, of the Midboro children had elder brothers or sisters by the same father; no doubt many later had younger siblings as well. Two out of ten had legitimate half-brothers or half-sisters living with them, and in some of these cases the woman was living alone and not cohabiting. On the maternal side six out of ten had, even at the time of the survey, either brother or sisters or half-brothers or half-sisters. This point needs to be borne in mind in the framing of adoption policies, lest an illegitimate child be made an 'only' child artificially.

The percentage (41.0) of the Midboro women who had had no previous child may be rather below average. Although there is no national figure to show how many illegitimate children are their mother's first child, figures for individual cities at a variety of dates suggest that it might be somewhere between 55 and 70 per cent. For example, in 1933, surveys suggested that it was 70 per cent in *London* and 61.5 per cent in *Manchester*.[1] In a study of the women who gave birth to children in England and Wales in one week of 1946—and the study covered 60 per cent of these—it was estimated that of the unmarried mothers who gave birth to children during that week 68 per cent were primiparae.[2]

THE DEEPER QUESTION

In this chapter we have tried to set together the few firm facts that are known about the men and women who have illegitimate children, and to sketch in the broad outline of a general portrait of them. Inevitably at this stage it must be a superficial picture, limited to the facts that are known about a few comparatively large groups of unmarried mothers and their lovers, and any national statistics that are available. A 'sociological portrait' of this kind certainly has its value. It is very broadly based and so acts as a corrective to any deeper studies and may help one to judge how far more intimate studies made at close quarters should be accepted or regarded as typical. But it does not in itself tell one very much about the character and motives of the men and women concerned. It may show *who* have illegitimate children, but it largely ignores the far deeper question: why? To answer this we must first know who conceive their children outside marriage.

[1] A. C. Stevenson, *Recent Advances in Social Medicine*, p. 114 (1950).
[2] *Maternity in Great Britain*, a survey by a joint committee of the Population Investigation Committee and the Royal College of Obstetricians and Gynaecologists (1948).

CHAPTER 3

THE PREGNANT BRIDE

PRE-MARITAL CONCEPTIONS

One child in twenty is born illegitimate. But that is only the tiny fragment of a larger problem. One child in eight is conceived outside marriage—two and a half times as many as those who are born illegitimate. And the proportion of first-born children conceived outside marriage is higher still: one bride in five who ever gives birth to a child is pregnant on her wedding day.[1]

These disturbing facts first broke upon the public when the Population (Statistics) Act of 1938 enabled registrars for the first time to ask all parents registering births to inform them of the date of their marriage. This date is not required for the birth certificate—that is to say, it does not appear on it in England and Wales, though it does in Scotland—but is needed to help in the general statistical analysis of women's fertility by showing the various intervals after marriage at which children are born. Children born within eight and a half months after their parents' marriage are classed for these purposes as 'pre-maritally conceived'; if some of them are prematurely born, this is statistically counterbalanced by the omission of children born in the last two weeks of the normal term of pregnancy—that is, between eight and a half and nine months after the marriage. There is no national figure to show the number or proportion of first-born illegitimate children.

Basing his calculation on the number of maternities[2] within eight and a half months of marriage *plus* the total number of illegitimate maternities (on the assumption that nearly all were first children), the Registrar-General arrived at an unexpected conclusion.

'The revelation, made possible by the new records, that one-seventh of all children now born in the country are products of extra-marital conceptions, or to go further, that nearly 30 per cent of all mothers conceive their first-born out of wedlock, is

---

[1] Tables 10 and 11 apply.
[2] See footnote, Table 10.

sufficiently startling to render the matter of more than statistical significance. These are records of sexual irregularities which actually result in the birth of children.'[1]

On this basis the equivalent figure for 1950 would be 33.7 per cent, which may be a slight over-estimate; as we saw in the last chapter, the first-born percentage of the total number of illegitimate births is probably somewhere between 55 and 70 per cent. But if even one illegitimate child in two is a first baby, one mother in four (25 per cent in 1957) conceives her first child outside marriage.

High though this proportion seems, it is not exceptional. Only a limited number of countries keep separate records of pre-marital conceptions, but where figures are kept the picture is much the same. In *Australia* in 1947 about one-quarter of all first births were either extra-nuptial or occurred less than nine months after marriage.[2] In *New Zealand* in 1939 one bride in six—as compared with our one in five—was pregnant at marriage, the percentage (16.5) being based only on births taking place within seven months of marriage. In *Sweden* a bare generation ago as many as one in three of *all* children were conceived out of wedlock,[3] as compared with our present figure of one in eight. According to an article in the *Manchester Guardian* of 23rd September 1954, in *Western Germany* the 'most usual time for the first child to be born is during the seventh month after marriage'. As a Government measure interest free loans were raised in Western Germany 'to help young married couples to set up house and to discourage the widespread habit of living together before marriage'. Professor Binder mentions that investigations in *Saxony* proved that on average 57 per cent of first-born children were conceived before marriage.[4]

AGES OF THE MOTHERS

But we have not yet reached the most revealing figures. These emerge when we consider the ages of the women who give birth to irregularly conceived children. In *England and Wales* in 1950, 49 per cent of all live-born children born to married women in their

---

[1] *Statistical Review of England and Wales*, 1938-9.
[2] *Australian Vital Statistics*, 1947.
[3] Nils Nilsson, speaking at the International Congress of Population and World Resources in Relation to the Family (report published by Family Planning Association, 1948). Dr Nilsson apparently refers to the period 1926-30.
[4] *Uneheliche Mutterschaft*.

78   THE UNMARRIED MOTHER AND HER CHILD

teens were pre-maritally conceived; and 67 per cent of all first-born children in 1954 to married women of the same age. In *Scotland* the proportions for the first-born were 65.5 per cent in 1950 and 59.8 per cent in 1954.

These girls of under twenty conceived pre-maritally to a far greater extent than any older age group. The figures below show the percentage of first maternities that took place within eight and a half months of marriage in 1950.

AGE OF MOTHER	% England and Wales[1]	Scotland[2]
Under 20	67.2	65.5
20-21	23.5	27.7
25-29	9.9	11.8
30-34	9.0	9.7
All ages	20.4	22.7

If we look at the younger girls' ages in more detail we see this even more clearly. Table 13 does not show the relatively small number of live births to girls under the age of sixteen—two hundred and seventeen in 1950, or 0.6 per cent of illegitimate births—since, marriage being legally barred before the age of sixteen, all their children are inevitably illegitimate. But it will be seen that by far the greater number of births to women aged eighteen or under are the result of pre-marital conceptions. Professor Crew has commented on these births in *Scotland*:

'The proportion of pregnant brides, especially among the younger age groups, is astonishingly large. It has to be assumed either that pre-marital relations were entered into without any thought of marriage and that when conception occurred the partners decided to contract a "cover-up" marriage, or else that, marriage having been decided upon, the partners saw no reason for abstaining from sexual relations. Whatever the situation it means that the marriage ceremony is lightly valued and the absence of it not regarded as a deterrent to sexual activity.'[3]

It is striking how much higher a chance of marrying before the child's birth a girl has at some ages than at others. Table 13 seems

---

[1] *Statistical Review of England and Wales*, 1950. These figures are summarized in column 1, Table 12. Table 13 compares the ages of mothers conceiving irregularly with those of mothers conceiving within marriage.
[2] Adapted from annual report, 1950, of Registrar-General for Scotland.
[3] *Measurements of the Public Health*, p. 64 (1948).

to suggest that at sixteen either her parents may think her too young to marry or the man tends to be too young to support her: only 47 per cent of the girls who conceive irregularly at this age and carry the child to term marry before its birth. Probably many of these girls are persuaded by the plain economic facts of the situation to give the baby to adopters. In the later teens, and especially around the age of twenty, over three-quarters marry. After twenty-five the number drops rapidly, perhaps because the man is already married or because her parents can bring less pressure to bear than on behalf of a younger girl.

'FORCED' MARRIAGES

Is there any evidence as to how many marriages result from pre-marital intercourse among engaged couples, and how many are 'forced' marriages, decided upon by the couple, or under pressure brought to bear by the girl or her parents on a more or less reluctant male, because a child is on the way?

A hint may be contained in the fact, referred to by Mrs J. Mann, M.P., in the House of Commons on 7th February 1958, that a quarter of all the marriages made by girls under the age of twenty-one end in divorce. Either, one may guess, they were too young to make a success of marriage, or they entered into it somewhat unwillingly. Surely, then, it is not a coincidence that a third of all the women who marry at this age are pregnant before their wedding. If so many end in actual divorce, one does not like to think of how many end in unhappiness or separation.

Another hint may be contained in the *Statistical Review of England and Wales*, 1950,[1] from which these details of brides pregnant at marriage have been extracted:

STAGE OF PREGNANCY AT WHICH MARRIAGE TOOK PLACE

FIRST THREE MONTHS			SECOND THREE MONTHS			LAST THREE MONTHS		
1st	2nd	3rd	4th	5th	6th	7th	8th	9th
11	19	24	18	12	8	5	2	1
54%			38%			8%		

It is true that the early months of the pregnancy are reputed to be

---

[1] *Part II, Civil*, Table 60.

the hardest to bear psychologically (see page 107), so probably a number of panicked girls persuade their lovers into marriage even at this early stage; but some of the 11 per cent who married in the first month of pregnancy may well not have been aware that they had conceived. Even those who married in the second month—another 19 per cent—must have been uncertain. A doctor does not often give a decided opinion until the third month. Among married women expecting their first child, less than half (43.9 per cent) consult a doctor within the first three months,[1] and unmarried mothers tend on average not to attend for ante-natal care until well into the fifth month of pregnancy.

It seems as though—unwilling though they are to visit doctors—many of the girls may try to persuade their lovers into marriage as soon as they miss their first period, but may still have to wait another two or three months before the marriage takes place.

THE INCIDENCE OF PRE-MARITAL CONCEPTIONS

No analysis has yet been made of the pre-marital conception rates of individual towns and villages of England and Wales, but there is a broad regional analysis (Table 14) and in addition a few local studies such as Alwyn Rees's description of a village in *Montgomeryshire*.[2] It will be seen from Table 14 that in the north of England and in Wales the proportion of pregnant brides is especially high. This does not necessarily mean that the illegitimacy rate follows the same pattern, and while sometimes both rates are high—as in the East and West Ridings of *Yorkshire*, the north-west counties and the north midlands—in other parts—for example, in *South Wales*—a very large number of girls conceive before marriage, but relatively few are still unmarried when the child is born. Again, there are parts of the country in which illegitimacy is comparatively rare—the farm lands of *North Wales*, the mining districts of *South Wales* and *Durham*, the dormitory areas around *London* (also, surprisingly, in London's East End)—but this does not mean that fewer children are conceived outside marriage.

Detailed studies are still be be made—and they should prove both rewarding and fascinating—of the factors that may lie behind these differences between regions: the relative scarcity of men of

---

[1] *Maternity in Great Britain*, p. 32.
[2] Alwyn D. Rees, *Life in a Welsh Countryside* (1950).

marriageable age, or of young women, in a neighbourhood; the age at which the local men attain a wage on which a family can be supported; the stability of a neighbourhood or its tendency towards a shifting population; the infinite variety of local customs, ancient or modern, and of underlying philosophies and points of view on courtship and marriage; the influence of the Church.

In the parish described by Alwyn Rees: 'The number of pre-marital pregnancies shows that sexual intimacy is frequent during courtship . . . All extra-marital pregnancies were considered improper and extremely unfortunate unless the situation was saved by marriage. But public censure seems to be less severe than, for example, in the Welsh industrial communities of South Wales . . . Within marriage, on the other hand, cases of unfaithfulness appear to be extremely rare and broken marriages are almost unknown.'[1]

In many parts of the Welsh and Scottish countryside, as in parts of rural England, it seems still be be quite usual for a couple who are going together to have intercourse, but to postpone marriage until a child is conceived. One Welsh woman is reputed to have said to her neighbour one morning over the garden wall:

'My Bessy is to be married.'

'Why,' said the neighbour, 'we did not even know she was expecting!'

Just as the Welsh seem to make honest women of the girls they lead astray—but do lead them astray in a big way—so the Durham miners seem to have very few girls to lead astray and consequently also have a very low illegitimacy rate.

It is said still to be quite usual to delay marriage in rural districts and this may possibly be traced to the farmer's realistic sense, that perhaps some share with Abraham, that his need of sons from his wife is as much an economic reality as his need of calves from his cow, so it is as well to be sure that his bride-to-be will be able to bear him children.

As typical of one philosophy underlying pre-marital conceptions, Rowntree and Lavers instance a city-bred young Englishwoman.

'Miss Y. is an attractive working-class girl of about 21. She is now being courted by a young labourer. They habitually sleep

---

[1] *Life in a Welsh Countryside*, pp. 87-8 and p. 28.

together and intend to get married as soon as Miss Y. is pregnant.'[1]

Marriage is regarded in some working-class homes not so much as a matter of legalizing a sexual union as the setting up of a new household. Parents will sometimes bring little pressure on their sons and daughters to marry until they are able to move to a place of their own and so, if housing difficulties are acute or financial resources inadequate, a child may even be born in the grandparents' household with both generations feeling that marriage must be postponed until the parents can find themselves, or afford to set up, a separate home.

A study made in 1939 shows that, at any rate before the war, it was very rare for middle-class parents to conceive their children before marriage.[2] Similar results were obtained from the 1911 fertility census. Few employers, professional men, clerks or foremen made their brides pregnant before marriage. It is probable that in the time of the great 'bottle-neck' in the divorce courts after the war, more middle-class couples anticipated marriage while waiting for a divorce from a previous partner, and certainly there were some children conceived of such unions, but the position today is, as far as we know, a matter for conjecture. How far professional and black-coated workers become the fathers of natural children is also unknown, but if they do cause a girl to conceive outside marriage it would seem likely that the child must be born illegitimate or the pregnancy ended with an abortion, if 'cover-up' marriages are rare.

The regional differences we have described derive in part from traditional occupations in the various districts. In the London region, where there is a high proportion of clerical workers, pre-marital conceptions are relatively few. Whether this stands for a greater sexual restraint or merely a more widespread knowledge of birth control, or even more abortions, it is not possible to say. Among shop assistants and manual workers throughout the country, pre-maritally conceived children are rather more common, especially among the unskilled workers.

But it is among farm workers, miners and, to a lesser extent, textile workers that by far the greatest number of pre-maritally

---

[1] B. S. Rowntree and G. R. Lavers, *English Life and Leisure*, Case History No. 81 (1951).
[2] W. A. B. Hopkin and J. Hajnal, *Analysis of the Births in England*, 1939 (*Population Studies*, September 1947).

conceived children are to be found. In the mining areas particularly, and in spite of the strong influence of the Methodist and Baptist Churches, local tradition is evidently tolerant of pre-marital intercourse. Since they are on full adult wages at the age of eighteen, the men marry young, and since there are few light industries offering employment to women, there is a shortage of girls of marriageable age and so conception is normally followed by marriage. Textile workers also tend to conceive before marriage, but as the illegitimacy rate is high in *Yorkshire*, the north-western counties and the midlands, it may be that fewer marry before the child is born.

Broadly, pre-marital conceptions follow almost exactly the pattern of fertility.[1] As with that other measure of fertility, the total number of children in a family, conception before marriage tends to relate directly to the heaviness of a man's physical work. It is the miners and agricultural labourers who have the largest families, followed by textile workers and unskilled labourers, and it is foremen, clerical and professional workers whose families tend most often to be small.

The study made by Barbara Thompson in *Aberdeen* (see page 62) was largely based on medical records, so it was possible to define pre-marital conception a good deal more accurately than in the Registrar-General's tables, which are confined to the information given in birth registrations. By Barbara Thompson's definition, a conception is pre-marital if the first day of the last menstrual period antedated marriage by more than four weeks.

The incidence of pre-marital conception was found to rise progressively in the first six groups, from 9 per cent of all maternities in the professional and technical group to 40 per cent among fish workers. When illegitimate births and pre-marital conceptions were combined, there proved to be 'a steady gradient from 11 per cent in the professional and technical group to 58 per cent among fish workers'. The combined rate in catering and cleaning workers was 40 per cent. Although this group occupied a position between skilled and unskilled workers, 'the ratio of illegitimacy to prenuptial conceptions is higher than in any other group'. The conclusion that illegitimacy tends—at any rate in Aberdeen—'to be associated with unskilled, unattractive or menial occupations'

---

[1] Hopkin and Hajnal *op. cit.*

applied with equal force to pre-marital conceptions. How far the facts apply outside Aberdeen or outside Scotland is still unknown.

CHAPTER 4

THE HUMAN BACKGROUND

We come down now closer to the individual girls and women who have illegitimate children. Can we understand something of the hundreds and thousands of human situations that lead up to the children's conception and birth? In the previous chapters we discovered to some extent *who* have illegitimate children. Can we throw any light on *why* they have them?

If we are to attempt this we must shed any superficial habit we may have of judging people's actions, as a Maths master confidently marks his ticks and crosses, his 'right' and 'wrong', in a child's exercise book. We must bring to the story of other people's lives something of our approach in a very mixed art gallery: an effort to see and feel through others' eyes, to catch something of their vision, to share their anger and love.

WESTERN AND CHRISTIAN MARRIAGE

Each human being has to work out in his personal life an individual solution to problems that face the whole human race: the child must learn to walk, men and women must learn for themselves the art of loving. They experience on one side a straight biological drive towards sexual intercourse, part of an instinctive urge to continue the race; they desire this as the greatest of all physical pleasures, and a man longs to prove his manhood, a girl her womanhood, through this adult experience. But there is also the urge—slower to develop but often no less strong—to love and to protect; to rear children, not merely to beget them; to be fulfilled through a deep personal life in loved company, an experience more satisfying in the end than passionate episodes. The first of these instincts ensures the continuity of the human race, its *esse*; the second its stability, its *bene esse*.

These two instincts, both good, both necessary, often come into conflict; they have to be brought deliberately into harmony. Different civilizations have at various times evolved different solutions. It is perhaps a matter for wonder that so early in our development from animal ancestry through primitive to so-called civilized man our own society should have chosen, not merely as an ideal but as a standard for the ordinary citizen, such a high principle as that of faithful, monogamous, lifelong partnership, the ideal of Christian marriage.

The public morality that our culture has chosen rests on two bases, a practical and a spiritual, the State and the Church. The State supports it because it is the best foundation for social stability: it is incomparably the best way of rearing children and it creates closely knit families who help each other out in time of need or trouble, so that fewer have to fall back on the State for support. It canalizes powerful emotions and helps them to become protective and cohesive instead of irresponsible and disruptive to society.

To the Church, it is man's apprenticeship to Christ's vision of a perfectly loving relationship: it is the setting in which the ordinary Christian can best learn to practise a love that is active and realistic; not a projection of dreams, but an exercise in seeing and accepting people as they are; loving them 'for better for worse', not 'on good behaviour only'; laying down life if necessary for the other's sake, and certainly forgoing many minor pleasures for the sake of a greater happiness.

Western marriage, however, the actual practice of Western men and women, generally falls far short of the Christian or even conventional ideal: the gap between public morality and private practice is very large. Clearly that must be so if one mother in five still conceives her first child outside marriage, if one child in twenty is born illegitimate, and if unofficial families exist in their tens of thousands.

Whatever view one may hold upon this issue, one is forced to recognize that many in the West have come out of 'realism' to accept a standard lower than the Christian—to regard occasional pre-marital intercourse between men and women who love one another as permissible—or very apt to occur—and to accept the possibility that, if a marriage should fail, it may be replaced, legally or privately, by a new partnership.

In England this 'realist' philosophy is not always acknowledged by those who hold it: many pay lip-service to the Christian ideal while acting according to the less demanding standard. But the adolescent tends to be less easily taken in. As he grows up he usually becomes aware that he has the choice between the two standards and, as if the choice were not already difficult enough, Western civilization allows commercial and other pressures to grow up, which work with great skill towards confusing him. During the long period between sexual maturity and the time when a man is in a financial position to marry, sexual longings are calculatingly stimulated through advertising with no concern for the social results, though with a lively concern for the financial ones. As G. W. Jordan and E. M. Fisher write:

'While Society says to its potential Romeo and Juliet, "Wait till your apprenticeship is finished and you have a secure job," those in charge of mass-produced entertainment, advertising and the popular press, keep up a ceaseless sex bombardment. Even shoe polish, apparently, will sell better if backed by sex-appeal. and modern mob-thinking can produce an early awareness of sex even in the audience of a children's cinema show. Books and periodicals emphasize the romantic and erotic in captions and illustrations. In fact, a "mass-observer" from some simple society might note what would appear to him the strange form of torture prevalent in a society which decrees that the young shall postpone all expression of sex until economic security is attained, and at the same time by its advertising provides mass incitement to break the law.'[1]

Other factors too have changed the attitude of many young people towards the traditional morality. The development of contraceptives has taken away much of the risk of having an unwanted child. Many people in all honesty feel that the old morality is therefore out of date. 'Why shouldn't we?' they ask. 'It is our own private concern; it doesn't hurt anyone else.'

The Church's values carry less weight since society has become increasingly secular. A recent inquiry of the Church of Scotland's Committee on Religious Instruction of Youth found that 38 per cent of the young men questioned saw nothing wrong in pre-marital relations if the couple were engaged, nor did 11 per cent of the young women: 17 per cent of the men and 4 per cent of the women saw nothing wrong even if they were not engaged. Geoffrey Gorer also found, in his large sample of all ages, that only about 63 per cent of the women and 52 per cent of the men positively disapproved of pre-marital experience.[2]

[1] G. W. Jordan and E. M. Fisher, *Self-Portrait of Youth*, p. 108 (1955).
[2] Geoffrey Gorer, *Exploring British Character* (1955).

The rule in some professions that a woman should give up her job on marriage, and the far heavier taxation that falls on a married couple who are both earning than on the same couple living together without marriage, is a strong incentive to an influential few to 'live in sin', and the wayward emotional lives of Hollywood stars and of certain other public figures influence any who are stirred by them or who tend to imitate their values as well as their hair styles.

These are a few of the cultural factors that influence sexual behaviour. It seems reasonably certain that behaviour has become more lax in the last fifty years, since the figures for illegitimacy are higher than in 1900, although the use of contraceptives has spread.

THE SOCIAL GROUP

Some of the influences upon a child as he develops his personal values and habits are widely recognized—the general pressures of modern Western society and the more intimate influence of his parents. But hardly less important, though less studied, are those in between: the influences of the little community or social group in which he is brought up, and the group that he may later join or find himself in: his church, his neighbourhood and street community, the social set among which he spends his leisure time, the village or factory or ship or shop he works in, his profession, occupational group or trade union—each of which may have its own separate values and customs. The outlook of every one of us is strongly influenced by the group to which he or she belongs, and the public standard of morality as we have described it affects us mainly in so far as it is filtered down to us through our group. Few of us know much about the feelings and customs of other groups. The values, customs, hopes and fears of a Welsh farming community, a cathedral close, an East End parish, a West End professional circle, a Manchester cotton mill, an Aberdeenshire fishing port, a group of Cornish artists, or a group of young Notting Hill toughs may be very different. A boy or girl growing up in one of these communities—now passive, perhaps overwhelmed, now actively choosing or rebelling or accepting—develops a highly personal outlook that must affect the deepest decisions of his or her life.[1]

---

[1] A rather pompous little girl wrote of how she 'fell into the dark haze of what is called "Juvenile Delinquency"'. 'At the time of my thirteenth year I decided to be a wild chick as I had seen many of my friends doing . . . I was the type that wanted to follow the crowd, I did but got stuck.' (Review in *Listener*, 24th May 1956, of *1,000,000 Delinquents*, by Benjamin Fine.

In a paper given at Peebles in 1957 to the Scottish Marriage Guidance Council, Dr Illsley, the sociologist of the Medical Research Council in Aberdeen, observed that 'the content of marriage is largely determined by the social context in which it occurs; attitudes and values imported from a different context may be not merely inappropriate but even harmful'. He contrasted especially the way of life of professional people and those having high responsibility in industry and government, with that of the semi-skilled and unskilled workers. One of the most striking differences between these groups is in the length of their education: the professional and managerial classes receive long schooling and generally a university or technical education that demands long-term planning and the sacrifice of leisure and money for a distant goal. Even when they enter upon their working careers it is often some years before they can afford to support a family. In both their adolescence and early adult life, they are often too deeply occupied in preparing for and learning about their main life's work to be as concerned with courtship and marriage, or to be as ready to experiment as less educated groups.

One could add that their values and standards tend to be more consciously held; that self-control for the sake of a distant goal is often felt to be a more acceptable hardship; that it is in the nature of their work to take responsibility, to look ahead, to consider the consequences of their actions; that they are probably paid by the month and pay their rates and taxes by the year. In short, they plan.

The occupational risks of these classes might therefore be assumed to be not so much illegitimate babies—though they do indeed have them—as the worship of success, nervous strain, or self-satisfaction with their own behaviour.

But an adolescent who enters semi-skilled employment has quite a different experience, He may leave school feeling that he has at last reached adult status, but when he starts work 'he appears to be taught none of the interesting processes he longs to work at, but he runs errands and makes tea or dusts the shop; he is given no responsibility at all, and then accused by his elders of being irresponsible.'[1]

For this class of boys and girls the risk may be boredom and frustration, from which may follow the adolescent's attempt to prove his manhood in another direction. Little thought is given

[1] *Self-Portrait of Youth*, p. 31.

to the risks attendant upon pre-marital intercourse. Their life has not trained them to think in terms of the future. They are paid by the week and so are their parents; the money that comes in one Friday night is gone by the next Friday morning. The family buy their furniture and TV on hire-purchase; you get your satisfaction first and pay up later. Brought up in that kind of milieu they never learn to look ahead.

THE FAMILY

When we come to the girl's response to the influences around her and to her relationship with her family, we often discover again a conflict of forces that ends in her becoming an unmarried mother. She may be an unhappy rebel in a correct, self-controlled but unloving family and a respectable neighbourhood. She may be an unusually sensitive and intelligent girl from a narrow suburban family who, in groping towards something better, loses her way and gets into an emotional tangle. She may be a carefully brought up girl who, far from home, finds herself in a community that accepts extra-marital intercourse as normal. She may be a tough girl, from a cynical family out for the main chance, in a society without standards.

Even when a family appears united to the outside world, it may happen that a child within it has never known security or real affection: one girl may be resented because her parents wanted a boy, or be thrust into the background when the longed-for son is born; another may be unwelcome from birth because her mother did not want her pregnancy, or because she wrecked her father's budget; another may be the gifted but unbalanced child of a family too preoccupied with their own pleasures and problems to give her the understanding she needs; another may be a girl who feels herself the stupid one or the ugly duckling in a socially gifted family, where all but she seem to attract love and friendship; another may have a cold father, or a dominating mother in whose shadow she never feels a person in her own right.

And yet, with all this diversity, we must inderstand these women, and this for three practical reasons. First, illegitimacy leads to so much unhappiness and to so many problems for mother, child and society. Secondly, she and the child are human beings who may need help—understanding help that fits their practical and emotional needs and works towards reintegrating them both into society. And thirdly, the child needs a good, loving and stable upbringing. Will its mother be able to provide this, alone or with her family? As the girl she is, in the situation in which she finds herself, should she be helped to keep her child, or is early adoption better? The decision must be hers, but any who help to clarify her mind carry heavy responsibility and should know a great deal about not only the girl herself but also her family and social setting.

DIFFICULTIES OF PSYCHOLOGICAL STUDY

In trying to study these mothers one is faced with two sets of difficulties, one practical, the other emotional. On the practical side, as we have seen, it is impossible to build up a picture that does not tend to be either superficial or unrepresentative. On the emotional side it is hard to view these things dispassionately. We each bring with us our own background of struggles, ideals, successes and failures. We are akin to the Puritans castigated by Samuel Butler, who

> 'Compound for sins they are inclin'd to
> By damning those they have no mind to',

or, if we have had difficulties, we may have grown unmerciful to those who struggle unsuccessfully: it does not always make us tender towards those who have them.

But supposing we are prepared to face the facts, they may still prove almost impossible to discover. No deep enough character study has been made of a fully representative group of unmarried mothers or fathers, and it is not easy to see how one can ever be made. Who will ever know all the women of a single area sufficiently well? Many of the *Midboro* parents were living an apparently normal life as 'husband' and 'wife' although their union had never been legalized. Men and women in that position do all they can to remain anonymous. Many of them are as capable as any other citizen of solving their problems without the help of outsiders, so comparatively few of them are likely to seek the advice of social workers; if they do, they may not mention that they are not legally married. Health visitors call on these families in the course of their work; later the parents may become known to he teachers at the schools their children attend; but what teacher or health visitor would welcome an invitation to give an intimate psychological portrait of every such parent? Of the members of this group one cannot ever hope to obtain an adequate portrait. It is doubtful if one has even the right to know who they are.

There are, perhaps, only three ways in which one could attempt to build up a psychological portrait of unmarried mothers. One might base it on women well known to some case-work agency, or on all those willing to co-operate with a skilled research worker, or alternatively, a psychiatrist might compose a questionnaire that would elicit, say from schools or health visitors, the most relevant information from a statistically complete group. Each method has its limitations and one should not regard any as likely to give one a complete, generally valid result.

A random sample of the women known to a case-work agency would be invaluable as a study of the problems with which that agency chiefly has to deal and one of the best of all methods of enriching case-workers' understanding of their work; but it would not give an unbiased portrait of unmarried motherhood. For who consults the agencies? Not a fair cross-section, but those who need help. In *Midboro* the Moral Welfare workers, who also acted for the Adoption Society, knew 40 per cent of the mothers—one hundred and ten out of the two hundred and seventy-eight—though some of these contacts had been brief. They had been consulted by over 70 per cent of the mothers under twenty-five, but by only 14 per cent of the women over thirty; by 20 per cent of those cohabiting unstably, but by as few as 5 per cent of the much larger number who cohabited stably. This double bias, both of age and of status, is fairly general in the work of the Moral Welfare agencies and is one that they acknowledge. There might be other sources of bias in their sample: girls whose homes are happy, and whose parents are willing to stand by them in their troubles, have less need to consult social workers. They may do so if they wish to go to a Mother and Baby Home around the time of the confinement or if they wish to have the child adopted, but many never come at all. Some of the more anti-social women, such as prostitutes, prefer to steer clear of the agencies, and at the other extreme, the more educated professional women have less need of help. Just as no one would claim that the people consulting case-work agencies give a balanced portrait of the population as a whole, the unmarried mothers known to agencies are not typical of unmarried mothers at large. But, as doctors in practice have to study illness rather than health, social workers give attention to the women who create most problems and who suffer most.

The second method, to base the study on those women willing to co-operate with a skilled research worker, is also liable to bias. Professor Binder, who used this method in the *Swiss* study we shall later describe, did not obtain an entirely 'random' sample of women; as a research worker he had to limit his material to 'effective contacts'.

The third method, though indubitably more superficial, might be promising in certain circumstances: that is, to give a sociological survey rather greater depth by compiling with a psychiatrist a questionnaire of such a kind that a health visitor, or any other social worker in touch with the mothers and children, could reasonably fill in over a period of time from limited observation and knowledge, yet the psychiatrist, analysing the returns, could assess from them something at least of the women's deeper character. In his questionnaires about disturbed children in schools and observation centres, Dr D. H. Stott has shown how much can be done by directing the observation of relatively unskilled workers to the right points. An enormous advance of knowledge might be made if his methods were used, through the schools, to assess the comparative development of natural children who have grown up in different home circumstances; who have been adopted or fostered or remained with their own mothers, or have gone back into the grandparents' home. To assess the mothers themselves would be much more difficult, though it might conceivably be attempted in quite a small town, for example, that had good social services and good records, a reasonably static population, and where the mother's own family background and childhood circumstances were adequately known, or the facts—broken homes, early nervous difficulties, and so on—could be ascertained. But that survey too would certainly remain incomplete and in some ways superficial. Unmarried mothers move from place to place, and many do not wish to be known even to the most discreet and sensitive of social workers. They have a perfect right to their privacy.

THE EMOTIONALLY DISTURBED

We cannot, then, at present get a really representative psychological picture of men and women who have illegitimate children. This fact may be at the root of a strong division of opinion among workers in the field over the degree of responsibility that these men and women have for their actions. The group that psychiatrists know best is somewhat weighted by the mentally or emotionally disturbed; the larger group with whom social workers are in contact includes, or seems to include, many who can get along better in the normal world; and we know very little as yet of those who perhaps manage best, the group that slips by quietly and is seen by neither.

One notable piece of research has already been done, using the first of the three methods we have described. Dr Leontine Young, of the New York School of Social Work, made a study in 1945 of a random sample of one hundred mothers aged eighteen to forty from an unmarried mothers agency, excluding only those who came from a background where illegitimacy was socially acceptable and any mothers under the age of eighteen.[1] The girls, though they came from a variety of backgrounds, tended in consequence to be somewhat above average as regards age and background, for it is more often at the lower social levels or in isolated country districts that the birth of a natural child is, if not approved, at least quickly accepted and the parents' behaviour not held against them.

All except six of these hundred women proved either to have come from broken homes (forty-three instances) or to have had dominating mothers (thirty-six) or dominating fathers (fifteen). The 'broken homes' included homes where one or both of the parents had died, or where they had separated or been divorced. In all, as many as forty-eight of the girls were described as having 'dominating and rejecting mothers' and another twenty 'dominating and rejecting fathers', and the girl's relation to the dominant parent was 'a battleground on which a struggle was fought, and the baby was an integral part of the struggle'.

Dr Young claimed that the great majority of unmarried mothers were more or less seriously neurotic. Among the women in her study:

'One of the most frequent tendencies to be found was that of self-punishment. Almost none of the cases was completely free of it and with many of them it represented the major force in their lives. So deeply ingrained and so powerful was this force that often

---

[1] Leontine Young, *Personality Patterns in Unmarried Mothers* (*Family Journal of Casework*, Family Service Association of America, New York, 1945).

the girl would permit nothing and nobody to interfere with its self-destructive progress.'

Dr Bowlby, who drew upon Dr Young's research and other studies in the *United States* and *Canada* in his important book, *Maternal Care and Mental Health*, concluded: 'Preliminary studies such as these go far to demonstrate that, in a Western community, it is emotionally disturbed men and women who produce illegitimate children of a socially unacceptable kind.'[1] And again, 'the girl who has a socially unacceptable illegitimate baby often comes from an unsatisfactory home background and has developed a neurotic character, the illegitimate baby being in the nature of a sympton of her neurosis.'[2]

'There can be no doubt', wrote Dr Young in a subsequent book, 'that the drive which propels an unmarried mother results in compulsive action. To say that her behaviour is the result of immorality or of free choice is to ignore all the evidence. The logical and seemingly inevitable result of her psychological development is an out-of-wedlock child, and like a sleepwalker she acts out what she must do without awareness or understanding of what it means or of the fact that she plans and initiates the action.'[3]

In this later book Dr Young made it quite clear that she did not claim that her study necessarily had validity outside the United States.

'The unmarried mothers so far described', she wrote, 'have been with few exceptions people with more or less serious emotional difficulties. The question is frequently raised, "Is this necessarily the case?" In other words, does a girl have to be neurotic or psychotic to bear an out-of-wedlock child? Europeans, particularly, question this and have pointed out that in some European countries this is not true of the unmarried mothers. In these countries social workers have observed some unmarried mothers with personality problems like those described here, but the large number of girls having out-of-wedlock babies are not like this. They seem to be much healthier, emotionally, have usually had a more enduring love relationship with the baby's father, and are generally devoted to their children. Many of them keep their babies, and, if they marry later, bring up the children in their own homes . . . The difference

---

[1] *Maternal Care and Mental Health*, p. 95 (1952).
[2] *Ibid*, p. 93.
[3] *Out of Wedlock*, p. 36 (1954).

has its source, pretty clearly, in the cultural background . . . Unmarried mothers mirror faithfully the degrees of social disapproval existing within the over-all cultural setting . . . Thus a girl brought up in a strict middle-class home is usually emotionally sicker than one from a more flexible and permissive environment . . . For the same reason the older woman tends to be more neurotic than the young girl. Public opinion may excuse if not exonerate the girl . . . Married women having out-of-wedlock children are often extremely sick psychologically. Our culture condemns them with more violence than the girl . . .'[1]

It is not surprising that her thesis met with strong opposition on many levels over here when it was first advanced—notably, though not only, from social workers. As one woman, not herself a trained worker, put it:

'In my young days these women were thought of as "bad women". You were sorry for them, you tried to help, but they had to be brought to realize they'd gone wrong before you could help them to go right. Now it seems that they're all mad, not bad. They can't help themselves. There's no freedom of will any more, no point in moral effort. If you're born to have an illegitimate baby, have it you will.'

The stubborn reluctance of social workers in this country to accept this thesis that a majority of unmarried mothers are neurotic is, of course, based on more than this; it is based on a very wide practical experience. They have watched difficult choices being made and have been impressed by the capacity of these women to triumph over handicaps and to bring up apparently healthy and happy children: they are not determinists. They claim no special knowledge of the psychology of the unconscious, but their impressions cannot be wholly written off.

Sociologists have also added their voice. Extra-marital intercourse, they stress, is very widespread. Are most of those who have extra-marital relations to be thought of as neurotic, or only those who conceive children outside marriage? Is failure to use birth control, and the ignorance of contraception among the young, always to be classed as neurotic?

The 'average citizen' adds another point of view. In other spheres of life, most people fall down sometimes on their adult responsibilities and do things they do not mean to do. Most of them—most

[1] *Out of Wedlock*, pp. 114 and 116.

of us—may be lucky enough to keep such immature behaviour within socially approved limits; but if we are not, are we always to be called neurotic?

Common sense would suggest that women who have extra-marital relationships probably do, in our present society, include a rather higher proportion of neurotics than those who do not. The women who conceive a child by a man whom they are then unable to marry, probably include a distinctly higher proportion. In our present state of knowledge it may be better to leave the matter there and to say that *among* unmarried mothers, as almost everyone would agree, there are an important number who are in general terms neurotic, immature, not fully responsible for their actions.

The old mystery of the degree to which man has freedom of the will is brought sharply before us today by the recent advances in understanding of unconscious drives that lie beneath human actions, even when they do not entirely govern them. So if we try to study why illegitimate children are brought into the world we must do it very humbly. No one ever completely understands another; motives are complex; forces of social pressure, religious belief, emotional relationships within the family, private fears and longings, act in an entirely individual fashion on the individual girl, according to her hereditary make-up, her upbringing and the degree of her integration as a person. The statistical method used in previous chapters is no longer apposite here. People cannot be fitted with any accuracy into psychological categories with such-and-such a proportion in each. There are too many border-line cases, too many insufficiently known, too many who move from one class to another, who have spells, but only spells, of neurotic behaviour in an otherwise normal life. Any figures, then, that may be quoted in the rest of this chapter are given without any claim that they are representative in this country. They will give some indication of important psychological groups, but since those in stable unions enter very little into psychological studies and the psychotic are also generally omitted, they fail to do justice both to those most likely to have weighed up pros and cons and decided to rear an illegitimate family, and to those who certainly did not—the freest and the least free.

A SWISS STUDY

The most detailed and authoritative study to date of the psychological make-up of any large group of unmarried mothers, and the effect upon them of their experience, was published in *Switzerland* in 1941 by Professor (then Doctor) Hans Binder under the title of *Uneheliche Mutterschaft*. This book, already referred to on pages 56 and 77, has not been translated into English and does not seem to be available in English libraries. It is out of print in Switzerland, so a copy was kindly lent by the author. Only certain sections of this highly technical and absorbing study are summarized here.

Professor Binder, at that time Director of the Psychiatric Policlinic and the Ehe-und Sexualberatungsselle (Marriage and Sex Advice Bureau) in *Basle*, wished to study how frequently and in what types of personality unfavourable psychic developments may *follow* unmarried motherhood. The inquiry was undertaken for a strictly practical reason: to assess in what circumstances women who bear children outside marriage sustain psychological damage so severe and permanent that a doctor would have been justified in performing an abortion, and whether it is possible to foresee, from the beginning of the pregnancy, of which women this will prove true. In order to decide these questions, he had to examine the whole social and psychological background of as large and representative a group of unmarried mothers as was practical.

In Switzerland all natural children come under a system of official guardianship, and Professor Binder aimed at a 'random and typical selection' of three hundred and fifty cases from the files of the Amtsvormundschaft (Official Guardianship) Bureau of Basle, the organization through whose hands all the mothers of natural children born or resident in the city automatically passed. He thus had a unique opportunity that would not be open to anyone in Great Britain. Official files and the possibility of official contact existed for all unmarried mothers in the city and he, as accredited psychiatrist, could make the maximum of any interviews that were arranged.

The cases were taken from a register of three thousand notified illegitimate births that had taken place in the city since 1912. Wholly 'random', however, the selection could not be, since he naturally included only effective contacts. Some children had died, others had passed out of the jurisdiction of the Bureau on

coming of age, or on being legitimated or adopted, or by moving away from the city; some mothers were psychotic and could not be effectively interviewed; some mothers' addresses could not be traced, some did not respond to the letter of invitation to come to the clinic and others, finding on their arrival the purpose for which they were required, were unwilling to co-operate. The number that fell out for these various reasons is not given. A reviewer in the *Lancet* of 14th March 1942 commented:

'His claim that his group is unselected and representative may be questioned; there is good reason to suspect that many of those who did not answer his letter or refused to attend for interview were of higher mental and social level than those who did.'

In the absence of evidence it is difficult to assess what bias, if any, the book may contain, but although Professor Binder stresses that the findings and conclusions apply only to conditions in Switzerland at that time, this close study of three hundred and fifty personalities is at least formidable evidence for the existence and importance of such character traits among unmarried mothers as he describes.

Each mother was invited to the outpatient department of the municipal hospital, where he examined and interviewed them, usually for one and a half to two hours. The stories that emerged were carefully checked where possible against extensive reports from the elaborate Swiss social and welfare services, which included annual reports on the welfare and home circumstances of every illegitimate child, and also against case-histories and court records of affiliation and other proceedings. In his talk with each woman, he followed the course of events from the first meeting with her child's father, through her pregnancy and its birth up to the time of the interview. He was thus able to deal statistically in the book with many external and inner difficulties of the woman's social and personal position, and, since one hundred and sixty-one of the women had had their child ten or more years before, was able to study the later consequences upon the mother.

He found overwhelming evidence that those women in Basle who became unmarried mothers were far from being a psychologically average cross-section of society. They tended to start with a poor inheritance and were then exposed, even before their pregnancy, to quite abnormal strain. He was led to the conclusion that 'growing up in disturbed, shaken, chaotic relationships to a certain extent predestines a girl to unmarried motherhood'.

The mothers studied were of every social class; as many as 18 per cent came from middle- or upper-class homes. As compared with the population as a whole, however, a rather large number came from the lower social levels:

	GIRLS' FATHERS %	MEN IN SWITZERLAND %
Upper class (i.e. higher professions)	1.0	3.0
Middle class (middle and senior officials)	17.0	29.0
Small middle class (shop-keepers, farmers, etc.)	39.0	43.0
Unskilled workers	43.0	25.0
TOTAL	100.0	100.0

Few, only 15 per cent, belonged to families who had lived all their lives in one place, and as many as two-thirds came from chronically impoverished families. Typically it was the unskilled, ill-paid, uprooted families that produced illegitimate children.

The following table, which compares the home circumstances at the time of the birth of the children with those at the time of the birth of the mother, shows an economic decline during that space of time:

HOME CIRCUMSTANCES

	AT TIME OF MOTHER'S BIRTH %	AT TIME OF CHILD'S BIRTH %
Good	7.0	4.0
Simple but respectable	26.0	19.0
Needy but respectable	39.0	42.0
Poor and slovenly	28.0	35.0
TOTAL	100.0	100.0

The psychiatric record of their families was relatively poor. Among rather over two thousand brothers and sisters of this group whose history was traced, abnormal personalities were more than twice as common as in the population as a whole; psychopathic and psychogenic personalities were two and a half times as common, endogenous psychoses and alcoholism each one and a half times as common, mental deficiency twice as common. Epilepsy and organic psychosis were not found more often than in the rest of the population. As many as 19.6 per cent of the siblings over ten years old and 14.7 per cent of the parents were psychopathic or psychogenic; 8.4 per cent of these siblings were mentally defective and 4.5 per cent of the parents; 1.8 per cent of the siblings and 1.2 per cent of the parents were psychotic.

As for their psychological background, as many as 12 per cent of the women themselves were illegitimate, another 62 per cent came from homes in which open domestic conflict was serious and frequent, nearly another 18 per cent from homes in which there was hidden conflict (together over 91 per cent), and fewer than 9 per cent came from homes that could be described as undisturbed. The chief sources of unhappiness in the two hundred and seventeen seriously disturbed homes (61 per cent of the total and 70 per cent of the homes in which the women had been born legitimate) are shown in the following table:

	%
Father an alcoholic	20.0
Psychological abnormality of one or both parents	17.0
Economic distress	12.0
Previous death of one or both parents	9.0
Separation or divorce of parents	7.0
Physical illness of one or both parents	5.0
TOTAL	70.0

Separation and divorce, it will be noted, play a smaller part in this Swiss setting than they do in American and British studies.

That such heavy handicaps, both in nervous inheritance and environment, should have some ill effect on the women is only natural, yet the extent of their nervous and mental abnormality is perhaps surprising. Professor Binder describes the women at the time of the interview as:

	%
Normal (including 6 per cent who were unintelligent)	37.0
Mentally defective	14.0
Imbecile	2.0
Psychopathic	22.0
Psychogenic	25.0
TOTAL	100.0

The term 'psychogenic', as used here, refers broadly to nervous abnormalities and disorders of, at any rate in principle, a temporary character; 'psychopathic' to those more deep-seated neurotic disorders that have become a permanent part of the personality. The psychopath's disorder consists essentially in an emotional immaturity; a failure to develop emotionally, just as a mental defective fails to develop intellectually, which prevents him from adapting himself to reality and profiting from experience.

Many of the psychopaths (7 per cent of all the women) had acute morbid feelings of inferiority, but in some it took the form of apathy, hysteria, acute irritability or impulsiveness, infantilism or a general lack of balance. If one adds that, among the three thousand registered, there were also another ten (0.3 per cent) who were psychotic and therefore omitted from this survey, the picture is, as the *Lancet* remarks, extraordinarily pessimistic. It would certainly be encouraging if one might hope that some of the other women who were not included in the survey would have lightened the gloom of this impression.

But to speak of their condition at the time of the interview is jumping ahead in time. In their childhood, only 10 per cent had had a normal relationship with their parents. As many as 55 per cent had received too little affection (27 per cent from their fathers, 16 per cent from their mothers, 12 per cent from both), while 10 per cent had too much affection of an exaggerated kind. The other 25 per cent had had a thoroughly inconsequent upbringing—too much one day, too little another.

This had its results in their sexual development. Up to the time of their extra-marital pregnancy, the girls' experience had been:

	%
Entirely ignorant sexually	3.0
Sexual relations with child's father only	22.0
Only isolated sex experience	16.0
Frequent sexual relations in one or more love affairs	35.0
Entirely promiscuous	17.0
Sexual relations within marriage	7.0
TOTAL	100.0

The proportion of relatively promiscuous women (52 per cent) is very high and gives a decidedly different impression from either the Midboro survey or Young's study, though neither of these went deeply into this aspect. In Binder's sample, only 25 per cent of the women had had no sexual relations with anyone except the child's father. A study of unmarried mothers in *Germany*, published by Weinzierl in 1925, has claimed that 80 per cent of the unmarried mothers had had no other lover, but Professor Binder was inclined to attribute this to the fact that Weinzierl had only the mother's own evidence to go by.

One of the most interesting aspects of Binder's book is his characterization of the women in these different groups. Although unmarried mothers are a very varied group, those who had much and those who had little sexual experience behind them were naturally of rather different type. Hardly any of the women who had had 'only isolated sex experience' had had these in the course of longer love affairs; they had been chance sexual contacts at parties, dances, expeditions, etc., made often enough by quite immature and inexperienced girls out of curiosity, bravado or the urge to please, and often under the influence of alcohol. It could rarely even be described as deliberately undertaken seduction by the man.

'Anyone who realizes how completely unprotected the working-class girl is in sexual matters by the actual customs of the people, how little it takes in their upbringing to yield to the quite obvious open pressure of the men, will not be surprised that in so many cases a girl's first sexual experience is a pure matter of chance without passion or love, yet quite without its implying any light-mindedness.'

And because these acts were relatively meaningless and did not touch the women deeply, this particular group were much less deeply conscious-stricken later if they found themselves pregnant.

The largest single group, those who had had frequent sexual relations in one or more love affairs, tended to be of a rather different type. Many of these had given themselves to a man out of love for him, but deceived themselves as to his attitude, romanticizing the relationship and—because of their own exaggerated hunger for affection—making too great demands upon him. Often these were girls who had been starved of affection or spoilt in their own homes, and who therefore fell in love violently, yielding themselves with an almost exaggerated surrender. When the man, not surprisingly, disappointed them, they were only too apt to repeat the whole pattern with someone else. It was these women who were particularly prone to reproach themselves afterwards; disappointed love led more easily than a superficial sexual relationship to a self-castigating conscience. If the experience repeated itself, their balance was often severely shaken.

The 'entirely promiscuous' women tended to be of a rather different type again. Some had superficial characters and were of low intelligence; others had originally had a good capacity for love and deep feeling, which had been injured, until nothing was left in their relationships with men but pure sexuality. These were rarely women who could be described as 'highly sexed': on the contrary, they were often frigid and received no pleasure from the act, their feeling closely linked with an instinct to take flight. Often what seemed to be at work in them was a kind of vanity, an attempt to reassure themselves, to compensate for some deep feeling of personal worthlessness. In this Professor Binder's book agrees with other studies of promiscuous women.

Only a few types of personality among an almost endless variety have been described here, but they are types that are certainly familiar to case-workers.

The girl's sexual relations with the child's father often began soon after her acquaintance with him. Only 16 per cent had known the man for a year or more before intercourse took place, and among 45 per cent it had occurred at their first or one of their first meetings.

Of the three hundred and fifty mothers in the study, few should be thought of as 'moral defectives' in the sense of not being able to distinguish between right and wrong. This was true of only one in a hundred, and in Professor Binder's view the moral understanding of about half of the women was completely intact, and at all seriously deficient in only about 15 per cent. Most of the women had had only one illegitimate child, 11 per cent two and 3 per cent more than two.

If there seems to be a contradiction in terms by speaking of women with so confused a sexual history as women with 'a perfectly intact moral understanding', one must remember how relatively homeless a group they were, and how much harder it was for them than for a girl with a normal upbringing to live up to their ideals. Nearly 40 per cent of them had lost one or both parents before they became pregnant, and 28 per cent before they were fifteen years old. When they became pregnant, 42 per cent had no connexion with their homes at all, another 21 per cent had long left home, though they were still in contact with their families, and only 37 per cent were actually living with their parents or foster-parents.

They were living a relatively unprotected life and few had come from homes that were happy or normal.

The children's fathers also seem to have been an unstable group. They were of the same social level as the women. In regard to character, there is little to go on except the girls' evidence, but apparently 16 per cent had a criminal background, another 17 per cent were alcoholic, another 20 per cent were described as work-shy or 'socially irresponsible' and 15 per cent had other psychic abnormalities. Only a quarter of them seem to have been normal.

Although fewer than half of the girls had surrendered to the man out of genuine love, only one in a hundred had been forced. The general picture was one of irresponsibility on the men's side and of too little sense of reality on the women's. Nearly half of the women were, in Professor Binder's view, psychologically incapable of a real surrender and an extraordinarily high proportion—90 per cent —had an exaggerated desire to be loved. (It may be here, in the urge to be loved, only too commonly associated with some real feeling of inferiority, that one finds one of the chief explanations of unmarried motherhood.) When they became pregnant, their feeling of personal worth was often deeply shaken. Even in working-class circles they frequently suffered a much greater hostility and humiliation than may be generally appreciated. One woman graphically described her experience to Professor Binder. 'The whole world turns away from me,' she said, 'and leaves me standing outside.'

Some momentarily experienced complete despair and emptiness, and very few came through without inner conflicts. There were good reasons for this: to their unhappy home backgrounds was so often added an unhappy love affair and the experience of being abandoned by their lovers and their own families. Even parents who came round afterwards often reacted at first with shock and unkindness. On top of this there were often acute financial worries: the prospect of being without a job for a long period with no money coming in and often with no prospect of financial help from the father or their parents. Five per cent actually attempted suicide and another 17 per cent thought of it really seriously. (In Weinzierl's study 17 per cent of the women made serious attempts to commit suicide, gassing themselves or taking an overdose of sleeping tablets.) Twenty-six per cent attempted abortions. Easily the majority had seriously thought of abortion and consulted doctors or others at some stage, often urged to do this by the child's father. But they did not in fact end their pregnancies. Had they done so they would not, of course, have been included in this study. The wish to destroy was simply a desperate attempt to break out of the situation, an outward expression of the mother's whole unhappiness. Her true feeling for the child was often ambivalent, as the following table shows:

	REVULSION %	PLEASURE %	AMBIVALENT ATTITUDE %	INDIFFERENCE %
First half of pregnancy	63.0	9.0	9.0	19.0
Second half of pregnancy	19.0	48.0	20.0	13.0
First months after birth	10.0	60.0	21.0	9.0
Dominant attitude in later life of child	23.0	30.0	40.0	7.0

Once the child was born, the mother's ability to regain her inner balance naturally depended upon circumstances. The women who were least successful in this—at least in this Swiss setting—were those who kept the child but had to bring it up alone, of whom three-quarters remained chronically psychologically disturbed; and those who married some other man, of whom more than two-thirds could not shake off their inner conflicts. Where the girl remained with relatives the position was a little better, though in general the women who best succeeded in regaining their inner balance were those who had the baby adopted, or placed it young with foster-parents. Those who later married the child's father were a less happy group: no doubt many had made forced marriages, for the few who cohabited with the child's father tended to do well.

The women on whom unmarried motherhood tended to have the most permanent ill effects were those who had their babies while they were still very young—eighteen years of age or less. But at the time when Binder interviewed them, as many as half of all the women in the survey had still not regained their inner balance and had developed into more or less abnormal people as a result of their chronic inner conflicts and their social and economic struggle. A third of the women were becoming fairly seriously warped psychologically, and in 7 per cent the damage was really severe. 'Favourable psychic developments as a result of unmarried motherhood are rare', he writes, and only occur in women who are already relatively well endowed by nature.

We would re-emphasize here that these conclusions concern a group of women in a largely pre-war and Swiss setting, and also that many of them had tended, even initially, to have somewhat disturbed personalities. English social workers, by contrast, might claim that some of the most serious psychological disturbances seem to follow adoptions too hastily made—although mothers distressed after passing a child to adopters are, of course, more likely to seek out social workers concerned with illegitimacy than are those who are disappointed in their marriages. In the absence, however, of any authoritative English studies, Binder's findings remain challenging. He had never himself expected to find the picture so dark.

He makes various cautious recommendations. The hardest time for the women to bear psychologically, the time when most suicide attempts are made, is the first part of the pregnancy. Action to help them needs to be taken in those early months. None of the women who suffered severe and lasting psychic damage had been normal before pregnancy, and it could be said with some confidence that when an already nervously abnormal woman took the first part of her pregnancy badly there was at least a 50 per cent chance of her sustaining severe and permanent damage, whereas there was practically no danger of this if she had been normal before. Professor Binder concluded that in the early months of the pregnancy such a prognosis could reasonably have been made about 8 per cent of the women and that, as it later worked out, 7 per cent were so severely and permanently injured by the experience that an abortion might have been justified.

The point that is of interest to us here is not the view that may be taken in another country upon abortion, but simply the fact that as accurate a prognosis of the development of some of these women could be made even so early in pregnancy. This is one of the chief questions with which social workers in England are now concerned: can one or can one not foresee which women will make good or adequate mothers, or which should be advised from the start to make no attempt to keep their children? The whole tendency of Professor Binder's book is to suggest that such a prognosis can sometimes be made even before the child is born. Further research into this is most urgently needed.

STUDIES OF THE FATHERS

It would be valuable to know far more than we do at present about the men who become fathers of illegitimate children. Dr Bowlby gives it as the opinion of social workers that many are unstable, that they often promise marriage irresponsibly and that, compared to the unmarried mother, they are more often promiscuous and get several girls into trouble within a short time.

Quoting from studies that have been made of habitually promiscuous men in connexion with the prevention of venereal disease, he notes Wittkower's conclusion that 'venereal disease patients are often emotionally, sexually and socially immature'[1] and that as few as 11 per cent in a group of two hundred studied, as compared with 62 per cent in a control group, were found to be emotionally mature personalities.

'Among factors which make for promiscuity', Dr Bowlby writes, 'Wittkower lists the need for affection, situations which arouse anxiety and situations which arouse resentment. "The so-called biological sex-urge, strange though it may appear, plays a minor part in most cases of promiscuity", in the same way that thirst has little to do with chronic alcoholism.

'In seeking to understand the origin of these unstable, immature characters, whose anti-social behaviour brings so much misery in its train, one is led back, as in the case of many of the unmarried mothers, to their childhoods and their relations with their own parents . . .'[2]

Although these comments may well be valid of the men Wittkower studied—men in the Forces suffering from venereal diseases—or those who are habitually highly promiscuous, there is no evidence that they apply to putative fathers in general. The first serious study of putative fathers in this country suggests that

---

[1] E. D. Wittkower in *British Journal of Venereal Diseases*, 1948.
[2] *Maternal Care and Mental Health*, p. 95.

they are a far from homogenous group.[1] In their psychology, as in other respects, they may still prove to be quite as varied as unmarried mothers.

---

[1] Cyril Greenland, *Unmarried Parenthood: Putative Fathers* (*Medical Officer*, 16th May 1958), a sociological analysis of the records of N.C.U.M.C.

they are a far from homogenous group.[1] In their psychology, as in other respects, they may still prove to be quite as varied as unmarried mothers.

---

[1] Cyril Greenland, *Unmarried Parenthood: Putative Fathers* (*Medical Officer*, 16th May 1958), a sociological analysis of the records of N.C.U.M.C.

PART II

HELP FOR THE MOTHER AND CHILD

CHAPTER 5

THE MOTHER'S STRUGGLE

THE UNWELCOME LODGER

An unmarried mother who decides to keep her child with her may not always realize how difficult her struggle will be. First she must find somewhere to go for the last weeks of her pregnancy, and some way of paying for it. She rarely has adequate savings; the child's father has no responsibility towards her; and even if she has been working and is entitled to National Insurance maternity benefit, she cannot live on this alone. When the baby is born, she must regain her strength and find lodgings to which she can take the child. This may be the most difficult problem of all; many landladies do not want babies, and a young mother who is suspected of being unmarried and penniless is rarely a welcome lodger.

Tramping the streets to find the lodgings; seeking work; finding —and paying for—a daily minder for the baby or, if a place can be found for it in a day nursery, bringing it early in the morning and fetching it on her way home from work; doing a day's work and coming home to a night of laundering and of looking after a possibly fretful child; up early again in the morning to feed the child—there is all this and much more to be done, so that a great deal will depend upon the mother's natural health and vitality and, if the baby falls ill, she will probably lose her job in any case. When the child grows to be a toddler, the landlady may not wish to keep her and the hunt for lodgings will begin again. School will create new problems: the school day ends early, while the mother is still at work; every childish infection may threaten her job, since she may have to stay at home to look after the child; and on top of all there are the long school holidays.

All these difficulties may be shared by others, especially widows and deserted wives with young children, but few young mothers are so entirely forlorn as some of the unmarried—so cut off from family and friends and from the neighbours who would normally lend a hand in times of trouble. Many of the unmarried mothers are living, too, in a state of nervous tension, owing to the unpleasant subterfuges of their position, their feeling that they have been rejected even by their own family and friends. Some are deeply worried by self-reproaches and, not least, by the fear of what the child may come to think of them when it is old enough to understand, or fear the cruelty of neighbours. All these things can undermine the mother's nervous health.

EARNING CAPACITY

But the first difficulty to be surmounted is economic: how is she to support herself and the child? For each mother there is a different problem, since they come from such widely different backgrounds. In the course of this study we have come across unmarried mothers who were teachers—several were headmistresses—doctors, nurses, social workers and members of the aristocracy and, at the other end of the scale, girls who worked in old-clothes shops, wet-fish shops, canteens or, as one described her job, 'turning over doughnuts in a bakery'.

So it is not easy to give any picture of their earning capacity, but five studies used in the course of this work may help. A group of ninety-three mothers who applied in 1952-3 for affiliation orders in a large city were earning an average wage of £3 18s. a week, and only three of them received as much as £5 or over.

In 1950 Valerie Hughes made a study of the circumstances of unmarried mothers in Mother and Baby Homes throughout the country. Among the one hundred and thirty-eight in her sample who quoted their earnings before the child's birth, the average income was £3 6s. a week; fifty-four earned less than £3 and only nine £5 or over. As for their hopes of the future, only eighteen expected to be earning higher wages and the average increase these anticipated was only 17s.; only six of them expected to be earning over £4. This group tended to be young and not all kept their babies: indeed, the decision as to whether the children were to be adopted or not was often influenced by their earning power. But one self-reliant fifteen-year-old earning £2 3s. 4d. in a box factory had every intention of keeping and supporting her baby.

In a poor district of north London in the early 1950's, the matron of a Hostel for unmarried mothers quoted the average earnings of fourteen who had recently left as £4 3s. in non-resident posts and £2 2s. in resident work. One mother had gone on the streets.

A group of forty-five in a local authority Hostel for unmarried mothers in 1951-2 were earning relatively well, their wages averaging £5 a week, varying from £3 10s. to £7 10s., but well over half of these were stenographers or clerks, skilled dressmakers or nurses. Only those with relatively good earnings could live in this Hostel, where the charge was £3 a week, with 10s. for the day nursery.

These four studies, then, show an average wage of well under £4 a week in the early 1950's—less than £200 a year for the support of two persons.

The Church of England Moral Welfare Council has also made an important study of the position of one hundred and eighty illegitimate children and of their mothers at the time when the children, all born in 1952, were three to four years old. The main occupations of the mothers both before and after confinement were factory, domestic and clerical work. The wages of single girls, other than those doing domestic work, were in 1955 generally at the rate of £4 to £5 a week, though some were earning less. Payment under affiliation orders often lapsed in part or in whole, so most of the burden fell on the mother or grandparents.

'Few of the putative fathers take any interest when the mother remains single. Relatively few affiliation orders are applied for and granted, and of those few are honoured to the full. The whole responsibility for rearing the child thus falls on the mother. Some of these have a very difficult time.'[1]

Many young mothers are aware that they will have to face a struggle. A fifteen-year-old Irish girl, the youngest of eight children, who dared not take her child home, replied to a questionnaire as follows:

Q. 'Will you go back to your old job?'
A. 'Doughtful.'
Q. 'What kind of work will you do?'
A. 'Well, I do not now see.'

A few more stories from Valerie Hughes's 1950 survey will show the problems some of the mothers faced and how they proposed to tackle them:

A student nurse aged twenty, who had no help from the child's

---

[1] *What Happens Afterwards?—A Survey of Unmarried Mothers and Their Children after Three Years* (*Moral Welfare*, January 1957).

father and had been earning £2 a week, hoped to get a post with her baby in a nursery, earning £3 10s. 6d.

A girl of nineteen entirely dependent on her own earnings—the baby's father was untraceable—hoped for residential domestic work with her baby, earning at least 25s. a week.

An extremely self-reliant fourteen-year-old, an orphan brought up by relatives and who had had the child by a casual acquaintance, and who was entirely dependent on her own earnings, proposed to take a residential domestic post with her baby at 25s. to 30s. a week.

A seventeen-year-old, who had been earning 12s. 6d. a week, hoped to earn £3 a week in factory work. The baby would have to go to a residential nursery, but the girl's mother would help her by teaching at evening classes; the child's father had also volunteered to help a little.

A seventeen-year-old, training as a typist, had thought her baby would have to be adopted, but when her parents saw their first grandchild they determined to help her keep it, offering, if she wished, to adopt it and bring it up as their own.

Another seventeen-year-old had the good fortune to find a landlady who was willing to look after the baby by day while she went out to daily domestic work.

A fourteen-year-old whose parents were divorced had a child by a middle-aged neighbour, but her mother—very proud of her first grandson—was ready to help her. Both would go out to work, arranging their hours so that one of them would be at home to look after the child.

A girl of twenty-five had twins by a man later in prison, so unable as well as unwilling to help her. She would take them home to her mother and would run the house while her mother went out to work to support them.

A sixteen-year-old, childish and irresponsible, determined against all advice to keep her baby, to which she became attached while she was breast-feeding it at the Hostel. Her attitude was, 'Someone will help: someone always does.' She had no plans, but the child —which she treated like a doll—was all in all to her.

A seventeen-year-old working in a fish shop, earning 7s. 6d. a week and her clothes, was most attached to her baby and hoped to keep it: no relatives were likely to help.

A nineteen-year-old, herself illegitimate and removed from her parents when she was three because of their neglect, also lost her foster-mother when she was seventeen and became pregnant in a period of great unhappiness. She was very happy to have a baby, for she felt that she at last had someone who belonged to her. She would take a residential job in a nursery with it, where the nursing staff would help to look after it.

Most of these stories are about very young mothers. They are worth giving, however, since many of the younger teen-agers who get into trouble are just those who are most determined to keep their children. In *Midboro*, for example, of the twelve teen-agers who might have had most difficulty in keeping their babies—that is, those who had lost a parent or whose parents had been separated —only three were willing to have the babies adopted: the others clung to their children as to their only anchor in the world.

The earning power of the older mothers is often little higher. One mother aged twenty-six planned to live with an aunt who would look after the child by day while she took factory work at £3 to £4 a week, but a thirty-four-year-old mother, whose own mother was an old-age pensioner and could not help her, could hope to earn only £2 a week and her keep in hotel work, placing the child in a residential nursery. An excellent mother aged twenty-eight decided to part with her child rather than go into domestic service with it: she would not let it go into a residential nursery and thought it would be happier with adopters. A mother of thirty, the youngest of a fairly large family, with no income of her own, had to part with her child, and go home to look after an invalid father. A research assistant aged twenty-nine, unsuitable for domestic work, had to place her child with foster-parents, since she had lost her post owing to the baby's birth. A social worker aged twenty-nine, earning £8 a week, had to resign from this post and take one at £6, placing her child in a residential nursery.

A number of the girls took residential work, earning anything from 25s. to £2 10s. a week as well as their keep, but there were many who were quite unsuited for such work. Anyone inexperienced finds it difficult to look after an infant or a toddler and be an efficient servant as well. Several girls, quite fond of their babies, decided to have them adopted rather than face such a life. It will be remembered that, although in *Manchester* in 1933 a quarter of the women who had illegitimate babies had been in domestic service when they became pregnant, in *Midboro* in 1949 only two women had been in such work. Domestic service may still be one of the simplest ways of keeping mother and child together, but for many of the mothers it is unfortunately unsuitable. One mother, the widow of a professional man with two older children in their teens and an illegitimate baby son by a man she could not marry, took a residential post when her baby was six weeks old, but had to give it up two weeks later: she had to be up at a quarter to six and work all day on her feet, and was soon in a state of exhaustion. She would not ask for help from the child's father, who had other troubles on his hands, and would not part with her baby son to adopters. The alternative seemed to be to place him with foster-parents, tiny though he was, and herself return to the clerical work for which she was trained.

It will be clear from the stories quoted that some of the girls who were most determined to keep their children had little hope of making a success of it. There were among them girls and women who in easier circumstances might have made good mothers, but because of their low earning power and housing difficulties and the need to be out most of the day earning their living, could not be the good mothers they longed to be. One of these, a married woman separated from her husband since the birth of her illegitimate baby, realized this herself when the child was two years old and wrote sadly:

'She is getting older every day and is in need of clothes badly which I am unable to get, as I am already getting into debt. It isn't fair to my child, as she is never able to go out or have in life as she should have, and that is why I want to get her adopted, and have a good home.'

It is often in this way, when mothers have had more instinctive affection and courage than realism, that children pass into public care or from one daily minder or foster-home to another.

DANISH AND CANADIAN STUDIES

No comprehensive study has been made in this country of the earning power of unmarried mothers, so it may be of interest to quote the findings of studies in *Denmark* and *Toronto*.

In *Denmark* 'solitary mothers'—that is to say, unmarried, separated, divorced or widowed women with children to support—form between 2.5 per cent and 3 per cent of all the adult women in the country. A study in 1949 of the circumstances of seven hundred and forty-four of these (39 per cent of them unmarried) who were living in *Copenhagen*, was published in 1953.[1] The average gross income of the whole group was £285 a year. Though 17 per cent were earning under £200 a year, nearly two-thirds had between £200 and £350. The average *net* income was £190, whereas that of male bread-winners was £405—rather more than double. The women's earning capacity was influenced by lack of training. Half of them had had no pupil or apprentice education and they were poorly represented in the occupation groups that can in general give opportunity for a higher or good and stable income.

The women in this study were questioned about their difficulties. It was found that when the children were ill, nearly a quarter of them had to look after themselves, though a sixth of the mothers stayed away from work as such times. When the mother was ill the child usually had to attend to itself. A third of the children were left on their own when the mother went out in the evening, but a fifth of the women never went out in the evenings at all. The mothers' average hours of work were just under eight, but since they had to go home to look after the child many had no free time at all. Very few had any help in the house, and only 25 per cent had a charwoman. The report concludes that the children's care 'both every day, in the evening and in sickness must wear out the solitary mothers' nerves'—in fact only half the mothers felt well, and as many as a sixth gave indications of illness. A good 50 per cent of the widowed and separated women, 45 per cent of the divorced and 33 per cent of the unmarried mothers (the youngest group) were actually under treatment for bad nerves.

The mothers were asked for their suggestions as to how conditions might be improved. Many of them would have been glad of some short course of training to enable them to earn a better wage.[2] Among their other proposals were: better nursing facilities for children with less serious illnesses, such as colds etc; places where the children can be accommodated when the mother is ill; financial help so that the mother can stay at home and look after

---

[1] *Den Enlige Moder* ("The Solitary Mother") (Det Danske Forlag, Copenhagen, 1953), the report of a commission set up by the Danish Women's National Council and Danish Women's Society (Danske Kvinders Nationalrad og Dansk Kvindesamfund).

[2] See VOCATIONAL TRAINING, p. 202.

a sick child; better possibilities for finding accommodation for solitary mothers; part-time work with a public subsidy to supplement it; paid work in the home; a free day every week or fortnight for shopping; priority for holiday places for the children; free-time activities in the schools to cover the period between the end of the school day and when the mother leaves work; a scheme for immediate visits from welfare officers when the mother becomes 'solitary', in order to help her with advice; occasional help in the care of children in the evening.

Perhaps of these various suggestions the three that would be most warmly echoed by mothers in this country are those for aid in obtaining accommodation, for training for better-paid work, and for increased opportunities of part-time work.

A study made in *Toronto* in 1943[1] also notes the economic difficulties.

'Undoubtedly the greatest struggle for the large proportion of mothers was in the first four years after the children's birth . . . The remarks made by the mothers at the interview, such as "it meant going without clothing and living on oatmeal", gave some indication of how little opportunity they had for normal living . . . There is little evidence that the mothers were helped by the caseworkers to realize all that is involved both for themselves and their children in their decision to retain custody . . . The implicit belief was that a mother who cares for her child during his greatest period of dependency will grow up attached to him and find some means of keeping him. Too little thought, however, was given to the question as to whether this planning was likely to offer any hope of normal living for the mother or security for her child . . .'

PROSTITUTION

The League of Nations Advisory Committee on Social Questions noted with satisfaction in 1943 that 'unmarried mothers no longer represent the chief source from which prostitutes are drawn'; but the League of Nations report on the prevention of prostitution, published in that year, stated that although 'the studies made . . .

---

[1] *A Study of the Adjustment of Teen-Age Children born out of Wedlock who remained in the Custody of their Mothers or Relatives*, made by the Unmarried Parenthood Committee of the Welfare Council of Toronto and District; summarized in chapter 13.

have suggested that illegitimacy plays a comparatively minor part in leading women into prostitution', yet 'the evidence produced . . . tended to prove that the fact of having had an illegitimate child is still an important contributory factor . . . Even in cases where the unmarried mother makes a brave stand against the psychological after-effects of her experience, her struggle may be defeated by the material impossibility of finding sufficiently remunerative employment to enable her to bring up her child in a normal way. The life stories of a great many prostitutes prove that it was not so much the impossibility of finding work as of finding sufficiently well-paid work to keep themselves and their children.'

Fewer mothers in England nowadays may turn to prostitution, but the financial problem remains, adding to the many nervous tensions and the constant insecurity in which natural children grow up.

CHAPTER 6

THE FATHER'S CONTRIBUTION

HIS RESPONSIBILITIES TOWARDS THE CHILD

A child normally looks to its father for financial support, but how far can an illegitimate child do so? In a country where perhaps about one man in every twenty-five is a 'natural' father, this is an important question.[1]

Even today English law is based on what Johan Castberg, the Norwegian social reformer, described in 1915 as 'the outrageous and unnatural fiction that the illegitimate child has only a mother'. Thus, except for a few specific purposes, a natural son has no legal kinship with his father—or with any other child of his mother—and has no legal right of accession to or claim against their estates. His grandparents—even on his mother's side—his aunts, his half-brothers and half-sisters are not bound to help him; he is not their relative. He cannot inherit titles or certain estates attaching to them, and though he may gain a surname by reputation he has none by inheritance.

The law asks little indeed of the father of an illegitimate child and it enforces less; much less than in many countries. His relationship to the child is at most a monetary one, but even this is limited. No legal obligation rests upon him to do anything for it at all unless the mother takes action against him in a magistrates' court (officially termed a court of summary jurisdiction, but commonly known as the police court), applies for a summons to be taken out against him, proves that he is the putative (the presumed) father and receives from the magistrates an affiliation order affirming[2] this and binding him to pay a certain regular sum towards the child's support.

---

[1] No one knows the real figure, but this is roughly calculated on the assumption that the number of men who have several illegitimate children is not very much greater (it may be a little greater) than the number of women with more than one.

[2] An order does not state that he is the actual father, since that is not susceptible of proof.

THE MOTHER'S ONLY CLAIM UPON HIM

The mother's sole claim upon him for her own support is for expenses incidental to the birth of the child. The practice of ordering him to pay these, and perhaps the practice of claiming them, seems to have fallen largely into disuse. Although we have come across courts that interpret their discretion under this head so widely that they include under it the cost of the mother's maintenance for a short time before and after confinement, this is rare. More typical are two large city courts where, in a recent year, there was no record of any incidental expenses having been paid by the father.

For the period of the pregnancy and the time when she is caring for the baby in its infancy she can claim nothing from him. To some extent her position may be compared to that of a deserted wife whose husband fails to support her: it is worse than that of a divorced woman, who rarely has a legitimate baby as young, and in England may be able to claim alimony, and it is considerably worse than that of a widow with a young child, who normally draws a pension. At first glance this may seem right, yet the formidable figures of mortality among illegitimate children compel one to question it. The infant mortality rate among illegitimate children is 27 per cent higher than among other children, and a natural child runs a considerably greater risk of dying in the first month of its life. These early deaths, often due to premature birth, which is the greatest single cause of loss of life among children, are often associated with poverty, malnutrition, lack of ante-natal care, and—another special handicap of the unmarried mother—the need to work too hard and too long during pregnancy. In the survey of women who bore babies in one month of 1946, it emerged that nearly half of the unmarried ones did not attend until they had been pregnant for six months or more. Less than one in five of the wives of manual workers had left it until so late; hardly one in nine of the wives of professional men.[1]

This survey showed also that the unmarried women stayed at work on an average more than two months longer than manual workers' wives, and that premature delivery was definitely more frequent among the women who worked in the second half of their pregnancy.[2] It found too that three-quarters of the unmarried

---
[1] *Maternity in Great Britain*, p. 33.
[2] *Ibid*, pp. 168 and 195.

mothers intended to return to work at an average period of two months after their confinement, whereas only 6 per cent of the manual workers' wives expecting their first child intended to return to work at all, and those few did not expect to go back until about the fourth month. As a result many more unmarried mothers have to bottle-feed their babies; at eight weeks nearly two-thirds (62 per cent) were doing so, compared with well under half (43 per cent) among the manual workers' wives. The need to return to work was given as the reason for weaning the baby by 28 per cent of the unmarried mothers in that survey, as compared with only 1 per cent of the manual workers' wives.[1] Most of the illegitimate babies will therefore have been separated from their mothers' daily care at the very time when they are most exposed to risk from infant diseases.

A position that leaves the unmarried mother without support at this time when the child's welfare is so closely linked with her own is, of course, very unsatisfactory. Certain voluntary societies help a little, and the National Assistance Board is usually prepared to give its aid if she is not working, but it would seem natural to expect the child's father to contribute. She can draw the maternity benefits offered by the Ministry of National Insurance, but this is not a complete solution, since the benefits, generous though they are (we shall consider them in the next chapter), were never designed to take the place of a husband's earnings—as one can quickly appreciate if one pictures the feelings of, say, a married woman whose husband stopped supporting her during her pregnancy and while the baby was in its infancy (and paid nothing for the baby's layette) because 'the State is already maintaining her adequately'. Nor should the psychological side be forgotten: some unmarried mothers have a quite unnecessarily difficult confinement owing to the physical tensions generated by worry, and by the feeling that the man on whose help they had relied has entirely abandoned them.

In many countries the child's father is expected to support the mother for a limited period. *Western Germany* and *Austria* have provisions obliging him to contribute to her expenses for the first six weeks after the birth. In *Switzerland* he must contribute for the first four weeks and also for the last four weeks of the pregnancy. In *Canada*, in the Province of *Ontario*, he is expected to meet her

[1] *Ibid*, pp. 148 and 150.

'reasonable expenses' for 'maintenance and care, medical and otherwise' for three months before the birth and 'such period after the birth as may in the opinion of the judge' be necessary. Under the *Polish* Family Code of 1950 the father is obliged to make a 'fair contribution' to the expenses of pregnancy and confinement, the woman's maintenance for three months at the time of the confinement and 'for reasons of substance' for longer, and to pay a proportion of other 'unavoidable expenses' or even 'special pecuniary loss'.

There are far-reaching and effective provisions in the Scandinavian countries. In *Norway* the father has to contribute towards the woman's maintenance for three months before the birth and six months after it. She receives a higher maintenance before the birth than for the rest of the time. In *Denmark* he must help defray, to the extent of about £1 a week, the expenses of her maintenance during the two months before and one month after delivery, and in case of illness due to pregnancy or confinement, for up to four months before and nine months after. A Danish provision that the father should pay 25 per cent more for the child's maintenance during the first two years of its life acts also in effect as an indirect payment to the mother for the care of the child in infancy.

In *Sweden* the Parents' Code of 1949 lays down: 'The father of a child born out of wedlock shall be liable to make such contribution to the maintenance of the mother for a period of six weeks before and six weeks after confinement as may appear reasonable in view of his situation and that of the mother . . . If pregnancy or lactation or any other care given to the child materially restricts the wage-earning capacity of the mother or she contracts a disease as a result of the pregnancy or the confinement, the father may be required to contribute to her maintenance for a period longer than aforesaid, but not exceeding four months before and nine months after the confinement.' Amounts paid under this head in 1953 usually took the form of a lump sum varying from £14 to £35.

It would be a great advance if we could see such provisions extended to Great Britain, though only if there were provisions as effective as in Scandinavia for securing payment. At present any addition to the small financial claims upon a natural father might encourage him to evade payment.

WHY DO SO FEW WOMEN APPLY FOR AFFILIATION ORDERS?

Any unmarried mother in Great Britain is at liberty to take action against the father in a magistrates' court but, poor though they often are, few do so. In 1953, a typical year, one unmarried mother in seven applied and only 12 per cent were granted affiliation orders. This would suggest that, on the basis of illegitimate births in that year, about 27,000 fathers were free of any *legal* obligation to support their children—unless they had contracted private agreements to do so. It seems an astonishingly large proportion, but one must understand it rightly.

In some cases, of course, the father is not known: even the woman herself may be in doubt when several men have been involved, or the relationship may have been so unpremeditated that she never learns the man's name. In *Midboro* the social records claimed that 93 per cent of the fathers were 'known' (that is, something—their age, profession, marital status—was recorded in the case-papers) and only three of the two hundred and seventy-eight mothers disclaimed all knowledge of the man's identity. But some may not have liked to admit their own doubts, and these vague claims could not all necessarily be substantiated in a magistrates' court. Even if the man *is* the child's father there may often be no corroborative evidence—letters, witnesses—and on this, under the present law, the courts insist. So a number of women could not have brought a case.

This, however, is far from explaining why so many men have no affiliation orders brought against them. A much larger part of the explanation is that a considerable percentage of men—perhaps more than 50 per cent—do in fact support their illegitimate children without the necessity for an order. We have seen that in *Midboro* 39 per cent of the couples were living in stable cohabitation; and 7 per cent unstably, the mother receiving irregular or uncertain support from the father. Again, many men agree, verbally or in writing, to send the mother regular weekly or monthly contributions for the child's maintenance. The sum may be large or small, but if it is guaranteed in a proper document (which may be drawn up with the help of a lawyer or social worker and duly stamped) it can be enforced through the county court if the man defaults, and until then the parents avoid the publicity and odium of court proceedings. Since they are made privately, no one knows how many of these agreements are concluded. They have the advantage that, if the father is well-to-do, a much more generous sum may be secured to the child than the thirty shillings a week that is the maximum a magistrate can impose under an affiliation order. But in practice few unmarried mothers can afford the cost of bringing a case in the county court, so if the man defaults the agreement may have no value except as evidence that the man has acknowledged paternity and—if he has ever made any payment under it—that he has supported the child, which are points that will help the mother if she applies for an affiliation order. These agreements do, however, suggest a way in which, with a few small alterations in the law, a secure income could be guaranteed to the child in privacy and decency. More will be said on this subject later.

Meanwhile there is a further group of fathers who should be remembered: those who are never asked to contribute because the mother has decided from the beginning to have the child adopted, action she can take without consulting the man if he is not contributing to its support. If she is a married woman living with her husband, she may think it unwise to keep the child; if she is very young, her parents may bring pressure upon her to part with it; or again she may be among those who feel that a child needs a complete home and secure childhood and will be happier if it is adopted; others are unable to face the social difficulties that an unmarried mother must face.

As soon as an adoption order is made, the natural parents cease to have any further financial responsibility, so a woman who plans to place her child in infancy is unlikely to apply to the courts for an affiliation order against the father. It is, however, hard to say in how many cases the man's failure or inability to support the child decides the woman to have it adopted. Some case-workers claim that a mother rarely parts with her child for purely economic reasons; if she is eager enough to keep it and willing enough to face a very uphill struggle, ways and means can usually be found to give her at least some help. Others state—and the two truths may not, after all, be incompatible—that financial difficulties lie behind most adoptions. Certainly it is true that a man's help or failure to help may turn the scales of her decision. At present about a fifth of all illegitimate children are in the long run adopted by someone other than their own parents, and one may be certain that if the mothers had complete financial security the number would be smaller.

It seems, then, that a very substantial majority of fathers give some monetary help, at least in the early months of the child's life. Valerie Hughes found in her *Midboro* study—made before the children were a year old—that only a third of the men had made no payment of any kind. About 13 per cent of the children had already been placed for adoption, and in three-quarters of these cases the men had made no contribution; about a third of the women who had already placed their children for adoption had had no help from the father.

Although, then, a father may recognize and act upon the moral obligation to support his child, he may be under no effective obligation to do so unless the mother obtains an affiliation order obliging him to pay so much a week for its maintenance. The entire initiative rests with the mother. The only exceptions to this rule are if the mother has applied to the National Assistance Board for financial help, when the Board may press her to bring a case or itself apply to the court, or if the child is in the care of the local authority, when the authority is empowered to apply. But unmarried mothers have become increasingly chary of taking this step. In 1924, soon after the maximum granted under an affiliation order had been raised from 10s. to £1 a week, one unmarried mother in every three or four applied; in 1950, when the limit was still £1, only one in seven. When the new Affiliation Act of 1952 raised the maximum to 30s. a week, there was no increase! In 1953 the proportion was one in seven.

Why should so few mothers apply? Over the last thirty years their own earning power has, of course, much increased, and adoption, not legalized until 1926, now ultimately affects many illegitimate children. The various national insurance benefits must also have made things easier. But women are not usually slow to claim the financial benefits to which their children are entitled, and, as Dr Chesser has pointed out, 'a class of parents so obviously in need of assistance would not so definitely decline the aid offered by the law if it were adequate'.[1]

The reasons given here for their reluctance are based on our own experience of unmarried mothers, on letters from mothers and on talk with social workers.

---

[1] Eustace Chesser, *The Unwanted Child* (1947).

THE CASE FOR SPECIAL COURTS AND PRIVATE AGREEMENTS

First of all the application must, as we have pointed out, be made to a magistrates' court. The charge in this country is still a criminal charge; police courts are associated in most people's minds with criminal proceedings, often of an unsavoury kind, are open to the public and the Press and are, in the view of many social workers, unsuitable places in which to hold these hearings. The thought of a police court appearance is in itself enough to frighten away quite a number of mothers.

Many social workers and others in the United States have long taken the view that any association with the court in the beginning may be felt by the putative father as a threat, arouse his fighting instincts and tend to make him deny responsibility. As the man and woman were often lovers a few months before the case is brought to court, it is natural that both may feel a revulsion against legal procedure, especially legal action taken in a police court open to the public. It is advisable to use the approach that is most likely to gain the man's goodwill. This is most possible if he is approached in a friendly way by someone with a fair and objective attitude, and where there is an opportunity for privacy and unhurried interviews.[1]

This difficulty is so generally felt that a number of countries have made provisions that avoid as far as possible the necessity of taking the case to court, and if it is unavoidable enable the mother to apply to a special court constituted for the purpose. The Children's Bureau and other national organizations in the *United States* recommend that jurisdiction of paternity cases and other family matters should be in a family court. The first course is followed in parts of the United States by some voluntary agencies, and also in *Sweden* and *Denmark*; the second course in *Norway*. If the father does not contest paternity and is willing to pay a regular sum towards the child's support and this sum meets with the approval of the specially appointed social worker and the court concerned, an agreement to this effect can be signed privately, then registered

---

[1] See paper presented by Maud Morlock at National Conference of Social Work, 1940, and published under the title of *Determination and Establishment of Paternity* by the U.S. Children's Bureau, Social Security Administration, Department of Health, Education and Welfare.

with the court without the necessity for further proceedings or for any appearance in open court. It can then be enforced and varied if necessary exactly like an affiliation order.

A somewhat parallel scheme is in force in *Ontario*. Here it is the responsibility of the director of the local Children's Aid Society to check that adequate provision is being made for all illegitimate children in his area. If a mother desires assistance in making a claim against the putative father, she must make a declaration of paternity before a commissioner of oaths. The man is then asked to appear before the local director and, if he admits to paternity, is expected to sign an agreement with the mother and the local director for a periodic payment or for a lump-sum settlement. The responsibility for enforcing the agreement thereby rests with the local director, the mother being relieved of the need of having any further dealings with the putative father. There are similar schemes in *Alberta* and *Manitoba*.

If, however, the man is not prepared to acknowledge paternity or to help to maintain the child, recourse to the courts may be necessary; but it need not be the open 'police court'. In the District of *Columbia* jurisdiction is vested in the juvenile court, in some counties in *North Carolina*, in the family court, and so on.

The National Council for the Unmarried Mother and Her Child, which has long pressed not only for legislative reform on individual matters but also for a comprehensive review of the law relating to illegitimate children, set up in 1950 a legal sub-committee for the purpose of studying the laws in force in this and other countries. The sub-committee's report, issued in 1954, made certain recommendations, one of which was that affiliation cases 'should not be heard at general sittings of the Magistrates' Courts but before specially constituted courts, under regulations analagous to those governing matrimonial cases, and before magistrates who have special qualifications for such duties'. In 1952 a Joint Committee on Psychiatry and the Law, appointed by the British Medical Association and the Magistrates' Association, recommended that when these cases are heard, magistrates of each sex should be on the bench.[1] The Legitimacy Act, 1959, provides for this (see page 135).

On the registration of private agreements the above-mentioned joint committee writes:

'We feel it would be a useful reform if the law permitted the

---

[1] *The Law in Relation to the Illegitimate Child* (1952).

mother of an illegitimate child to register her agreement at the local magistrates' court or in the High Court if the amount agreed is beyond the limit of the jurisdiction of magistrates' courts. Thereafter the parties should be in the same position as if the court had made a bastardy order. The amounts could then be verified by a court if the means of the parties alter. The advantage of the magistrates' courts for people of small means is that payment can be enforced more easily, cheaply and quickly than in a county court or the High Court.'[1]

The legal sub-committee of the N.C.U.M.C. recommends:

'It should be possible for the parents of an illegitimate child to attend a Magistrates' Court privately and record (a) an acknowledgment of paternity and (b) an agreement from the father to pay certain sums towards the support of their child, and such agreement should be in all respects equivalent to an order of the Court.'

APPLYING FOR AN ORDER

The Time Limit and Initiative by the Mother

Another difficulty facing the unmarried mother is that if she applies for an order, she must normally do so before the child is a year old. Exceptions are if the man has gone abroad or if she has evidence that he has at some stage paid something towards the child's support; and if the case is brought by the National Assistance Board or the local authority, there being then no time limit. In Scotland there is no time limit at all. The system has some advantages but it allows a man to be confronted after many years with an allegation of paternity that by that time he may be unable to refute. The N.C.U.M.C. recommends, however, that the time limit of one year should be extended to six, as in cases of civil debt, and that any acknowledgment of paternity—not only a money payment—should be accepted as a reason for extending the limit of time.

If the mother wishes to obtain maintenance for the baby from its birth, she must apply before it is two months old. This safeguards the father, who may be a weekly wage-earner, against a large accumulated debt. If the records of one large court are typical, three-quarters of the applicants let these first two months slip by. Often in these early months of the child's life—indeed, for longer

[1] *The Law in Relation to the Illegitimate Child.*

—the woman is passing through a highly disturbed phase of feeling about the father. Many are still unable to face realities: they privately nurse the hope of marrying him and naturally do not wish to take proceedings against him. On the other hand, they may be passing through a temporary violent reaction against him: they refuse to ask for money from a man who will not give them love, determining to do without his help and often almost seeming to deny his share in the child altogether. It is more often their pride than the child's interests they have at heart, and in this early stage they may underestimate the difficulty of supporting it alone and forget the forlorn position of the child if they fall ill or die. Even if they later reach a sense of reality, this first reaction may, because of the time limit, jeopardize the child's whole future. If to this are added apathy, fear, stupidity, one can understand how many mothers come to postpone action until it is too late. A married woman with her children's welfare at heart will often pass through years of indecision before bringing an unsatisfactory husband to court, so it is not surprising if case-workers among unmarried mothers have only a very limited degree of success in persuading them to take action for the child's sake. An interesting study of three hundred and eighty unmarried mothers made in the *United States* in 1934 showed that nearly half of the women who failed to apply for affiliation orders neglected to do so because they were fond of the man or still hoped for marriage and wished to protect his interests.

Many countries—among them *Western Germany*, *Norway*, *Sweden* and *Denmark*—are so impressed with these women's carelessness of the rights of their children that they have appointed official custodians of the children's legal and financial interests. In other countries there are certain doubts about a system that vests solely in the local authority as sensitive a decision as to whether, for example, to bring a case against a married man.

There is, of course, a possible compromise. The initiative in applying for a court order against the father might be vested in the local authority but remain subject to the woman's veto. This would make a realistic psychological concession to the woman who fails to protect her child's interests out of fecklessness or false pride; she would be unlikely to stop action taken by a third party if it was considered normal and automatic. But it would still leave an altruistic woman free to waive the child's right to alimony if she thought this essential in order to prevent the breaking up of the man's family life. Even such a course, however, has disadvantages. A scheme that would simply make it possible for privately made agreements to be registered with the courts and enforced by them might be considered more realistic at present.

The Status of the Mother
'The Bastardy Laws Amendment Act, 1872, provided that only a "single" woman may apply to a court for a maintenance order in respect of an illegitimate child. By a series of decisions, however, the High Court has found itself able to recognize as a "single woman", a widow and, in certain circumstances, a wife living apart from her husband.'[1]

The law is now found in the Affiliation Proceedings Act, 1957, and the Legitimacy Act, 1959, which made an important change. The mother who seeks an affiliation order must now be either a 'single woman' as defined at the date of her application to the magistrates, or a 'single woman' at the date of the child's birth, whatever her marital status at the time of her application to the court. Thus, a woman who has a child whilst a spinster may seek an affiliation order even though she later marries and, conversely, a married woman who has a child by a man not her husband may seek a like order if her husband turns her out or dies. While there are presumably some married women who are still debarred from obtaining affiliation orders, the Act of 1959 certainly improved the legal rights of mothers generally.

It may also be that, where the National Assistance Board or a local authority has obtained an affiliation against the putative father of a child whom it has been relieving or maintaining, the mother may have transferred to her the rights of the Board or authority in regard to enforcing payment under that order, once she has herself recommenced to maintain it in her own home. This procedure of transfer applies, however, only in cases where assistance has been given for the child by the Board, or a local authority has taken it into care; it will not assist mothers who are too proud or ashamed to go to the Board or Children's Officer for help, or those whose financial means are such that the Board will not give them money—an unusual example of one law for the rich and another, much more advantageous, for the poor.

[1] *The Law in Relation to the Illegitimate Child.*

A further reform is being introduced by the Matrimonial Proceedings (Magistrates' Courts) Bill, which it is expected will become law in the summer of 1960. If it is passed by Parliament without change on this issue, a husband, summoned by his wife for maintenance for herself, may be ordered to pay maintenance for any of her children by another man, whether legitimate or not, provided the husband has accepted them as children of his family. This reform will apply even if the wife is not awarded any maintenance for herself.

THE HEARING

When the date of the hearing arrives the woman must be present in court. The putative father is usually there also, although if he fails to appear on a summons, the case may be heard without him. Until the passing of the Legitimacy Act, 1959, it was usually held in open court. There were, however, some courts—among them one that we visited—that set aside a special day of the week for the hearings, in order to reduce casual visitors to a minimum: pressure might even be brought on them to leave, though they had a theoretical right to attend. A few courts that we came across heard the cases privately along with those taken under the Domestic Proceedings Act, clearing the court of all casual visitors except the Press, who had the right of admission.

The publicity of court procedure was often the woman's strongest objection to it. This was sometimes a risk rather than a reality, but one it might be difficult to assess in advance. Journalists rarely attend in the larger centres, since affiliation orders have comparatively little news value in the anonymity of a city, but in certain small towns the evening papers used to make a habit of publishing the names and addresses of the persons concerned and, more rarely, intimate details of the cases. The legal sub-committee of the N.C.U.M.C. drew particular attention to the 'great distress often occasioned to the parties and their familes by detailed reports in the local press and in the baser sort of Sunday papers'. Some papers claimed that publicity acts as an effective deterrent to immorality, though presumably few lovers think in terms of newspaper publicity at the time when the child is conceived. Only after the child is born may it act as a deterrent:

discouraging some of the best mothers from going to court to claim the maintenance to which the child is entitled.

To find an answer to this was not as simple as it sounds. The right of the public and the Press to be present helped to put a brake upon the giving of false evidence, which is only too common in affiliation cases, and upon blackmail to which a married woman is often open. It was felt that these objections would be largely met if the same restrictions were laid on the reporting of affiliation proceedings as those imposed on divorce proceedings and on proceedings in the juvenile courts, in which the names of the parties may not be divulged, and if the time and place of hearing were such as to discourage the attendance of casual onlookers. The joint committee of the B.M.A. and the Magistrates' Association was not in favour of the first proposal because so much false evidence is given in bastardy cases, but the legal sub-committee of the N.C.U.M.C. supported both recommendations.

The Legitimacy Act, 1959, has met a great part of the difficulty by providing that affiliation cases shall be heard in a court from which the public are excluded; the Press may remain but the amount reportable is limited and intimate details can certainly no longer be published. The case is heard by not more than three magistrates, both sexes being represented on the bench.

In *Canada*, it is worth noting, the exclusion of extraneous persons is taken farther. In *Alberta* 'no person other than the officers of of the court, the complainant and the defendant, their representative counsel and such other persons as the judge in his discretion expressly permits, shall be present at the hearing'; and in *British Columbia* 'all persons other than the officers of the court, the parties interested, and their witnesses and counsel shall be excluded therefrom'. There is a somewhat similar provision in *Saskatchewan*.

PROOF OF PATERNITY

English law assumes a man to be the father of an illegitimate child if he had sexual relations with the woman at the period of conception, unless he can produce evidence that any other man had intercourse with her at that time. If he can prove this, neither he nor any other man is held responsible. The woman's evidence must be corroborated in some material particular: the man's written admission, the evidence of neighbours, or proof that he has given her money for the child's support, or promised her marriage knowing her to be pregnant. A married woman applying for an affiliation order must prove her husband's non-access at the time of conception, and that she is still living apart from him.

The proceedings are still coloured by the fact that to prove the woman to be of bad character is the man's best defence, unless he can prove non-access. A number of girls therefore go through an ordeal in court, especially if they are attached to the man. Cases even occur in which witnesses—friends of the father—give false evidence that they slept with the girl, in order to destroy her case.

Various countries have evaded this difficulty by framing their law on different lines. In *Sweden* the man named is assumed to be the child's father if the evidence that he slept with the woman is clear, irrespective of whether any other man had sexual relations with her around the time of conception. Dr Alva Myrdal describes the intention behind this as being that even 'the illusion of a real father' is better than none.[1] Paternity is therefore more easily established in Sweden and proceedings are relatively innocuous.

In *Denmark* a distinction is made between being the child's father —determined as such by the man's acknowledgment or by process of law—and being only 'liable to pay maintenance' for the child, i.e. one of several men who had intercourse with the woman at the time under consideration. This distinction was also made until quite recently in *Norway*, each man being liable to pay the full sum fixed, though in practice the amount was shared between them as determined by the county sheriff. In *Denmark* each pays the full sum, one contribution being paid to the mother and the others into a special fund for child welfare. A somewhat similar system, apportioning the amount to be paid among several men, is in force in seven Provinces of *Canada* and was, for a period, adopted in the *U.S.S.R.* Such a distinction is foreign and perhaps antipathetic to English law and in *Norway* and *Denmark* has been under severe criticism as being confusing for the child, who may find itself faced with a series of possible fathers and may come to take a rather sceptical view of its mother. The Scandinavian countries have agreed that with the more accurate determination of fatherhood that has become possible since the development of blood tests and

---

[1] *Nation and Family*, p. 334.

anthropological tests (see next page), this double category of 'established paternity' and possible father[1] has become less necessary, and a revision of the law has recently taken effect in *Norway*. It provides that 'should it appear from the evidence in the case that the mother had had intercourse with two or more men during the period when the child could have been conceived, none of them shall be known as the father unless there is a greater probability that the child was conceived by him than by any other'. Judgment will then be given either for paternity or for full acquittal.

The English law, which assumes the man innocent unless he is proved responsible, is perhaps more equitable, though at present the process of attempting to establish that a man is the father is not by any means reliable. An article in the *American Journal of Police Science* of 1932, quoted and commented upon in the *British Medical Journal* of 5th August 1950, suggested that about half of the accusations made in the courts may be made against innocent men. This suggestion is based on blood tests made upon over six thousand men involved in bastardy proceedings in *Germany, Austria, Danzig, Denmark, Sweden, Norway, Switzerland* and *Lithuania*. According to this analysis, an innocent man involved in a paternity suit has only about one chance in three or four of being acquitted. Whether or not these figures are in any way applicable to this country at the present date, they do raise the question as to how far blood tests might contribute to a greater degree of certainty in deciding paternity cases.

A blood test is a careful scientific examination of samples of the blood of the mother, the alleged father and the child, to determine whether under the laws of inheritance it is physically possible that the accused man should be the father. All human blood falls into groups, which are inherited according to Mendel's law, so that a child cannot have a character of blood that it does not inherit from its parents. If, therefore, the child's blood is found to contain a character which is not found in the blood of the man alleged to be the father, it is clear that some other man must be the father. These tests cannot ordinarily establish that the accused or any other particular man is the father but they may prove conclusively that he is *not*. Experts put the chance of the tests excluding an

---

[1] We use this term as a convenient shorthand. In law, the man is described only as being 'liable to pay maintenance'.

innocent man falsely accused at 53 per cent.[1] A well-equipped laboratory, using seven blood-group systems, could do rather better and raise that chance to 60 per cent.[2]

A Bill to make blood tests compulsory in affiliation cases, when demanded, failed to pass in 1938. Under the present law either party may ask for a blood test, but it is undergone at the parties' discretion and the mother is entitled to refuse; nor may the court draw any conclusion from her refusal to take part in the test. The legal sub-committee of the N.C.U.M.C. has recommended that the defendant should, on receiving a summons in an affiliation case, have the right to demand a blood test.

'This matter is of the first importance, as reliable evidence in affiliation cases is notoriously hard to find, and the decision of the Court is only too often subject to a lingering doubt . . . The test may . . . be of . . . crucial importance to the defendant if it shows that he belongs to a blood group of which the child's father cannot be a member and the mother's allegation is therefore false.'

The completion of such tests, the sub-committee considered, would save the courts a considerable amount of time wasted in hearing evidence on false allegations of paternity. The joint committee of the B.M.A. and the Magistrates' Association was divided as to whether the tests should be a right of the defendant or optional at the discretion of the court.

In some countries—*Norway*, for example—blood tests are a regular part of the procedure when a case comes before the courts, unless the man has already admitted paternity. Recently a new procedure has been introduced in some countries, that of anthropological tests—scientific comparisons of such features as the pigment of the skin, hair, etc. of father and child. Tests along these lines—in which *Austria* has led the way and a number of countries, among them *Norway* and *Eastern Germany*, have followed suit—are yearly becoming more reliable.

PAYMENT UNDER AFFILIATION ORDERS

The Sum Fixed

The law provides, as we have stated, only for the child's

---

[1] R. R. Race and R. Sanger, *Blood Groups in Man* (3rd ed.), Table 93 and ch. XVII (Blackwell, 1958).

[2] Correspondence with Dr Norman Bailey of the Unit of Biometry, University of Oxford.

maintenance. Up to September 1952 the maximum sum that the justices could fix was £1 a week, payable until the child was sixteen. This compared poorly with the average maximum of £2 or actual average of £1 7s. 9d. that Children's Departments paid to foster-mothers—a figure notably free of any margin of profit. From 1st September 1952 the upper limit was raised to 30s.,[1] payable until the child is sixteen years old or, if he is still undergoing a course of education or training, up to the maximum age of twenty-one. There is no provision for its extension if the child is incapable of earning a living for any other reason, as there is in some countries. In pre-war *Danzig*, for example, the father had to maintain the child beyond the age of sixteen if it was unable to earn its living owing to any infirmity. In *Finland* the claim to maintenance lasts in any case until the child is seventeen years old and is prolonged in case of illness for so long as the child needs it. *South Africa* has made a provision for continuance of the maintenance obligation beyond the child's majority if it is a lunatic.[2]

Many lawyers think this ceiling of 30s. still too low in view of the income some men earn; others see no object in retaining a maximum. The upper limit was in fact set at that figure to bring the provisions for illegitimate children into line with the provisions in the magistrates' courts for the children of separated parents. Up to 1948 the upper limit in affiliation cases was higher than for legitimate children, a position that was not necessarily illogical, since the mother, who may have both to earn and to care for the child, receives no payment towards her own maintenance. An upper limit is usual for payments entrusted to the magistrates' courts, and so long as bastardy cases continue to be dealt with exclusively there, a limit must be expected to remain.

Few other countries set an upper limit. A *Norwegian* child, who is, for example, the illegitimate son of a doctor can expect to be maintained according to his father's social level, and a case was recently before a Scandinavian court attempting to compel a father with a salary of £3,000 a year to pay £6 a week towards his child. Indeed, some countries such as *Norway* and *Denmark* enforce a

---

[1] A change now being proposed in the Matrimonial Proceedings (Magistrates' Courts) Bill is that the weekly maintenance under affiliation orders should be raised to a maximum of £2 10s.

[2] These facts are quoted from the League of Nations *Study of the Position of the Illegitimate Child*, 1929.

normal minimum contribution. The common European tradition is that, at least in theory, the child should be brought up according to the standard of both parents or, in some countries, of whichever is the wealthier. In *Canada* the amount is left to the judge's discretion. The law of *Ontario* provides that 'he shall take into consideration the ability to provide and the prospective means' of the father.

'Obviously', comments the sub-committee of the N.C.U.M.C., 'the present maximum of thirty shillings a week is low, but the Committee were impressed by the warnings of very experienced magistrates (endorsed by others familiar with the Courts) that it would be very difficult to get the average wage-earner, who is the subject of most affiliation orders, to pay more. If orders were made on a higher scale they would probably only lead to the piling up of arrears. For these and other reasons it was considered that a ceiling for payments (on orders payable under present procedure) is desirable, but if special Matrimonial or Domestic Relations Courts, with jurisdiction to try affiliation cases, are established, no limit should be imposed. In certain circumstances, where for example the child of a wealthy man appears entitled to exceptional treatment, the Committee felt that it should be possible to take affiliation proceedings to the High Court, where there would be no legal restriction on the amount.'

It cannot be too strongly stressed, however, that the maximum is rarely the sum the justices actually fix. Before the 1952 Act came into force it was apparently granted in less than 20 per cent of cases and since then, in less than 10 per cent. These figures are based on an analysis of the files of two large city courts: in 1950-1 the maximum was granted in 17 per cent of the cases in one court and 19 per cent in the other: in 1953-4, in 8 per cent in one court and 9 per cent in the other. These were both highly efficient courts, so the national average may have been lower.

A study of the sums fixed in these two courts under orders granted during the year following 1st September 1953 may be of interest. (In a few instances the sum was fixed for each of two or more children, in one case 17s. 6d. for each of three children, in another 7s. 6d. for each of five.)

THE FATHER'S CONTRIBUTION

Sum fixed	COURT 1 (121 new orders affecting 138 children)		COURT 2 (127 new orders affecting 133 children)	
	Number	%	Number	%
30s.	10	8.3	11	8.7
25s.	9	7.4	1	0.8
20s.	35	29.0	37	29.1
17s. 6d.	5	⎫	—	⎫
15s.	21	⎪	28	⎪
12s. 6d.	5	⎬ 25.6	7	⎬ 29.9
12s.	—	⎪	2	⎪
11s.	—	⎭	1	⎭
10s.	17	14.0	23	18.1
8s.	1	⎫	—	⎫
7s. 6d.	5	⎪	4	⎪
5s.	5	⎪	2	⎪
2s. 6d.	4	⎬ 15.7	7	⎬ 13.4
2s.	—	⎪	1	⎪
1s.	3	⎪	3	⎪
3d.	1	⎭	—	⎭
	121	100.0	127	100.0

The average sum fixed in Court 1 was thus 15s. 6d. per child—or an average of 17s. 9d. per father, some of them paying for more than one child under an order. In Court 2 it was 16s. 4d. per child—or 17s. per father. The national average may have been lower.

There were only ten or eleven orders for 30s. in either court; and of the ten in Court 1 the men had in three cases offered the maximum, and in four more the woman was dependent on the National Assistance Board or had no other source of income. In the year 1950-1, when the maximum was fixed by this court in as many as nineteen cases, in eight the man had offered it, and in five others the woman was dependent on the National Assistance Board or out of work. These findings are a little disconcerting, although they are an improvement on the position before the 1952 Act came into force, when the average fixed in Court 1 was 13s. 4d. and in Court 2, 13s. per child.

Why are the sums named so low? The magistrates do not have to allow for further contingencies such as the defendant's marriage and further family, since the sums fixed are not irrevocable; either party may apply at any time for a variation of the order upwards or downwards, should circumstances change. An order is based exclusively on present circumstances—so exclusively that the following human note appears beside one of them: 'The man offers to pay £1 . . . but if a nominal order (for 3d.) is made there is every likelihood that the couple will continue to live together. If they part complainant to apply for increase.'

The new ceiling is not in itself regarded as an argument for increasing amounts fixed under previous orders, unless they were originally fixed for the maximum or the men's earnings have increased substantially meanwhile. Court 1, for instance, made fifty-four variation orders in the year after the Act came into force (thirty-six increasing and eighteen decreasing the amount payable), but only five were for 30s. Thus, under new and variation orders combined, the maximum was fixed in only 8.6 per cent of the cases. Court 2 in the same year made eighty-two variation orders, but in only three cases raised the sum to 30s.

Any very small sums ordered—those under 5s.—are fixed only to establish paternity when the man is out of work or otherwise unable to pay more, and it is open to the woman to apply later for an increase. We received an eloquent comment on this from a young mother aged nineteen.

' . . . Anyway I went to court and everything went all right he admitted it but he also told them of his numerous debts he has to pay so I only get 5/- p.w. but with the understanding I can claim any time if I know he gets more wages and paid his debts off. Well I don't think he is going to tell me that, also they told me my wages was quite good being £3 17s. 6d. I don't think they take into consideration the cost of fetching a child up decent and the debt I went into before I had baby.'

The Sum Received

It is clear now that the impression that a woman can expect 30s. a week under an affiliation order is incorrect. The usual sum fixed is about 16s. But is it paid? A simple division sum between the amount of money Court 1 received in, for example, 1951-2 and the number of orders then on its books reveals that the average man actually paid only 9s. 6d. a week. Most, it seems, fell seriously and successfully into arrears.

This, too, is only part of the story. If a man has failed to pay for six months and the mother has not asked to have him sued, Court 1 removes him from its books at the quarterly audit. Consequently of one hundred and sixty-nine orders made in 1935, only forty survived until the children reached the age of sixteen. Many truly fell by the way for good reasons: the child was adopted; the woman married and her husband preferred to maintain the child himself; payment was transferred to another court; the man was killed, or the child died. But in some cases it was another story: the man left the country—the best way of evading payment—or changed his address so that he could not be traced; or the woman herself lost heart after his constant failure to pay the amounts due, and ceased at last to ask the court to summons him. Many women feel each time the man fails to pay as a fresh wound to their pride: it would be easier for them if the court relieved them of the burden of taking renewed action.

One can set out the real picture, then, in a sum on the lines of the House that Jack Built:

12 per cent of fathers
pay less than two-thirds of the sum fixed,
which is half the sum that might be fixed,
and less than a quarter maintain payment.

The Men's and Women's Earnings Compared

It is sometimes argued that the men fail to pay because the sums fixed are too high. This does not explain why nearly all the orders surviving from 1935 were those for the higher sums, but since Court 1 conscientiously notes details of the men's and women's comparative earnings, outgoings and responsibilities, we will leave the facts to speak for themselves.

Only twenty-eight of the one hundred and twenty-one women were earning a wage. The rest were living on the following resources:

Maternity benefit (36s. a week)	5[1]
Sickness benefit	10
Widow's pension	1
National assistance (average receipt of woman with one child, £2 11s. p.w. apart from rent)	42
Maintained by parents	at least 2

[1] These women must have applied within a few weeks of the child's birth.

Maintained by child's father	4
Earning board and lodging only	2
Not earning, and no details	27
	93

The average gross earnings of the women receiving a wage were £3 18s. a week.[1]

£2 and over	2
£3 and over	10
£4 and over	13
£5 and over	3
	28

Of the men, about a third were bachelors who had no special responsibilities towards parents or any other person. These were earning a gross weekly average of £6 11s.

£4 and over	3
£5 and over	13
£6 and over	11
£7 and over	7
£8 and over	4
£9 and over	2
£10 and over	1
£11 and over	1
	42

They paid for their board and lodging from £2 to £2 10s. a week—in a few cases £3—and none was making any further contribution to his parents' maintenance; so they were, one supposes, handsomely provided with beer and tobacco.

In some instances the men's and women's position can be compared in greater detail. The following table includes every case where full details about both man and woman were available, except where the man was married or in the Forces, or the woman had other children to maintain, when their comparative burdens are more difficult to assess. The table refers to sums fixed and not to amounts actually received.

---

[1] See EARNING CAPACITY, p. 114, where other figures are also quoted.

THE FATHER'S CONTRIBUTION

	WOMAN'S INCOME	AMOUNT OF ORDER	WOMAN'S AND CHILD'S INCOME WITH ORDER (2 persons)	MAN'S INCOME	MAN'S INCOME LESS ORDER (1 person)
	£ s. d.	£ s. d.	£ s. d.	£ s. d.	£ s. d.
1.	— — —[1]	1 — —	1 — —[2]	9 10 —	8 10 —
2.	3 10 —	1 — —	4 10 —	6 10 —	5 10 —
3.	4 — —	1 10 —	5 10 —	8 7 —	6 17 —
4.	4 1 —	1 — —	5 1 —	8 — —	7 — —
	NATIONAL INSURANCE				
5.	1 16 —	1 — —	2 16 —	7 13 —	6 13 —
6.	1 16 —	— 15 —	2 11 —	5 7 —	4 12 —
	MATERNITY BENEFITS				
7.	1 16 —	1 — —	2 16 —	8 — —	7 — —
8.	1 16 —	1 — —	2 16 —	6 — —	5 — —
	NATIONAL ASSISTANCE				
9.	1 10 —	1 — —	2 10 —	5 8 —	4 8 —
10.	2 5 —	1 10 —	3 15 —	9 10 —	8 — —
11.	2 10 —	— 15 —	3 5 —	5 15 —	5 — —
12.	2 17 —	1 — —	3 17 —	6 15 —	5 15 —
13.	3 — —	— 15 —	3 15 —	6 1 —	5 6 —
14.	3 5 —	— 12 6	3 17 6	5 — —[3]	4 7 6[3]

THE PROBLEM OF ARREARS

If the men's earnings are so good, why are they allowed to fall into arrears? In part because the courts are overworked and the police are reluctant to add to their duties by trying to trace vanished men liable for comparatively trivial sums under these charges. In part, also, because the women get discouraged and do not go on pressing the case. But also because of the men's attitude; they have usually already indicated their unwillingness to pay: they have neither the custody of nor usually access to their children, so they have no opportunity to develop a personal affection or share the parental satisfaction that develop a feeling of responsibility.

---

[1] Board and lodging only.
[2] Plus board and lodging.
[3] Net.

What happens, then, if a man falls into arrears? Strictly speaking, the woman should be notified if the man is more than four weeks in arrears, but normally Court 1 waited until the man had not paid for six months and then, at the quarterly audit, if the woman had not expressed a wish for further proceedings, removed the case from its books. Occasionally, as in Court 2, it waited only until a month's arrears had accumulated and then wrote to ask the woman if she wished to take action. Sometimes at the end of a year it sent out a group of notifications. Court 2 offered to take action on the woman's behalf, and if she desired it, a summons would be issued and a hearing fixed. At such hearings both parties are expected to be present, though if the man has disappeared and the police are not prepared to take action or if he has gone abroad, nothing can be done until he returns.

If all went well, the court normally ordered the man to pay the outstanding sum or some weekly proportion of the arrears, and the case would then be adjourned for two or three months. Should he fail to pay or be irregular, there might be a further adjournment and finally he might be committed to prison. The maximum term is six weeks. His actual commitment was often suspended after sentence to give him a last opportunity to pay, but if then he fell into arrears for even a day, he was arrested and had to serve his sentence or a period representing the undischarged portion of his debt.

And then what happened to the debt? It was automatically wiped out. Although he was imprisoned for contempt of court rather than directly for non-payment, his imprisonment was regarded as discharging his debt to the child—the law had not forgotten the folly of the Debtors' Prison!—and current payments did not begin to accumulate until a week after his discharge. But the child did not benefit from this term in prison and the man often came out still more bitterly determined not to pay. In theory his goods might be distrained and sold to satisfy the debt, but this was so rarely done that an officer of Court 1 denied that the power existed. Was it thought unwise to kill even the wireless set of the goose that laid the golden eggs?

Unencumbered, then, the bachelors remained, or if the burden was too much for them, they would

> 'softly and suddenly vanish away,
> And never be met with again.'

The experience that the recovery of arrears is in practice a difficult task is not confined to England. In one study made in the *United States* in 1928 the records showed that 44 per cent of the men whose orders to pay had been in force for one or two years were in arrears, while no less than 73 per cent of those whose orders had been in force from five to seven years were in arrears. Records of children born in a year of financial depression, 1935, showed that within one or two years 80 per cent of the white fathers and 86 per cent of the negro fathers had already fallen behind in their payments, nearly half of the fathers being in arrears for 50 per cent or more of the amount due. These figures, an American social worker wrote in 1939, 'suggest that we have had false hopes of the efficacy of court orders as a means of actually providing support for children born out of wedlock. It is probable that only a small proportion . . . are supported until they are sixteen years of age.'[1]

The legal sub-committee of the N.C.U.M.C. reported in 1954:

'The practical difficulty which the unmarried mother experiences in actually securing the moneys due to her under affiliation orders is notoriously one of the greatest trials she has to endure. All persons experienced in her problems, whether magistrates or social workers, are emphatically of the opinion that the *prevention of accumulation of arrears* is the most effective way of safeguarding her interests. If the payments are allowed to lapse, the man finds himself with a hopeless burden of debt, he gets reckless and refuses to attempt to pay. Once he has served a prison sentence the debt is wiped out but he is now full of resentment and the whole miserable sequence starts again.

'Every effort therefore should be made to make the collection of payments as easy as possible, which the Committee think could be effected under existing legal powers by administrative action. Offices should be kept open at hours convenient to those making and collecting the payments, e.g. at lunch hours and certain evenings. Collecting officers' clerks should have some special training in the social implications of their work. Greater use should be made of Probation Officers to make enquiries about men who default, and in many cases before first orders or variation of order. The offer of social services may help as the man may be genuinely unable to pay.

'If payments fail, action should be taken *promptly* and before

[1] Maud Morlock, *The Fathers of Children Born Out of Wedlock* (1939).

arrears accumulate. In the case of deliberate and persistent refusal to pay a quick prosecution is the fairest all round and punishment of the recalcitrant, it was thought, should be speedy and effective. The hardship to the woman consequent on the law that imprisonment wipes out debt, was recognized by the Committee but they were unable to recommend any alteration, in view of its general application to a number of analogous cases.'

The report went on to consider the advantages of the *Scottish* (and *Scandinavian*) method of seizing the man's money at source, requiring employers to deduct payments from the man's wages. This was not at that time favoured by the sub-committee, since it was thought it might be detrimental to the man's reputation and possibly to his employment. However, it commented:

'This aspect of the matter would be less objectionable if the same method were used for payment of maintenance orders to wives and alimony', and meanwhile it put forward as an alternative suggestion, 'A much more agreeable proposal is that use should be made of PAYE either as a routine method of payments at the man's request, or for compulsory deductions if he became a defaulter.'

Parliament fortunately soon recognized that drastic improvements must be made in the procedure for recovering arrears due from married or divorced men to their wives and children, as well as from natural fathers, and in 1958 the English courts acquired through the Maintenance Orders Act an important new power, applicable in both situations. So today, if a man is four weeks in arrears, the court, at the woman's written request, may make an attachment of earnings order. This has the effect of stopping a proportion of his wages at source. It may prove a fairly effective means of recovery. But it is too early to say if it will do so. For will the courts in fact make any wide use of their powers? And are there not still too many loopholes? To evade payment the man has only to change his job and district, or become unemployed or even self-employed, or, as always, simply to disappear.

On the question of imprisonment, the 1958 Act provides that this does not wipe out arrears, but the man may not be imprisoned again for those arrears, though he may be for later ones.

A State Guarantee

The problem is of such long standing that as far back as 1888 steps were taken to combat it in *Denmark*. If a Danish father defaults upon the duty of maintenance, the amount that he owes is advanced to the mother from public funds. These advances—which were, by the way, the germ of family allowances—were at first introduced solely to help illegitimate children, though they are now paid also for children whose parents have been divorced or separated. Payment is at the so-called 'normal' rate for a father's contribution, i.e. three-fifths of what the decent upkeep of the child would cost in a good home in the locality in which it is living, assessed in 1955 at about 16s. a week, and in addition covers any special contributions due for its baptism, confirmation, education, professional training, sickness and burial and the additional 25 per cent due for the first two years of the child's life. It also includes any amount due for the mother's own support.

Payment is subject to a generous means test of about £6 a week. The advance is not recoverable from the mother, but is treated as a debt due from the father to the public purse. Well over a third of all illegitimate children probably receive these advances, and about half of the total advance made on behalf of out-of-wedlock children is successfully recovered.

The Danish Child Welfare Committee has power to order a person receiving these public advances on affiliation contributions to spend the money in a certain way, and if the directions are not complied with, or if conditions otherwise make it necessary, the Committee may arrange to draw the advance itself and either pay it over in instalments or itself apply the money for the child's benefit.

A similar scheme has long existed in *Iceland*.

Sweden introduced similar arrangements in 1938, although there the advances are not subject to a means test. Payment is limited to 600 kroner a year, or about 17s. a week, and does not include any amounts due for the mother's maintenance. Recovery is made from the father wherever possible by the Child Welfare Committee; but if the amount or full amount cannot be recovered from him, the State will examine the case and reimburse to the commune three-quarters of the unrecovered sum.

A *Norwegian* Royal Commission reporting in 1951 proposed the adoption of a similar scheme. In 1949 only about 20 per cent of all maintenance payments in Norway had been made punctually: about 55 per cent were sent late or had to be collected by force, and 25 per cent were never paid at all. It was therefore proposed that whenever the father was in arrears, the amount due might be advanced to a maximum of 50 kroner, roughly 50s., a month. A duty would lie on the Bailiff of Alimony—who handles the financial affairs of extra-marital children—in conjunction with the Child Care Office to see that the money is used in the child's best interests. This proposal has now become law.

These *Scandinavian* reforms are based on a true understanding of the financial difficulties confronting 'solitary' mothers with children to maintain.

'Over a generation ago,' wrote Alva Myrdal in 1945, 'public opinion came to consider it absurd that a child should suffer from irregularity of support when such support was promised.'[1]

Good ideas travel and the principle of maintenance advances has, interestingly enough, also been adopted since the war in one of the People's Republics. By an Act passed in *Czechoslovakia* in 1948:

'If agreement has been reached regarding the amount of maintenance payable by the father, or if such maintenance has been fixed by the court, and if the person legally responsible does not pay or if judgment cannot be executed against him, the State, on application of the person entitled to it, pays the whole amount to such person in monthly instalments. The State subsequently claims repayment of such sums, plus 10 per cent (for administrative expenses) from the person who should have paid them.'

The legal sub-committee of the N.C.U.M.C. wrote in its 1954 report:

'The Committee also considered a proposal which if accepted would sweep away all collecting difficulties as far as the mother is concerned. The suggestion is that when an affiliation order is made, it should be registered with the Local Authority (or the National Assistance Board) to whom the putative father would be required to make his payments. If the man defaulted, the responsible body would continue the payments to the mother (or other guardian) and would where necessary take proceedings against the man. Once an order had been made the mother would have security for her child and would be relieved of a continuing relationship with the Magistrates' Court.

'The scheme is not free from objection on the ground that (*a*) legal proceedings taken by a Local Authority require the consent of a Committee and are often much delayed and (*b*) it might

[1] *Nation and Family*, p. 335.

impair the man's sense of responsibility and discourage effort if he knew that his child and its mother would automatically receive the payments even if he defaulted. After discussion with a representative of a Local Authority who thought that the suggested method presented no serious administrative difficulties and would avert much hardship, the Committee by a majority decided to give it their support.'

It will be noted that this proposal would limit the advances to those cases where an affiliation order has been made but the man has defaulted. If a scheme were introduced whereby voluntary agreements could be registered with the courts or approved by the competent administrative authorities, advances would no doubt be made on these also, as is done in *Sweden, Denmark* and *Czechoslovakia*. But there is no suggestion that advances should be made where there is no legal obligation to pay; this is also the principle in *Scandinavia*. There are rare exceptions: in *Denmark*, for instance, when a child is born of an incestuous relationship, it may not be held to be in its interest to know its father's identity and in that case no affiliation proceedings will be taken and yet, by special arrangement, the mother may be permitted to draw the advances.

There is in any such scheme, which covers only a proportion of illegitimate children, a certain inequity: it is not the child's fault if its father is unknown or not bound by a legal agreement, but every child needs financial security. But the essence of the matter lies in our comment that the Danish scheme, though it survives till this day, was the germ of family allowances: it proved a step on the way to a far wider scheme designed to give greater financial security to all families. In England, where the family allowances are not at present paid for the first child, there is still no such minimum security for natural children, but a great need to provide it. State advances meanwhile place the economic shock of a father's dereliction upon stronger shoulders than the single mother and her child.

At a Parent's Death
If the child's father dies, his responsibility under an affiliation order dies with him. Proceedings cannot be taken to claim from his estate any payments due under the order—or even to claim any accumulated arrears. This is a judicial decision, based upon the principle that the father's liability is strictly personal and therefore

cannot be enforced against his estate, and it perhaps serves one good purpose: if the man is married and the wife did not know of the illegitimate child's existence, she is less likely to be faced with the fact suddenly upon her widowhood. It is questionable, however, whether the protection of a widow from mental suffering should be obtained at the price of the sudden loss of security for a child: few women would really wish to secure their own peace of mind at the price of a child's welfare. The alternatives would seem to be for the State to take over the liability (which raises difficult questions of means tests) or for the law to be changed.

The Joint Committee on Psychiatry and the Law, appointed by the British Medical Association and the Magistrates' Association, reported in 1952:

'It seems to us that the inability of mothers or guardians of such children to make a claim on the estate of deceased fathers reflects again the spirit in which the legislation has been passed. Poor people are not likely to leave substantial assets behind them on their deaths and only the illegitimate children of poor people have so far received the attention of Parliament.

'We see no justification for this law and if, as we recommend, power is given to the High Court to deal with bastardy cases, such a law would be definitely harmful. We recommend that the present state of the law in this respect should be reconsidered with due regard to the interests of the wife and any other children of the deceased.'[1]

The various attempts by different countries to solve this difficult problem are discussed in Part IV. But the law of one Commonwealth country may be worth quoting here. In *Canada*, in the Province of *Ontario*, if a putative father dies, an affiliation order is regarded as binding his estate; the judge is, however, required to see that the widow and legitimate children are not deprived of necessary maintenance.

If it is the mother who dies, the child's position is different. He may inherit from her, if she left no valid will to any other effect, but only if she has no legitimate children.

Foreign Fathers and Those Residing Abroad
A difficult problem arises if the father lives abroad, whether he is British or foreign. An Englishman who wishes to avoid paying

[1] *The Law in Relation to the Illegitimate Child.*

under an affiliation order may, of course, do no more than move to another town, leaving no address behind him, but if he emigrates, say to Canada or Australia, or takes up his residence in a foreign country, he passes out of the jurisdiction of the courts and there are no provisions for the enforcement abroad or in the Commonwealth of an affiliation order made in the United Kingdom. There are, it is true, reciprocal arrangements between some countries of the Commonwealth for the enforcement of orders for the maintenance of children born of marriage, but they do not apply to illegitimate children.

Similarly, when an English or Scots girl has an illegitimate child by a foreigner, an affiliation order may be made if the child was conceived and the putative father still resident in this country, but the order is not enforceable against him if he returns to his own country. Nor is it possible to prevent a British or foreign father from leaving the country if he is in arrears with his maintenance. In Scandinavian countries he may be refused permission to leave the country and the police may distrain on his property, even ensuring that before he departs a sum is deposited equivalent to the amount yet to fall due under the order. Indeed, if paternity has not yet been finally established, action on these lines is still possible, although if he is eventually discharged he may have a claim for compensation against the mother. But in the United Kingdom, as in most other countries, one of the easiest ways to be rid of the burden of a maintenance order is to go abroad.

This problem affects financially the illegitimate children born to *American* servicemen stationed in the United Kingdom. Up to the passing of the Visiting Services Act in 1954 a mother could not even take affiliation proceedings against an American serviceman, since he was expressly protected from bastardy proceedings in British courts. Since 1954 it has been possible to obtain an order, but service regulations still forbid deductions from his pay on behalf of an illegitimate child and when he returns to the States the order cannot be enforced.

The same difficulty arises for a German girl who has a natural child by a British serviceman stationed in *Germany*. Until recently no case could be brought against him in the German courts, and Army (though not Air Force) regulations still forbid deductions from his pay for sums due under an affiliation order. When he returns to Great Britain the order cannot be enforced.

The N.C.U.M.C. has done much noble work on behalf of the British children of foreign men and the foreign children of British servicemen stationed abroad: in tracing the fathers, negotiating voluntary agreements with many of them to pay regular sums towards their child's support and acting as a channel for the transmission of these sums to Germany and other countries. Over the last few years the Council has been sending abroad steadily increasing sums of £2,000 a year and over towards the maintenance of foreign children of British men. But the problem is too large a one to be dealt with on a voluntary basis. Some impression of its scope may be gained from the figures quoted on page 29. It has been greatly swollen since the war owing to the large refugee populations in some countries, the forced migrations and great rise in emigration. Satisfactory arrangements do not exist as yet even for the recovery of sums due from emigrant bread-winners to their wives and children born of marriage.

The problem was repeatedly pressed upon the United Nations as a matter of urgency by the International Union for Child Welfare, the International Social Service and other organizations, and in 1952 a committee of experts under the auspices of the Economic and Social Council of the United Nations met at Geneva to consider two draft conventions for the recognition and enforcement abroad of maintenance obligations, whether towards the dependants of married men or towards children born out of wedlock. This committee has had to face innumerable difficulties. Nations have very different legal systems, different definitions even of what constitutes illegitimacy, of how paternity should be established and of what obligations a father has towards his illegitimate child. Was the law of one land to be enforced in another even if it meant accepting evidence that would not be regarded as adequate in the country of enforcement, which might have quite different rules of evidence and procedure? or if it made a man liable to pay a sum that would not be required of him under the law of the country asked to enforce the order? These were only some of the obstacles in the way of drafting satisfactory conventions that could be adopted internationally.

As long ago as 1931, *Norway, Sweden, Denmark, Iceland* and *Finland* adopted a convention for the collection of maintenance allowances from nationals of their own countries who neglect their maintenance duty towards spouse or child, legitimate or illegitimate, and move to another Scandinavian country. Under this convention the authorities in the country to which a man moves will recover from him any outstanding maintenance contributions (by distraint if necessary), enforcing payment on practically the same strict terms as in his own country. A father's departure to any country can also be stopped by the authorities.

Since their laws, and in particular their social legislation, were very similar, it proved possible to draw up a convention with relative ease. The same condition has made possible effective mutual arrangements between the constituent States of the *U.S.A.* and recently within the United Kingdom.

For securing effective enforcement internationally, the United Nations committee of experts has suggested two alternative methods. One would provide for a maintenance order made in the mother's country to be registered in the father's country of residence, thus enabling the order to be enforced without the necessity of bringing a new suit and of obtaining a new judgment in that country. This, the simpler procedure, is possible between countries with a reasonably similar legal system and familiar with this method of exequatur. More widely applicable would be the proposal for a system of judicial collaboration, whereby a woman could file an application in her own country and be given a preliminary and summary hearing by a court, which could make a finding to the effect that there seemed to be a *prima facie* cause of action. This court would transmit the application and finding, with any necessary documents, to an agency appointed for the purpose in the father's country of residence, which would prosecute a maintenance action on behalf of the claimant in the courts of the respondent's country.

The committee proposed that bilateral treaties or a multilateral convention should be signed between interested countries, agreeing to procedure along these lines. The Economic and Social Council referred this report to the Secretary-General in 1954, and a multilateral convention came into force on 25th May 1957, signed by twenty-six governments, including several of the *Scandinavian* countries, *France, Italy, Western Germany* and *Austria*. But neither the *United States*, the *United Kingdom* nor any of the countries of the Commonwealth are signatories, and so in this country the position remains as before, with courts abroad powerless to enforce affiliation orders made in this country, and our own courts powerless to enforce those made abroad. In time, the conclusion of bilateral treaties, the policy preferred by the United States and the United Kingdom, may ease or solve these problems, but meanwhile the position is a tragedy for many young families, married and unmarried.

Approaching the Father
Legislation is always a limited way of trying to solve a human problem. Any father reading this chapter will ask why so little is done to enlist the psychological support of the father of the natural child. Social workers sit in judgment on him, the girl's family speak their minds to him freely; but he is often pretty young, and they combine to make him feel that he wants to get a long, long way from the situation and forget it. He, like the woman, is in need of society's support if he is to take on what is for him a new and rather unexpected role.

One of the best case-workers, recognizing this need and the men's—to put it at its lowest—curiosity about their children, has so enlisted the interest and help of many of the fathers that they come to her for regular news of their children and to ask if there is anything more they can do for the mothers' and children's support.

Here, then, is the problem: at present there are more than half a million children in this country under the age of sixteen who were born illegitimate, and too few of them receive adequate aid from their fathers. It does not seem too much to ask that the English law and practice should at least be brought into line with the best European legislation.

CHAPTER 7

THE STATE'S CONTRIBUTION

The development of the Welfare State has brought about a profound change in the position of unmarried mothers and their children, as it has in that of many other citizens threatened by poverty and insecurity. Unmarried mothers benefit, for example, from the national policy of full employment; from the improved wages for women; from the various social insurance benefits designed to cushion the shock of loss of wages due to sickness, pregnancy and childbirth; from the free health services; from the National Assistance grants made to those in want; from the improved care given to deprived children and those in foster-homes; from the development of day nurseries; from the stricter control of adoptions; from the various developments in school welfare services, etc. Indeed, the Welfare State impinges on their lives as closely as upon any group in the community.

None of the new services was specifically designed to meet the needs of illegitimate children and their mothers, although as a matter of policy they qualify like any other citizen for the benefits. But if one were to try to assess the achievement of the Welfare State in the last decade, one could hardly choose a more sensitive index than its effect upon unmarried mothers and their children. In them the sensitiveness of the State machinery to the needs of the individual is fully tested. No other group presents so many, such varied and such intractable problems; none is less amenable *as a group*, since the women and their backgrounds, needs and difficulties are so individual. No women are shyer of making use of the services offered, if they wish to conceal their condition or suspect any of the help of being at all insensitively administered; they make exceptional demands upon the personnel for sympathy, imagination, shrewdness and skill, for discretion and ability to adapt the help to the needs of the individual and see her problem as a whole. These are severe standards by which to test any services, yet they are the final ones by which their value must be judged.

The aim of the post-war schemes of social security was, in the words of Lord Beveridge, 'to make want under any circumstances unnecessary'. The unmarried mother with a child to support may only too frequently suffer from want. What help can the State give to her?

NATIONAL INSURANCE

Among the social insurance benefits administered by the Ministry of Pensions and National Insurance the two that are of particular interest to unmarried mothers are the *Maternity Benefits* and the *Family Allowances*. The mother's unmarried status and the child's illegitimacy do not disqualify her from claiming these or any other benefits paid by the Ministry if she is otherwise entitled.

Maternity Benefits
An unmarried mother may claim the maternity benefits if she is herself insured and has paid the necessary number of contributions. To do this she must normally have been insured for about a year, so the younger mothers or those who have been living at home looking after relatives or acting as housewives usually do not qualify —unlike married women, who may claim on either their husband's insurance or their own. But those that do qualify—and it includes most women who were working for the year or eighteen months preceding the period for which the benefits are drawn—are entitled to generous benefits: the *Maternity Allowance* of £2 10s. a week for eighteen weeks, normally beginning eleven weeks before confinement; the *Maternity Grant*, a lump sum of £12 10s. to help with the general expenses of having a baby; and, if the child is not born in hospital accommodation provided at public cost, a *Home Confinement Grant* of £5 to help to meet the extra cost involved. If the mother has other dependent children, she may also claim an increase of the maternity allowance of 15s. a week for the first child and 7s. a week over and above any family allowance for each of the others for the whole eighteen weeks, and also an increase for the new baby as soon as it is born, for the first weeks of its life.

These benefits, which are primarily designed to help married families where the husband is normally earning a full wage, are not enough fully to support a woman living on her own, although they may make a very great difference to her position. They may enable her to manage with the help of any small savings she has made. If she goes to a Mother and Baby Home run by a voluntary society, the maternity allowance will in most cases enable her to meet the small charge. Her family, so often torn at first between their distress and their affection, may be willing to have her home if they know she will not be a financial burden but can pay her way until she is able to go out to work. The allowance thus gives the young mother greater self-respect and her family less financial anxiety, and there is a far better hope of avoiding friction and of rebuilding the strained family relationships so that the child may grow up in a relatively happy and secure atmosphere.

Family Allowances
A family allowance is not payable for the first dependent child of a family, so the majority of unmarried mothers, having only one child, do not qualify. If a woman has several children, legitimate or illegitimate, the fact that she is unmarried or uninsured is no bar to her drawing the allowance, which amounts at present to 8s. a week for the second child and 10s. a week for the third and each subsequent child. A child is within the age limit whilst below normal school-leaving age (fifteen) and for any subsequent period before the age of eighteen whilst receiving full-time instruction in a school or as an apprentice. Thus a deserted wife, for instance, with several legitimate and one illegitimate child, or a woman who is cohabiting with a man to whom she is not married and has more than one child by him, or a promiscuous woman with a number of natural children by different fathers, may draw the allowance.

But the typical unmarried mother, who has only one child but often a severe financial struggle to bring it up, does not benefit. This situation might seem a little absurd if it were not that the children's welfare rather than the mother's ethics must be paramount—the child of a large family has no less need for food and clothing because it is illegitimate or its mother's morals dubious— and that the allowance is not, of course, in itself large enough to act as an inducement to have an illegitimate child. The inclusion of illegitimate children on equal terms under insurance benefits and family allowances is a matter of general policy in most countries and is supported by the trade union movements. The anomaly is therefore inevitable until such time as the allowance is extended to the first child of the family.

Family allowances were of course primarily designed for the help of married couples. A married man earning a normal wage is regarded as capable of supporting a wife and child without assistance, and it was felt that the country could not afford the extra cost of paying an allowance for the first dependent child, which Lord Beveridge assessed at nearly £100,000,000 a year, even at the much lower rate of allowance then proposed. However, there is pressure for its extension to first children when the country can bear the extra cost. The Royal Commission on Population reported in 1949 that 'it is usually the coming of the first child that makes the most significant addition to a married couple's expenditure and the most radical change in their way of life', and therefore regarded the exclusion of the first child as 'a serious defect', suggesting that it would be preferable to exclude the youngest rather than the eldest child of dependent age from the scope of the allowances, and to make even such a limitation only temporary. As a less expensive and more immediate improvement the Commission recommended a special lump-sum payment for the first child, in addition to the maternity grants and as a part of the system of children's allowances.

The maternity grant paid at the birth of each child has been raised from £4 to £12 10s. since that date, but the other proposals have not as yet been adopted. The Royal Commission's recommendations would, however, be of great benefit as bringing the great majority of illegitimate children within the scope of the family allowances scheme. In 1946, when the Population Investigation Committee made a study of the total expenditure on first births by different groups in the community, it was found that the average expenditure by unmarried mothers was only £17 as compared with £31 among agricultural workers, £35 among manual workers and £57 among professional and salaried workers.[1]

Certain countries do already include the first child in the family allowance—notably *Sweden* and *Denmark*, though in Denmark the allowances are subject to a means test. In a few countries, where wages are for one reason or another exceptionally low, these are paid on a very generous scale. For example, at the time when the Royal Commission reported, a *French* worker who was the sole bread-winner in his family received allowances, under one heading or another, amounting for the first child to 20 per cent of the average wage, whereas in *Great Britain* a worker with even three dependent

[1] *Maternity in Great Britain*, pp. 113 and 196.

children received an amount equivalent to only about 10 per cent of the average adult male wage. In *Jugoslavia*, where a skilled worker's wage in 1955 was about £12 a month, the family allowance for one child amounted to about £4 10s.

In *Sweden*, where all children, including the first and those born out of wedlock, are entitled to the normal children's allowance of 400 kroner a year (about £30), an additional sum, the *Special Family Allowance*, is also payable for certain groups of children who have lost their normal bread-winner. This supplementary pension, which amounts to a maximum of 600 kroner a year for each child, is not simply an orphan's pension but covers a considerably wider scope. It is payable if the father has died (or the mother, if the child does not live with its father after her death) or if the father draws a national pension, e.g. for old age or disability (or the mother if she draws a national pension and if she lives alone and has the care of the child) or where the child's paternity has not been established. An illegitimate child may therefore qualify for this pension if it has a recognized father and he dies or draws a pension (or in certain circumstances if the mother does so). There is a certain means test before this additional allowance is payable, but only upon the child's own means. If the child's paternity has not been established, and it thus has not its normal male breadwinner, the child may also be entitled to the pension, but only if its mother's means are small. The means test in this case is very strict; the full amount is payable only if her resources do not exceed 2,400 kroner a year and only after the child is three years old, since it is assumed that up to that date there may still be some possibility of establishing the father's identity. For a child under three she may, if she is in need and not working, claim national assistance.

These special *Swedish* children's allowances are relatively small and each subject to some kind of means test, but they constitute a type of help that has more the character of a right and of a pension than national assistance, and so can be accepted with greater self-respect. Taken in conjunction with the advance payments of alimony that are made by the local authority and partly reimbursed where necessary by the State—where a father, that is, is liable to pay alimony but fails to do so—they constitute the beginnings of a general State pension for children, legitimate or illegitimate, who for any reason—such as death, disablement or desertion—are deprived of their normal bread-winner. This is a large and fairly easily definable group, most of whom in Great Britain have no official resource at present except national assistance.

Sweden also has a provision that is of interest in connexion with the Royal Commission on Population's proposal that there should be an additional lump-sum payment under the family allowance at the birth of every first child. The costs with which an unmarried mother may be faced are not only the layette and actual expenses in connexion with the child's birth but also quite often the need to set up an independent home. In 1938 Sweden introduced a programme of State marriage loans for furnishing a home, to assist young people to start family life on a sound economic basis and without unreasonable resort to hire-purchase.[1] Since 1953 unmarried mothers have been included in this scheme. The loans are granted up to a maximum of about 3,000 kroner (or about £200), although smaller sums up to a maximum of about 1,000 to 2,000 kroner are more usual. Their size depends on the amount that the borrower is deemed able to repay; the annual interest is 4 per cent and repayment is normally required within five years, though it may sometimes be written off wholly or in part. These loans often assist an unmarried mother to set up an independent home with her child very much earlier than she otherwise would.

If an unmarried mother in *Great Britain* wishes to keep her child with her, but is unsuitable for a residential domestic job and her family cannot have her home or strains arise there, her position may be difficult. There are hostels where an unmarried mother may live with her child and go out to work by day, but there are not many of these and they offer lodging only for a few months—in some cases, for two or three years—and the time comes when the mother must and should begin an independent life of her own. The Royal Commission did not recommend the introduction of marriage loans in Great Britain, but perhaps if there were a small voluntary fund run on somewhat similar lines to the Swedish scheme, it might be of considerable assistance to women well deserving of help.

Sweden is a relatively well-to-do country, but even *Norway*, with its much more limited means, has tried to give special financial help to fatherless children. There the family allowance is, as in Great Britain, normally payable only if there is more than one child;

---

[1] *Freedom and Welfare, Special Patterns in the Northern Countries of Europe*, edited by George R. Nelson (Ministries of Social Affairs of Denmark, Finland, Iceland, Norway, Sweden, 1953).

but if the first child is in the care of a mother who is widowed or divorced, deserted or unmarried, she may claim the family allowance for it, and sometimes, if she is in need, an addition to her maternity allowance is also payable, though this latter provision has various restrictions and not many women take advantage of it.

Sickness, Unemployment and Injury Benefits
If the child's mother is working and has paid sufficient contributions she may at need claim the *Sickness Benefit* of £2 10s. a week for herself and 15s. a week for the first dependent child, with 7s. a week, over and above any family allowances, for each other dependent child; or *Unemployment Benefit* of £2 10s. a week, with the same addition for dependants; or in an appropriate case the allowances payable for industrial injury or to a tubercular or blind person. The child must be living with her for the addition for a dependent child to be payable or she must be contributing at least 8s. a week towards its maintenance. If it lives in another family and she pays less than 8s. a week towards its maintenance, the insured householder of the family in which the child is living may claim for it as a dependant. Similarly, if she has married since the child's birth, her husband may claim for it as a dependant.

Should the mother fall ill, this sickness benefit, amounting to £3 5s. for herself and one child, may tide her over a crisis; but in normal family life it is at least as often the child as the mother who falls ill and there is, of course, no insurance to cover such a situation: neither unemployment nor sickness insurance was designed to meet it, since in the normal family the main bread-winner, the father, will continue to earn and the mother will stay at home to look after the child—so that, even if she were normally at work, this temporary interruption is less likely to cause a vital loss of earnings. But the position of a widow or a deserted, separated or divorced wife with young children, or of an unmarried mother, is very different. She must accept the combined roles of bread-winner, home-maker and nurse, and for her a child's illness, even a minor illness, may cause acute hardship. She may well have to take time off and possibly resign or lose her job in order to look after the child.

A widow is nowadays to some extent safeguarded in such a case. If she has young children she will normally draw the *Widowed Mother's Allowance* referred to on page 166; even if she supplements it by earning, she can fall back upon it in a time of crisis. A separated or, in England, a divorced wife may draw alimony, but a deserted wife or unmarried mother may have no resort except national assistance. Unless she is lucky enough to have a friend or neighbour who can look after the child, minor crises of this kind may repeatedly interfere with her earning power. If a child is at school or day nursery, even a period of quarantine when a child cannot attend may cause a crisis. The frequency of minor ailments in a normal childhood makes such crises fairly common. It is by no means easy for the mother to make adequate savings to meet them and they often lead, in our experience, to a nervous atmosphere of chronic strain and anxiety in the home, which is not at all good for the growing child.

However, as we have said, it is difficult to see how an insurance scheme could be redesigned to cover such a risk as 'interruption of earnings due to a child's illness'! The solution lies elsewhere and will be discussed later in this chapter.

Guardian's Allowance

The guardian's allowance, which superseded the orphan's allowance paid up to 1948, cannot normally be drawn during the mother's lifetime, but if she dies it may be of considerable importance for the child's future. It is an amount of 27s. 6d. a week paid to the person in whose family a child is included after the death of both its parents. 'Parents' in this sense includes both natural and stepparents, but if the child's paternity has not been established and the mother is dead, the person looking after the child may be entitled to the benefit, if the mother had been insured under the National Insurance Acts. It is not paid for a child living in a Home or institution if it is not included in any family.

The guardian's allowance may make a great difference to the child's future if, after its mother's death, it has friends or relatives who are willing to offer it a home but could not ordinarily afford to do so. It must be remembered that the grandparents and other blood relatives of an illegitimate child have no legal responsibility towards it. There may therefore be some conflict of view inside the family of the grandparents, or the uncle or aunt, as to whether to offer the child a home, and a child that is unprovided for may be an unwelcome burden—in some families only too likely to have its origins thrown in its teeth. The existence of this allowance may do much to ease the home atmosphere. By a wise provision also, the allowance continues to be payable even if the child is adopted, so that if an affectionate family who take in a child would like after a while to offer it fuller security, the loss of the allowance need be no bar to their doing so.

Child's Special Allowance
In November 1957 a new cash benefit was introduced. It is paid after the death of her former husband to a woman whose marriage has been dissolved or annulled, if she has a child towards whose support he was contributing. The benefit equals the amount of his contribution, but is limited to a maximum of 16s. 6d. for the first child and 8s. 6d. for any other. If this benefit were also made payable on the death of a putative father who was liable under an affiliation order, one more financial problem would be solved. At present an order lapses on his death and is not payable to the child from his estate.

Lack of Other Benefits
The benefits so far described offer an unmarried mother and her child very considerable help over the later weeks of her pregnancy and the first seven weeks of the child's life; they help her out in such crises as her own disability or unemployment; they may assist the child after her death, if the father is unknown or has died; and if she has more than one dependent child, they may give her some slight regular weekly help throughout its childhood and school-days, by way of family allowance. There is, however, no provision under the insurance scheme in this country for regular help throughout childhood for the child of either an unmarried woman or deserted wife if she has only one child.

Here it is interesting to compare the position of a widowed mother with dependent children. Up to 1948 her position, unless the husband had been privately insured or had made adequate savings, was nearly as bad as that of an unmarried mother today. She might draw the widow's pension of 10s. a week with an addition of 5s. for the first and 3s. for each other dependent child who might qualify, but this was quite inadequate to maintain the family, and if she was not able to go out to work she was usually dependent upon public assistance.

Under strong public pressure her position has been greatly improved. If her husband has paid the necessary national insurance contributions, she may now claim for the first three months after his death the *Widow's Allowance* of £3 10s. a week, a further £1 for the first child and 12s. as well as the family allowances, for every other child. This allowance is unaffected by whatever amount she may be earning or whatever her other resources may be. After the first three months and until her children leave school or complete their training (the maximum age to which a dependent child's allowance can be paid is its eighteenth birthday), she may draw the *Widowed Mother's Allowance*, a weekly pension of £3 10s. for herself and the first child, with an addition of 12s. a week plus family allowances for every child after the first. This pension differs radically from national assistance in that there is little bar to her earning a supplementary income while she draws it, and no other means test. By a series of amendments to the original provisions, she may now earn £4 a week[1] without the pension being affected. If she earns more than £4, the pension is still not at once reduced, shilling by shilling, by the extra amount she earns: for example, if she earns £5 her pension is only reduced by 10s. If she earns over £5 there is a shilling by shilling reduction in her personal allowance, but none in the addition made for a child. Thus a widowed mother with one dependent child who draws this allowance and earns between £5 and £6 10s. has a weekly income of £8 from the allowance and her earnings. Should she earn, say, £8 she still draws £1 for the child, giving her a total income of £9. If her earnings are interrupted due, say, to a child's illness she still has the allowance of £3 10s. a week to fall back upon. Nor is it ever affected by other resources such as savings or a pension from private insurance.

This sum—£7 10s. when she is earning £4, and £3 10s. when she is temporarily unable to do even part-time work—presumably represents the amount which it is considered that a woman with one child may reasonably need if she is to maintain it adequately without any other person's help. It is a very much larger sum than any that most deserted wives or unmarried mothers can rely upon and above all it is compatible with part-time work. It is, of course, paid upon the husband's insurance and although, if he dies after three years of marriage, it may bear little relationship to the actual premiums he has paid, this is a normal insurance risk. A widow has also a certain status in society and may be considered as deserving of every help and sympathy. The position of a deserted

[1] It is proposed to increase this, and those that follow, by 20s.

wife may be the same, but society regards the husband as still responsible. The unmarried mother is in an ambiguous position. She does not yet meet with much public sympathy and there are certainly a rather larger number of unmarried mothers than, say, of widows who have properly forfeited the right to sympathy, even if their children have not. But a very large number of unmarried mothers are making a genuine struggle to bring up their children well, and these still receive little encouragement. What they—or many of them—need, as does the widow, is to be able to rely on a small regular weekly sum and to supplement this with their earnings, falling back on the allowance when their earnings are interrupted.

A child under, say, three years old should not ideally be placed in a day nursery, separated from its mother for nine to twelve hours. It is usually too young to benefit from the social life of the nursery and although the care given to it may be excellent and loving, it is rarely that it can receive the close and steady personal relationship that helps a young child to develop rightly. The care given in many day nurseries is far better than the care given in many homes, and yet it is not an ideal arrangement for a small child with a mother personally capable of giving it adequate affection and care. When the child goes to school it is a tragedy if the mother is not at home to welcome it on return or to look after it during the holidays. For these reasons and because of the wear and tear of running both a home and a job when there are young children, it would be better for many unmarried mothers with small children, though not for all of them, if they could take only part-time work, leaving the child in a nursery or with a good neighbour for part of each day, and earning enough to supplement, as a widow may, a basic allowance.

There are at present various difficulties in the way of such an arrangement. First of all, day nurseries have been rapidly closing down since the war and comparatively few are available; and the pressure on them for full-time vacancies is so great that they are not normally permitted to take children for only part of the day. Secondly, part-time posts are still few and far between. A mother may go out to part-time domestic work, but this would not normally bring her in very much money. She may find a part-time post if she is a secretary, but only a small proportion of mothers have this training. Part-time work in shops or factories is still difficult to obtain. Thirdly, and this is by far the most important consideration, it would not be in every unmarried mother's interest to be able to draw such an allowance. It is still doubtful how far any but the most exceptional unmarried mother, living on her own, can offer a child a normal and favourable home life. It is proper that this decision should be left in the mother's hands so long as she has access to sound advice to help her to make up her mind realistically, but a system of general State subsidies to enable all these mothers to bring up their children might be of doubtful value. Unless there were proper safeguards the subsidy might in some cases be used to enable a woman to cohabit or have sexual relations with a series of men and have children by them, with minimum financial help from the man: there are cases in which it is hard enough to prevent even national assistance from being abused in this way. What is necessary is to give the right mother in the right circumstances all necessary help to make a success of bringing up the child alone; but neither to subsidize every unmarried mother to sit at home indefinitely and look after her child, nor, because the prospect seems to be without personal hardship, to subsidize her to keep a child with her in circumstances that are unfavourable for the child's happy development. Here, as elsewhere, the needs of each child and mother may be different. Finally, there is little doubt that at present public opinion would not stand for any such special subsidy of illegitimate children. If they are to be helped it can only be as part of a wider scheme, by the extension of family allowances to all first children or by the introduction of some programme of special allowances for children—whether orphaned, deserted or illegitimate—with no male or other full-time bread-winner. Such provisions may come, but they will be expensive and may not come soon.

At present, the fact that unmarried mothers and their children are thrown back in need upon the National Assistance Board has the great disadvantage that this restricts their right to earn.

NATIONAL ASSISTANCE

Lord Beveridge in his plan for social security laid down as two of its basic principles that the scheme for social insurance should be 'adequate' and 'comprehensive'. The national insurance benefits were designed to cover the main risks that threaten a family's financial security—unemployment, sickness, industrial accident, childbirth, the cost of bringing up a family, and old age—while the National Assistance Board deals with those who slip through the net for one reason or another: those who have failed to qualify for insurance benefits because they have not fulfilled the necessary contribution conditions, or who have exhausted their right to benefit, or for whose needs the standard benefit is not sufficient. There are still, however, certain other clearly definable groups that fall outside the scope of insurance benefit, among them the deserted wife unable to get an order against her husband and who cannot go out to work because she has young children to care for, the wife and children of a man serving a term of imprisonment, the unmarried mother and her young child. These are dependent upon national assistance, which is a necessary subsidiary to the insurance scheme.

'It was realized, of course,' wrote Lord Beveridge in the *Sunday Times* of 15th May 1957, 'that National Assistance subject to a means test could not be abolished at once or completely. But a central idea of the Beveridge Plan . . . was to reduce National Assistance to a dwindling minimum.'

The days when an unmarried mother claiming poor relief was usually parted from her child as a matter of course (the alternative being to live with it in a workhouse) are long past. The present national policy is to do everything reasonable in any suitable case to enable a mother and a child—if she wishes to keep her baby—to stay together; to this, in the family's times of special need, the National Assistance Board does much to contribute.

Assistance is normally given in cash and is dependent upon proved need. With certain rare exceptions it can only be given to someone who is not in full-time employment. For a mother who lives alone or is a householder and so directly responsible for rent and household necessities, her needs are assessed at £2 10s. a week, plus an additional amount for rent, which is normally the net rent paid, if it is reasonable, and from 16s. to £1 3s. a week for a child according to age. Thus the needs of a mother who lives alone with one child under the age of five would be assessed at £3 6s. apart from her rent. If she lives as part of someone else's household, the rate for her needs would be £2 6s. a week, plus a share of the rent (which will not be more than 15s.) and the 16s. for the child —a total of £3 2s. a week apart from rent. The standard rate for a girl of, say, sixteen or seventeen would be considerably lower—

30s. a week apart from the child, with no allowance for rent; for a girl of eighteen to twenty it would be 36s. and a share of the rent. In either case, if she is a householder and has a dependant, she is paid at the full rate for an adult. If she is under sixteen she cannot apply for assistance, but if she is dependent upon someone drawing assistance, provision for her needs may be included. If necessary she would be taken into the care of the Children's Department and, should there be no one to help her, the Department would assume financial responsibility for her.

We have described the position of a woman with one child under the age of five. If she has several, an addition is made for each at the rate appropriate for its age. For a child aged from five to ten, the rate is 19s. a week, and for a child aged eleven to fifteen, 23s. These figures are subject to a stringent means test: they are only the amounts to which the Board makes up any income the woman may have, subject to certain 'disregarded' amounts. Assistance is not payable if she is in full-time employment. Part-time earnings of up to £1 10s. a week net and half of the next £1 of any earnings above that will usually be disregarded, but if she earns more than this, the allowance will be reduced by a shilling for each additional shilling that she earns. The Board's addition for the child, and if thought necessary, the total joint allowance will also be reduced by the amount of alimony, if any, received from the father. A mother drawing assistance for herself and one child under five is therefore unlikely to have a total income, from all sources including assistance, of more than £4 15s. 6d. a week, or if she is a householder, £4 19s. 6d., unless she is drawing upon capital small enough to be disregarded by the Board[1] or not greatly to affect her allowance, or unless the putative father pays more for the child than the national assistance rates of 16s. to £1 3s. a week, or unless she has other income, e.g. an allowance from a charitable grant, of which part (not more than 15s.) may also be disregarded. But none of these eventualities is typical. If she is not earning but draws, for example, a maternity allowance, the first pound of this will also be disregarded, but that does not increase the total quoted above. No Government department or local authority has power to give financial help to the mother of an illegitimate child under five years

---

[1] This usually means under £75. The position regarding capital is in fact more complicated than this, but since few unmarried mothers have any capital to speak of, the details are not given here.

of age to enable her to keep it with her if she is earning more than £4 19s. 6d. a week apart from her rent.

If, then, she lives on her own with the child and is dependent on national assistance for any length of time, she must live at the barest subsistence level. The amount granted is supposed to cover the replacement of clothing etc., but the Board is nevertheless empowered 'where there are special circumstances' to adjust the amount 'as may be appropriate to meet those circumstances' and may also make 'an assistance grant of such a sum as is reasonable having regard to all the circumstances of the case . . . by way of a single payment, to meet an exceptional need for assistance'.[1] The amount of any such additional allowance or grant is left to the discretion of the Board—in the first place, to its area office. It is possible in an exceptional case (e.g. where an applicant has been dependent on assistance over a long period) for an area office to give fairly generous help—for example, where a growing child needs a bed or extra blankets, or for some special purchase of necessary household equipment or clothing that is beyond the applicant's means. Officials naturally vary in the amount to which they make use of this discretion; and inevitably one will still meet officers with rather different points of view as to the help which it may be advisable to give. Their experience may have been principally in the centre of great cities in districts where a number of the unmarried mothers who apply for help are highly promiscuous women, sometimes cohabiting with men who depend on their immoral earnings, or it may have been among unmarried mothers of a better type who are struggling valiantly to make a success of bringing up their children. Attitudes drawn from a different general experience may sometimes affect the extent of the assistance given or even, at times the spirit in which it is administered; but this is becoming less common as the headquarters of the Board develops its policy towards this thorny question, and as some of the older officers who grew up with a different outlook are succeeded by those with a more understanding point of view. In view of the immense trouble that a few unrewarding and 'chronic' applicants, with a high sense of their rights and little of their responsibilities, can give to the Board, and the difficulty of seeing that money given to such women is really spent for their own and their children's welfare, it is surprising how understanding and

[1] National Assistance (Determination of Need) Regulations, 1948.

sympathetic the majority of the Board's officers are. In general, the assistance given by the Board must have helped many thousands of unmarried mothers and their children to weather the more acute crises in their lives, and it remains the sole source of income for many of them while the mother is unable to work.

Since it is allowed some discretion in the making of grants of assistance, the Board may make it a condition that the mother registers at the employment exchange—for instance, where she lives with her parents and the child is no longer a baby and the grandmother is quite fit and able to look after it by day. But the Board's general policy is that it is best for a mother and child to be together by day, and if exceptions are sometimes made this is often because of the rather special circumstances that face an unmarried mother.

An unmarried mother living on her own with the child has no very complex household to maintain: to do a full-time job and to look after the child may be difficult and exhausting, but to do nothing but look after the child, and this at a very low standard of living on national assistance, may not be in the interest of either child or mother. Many unmarried women who have had a baby feel a need to 'work their passage' back into society again and to prove in their efforts to maintain the child that they are responsible women: they try to clear themselves from their feeling of guilt towards the baby by struggling to support it. This can be a natural and good impulse: the question is simply how far in any *individual case* it is in the child's interest—how far it will suffer or not from being deprived of its mother's daily care. It is not easy to decide such a question, but to some extent it is determined by the simple fact that the rate of assistance is so low that few self-respecting women who are capable of work wish to live on it indefinitely.

The question of how far and to what age a young child needs its own mother to stay at home with it, or a warm and adequate substitute, and how far it may be upset by long periods in day nurseries or with a succession of daily minders, may still be disputed. Unquestionably we have seen illegitimate children who suffered considerably from the long daily parting from their mothers, and others too whose nervous tension relaxed appreciably when their mothers went out to work and they were left in the care of someone less anxiety-ridden. The mother sometimes made new interests, new contacts that led to a better life for herself and the child, and the family's standard of living naturally rose. But these are all vexed questions, and principally because in any particular case there is rarely an ideal solution available. It might certainly be better for some mothers at some stages to do well-paid part-time work and have their income supplemented by an allowance from either the father or the State. Daily minders might in theory be excellent mother substitutes, but it is rarely that so good a person can be found. What personal relationship with a mother substitute a child can find in a day nursery must vary, and be much affected by the time the hard-pressed workers can give to the child. There is, in fact, no complete answer to the problem of how to be an effective mother and an effective bread-winner at once, or how, if she decides to be chiefly the bread-winner, to find an effective temporary mother substitute: so the Board's officers often have the responsibility of helping her to make the best compromise.

There is another difficulty about leaving unmarried mothers with no resource from the State but national assistance. This is that many of the best mothers are unwilling to apply to the Board. Some still feel the ancient prejudice that used to attach to the poor law against claiming what many still think of as 'poor relief'. Many dislike the investigation of their means that an application invariably involves. Others have a natural pride that makes them prefer to stand on their own feet in any circumstances, and often prevents them from turning even to the child's father for help. The number who feel in this way is not known, but a Labour Party survey in Bethnal Green showed that for every old-age pensioner, for example, who drew national assistance in order to keep alive, another pensioner, entitled equally to national assistance payments, was too proud to draw the money.[1] This attitude of old-age pensioners may repressent in part the attitude of an earlier generation, yet unmarried mothers are so vulnerable and sensitive that it is quite possible that as many of them refuse to apply for the help they need. There are districts where, in our own experience, some women prefer to apply to the voluntary societies for help rather than to the Board. This presumably reflects some difference of personnel, where the voluntary workers have proved to be more sensitive in the handling of the women, and such difficulties are, of course, passing as a new generation of officers grow up. But the natural, and in a sense very healthy, prejudice against claiming

[1] *Manchester Guardian*, 16th June 1957.

relief bars from help many of the best and most self-respecting mothers who, nevertheless, would often gladly accept and most deeply welcome any small pension or allowance that they could think of as automatic and the child's natural right—a family allowance for the first child of a family, or a State advance of alimony, or a special allowance for children with no male bread-winner, on the lines of those paid in *Sweden*.

In November 1953 the National Assistance Board undertook an inquiry that showed that more than 20,000 unmarried mothers received allowances amounting to £2,359,000 yearly—a subsidy from public funds of £2 5s. per week for each mother.[1] But a large number of these receive help to cover their maintenance in a Home or institution run by the local authority, or by a voluntary society on its behalf, which offers her shelter or temporary accommodation, generally during the last months of her pregnancy or while the child is a baby. If the mother is not insured and cannot meet the fees charged by a voluntary society for such accommodation, or if it seems desirable for her to stay on in a Home after her maternity allowance has expired, the National Assistance Board may help. If she is without means they may also pay her, or any other person in such accommodation, a small sum of 10s. a week by way of pocket money while she is in the Home. In this way the facilities of the Mother and Baby Home can be made available to most of the women who need them.

It is the National Assistance Board that gives its help, where it is needed, to that most discouraging of all groups in the community, the problem families who so rarely seem able to rise above their troubles without rapidly sinking again: the families whom a series of misfortunes or some inherent weaknesses of mind or character have brought to a very low level from which they find it very hard to rise. Unmarried mothers from these families can be exceedingly difficult to help. They take up much of any welfare officer's time and sometimes end by colouring his view of unmarried mothers as a whole. It is the existence of this group that often proves a bar to improving the position of illegitimate children and their mothers as a whole. People are quick to say that if one gives any 'more help' to unmarried mothers, this problem group will take advantage of it and prove both ungrateful and unrewarding. Even experienced

[1] Cyril Greenland, *Some Ecological Aspects of Unmarried Parenthood* (*Lancet*, 19th January 1957).

social workers use this argument if their experience has been principally among such people. But someone has acutely remarked that in a democracy it is almost impossible to avoid having a small 'leisured group' at the top and at the bottom of society! In any case their existence cannot in the long run be a bar to the introduction of measures that would really benefit many other citizens. The fact that some mothers would certainly spend the family allowance on cinemas or beer was not allowed to prevent the introduction of family allowances. The fact that some people put coal in their baths proved no argument against providing baths. If a few abuse a new service, that is less an argument for abandoning it than for exploring their special needs separately: with a better understanding of *how* problem families can be helped, the community may become less nervous of helping them.

A far more serious difficulty is that any additional help from the State for unmarried mothers who have to provide alone for their children might at the present stage irritate their married neighbours beyond endurance and so delay the growth of the understanding and tolerance that is needed if the children are to be given a better start. This has not happened in Scandinavia, but in our country it might well do so: unfortunately we have at present far less tolerance and understanding of these problems. This, then, may be the time instead for pilot schemes and experiments backed by voluntary rather than State funds, paving the way for the stage when public opinion is ready to face the problem more simply. Faced it ultimately must be.

CHAPTER 8

THE LOCAL AUTHORITIES' AND VOLUNTARY SOCIETIES' CONTRIBUTION

AROUSING PUBLIC INTEREST

Pioneer social work tends to be initiated by some individual whose conscience has awoken to a great need while the mass of the people are still indifferent to it, and who gradually succeeds in rallying strong public support. This is how Castberg achieved his great aims in Norway, and how Josephine Butler initiated some of the first voluntary social work among unmarried mothers and 'fallen women' in the last part of the nineteenth century.

Today the position is happier: a great many public servants have consciences at least as sensitive and ideas as advanced as any independent person, and one cannot forecast whether a new idea or pioneer scheme will come from a Government department, an enterprising local authority, a voluntary society or trust, or from some solitary enterprising person. Government departments and local authorities are limited by public opinion in what they may do, but increasingly the drag-chain lies in the public mind, not in the public servant's.

The ordinary citizen—the ratepayer—has very little interest in unmarried mothers and often scant sympathy with them. At a conference on 'Homes and Hostels of the Future'[1] organized by the N.C.U.M.C. in 1945, the Medical Officer for Guildford, who was then establishing in the city a special local authority Hostel for unmarried mothers and their children, described some of his difficulties.

'One has to remember,' he said, 'the married women of the town. Although the home has not got going yet, I have received complaints from the married women: "It is all very well providing things of this sort for the mothers of illegitimate children. Why is nothing done for us?"

[1] Published as a booklet under this title by the N.C.U.M.C., 1945.

'That is a very difficult question to answer. My only answer is this. "You have husbands who are legally bound to support your children. These girls have not anybody, unless you can count the putative father. They are mothers. That is an established fact which no amount of moralizing will undo. The children are children who may be as good as the next one. They may be future Prime Ministers, anything you like." '

But that is a mature point of view and not the natural reaction of the ordinary woman struggling with her own difficulties, who is quick to resent help given to those who, in her view, are so much less 'deserving'.

STATUTORY DUTIES OF LOCAL AUTHORITIES

Fortunately the local authority has definite duties towards illegitimate children and their mothers that cannot be avoided, whatever the reaction of the ordinary citizen.

Up to the outbreak of World War II there were few Homes for unmarried mothers other than those run by religious organizations, and nearly all the specialized case-work among the mothers was done by these bodies, who alone employed specialist workers. But the very great increase in illegitimate births during the war strained the resources of the voluntary societies to the utmost. To ease this the Ministry of Health opened Mother and Baby Hostels for girls from the three Services, and local authorities were empowered and strongly urged to make provisions for the welfare of illegitimate children. On 16th November 1943 the Ministry of Health issued the very important Circular No. 2866 to all welfare authorities in England and the London County Council. It ran as follows:

1. I am directed by the Minister of Health to state that he has had under special consideration the problems arising under war conditions in regard to illegitimate children. He referred this matter for consideration to one of the Sub-Committees of his Advisory Committee on the Welfare of Mothers and Young Children and he has taken into account recommendations recently made by them.
2. He now desires to call the attention of all welfare authorities to the importance of this matter and to ask them, even in the present difficult circumstances, to give their earnest consideration to the

problems presented. He suggests, below, some lines on which the difficulties may be dealt with.

3. It is clear that there can be no complete solution of the problem, since every child needs both a father and a mother, affection, security and the shelter of a normal home, but the successful work of voluntary agencies and moral welfare workers attached to diocesan and other religious bodies has shown that much can be done to help the mother and to safeguard the child.

4. In most cases, the Minister thinks, the most promising line of attack would be that the welfare authorities should co-operate with and reinforce the work of existing voluntary and welfare associations, and he suggests therefore that every welfare authority should formulate a scheme for this purpose. The range of work will be a wide one, and the appointment of a trained worker experienced in the special problems she will have to handle will probably form an essential part of the organization and administration of this scheme. The Minister recognizes that it may be impossible to find enough suitable people to undertake the work while the war lasts, but he thinks that a beginning might be made in some areas at least. The worker to be appointed should have taken one of the recognized courses of training in social service and also have some knowledge of moral welfare; experience in probation work would be valuable. Some authorities may have a worker already on the staff who could suitably undertake the work, e.g. the welfare worker engaged in the Evacuation Welfare Service or the social worker whose appointment is recommended in Circular 2834 of the 23rd July, 1943, who might combine the duties now outlined with those set out in the earlier Circular. It is essential that whoever is appointed should work in close co-operation with the Health Visitors.

In Country Districts it would probably be desirable to arrange for a combination of areas, and I am to suggest that the County Council might call a Conference of the separate welfare authorities within the County in order that a joint scheme might be prepared.

5. It is suggested that the duties which the special worker might undertake, in co-operation with the existing workers in voluntary societies, are:

(a) Wherever possible to persuade the girl to make known her circumstances to her parents and, if the home is likely to be a satisfactory one, to persuade the grandparents to make a home for the little one.

(b) Advising the expectant mother on suitable accommodation before and immediately after confinement.

(c) Assisting the girl to obtain an affiliation order or otherwise to secure assistance from the father of the child.

(d) Assisting the mother to find employment preferably with her baby, in an institution or in private employment.

(e) If a home cannot be found for the baby with the girl's relatives (see (a) above), finding lodgings for mother and baby when the mother desires non-resident work. This accommodation might be in a special hostel set up by a voluntary body or by the welfare authority itself. If in ordinary lodgings, it would be necessary to arrange for the baby's care by day, e.g. in a war-time nursery.

(f) Finding a suitable foster mother if it is necessary for mother and baby to be separated. In such cases it may be desirable for the authority to guarantee payment to the foster mother, recovering from the mother. (This scheme works satisfactorily in Birmingham.).

(g) Arranging for places in a residential Nursery or Home, for babies whose mothers cannot look after them and for whom accommodation cannot be found by other means.

(h) In special cases, e.g. where the mother is very young, or is the wife of a man not the father of the child, giving advice about legal adoption.

In nearly all these cases it will be desirable to follow up the advice given, in co-operation with the Health Visitors and to see that the mother keeps her baby under observation of the Infant Welfare Centre until it is handed over to the education authorities.

6. I am to ask that welfare authorities will give very early and urgent attention to this matter and will submit proposals to the Minister, in accordance with Section 204 of the Public Health Act, 1936, within the next few months.

By the end of 1945 one hundred and eight local authorities had appointed social workers as proposed in this circular, independently or in combination with other authorities, and another two hundred and eighty-one had made arrangements for Moral Welfare workers to undertake the work on their behalf, and were making a financial contribution towards their salaries and office expenses.

Twenty-two local authorities had established Mother and Baby Homes or Hostels (paragraph 5(e) of the circular) of their own, and many others were making substantial subsidies, in the form of block or *per capita* grants, to voluntary Homes and Hostels. Some block grants had already been paid on a smaller scale through the Maternity and Child Welfare Departments, but this new departure involved a considerable increase in them.

The Ministry of Health returns show that in 1956 there were, apart from Hostels, twenty-seven local authority Mother and Baby Homes (397 beds). These Homes made no charge to the mothers, being provided as part of the National Health Service. One hundred and seven voluntary Homes (1,666 beds) were also being used by local authorities.

Before we go on to discuss specialist case-work among unmarried mothers and the organizations and administration of Mother and Baby Homes, some reference must be made to the voluntary societies working in this field of social service.

THE VOLUNTARY SOCIETIES

The National Council for the Unmarried Mother and Her Child
The N.C.U.M.C. came into being in 1918 to help illegitimate children and their mothers. Although it is entirely independent, members of the local authorities, of religious organizations and of many voluntary societies concerned with both voluntary and statutory social work are represented on the Council. It is a central, co-ordinating body, non-denominational and recognized by the Ministry of Health, which acknowledges by an annual subsidy the value of its steadily expanding work. Its help, based upon years of experience, is shrewd and understanding, and directed to the points of greatest need. To further its end it has, in its own words:

'Worked for *legislative reform*, especially in connection with the Bastardy and Affiliation Acts, and has also kept a close watch on all legislation that was likely to affect the illegitimate child.

'*Administration* has also been carefully watched and the Council has tried to do what it can to encourage local public authorities to make full and wise use of their powers for the care of mothers and children.

'The Council tries to promote and encourage hostels, homes and other suitable *accommodation* to meet the varying needs of mothers and babies throughout the country, with the special aim of making it possible to keep mother and child together.

'It has a *Case Department* which deals with individual enquiries for or on behalf of mothers of illegitimate children. During its existence it has dealt with thousands of cases: it is in touch with moral welfare workers and with other organizations all over Great Britain, so that mothers can be helped and advised as speedily and thoroughly as is possible. The Council works in close co-operation with kindred organizations throughout the world.

'Lastly it tries to educate public opinion, by speeches, through the press, in any possible way, upon the needs of the illegitimate child, and its claim upon its fellow citizens to do everything possible to promote its well-being and to enable it to attain full and worthy citizenship despite the handicaps of its birth.'[1]

Every year the N.C.U.M.C. receives thousands of letters and many visits from mothers of illegitimate children, whether married or unmarried, who turn to it for help in their emergencies. Some are expecting their babies in a few days or hours, having left their plans until late; some are those who have written in desperation to the advice columns of women's papers and have been referred to the N.C.U.M.C.; a few are women just released from prison; some are married women with older illegitimate children, who may at first come seeking material help, such as clothing for a growing son or daughter, but often also need advice on some difficult personal matter, e.g. how to explain to the child about its origin. Grown-ups born illegitimate also consult the Council. Some years ago the Council took part in a television broadcast on the subject of illegitimacy, in which was mentioned the shortened form of birth certificate, which excludes reference to parentage, introduced under the Births and Deaths Registration Act, 1953. Immediately after the broadcast a number of elderly men and women rang up the office for details of how to obtain these certificates; they had been entitled to old age pensions, but had been afraid to apply if it involved revealing their illegitimacy.

The number of applications is steadily growing. In the year 1956-7 the Case Department dealt with 3,241 new applications, while still in touch with 592 former applicants. Most of the new

[1] Statement published in the annual reports of the Council.

applicants (2,645) were pregnant women or mothers who had themselves got directly in touch with the Council. Inasmuch as it is only incidentally a case-work agency, the majority of these (2,519) were referred to Moral Welfare workers in the dioceses in which they lived. A number (126), however, were dealt with by the Council directly, since they presented specialized problems or had expressed a desire to be helped and advised by the Council. There were also 352 requests for grants of money, legal advice and so on from Moral Welfare workers and other organizations acting on behalf of mothers and children.

At present the N.C.U.M.C. is so short of funds that its Case Committee is limited to making grants to a total of £50 a month, a typical grant being £3 or £5 towards the purchase of a cot or pram. With this £50, help has to be given to those in need among many thousands of mothers of illegitimate children. Divided among the 600,000 children under school-leaving age in this country who were born illegitimate, it would amount to less than a farthing a head per year. Not a royal sum! The shortage of funds has always run like a refrain through the annual reports of the Council: 'Our financial position is the source of the most acute anxiety' (1946-7); 'There is so much that we could do, so much that we try to do, and never nearly enough money with which to do it' (1949-50); 'The Council's finances . . . give rise to increasing anxiety, our major problem being how to raise funds to meet commitments which grow as the work of the Council expands . . . This year . . . the account shows a deficit' (1952-53); 'In spite of heroic efforts to increase the financial support of the Council, the year ended with an adverse balance' (1954-5); 'The need for more subscriptions and donations is urgent' (1956-7).[1]

Two aspects of the N.C.U.M.C.'s work, for which it is particularly fitted by its wide international contacts, have in recent years become increasingly important: the tracing of men who are the putative fathers of children in other countries, and the collation of reports for the Home Office upon foreign unmarried women who become pregnant in this country, or arrive here pregnant. The Council reports that these women present many difficulties.

'. . . their background is often tragic and sometimes their lack of knowledge of the language and customs of this country makes it hard to help them. We feel we have a definite responsibility

[1] The address of the Council is 21 Coram Street, London, W.C.1.

where the putative fathers are British, although instances where women arrive here from abroad already pregnant are not unknown. In these cases we are able to help with their repatriation'—which is often a sad task—'by putting them in touch with welfare organizations in their own countries.[1]

'The girl from abroad faces many difficulties when she becomes illegitimately pregnant; her background and upbringing may make it hard for her to adjust herself to life in this country; she may have lost her family during the war, is limited in the kind of employment she may take and must have Home Office permission for a continued stay in this country. There seems to be an increase in the number of girls in the late teens and twenties coming to England to work and becoming pregnant shortly after their arrival.'[2]

In the year 1955-6 the N.C.U.M.C. dealt with eighty-six queries from the Home Office about foreign expectant mothers in this country, and in 1956-7 with as many as a hundred and forty.

This mention of the Council's work is very brief and covers only one of its activities, case-work, but a published account of its growth and work from 1918 to 1946 and its untiring efforts for improved legislation and a better understanding of the whole social problem of illegitimacy has been written,[3] and a further account, bringing the story up to date, is being considered.

The Moral Welfare Associations

In the Church of England there are about three hundred and fifty moral welfare workers, who cover the whole of the country. They are employed by the Moral Welfare Association of their own diocese, which is affiliated to a central body, the Church of England Moral Welfare Council, but remains an integral part of the diocesan organization. The Roman Catholic Church has its own moral welfare workers—some of them priests and some of them nuns—but these are less numerous than in the Church of England. There are also a few workers employed by the Methodist Church and other bodies.

The strong Moral Welfare movement within the Church of England derives principally from the pioneer work of Josephine Butler. Many of its workers are trained at Josephine Butler

[1] Report for the year 1951-2.
[2] Report for the year 1954-5.
[3] Lettice Fisher, *Twenty-One Years and After*, 1918-1946 (N.C.U.M.C.).

184   THE UNMARRIED MOTHER AND HER CHILD

Memorial House in Liverpool, some of them taking two- or three-year courses in theology and the social sciences, others shorter courses. Almost all the workers are women, for in the Church of England few men take up this work except on the educational side.

Moral Welfare workers are not concerned only with problems of illegitimacy, but with Christian education and case-work among children, adolescents and grown-ups throughout the whole field of family life and sexual relationships. They are described as 'indoor' and 'outdoor' workers according to their functions; normally 'indoor' workers include those who have resident posts in Homes and Hostels, such as the matrons and superintendents of these institutions; 'outdoor' workers concern themselves with girls and women not resident in the Homes and with their relatives. A few specialize in helping adolescents and children.

CASE-WORK AMONG UNMARRIED MOTHERS

Voluntary Societies
Through their network of case-workers and Mother and Baby Homes, the Moral Welfare Associations help many mothers around their first and often principal time of crisis, the baby's birth. These diocesan workers are consulted every year, at a very conservative estimate, by over thirteen thousand parents of illegitimate children (in 1954 sixteen thousand did so out of nearly thirty-one thousand) and about one in ten—over three thousand a year—spend some time in one of the Church of England Mother and Baby Homes.

A few women get in touch early in their pregnancy, but most do so rather later, some even after the child's birth. Among a group of seventy women who consulted a Moral Welfare worker in 1950, a third paid their first visit some time during the first six months of their pregnancy; a third during the last three months, eighteen as late as ten weeks or less before the baby was born; and a third after the baby's birth, usually during the first year.

In general, both Moral Welfare workers and Homes tend to help a rather specialized group of unmarried mothers. They deal chiefly with the young. Relatively few of the religious Homes, apart from those run by the Salvation Army, are ready to take the older women or those having a second illegitimate baby. They are trying to rehabilitate the young and do not wish them to be confused or injured by contact with more sophisticated or perhaps more hardened women.

About a third—say ten thousand a year—of the women who bear illegitimate children are aged twenty-two or less. Something like four out of every five of these consult the Moral Welfare workers. In Midboro over 70 per cent of the girls aged twenty-four or under did so, but as few as 14 per cent of those above the age of thirty. Some divorced or married women expecting illegitimate babies consult the workers, but—perhaps not surprisingly—relatively few of those who are cohabiting with the child's father or who are expecting a second illegitimate child. In Midboro only 5 per cent of the many who were cohabiting came near the Moral Welfare worker; presumably they had no economic or housing problem and no thought of parting with the child to adopters—the three chief practical reasons that lead women to consult case-workers.

Many, then, never make contact with case-workers, either because they do not need help or because they like, for good reasons or bad, to manage on their own. In 1954 the N.C.U.M.C. and the Moral Welfare Associations of the Church of England were together in touch with rather over sixteen thousand cases, but nearly twice that number of women had illegitimate babies (see Table 5). The special case-workers attached to Maternity and Child Welfare Departments were consulted by some further large number, and others will have been in touch with Roman Catholic and other case-workers, but certainly many thousands in that year, as in any other year, did not see a case-worker at all.

Most of these may be women who are cohabiting. Some may have married the child's father almost immediately after the birth. Some may be educated women who go abroad over their confinement or arrange it privately. Others may be mothers for whom an illegitimate child creates no problem, since they live in a milieu where such things are taken for granted. A few anti-social women, such as prostitutes, prefer to steer clear of case-workers whenever possible. We remember a girl, quite a young prostitute, who, a week before the baby was born, was still plying her trade on the lorries that ran between two industrial centres. An older prostitute, feeling anxious about her, took the unusual step of visiting a Church of England Moral Welfare worker to see if she could be given a vacancy in a Home; but the girl refused and was delivered a few days later in the local hospital, and the baby was taken for adoption by one of her friends.

The thousands of mothers or expectant mothers who do seek help are referred to the Moral Welfare workers from many sources. In the group of about seven and a half thousand cases dealt with in 1952 (see page 54) and later analysed in detail, 44 per cent were referred to by official agencies—hospital almoners, health visitors, clinics, the National Assistance Board, the employment exchanges, the police or the Children's Departments—and nearly 30 per cent by the N.C.U.M.C. and other voluntary agencies and social workers. Direct personal application to the workers was made by 4 per cent of the women, and less than 4 per cent got into touch through their churches. Others came through doctors, employers or friends.

Many come at first with one idea in their minds: to seek advice about how to have the baby adopted, but after a talk with the worker their minds may be open to other alternatives. The welfare worker may be able to give them much practical assistance. Some of the types of help given are shown in the following analysis, quoted from the same source as the above:

	CASES
Admission to voluntary Homes and Hostels	3,159
Provision of clothing, cots, prams, etc.	1,121
Finding lodgings for mothers	319
Finding foster homes for babies	398
Finding work for mother	549
Placing children in voluntary Homes or nurseries	381
Help in obtaining affiliation orders	519
Help in arranging private financial agreements with the fathers	591
Help in obtaining financial aid through voluntary societies	259
Advice and guidance on questions of adoption, affiliation, confinement arrangements, etc.	5,969

Miss Barbara Reeve and Miss Ena Steel of the Church of England Moral Welfare movement have given this vivid account of a 'typical' interview with a Moral Welfare worker:

'A girl of twenty-three comes by appointment through an almoner, because she is expecting a child. She is a superior type of girl who wants to get away before her people and her employer find out her condition. The worker listens and draws out as much of the story as may be told willingly at that stage, sufficient probably to show that the girl must first be helped to tell her family. After outlining various forms of help and promising to make enquiries about vacancies in Mother and Baby Homes, the worker manages to suggest, too, that most parents would prefer to know when their child is in trouble and would be anxious and greatly hurt if she disappeared. The girl gains courage from the interview and goes away with plans to put before her parents when she tells them.

'It may well happen that next time she comes she will bring her mother with her and that her mother, though greatly distressed, will be comforted a little by having someone to help with practical arrangements, and by the knowledge that there is someone who does not think ill of her daughter in spite of her failure. The attitude of mothers in matters of sex behaviour vary from the mother who says: "I'd rather have seen her dead", to the fiercely defensive mother who says: "After all, she is not the first". In both cases there is an affront to their sense of respectability and the offence is seen out of proportion. To help such mothers to understand another point of view is sometimes the main part of the work, but the father presents another difficulty. He may have thrashed his daughter or he may be fiercely defensive: "No girl of mine is going to be turned out of my house". In some families, however, the girl's predicament exacerbates some existing tension between the husband and wife and they oppose each other in the attitude each adopts towards the girl.

'If it is agreed that the girl should go away to have her baby the worker keeps in touch with her parents as well as with her, and it is at this stage that time works such wonders. There are not many families where the parents remain implacable and insist that the baby must be adopted. After the birth of the child the worker can see the father and mother adjusting themselves to the fact that they are grandparents until it becomes comparatively easy for them to face the situation and decide that the girl should return home and bring her baby with her. They have learnt to react differently to "what the neighbours will say" and the love of their own child deepens through the suffering they share with her.

'But perhaps there are further considerations in this case. The presence of younger brothers and sisters may make it desirable for the girl to go away for a time; there is the older brother who says he will leave home if she returns; or she may be the only child of a widow who needs her earnings. How can she manage, and how *can* they keep the child afterwards when both have to work and when nurseries are so scarce? Or perhaps she is not very intelligent and is rather weak. Has she sufficient strength of character to bring up her child under difficulties? What made her get into this trouble? Was it unhappiness or is she "man-mad" as her mother says? If she is, will she have a strong maternal instinct? Or is the girl's mother the managing type who will annex the baby as if it were her own and then complain that her daughter does nothing for him? From questions like this it is clear that it is quite impossible to help the illegitimate child in isolation from the other members of his mother's family, and indeed not only the mother's family, for there is the father of the child and *his* family to be considered. The two families become involved when there is any question of a forced marriage and feelings run high if one wants it and the other does not. A marriage which takes place merely to hide the illegitimacy of a child is no solution of the problem for either of the partners concerned. The worker may act as a useful intermediary in helping the boy and his family to face their responsibility for the child.'[1]

Moral Welfare work is based almost invariably upon a religious interpretation of life. The worker recognizes the urgency of an unmarried mother's practical problems and is usually fully occupied in trying to solve them, so she may rarely speak to a mother about religion, but the unspoken faith expressed in her whole approach and personality may make a deep impression upon some of the women; later many will experience the more openly religious atmosphere of the Mother and Baby Homes. Few tasks are, perhaps, more difficult than a Moral Welfare worker's. The quality of those employed in it varies widely, a few still narrow and old-fashioned, others broad in their outlook and profound in their understanding. As is the fate of today's church workers generally, they are among the most hard-worked and most poorly paid social workers in the community.

Local Authorities
In 1959 sixteen authorities had their own social workers, usually specially trained or appointed welfare workers or health visitors working within the Maternity and Child Welfare Departments

---

[1] Barbara Reeve and Ena M. Steel, *Moral Welfare*, chapter 7, *Social Case-Work in Great Britain*, edited by Cherry Morris (1950).

and specializing, solely or largely, in helping mothers of illegitimate children. Whether a local authority chose this course or helped to subsidize the local Moral Welfare organization depended partly on the attitude of the individual Medical Officers, partly on the past relations between the Maternity and Child Welfare Departments and the voluntary organizations, but perhaps chiefly upon the quality of the individual Moral Welfare worker—including her capacity for record-keeping!

The Maternity and Child Welfare Departments had the advantage over voluntary organizations in that it was the duty of their health visitors in the ordinary course of their work to keep in touch with children in the area under the age of five and advise on their health and welfare. They thus had an excellent opportunity to keep a discreet general superintendence over the younger illegitimate children. Their training in social work was limited but, if the Department arranged with the local registrar of births to notify them at once of the birth of an illegitimate child, they could visit it promptly without exciting any curiosity among the neighbours and report back any unsatisfactory features to the special welfare worker attached to the Department, or to other local caseworkers. How fully this opportunity for 'preventive' social work was taken depended on the Department; in many areas it could have been taken further.

There is a certain group of women whom both voluntary societies and local authorities find it difficult to help: the mothers of several illegitimate children; the Roman Catholic girls who will not turn to their Church; the morally or mentally defective; the older women or those of crude and rough character; those who have had illegitimate babies and have left their husbands; those who have been ejected from their homes for non-payment of rent, or turned into the street by their parents or landladies; those late in making their plans. Many illegitimately pregnant women conceal their condition until the last moment. Some do so successfully, and give birth to the child alone. Others, less 'strong-minded', merely fail to make arrangements for their confinement and are admitted to hospital as emergency cases. If they are far from home or have no home, yet must be discharged from hospital as soon as they are well enough to leave, where are they to go?

INSTITUTIONS AND HOMES RUN BY LOCAL AUTHORITIES

The department of the local authority that is deeply concerned with this crisis in these women's lives is the Welfare Services Department, which is responsible, under Part III of the National Assistance Act, 1948, for providing lodging for the homeless. When faced with the difficult problem of finding temporary accommodation for mothers with illegitimate children, the Welfare Services Department has three courses open to it. First, it may place mother and child in what is known as 'Part III accommodation'; secondly, if it has a Mother and Baby Home of its own and the baby is young enough to go there, mother and child may be sent to it: and thirdly, it may have effective arrangements with the voluntary societies for their speedy transfer to a diocesan Home, subsidizing her while she stays there. There is generally room for improvement in these arrangements.

'Part III accommodation' is usually a large Home of a strictly institutional kind, sometimes still housed in an old workhouse building. Here all the evicted and homeless of the neighbourhood are given temporary shelter. Few of these Homes seem to have resident case-workers, and many have not even a local authority case-worker attached to them. Some of the Moral Welfare workers do not seem to visit them. This is surely a place where the Family Service Units might be brought into action, and it is difficult to see why some of the local authorities could not themselves undertake more effective case-work among them and concern themselves more deeply in the question of rehabilitating and resettling some of the families who use them.

Certainly these local authority 'large Homes' cannot provide a proper atmosphere for a young girl with a baby; she may be living with the old and feeble-minded, the mentally deficient and the roughest types of women. Some of the unmarried mothers might be helped effectively if there were in the neighbourhood a working Hostel where they could live for a year or two and go out to work daily, or a training Hostel where they could be taught the elements of domestic skill and of hope and self-respect, and where they could live for a while in a more invigorating environment. Failing this, some of the inmates may get discouraged and go morally to pieces.

It is the policy of the Home Office and the Ministry of Health that no pregnant women or woman with a young child should be placed in such a home if any alternative accommodation can be found. Despite their vigilance it still sometimes happens. For example, in 1950 the L.C.C. was faced with the problem of well over a hundred such girls, many of whom had come from distant parts of England and 'hidden' themselves in London lodgings until the child was due to be born. They had to be placed direct from hospital into some of the L.C.C.'s 'large Homes'. Their welfare officer took active steps to find suitable accommodation for them, but it was no easy task.

The opening of special Homes for unmarried mothers helped to solve some acute problems. In 1949, for example, one populous county in England had twenty-one unmarried mothers and twenty-two illegitimate children living in large institutional 'Part III accommodation'. By 1950 there were only nine mothers and ten children, and some of these owed their presence to what was tactfully termed 'an administrative accident'—lack of foresight, say, on the authorities' part when arranging for a transfer of population from a city to a neighbouring dormitory town.

The following brief histories of these nine women shows them to be members of the group that local authorities and the voluntary societies find it difficult to help.

1. Aged twenty-six, born in the institution and in and out of it all her life. Three illegitimate children by married man, two in Children's Homes, third with her.

2. Aged thirty, Roman Catholic. 'A bad lot,' said the superintendent. Two illegitimate children by different fathers. Elder child living with mother's sister.

3. Aged twenty-seven, Roman Catholic. Three illegitimate children by single man, but his parents opposed marriage. One child with relatives, one in Children's Home.

4. Married Roman Catholic with four legitimate children and one illegitimate. Two of legitimate living with father, two in Children's Home. Illegitimate baby with her. Father of it a neighbour who wrote threatening letters to her. Husband would not have her home.

5. Aged forty-two, Church of England, formerly voluntary patient in mental hospital—about time of illegitimate child's birth. One other child, aged four, in Children's Home and another adopted in infancy.

6. Aged thirty-five. Classed as 'moral defective', had been in Home for at least ten years. Only illegitimate child born fifteen years before—a girl brought up by grandmother and not turning out very well. Not clear why woman was in an institution unless authorities had originally taken view that safest thing to do with a moral defective was to shut her up until past child-bearing age.

7. In late twenties, was having fourth illegitimate child by married man living apart from wife. Always returned to this Home to have them. Other three adopted.

8. Last remaining girl in institution that in past eighteen months had had five unmarried mothers, four of them mothers of their first child.

9. Mother of two illegitimate children, had been in Home for three and a half years. Second child born while she was there, apparently also conceived while she was an inmate.

A number of the women were probably in institutions because of the unwillingness of most of the denominational Mother and Baby Homes to take 'rough types' or the mothers of second or subsequent children. This works out harshly on some mothers who are no more hardened in character than good-time girls of sixteen and, even if they are, need somewhere to go with their babies. One can perhaps sympathize with the reluctance of the religious societies to mix these women in with others in their Homes, but they had failed to make any other provision for the nine referred to above and were not even, in most cases, making any effort to rehabilitate them. Yet these women were surely among the first whom a Christian community might be expected to help. They are certainly those whom the great saints of the Church would always have been the first to help: the desperate cases, in need sometimes of skilled and long-term rehabilitation at the deepest level. This is a question that deserves further thought, both by the voluntary societies and the local authorities.

MOTHER AND BABY HOMES
RUN BY VOLUNTARY SOCIETIES

In 1958 the Church of England Moral Welfare Associations had forty-five Mother and Baby Homes, fifty-two diocesan shelters open to women and girls in need of temporary refuge in an emergency—when, for instance, there is no vacancy in a Mother and Baby Home—and twelve maternity homes, providing for the confinement as well as before- and after-care. There are also a number of Homes run by other religious bodies—the Roman Catholic Church, the Methodist Church, the Salvation Army—and a small handful of non-denominational organizations such as the Crossroads Club in London, which is chiefly for professional girls. In some country areas where the Roman Catholic population is small there are arrangements with the Church of England Moral Welfare workers to help Roman Catholic girls: indeed, most denominations are quite prepared to help or take in members of other faiths at request and co-operate generously with one another.

There are one or two Homes run specially for professional women; some for the very young; a few principally for high-grade defectives. It is essential that there should be this variety, so that the individual needs of girls may be met as far as possible, and the loneliness of their existence lightened—sometimes, at any rate—by finding themselves in more or less congenial company.

These Homes are subsidized partly by the funds of the voluntary societies and partly by substantial block or *per capita* grants from the local authorities, who in turn seek partial reimbursement from the State. Between them they have largely solved the financial problem of the later weeks of pregnancy and the first weeks of the child's life, at least for any women who make use of them—about one in ten of all unmarried mothers and probably almost one in five of those under twenty-five years of age. Only the smallest fees are generally charged and it is rarely necessary to turn a girl away for financial reasons. The maternity allowance from the Ministry of National Insurance will normally meet the cost of her stay, and if she is not entitled to this, the National Assistance Board, the local authority or the voluntary society itself may help her. Homes for professional women make slightly higher charges, but they are fixed on the assumption that few mothers have large savings. The abolition of acute poverty over this period is a very great achievement, due originally to the efforts of the voluntary societies, but now also to the backing of the Welfare State.

Most of the Homes like to admit the girls six or eight weeks before their confinement and to keep them for six weeks at least after the baby is born—in some cases for three months or longer. This is in order that they may breast-feed their babies if possible, and have an opportunity to regain peace of mind and make plans for the future.

Mother and Baby Homes vary greatly in quality and character. In one a young matron, a deeply believing Christian, may be in charge of sixteen or twenty young mothers in a Home run on modern lines with a warm and intimate atmosphere. The rooms may look gay though they are inexpensively furnished; the girls are encouraged to keep personal possessions and photographs in their bedrooms to help them feel at home; the baby's cot may be at the end of the bed. The mothers are encouraged to attend the classes arranged in cookery, sewing and baby care. A small chapel is the true centre of the Home's life but attendance is entirely voluntary. The children's fathers are encouraged to call and take an interest in their babies. The matron's room is full of happy photographs of growing children who have left the home, and of wedding groups sent by recently married mothers. In a Home such as this some of the girls may experience for the first time the affection, serenity and trust of a true Christian 'family', and some of them will keep in touch with the staff for many years afterwards.

But by no means all the Homes are of this quality. It is difficult to find women with the right personality and training who are prepared to take on the very exacting and self-sacrificing work of matron or warden for the small salary and scant time off that are usually all that can be offered. There are still some Homes pervaded by a strict, old-fashioned, almost penal atmosphere, where the mothers work in old-fashioned laundries, do exquisite embroidery that is not for their babies to wear, and live under rigid discipline, forbidden to go outside the gates without permission or to wear such luxuries as lipstick. In some of these Homes the babies' fathers might be assumed not to exist. The matrons are, however, often in a difficult position, since some of the mothers may have been sent there on probation from the courts, so a girl from a good home background may be sleeping next to a girl on probation for theft, or to a young prostitute. It is a very skilled matron who can handle each of these mothers according to her individual needs and without creating any restrictive atmosphere.

The Roman Catholic Homes stand in a class apart: many are run by nuns. But in these also one may still come across wide contrasts. Often in the chapel the beauty and atmosphere deeply affect a visitor; in the nursery nuns appear to give the babies most loving care: but the dormitories, with their floors shining with polish, will sometimes seem as bare and impersonal as a convent cell and one may wonder whether the nuns are aware how deeply the girls are longing for a homelike Home.

As with Moral Welfare work, the basis of nearly all voluntary Homes is religious. Criticism has been made of the approach to proselytizing in some of them. In a P.E.P. broadsheet issued in 1946 it was stated that in some Homes 'there is a tendency to combine moral welfare work with compulsion to attend religious service, moralising and attempts at making converts for particular religions. Unmarried mothers should not have to pay the price of a pseudo-conversion for the help they receive, and from the point of view of the mother's resettlement such methods are not only objectionable but usually also ineffective.'[1] This is appreciated by many Homes, and a booklet published by the N.C.U.M.C. in the same year particularly stressed that 'the most successful Homes are those where a girl is welcomed whatever her religious allegiance, and often she has none. No compulsion should be brought to bear on her to attend any service that may be held.'[2] It is in the underlying spirit of the Home that a Christian ideal reaches, or fails to reach, the mother, rather than in any words that are said to her.

The need for many Homes to have a religious basis is, however, a very real one if the girl's own needs are to be met at the deepest level. The Home may 'have to help her to find a purpose in life, to realise that she is a child of God and that her child is a child of God, and for these difficult things, we need something more than just humanism'.[3] A mother may, of course, have developed a neurotic sense of guilt through her disturbing experiences, or the feeling of being a social outcast, which is a social reaction, not in any sense Christian. The staff need to have enough understanding and spiritual maturity to distinguish between this and a true religious response, often starting with the experience of being accepted and welcomed within a loving Christian 'family'; 'repentance' can then be the response to a vision of God and man, a happy thing and not a mere act of self-loathing.

---

[1] *Planning* No. 255, *The Unmarried Mother* (Political and Economic Planning, 1946).
[2] *Scheme for Homes and Hostels* (N.C.U.M.C., 1946).
[3] Miss Ena Steel at the N.C.U.M.C. conference on 'Homes and Hostels of the Future', 1945.

In visiting these Homes one is struck by the contrast between those where the girls creep around the passages avoiding every eye and those where they come up at once with a warm smile and loving pride in presenting their babies, sure of appreciation.

STATUTORY AND VOLUNTARY HOMES COMPARED

When local authority Mother and Baby Homes were first opened, it seemed to some people that local authority Homes and the direct appointment of local authority workers foreshadowed 'the shape of things to come', and that much of the work of the voluntary organizations might be superseded. There had been a feeling in certain circles that some of the work of the Moral Welfare Associations was old-fashioned and took too little note of the facts that many intelligent women who conceived extra-maritally were not churchgoers, did not desire 'moral' guidance and had no feeling that pre-marital intercourse was wrong as such: they wanted only practical help such as a well-designed medical service might provide. But time has proved that this viewpoint was as limited as its opposite. The State and the local authorities certainly had larger financial resources, and if the voluntary associations were to survive they had to work closely with the statutory bodies, but the voluntary associations undoubtedly had a vital individual contribution.

Certain special contributions that the voluntary Homes could make became quickly apparent. Homes run by the local authorities were subsidized by the ratepayers with some help from the State: an unmarried mother leaving home during her pregnancy often wished to go far away from her own district, but the ratepayers might see no reason to subsidize a woman from another county. Voluntary Homes, on the other hand, would take women from any part of the country: in this they are more realistic and are meeting the mothers' needs. Again, individual voluntary Homes often specialize in certain types of case or certain age groups; very young or difficult mothers may be sent to them by religious organizations from all parts of the country and may be sent to a Home of which the matron is, by her personal qualities, best able to help them. The local authority, responsible solely for its own area, cannot afford to specialize so fully. Above all, the critics of the religious point of view had failed to realize how much more intimate and homelike some of the small voluntary homes might seem to the mother: even girls who strongly objected to attending prayers in chapel often asserted that they were moved and grateful at the warmth and simple friendliness and tolerance they met with from the staff. They were unconsciously moved, it seems, by their Christianity. But, as a local authority official has rather plaintively expressed it, 'You can be an officer of a local authority and still be a Christian.' All depends on the individual worker's approach. A Christian outlook is not confined to voluntary bodies—indeed, most of the local authority Homes have chapels of their own.

At present there are at least four times as many Homes provided by the voluntary societies as by local authorities, and most of these voluntary Homes are run upon a religious basis. It may perhaps be a limitation still that so much of the work is in the Church's hands, since in any district where the local authority has not opened a Home of its own, there may be too strong an inducement for a mother to make use of a Church Home, even if she herself is not a believer or a church-goer. The Church offers its help generously, but some of these women make use of it with reluctance, feeling uncomfortable and out of place in a religious atmosphere. Some Roman Catholic girls welcome the more detached attitude in Homes run under the National Health Service. Those late in making their plans or those too rough in type to fit in well in most of the voluntary Homes can also be assisted by the local authority, which sometimes welcomes an opportunity to set up a proper organization to help them. Though some women will never fit happily into a Home with a religious atmosphere, others seem to prefer it, so if local authorities open Homes, they should still be prepared to subsidize women who wish to go to a diocesan Home, even if it should be in another area.

WHEN THE MOTHER LEAVES THE HOME

Thanks to the help of the Moral Welfare Associations and other voluntary societies, backed by the Welfare State, a young mother's financial problems may be delayed until she leaves the Home, or, if she is lucky enough to live in one of the few areas served by a working Hostel for unmarried mothers, perhaps for longer. The struggle begins when she has to face the future on her own. She has probably had time to talk over her plans with the case-worker attached to the Home, and, if there is a good after-care system, may be able to stay in touch with the Moral Welfare worker in the area to which she goes.

If she has decided to keep the child, but cannot return with it to her parents' home, she will have to find lodgings. She will need a pram, a cot, baby clothes. She may need bedding, perhaps a few cooking utensils, or a little simple furniture. While she is looking for a job and a room, she may need temporary help with foster fees. Perhaps she needs some money with which to set up a small business in her home: to buy a sewing-machine, for instance, to earn her living as a dressmaker. She is unlikely to have financial resources of her own, unless she is an older woman, and the National Insurance maternity grant of £12 10s. will not last her very long.

Her first search may be for a pram. Here the Moral Welfare Association may quite possibly be able to help her; it may have tiny funds of its own sufficient for this purpose, or will perhaps get into touch with somebody who can help her. But the Moral Welfare Associations have to concentrate their slender resources on keeping open their Homes and providing case-workers; some of them work on a deficit and few, if any, can make a mother any large grant or give her steady financial help. They may even have to apply to the National Assistance Board or the N.C.U.M.C. for help over a pram or cot, or later for a child's school uniform or the fare for the mother to visit her child in a residential nursery. That they should apply to the N.C.U.M.C. for funds is a measure of how small their own resources are, for few bodies of the N.C.U.M.C.'s national status and responsibility are so poorly endowed.

Besides finding lodgings when she leaves the Home, the young mother who has decided to keep her child will have to find someone to look after it while she goes out to work. A few landladies are prepared to care for the baby by day, but the 'care' that is given varies very greatly in quality, and the mothers may be too grateful to have found any lodging at all to afford to be particular.

Foster-homes are exceedingly hard to find and, on a wage that is often barely sufficient for herself alone, it is difficult for the mother to pay the fees. Some social workers have suggested that one sound way to help these mothers would be to find foster-homes where they could live *with* the baby, where the foster-parents would take a parental interest in the mother and treat her as a daughter of the family. Not many foster-parents would have the tact, skill or patience to handle a difficult girl if she began to keep late hours or seemed to be neglecting her child; a good many foster-mothers would become possessive, exasperated or resentful. But if good homes of this kind could be found, it might prove a valuable way of helping one group at least of unmarried mothers: those who, perhaps because their own homes were unhappy, still crave the affection and stability of a 'parental' home.

Sometimes it may be necessary to take the child to a daily minder in the neighbourhood who takes in one or more children for profit, and collect it in the evening on her return from work, but many of these daily minders are of extremely poor quality, more interested in the money than the baby, and, unless they take in for reward more than one child under the age of five from different families, they are not subject to inspection under the Nursery and Child-Minders Regulation Act, 1948.

A better alternative may be to take the child along to the nearest day nursery run by the local Maternity and Child Welfare Department, which gives priority to the children of unmarried mothers, and other women who have no bread-winner and have to go out to work. It is not ideal for a baby or a small toddler, at an age when it still needs one person's constant affection, to spend ten or twelve hours a day in a place of this size, but they are not admitted for part of a day. Alternatively she may try to place the child in a residential nursery. These, like day nurseries, are few in number. Some keep children only up to a certain age, so the child may find itself uprooted just when it is growing used even to this temporary home, and at best they generally offer a somewhat institutional atmosphere.

Sometimes even an unpractical mother may be forced against her gifts and inclination to look for residential work in a private house or institution if she wishes to keep her baby with her. A plan of this kind may break down when the child becomes an extremely active toddler, and it is difficult for an untrained girl to be at one and the same time a good mother and a good domestic servant. Living in someone else's home leaves her, too, with a certain feeling of insecurity, and now that there is a general reaction against domestic service, the work does little to meet one of her deepest needs, which is to recover her self-respect.

None of these courses is really satisfactory except for a few women. They are forced upon the mothers by the great difficulty of finding suitable lodgings to which one may take any child at all, especially if one is unmarried. The chief need of many women, particularly over the first year or two of the baby's life, is well-run lodgings at a price they can afford and where the child will be well looked after.

THE PROVISION OF HOSTELS

The voluntary societies and a few of the local authorities recognize this need and are doing their best to meet it by the provision of special Hostels for unmarried mothers and their children, from which the mothers go out daily to various kinds of work in the neighbourhood, while the children are looked after either in a nursery run by the Hostel or in the local day nursery.

These Hostels are expensive to set up and to maintain and at present there are only eight in the whole country. Six of these are run under the auspices of the Church of England Moral Welfare Council; the other two have been opened by local authorities. The usual practice is for these Hostels to take the women only after the child's birth. They have room for some fifteen to twenty-five mothers and sometimes for rather more children (in case the mother wishes to leave the child there during the day, even when she has found herself lodgings nearby) and permit them to stay for six months or a year—even, in one or two Hostels, for as long as three years. But these Hostels are thought of somewhat as 'transit camps', only a passing expedient until the mother is settled in her work and in suitable lodgings, for the somewhat institutional atmosphere might in time sap her self-reliance and make it harder for her to face the normal world. If unmarried mothers live together for too long, they sometimes come to think of themselves as a race apart.

At the 1945 conference on 'Homes and Hostels of the Future', Dr Letitia Fairfield commented:

'There is . . . the Home where the girl goes out to work . . . I do not think that this is the complete answer . . . Neither the mother nor baby are happy as the permanent inmates of an institution and the mother-child relationship does not grow up happily where the child sees its mother as the inmate of an institution. It is not the ideal solution, but it may suit the mother for a year or eighteen months while she is looking round for something more permanent.'

But at present more of these Hostels are certainly needed most urgently and new forms of help for unmarried mothers would be deeply welcomed. One large local authority has, for example, its own Hostel for unmarried mothers, mostly girls of reasonably good earning power who are thought to have it in them to be good and capable citizens, if they are given the right help. An experienced case-worker keeps in close touch with the Hostel and, with the help of the Ministry of Labour, helps to find jobs for the women. When they are ready to leave she may help them to find lodgings, and even, with the assistance of certain funds, be able to loan or give some of them a little basic furniture to set them up in their own homes or to help them with some simple equipment—with, say, a sewing-machine—that will enable them to earn a living. Such work could be extended; it is done by a few authorities with imagination and is dependent chiefly on two absolute essentials: a first-rate case-worker, who should be encouraged to do any necessary after-care, and an adequate fund of money from which to help the women.

FLATLETS FOR UNMARRIED MOTHERS

Sweden has gone much farther. For years there has been in *Stockholm* a block of forty to fifty flats, built by a voluntary society, the Frederic Een Foundation, specially designed for the use of unmarried mothers, though sometimes also available to divorced or other solitary mothers who are forced to support their children. The flats are independent; furniture is provided, though some of the women prefer gradually to buy their own. There is a matron and a fully staffed nursery on the premises. A mother may apply to rent a flat inexpensively in the block from the time when her child is three months old, and she may stay there, as many do, until it enters school at the age of seven.

At the 1945 conference organized by the N.C.U.M.C. Dr Albertine Winner suggested the provision of something along similar lines in England, but giving the women still more independence.

'What I would like to see,' she said, 'is a collection of small flatlets, nice little rooms, if possible with a gas ring, where a girl could live completely freely. I do not want her under supervision or in a hostel. Let there be those places, where she can have her child, where in the morning she can bath it and dress it, and leave it at the day nursery. It would be very simple in those cases for someone else to mind the child if she wanted to go out for the evening . . . '

'I do not like this idea of landladies. I do not think girls like landladies poking their noses into their business. It would be better for the girls to be completely independent in a community of which the members are not under a single head or any form of discipline.'

A local authority that provided such a service for separated, divorced, unmarried mothers and widows in its area who have children to maintain would be performing a most rewarding service. A requisitioned house could perhaps be taken over in the neighbourhood of a day nursery and converted into small flatlets. No supervision would be needed, but some organization such as the Family Service Units or a fully trained case-worker might be at hand in the district to give help to any mothers who needed it. In this way a number of flatlets might be used as a method of rehabilitating families, legitimate and illegitimate, who are at present so discouraged and demoralized by their experiences that they are a very great burden upon the social services.

Indeed, there is much that local authorities could do if they had the backing of public opinion in the provision of such accommodation, in the encouragement of skilled long-term case-work with some families, in helping to finance mothers who wish to stay in Homes outside the authority's borders, and in helping them to find lodgings where they can have their children with them.

VOCATIONAL TRAINING

The survey made in *Denmark* in 1949[1] of solitary mothers—divorced, separated, widowed or unmarried—showed that as many as a third of them desired help with specific training. The Danish Maternity Aid Institution, which exists to help married and unmarried women, and is subsidized by both public and voluntary funds, is authorized to grant such help—as too are the local social welfare committees. Although it is still on a restricted scale, it is vastly greater than anything of the kind than has been done in England.

'What sort of training is it,' wrote the Maternity Aid Institution, 'for which the solitary mother desires help? . . . Bookkeeper's course; seamstress or fitter's course; housework; home

[1] See page 118.

help; nursing orderly; kindergarten teacher; teacher for children's "free-time home"; children's nurse; hospital nurse; masseuse; midwife; ladies' hairdresser . . . As a rule the training concerned is quite a short one, or in the case of longer courses, a supplement to or completion of a course already begun.'

It was thought unlikely that a mother would complete a long course unless she had already begun it, since there are many difficulties bound up with taking a training when she has a small child on her hands, and the general principle adopted was to expect a mother to save something herself towards her training.

In the year 1951-2 the Maternity Aid Institution spent about £1,500 on the training of about ninety solitary mothers—this in a country with a population less than a tenth the size of that of England and Wales. Many more had sought help, so only a small contribution could be made towards the cost of any one woman's training. A limit of about £30 was at first placed on the grant made to any one mother, but it was considered a pity that the help had to be restricted to such a low figure.

The commission of the Danish Women's National Council and Danish Women's Society that made the survey in 1949 reported in 1953 that means should be found to give greater help to solitary mothers over their training and that even if the training itself were provided from public funds, mothers would require assistance with living expenses.

In addition to helping unmarried mothers financially with their training, the Maternity Aid Institution in *Copenhagen* provides a certain number of flats in its building for mothers who are undergoing a course of training; some unmarried mothers have been helped in this way to take courses as kindergarten nurses, dieticians, shorthand typists, etc. and have been housed there during their course of training for as long as two years. In England existing Hostels for unmarried mothers might sometimes be used in this way.

The N.C.U.M.C. too would like to enable mothers to earn a more secure living for themselves and their children. In 1948 a generous grant by the Lord Mayor of London from his Children's Fund made it possible for the Council to fulfil part of this ambition, and for a few years to make quite substantial grants towards the expenses of some unmarried mothers who needed, for example, to complete a long professional training that had been interrupted by the birth of a child. Through these grants a number of capable women qualified as nurses, secretaries and social welfare officers.

After 1953 the Council was able to draw upon the interest, amounting to about £200-250 a year, of a small Foster Fund to help with the fostering expenses of first children under the age of four; this was used primarily to meet the cost of maintaining children in foster-homes while their mothers were taking a training course, or during a mother's illness. The Foster Fund is still in existence, but unfortunately by 1956 the whole of the grant from the Lord Mayor had been expended. But as a memorial to the Council's founder, Mrs H. A. L. Fisher, a new Training Fund was launched in that year and totalled over £400 in its first twelve months. The first grant made from it went towards text-books and equipment for a young girl training to be a nurse. The Council describes these grants as 'one of the most constructive pieces of work we have been able to do', and keenly regrets that they have had to be confined to such a tiny handful of mothers.

FOSTER GRANTS

By the Local Authority
In paragraph 5(f) of Circular No. 2866, the Ministry of Health commended to the notice of other authorities the imaginative scheme initiated during the war by the *Birmingham* Health Department. This was an arrangement whereby the Maternity and Child Welfare Department kept a panel of approved foster-homes and, if the unmarried mother made application, would advise her as to the placement of the child and, should she fail to keep up the payment of the fees, would advance these to the foster-mother, afterwards recovering them from the mother of the child. By this arrangement children were not moved unnecessarily from home to home, 'such changes being detrimental to young children', and were less likely to be placed in unsuitable homes from the start.

There is one other form of direct financial assistance, which has been briefly mentioned on page 139. If a child is living with relatives or friends and they can ill afford to keep it, but because the parents are living, cannot claim a guardian's allowance, the Children's Department may be able to help. If it receives the child into care on the ground that its parents have deserted it—or are destitute or incapacitated—it is in a position to pay the family who are looking after the child a foster fee. A number of illegitimate children who have been deserted by their mothers have in this way been enabled to stay with friends or relatives. Some Children's Officers wish that their powers went further, and that they could pay the mother herself to look after the child, and so keep it in what might be the most suitable home of all.

In the *United States* there is a fund for Aid to Dependent Children administered by the national government, from which a State can claim financial assistance for a needy child in its own home if it has been deprived of parental support or care through a parent's continued absence. This help may enable a mother to look after her own child if the father has deserted it. It may even enable her to do so without going out to work if her health or the child's well-being demands her presence at home. Aid is available for legitimate and illegitimate children on the same terms. Public opinion in England would probably at present not approve of any such statutory provision for illegitimate children over here, and so the burden falls upon the voluntary societies.

By Voluntary Societies
Below are a few details about some of the schemes in operation at the present time.

Dr Barnardo's Homes have an 'Auxiliary Boarding-Out Scheme', which is administered through intermediaries, the majority of whom are Moral Welfare workers. Under the orginal scheme, started in 1891, grants were given to supplement the wages of unmarried mothers in domestic work to help them pay reliable foster-mothers to look after their babies. The chief development in recent years has been the granting of allowances to mothers who arrange for their children to live with them or with their relatives, rather than in foster-homes. Help is given to the children during their schooling and when they start work.

The *Church of England Children's Society* (formerly 'Waifs and Strays') has a 'Grant Scheme' for providing financial assistance through intermediaries (again, usually Moral Welfare workers) to enable children to stay with their mothers or relatives, or with approved foster-parents found by the mothers. The amounts paid are fairly modest. In the latest year for which we have figures, the maximum grant given was 30s. a week, and the average payment worked out at 12s. 6d. a week. But many thousands of pounds a year are paid out in this way, and through this imaginative and generous help many children are enabled to stay at home with their mothers who in the past would certainly have been parted from them. Help is also given in other ways, such as providing clothes, bedding or furniture.

The *National Children's Homes and Orphanage* have a 'Family Aid Scheme' to enable children to remain with their parents, but this applies mainly to widows and deserted wives.

The foster grants paid to unmarried mothers by Dr Barnardo's Homes and the Church of England Children's Society have the advantage over any general State subsidy that they are paid only where it is clearly in the child's interest to stay with the mother. They are also accompanied by a minimum supervision. Even the National Assistance Board, which is free to use its discretion in the payment or non-payment of assistance, might have difficulty in defending itself against criticism if it had power to help these women when they were earning and then gave help to some and not to others. Women might suspect, perhaps not incorrectly, that discrimination had been made against them under something even more unpopular than a means test—a morality test; and the authorities may be glad that such invidious distinctions have to be made by voluntary societies rather than by themselves.

But there is room for a considerable extension of these grants. The working party set up by the N.C.U.M.C. in 1952 to consider the needs of unmarried mothers reported in 1953 that they felt very strongly that the payments of grants to mothers to enable them to keep their children with them was 'a field of action which the voluntary societies ought to consider very seriously, because the voluntary society has got the power of discrimination, and the power of exercising some sort of supervision over such payments, and there are, in their opinion, certain mothers who ought to be looking after their own infant babies and not going out to work'.[1]

The need for this may become clearer when there has been further research into the later history of these children and their mothers.

---

[1] Miss Ena Steel reporting on behalf of the working party at an extraordinary general meeting of the N.C.U.M.C., 26th July 1953.

HELP GIVEN BY OTHER VOLUNTARY SOCIETIES

Financial help given by other voluntary societies should be briefly mentioned.

The *Buttle Trust* makes generous grants towards the maintenance and education of legally adopted or illegitimate children in the care and custody of their unmarried mothers, where for some valid reason the adopters or mothers are unable to bear the full cost of maintenance and education. Assistance may not be given in respect of illegitimate children who are in institutions or orphanages, or are receiving a boarding-out allowance from a children's society nor has it power to make grants for unmarried mothers themselves.

A voluntary fund on which the N.C.U.M.C. is represented is the *Margaret Club and Day Nursery Fund*. It is restricted to helping unmarried mothers who live in or near the borough of St Pancras, London, N.W.1. Between 1954 and 1956, the first three years of its functioning, it made some fifty-seven grants totalling £781 towards holidays, fares, equipment and clothing. These included one or two quite substantial grants for furnishing houses for mothers who had been rehoused by the local authority and so at last acquired homes of their own. The *Church Army* has also given some generous help towards furnishing unmarried mothers' homes, but there are few other sources to which a mother can turn for such help with any hope of success.

That grants to the amount of nearly £800 proved necessary in the vicinity of one borough alone is some measure of the real need for very substantial voluntary funds to help illegitimate children and their mothers throughout the country.

AFTER-CARE AMONG UNMARRIED MOTHERS

At the 1945 conference on 'Homes and Hostels of the Future' Lord Gorell stressed that much attention is given to the period when the baby is about to arrive and very shortly after it has arrived, but that a mother's problem is not confined to that period, but 'goes on year after year, in some cases until the child is old enough to have its own separate life. I know of some cases where some of the greatest difficulties have come several years after the child had been born, where the mother is striving still to keep a roof over her head and to keep the child with her. I would like as much attention as possible to be given to this . . . whole question of after-care, stretching on as long as the mother needs the help, and that may be a very long period indeed.'

It is a sad feature of the case-work among unmarried mothers at present that welfare workers tend to lose touch with the mothers long before their troubles are over. In the vast majority of cases, Moral Welfare workers lose touch soon after the mother leaves a Home to take her first job, or when an affiliation order or agreement with the child's father is safely negotiated. Some mothers keep in contact longer; some return later, in gratitude or in trouble, but the majority do not.

Moral Welfare workers lose touch with those they have helped chiefly because they are over-pressed; many of them carry a caseload of about a hundred new cases a year, nearly all involving a great expenditure of time and of energy. They are quick, too, to appreciate that some of the mothers would rather push out of their minds the whole troubled memory of their illegitimate pregnancy and feel it is easier to do so if they lose contact with the person who helped them. Some Moral Welfare workers even have something of the psychiatrist's instinct that the initiative in seeking help should always come as far as possible from the mother herself.

But the mother may in fact have lost touch for some quite trivial reason. Often she is simply too busy to come and visit the worker and is no hand at writing letters. Or she may have been disappointed rightly or wrongly, with the help she was given—a thing that can easily happen if a worker takes too moralistic an attitude, or if the mother is in a mood to think that she did. Some lose touch because they have returned to live with the child's father but prefer not to say so; others perhaps because they have had an experience of life or of motherhood that they feel they can no longer share with an unmarried church worker. On the other hand the reason may be a serious one: she may be too ignorant to recognize when trouble is brewing, because it is the child who is suffering and not herself. However it may happen, somehow the contact tends to be dropped.

In the case of the Maternity and Child Welfare Departments the reasons tend to be different. They have, as we have mentioned, a responsibility for the health and welfare of all children under five in their areas, and the health visitors, busy though they may be, are sometimes specially instructed to keep an eye upon under-fives

LOCAL AUTHORITIES AND VOLUNTARY SOCIETIES 209

who are illegitimate, and visit them rather more often than other families, since they are a group 'at risk': yet only too often they call upon an unmarried mother to discover that she has suddenly left the neighbourhood, perhaps leaving no address. Indeed, they may be notified of a birth but never succeed in seeing the child at all because of this.

One result of the loss of contact is that when a case-worker has to decide whether to advise a particular mother and child to stay together, she may not be sufficiently aware of the troubles the girl has to face at home, in her work, or in her day-to-day living. One sometimes notices a tendency to assume that if the mother has returned to her parents' home, or gets married and keeps the child with her, all is well, unless the mother complains, and the file on the case may with reasonable safety be closed. This attitude is probably chiefly due to pressure of work, but ignorance of the actual fate of the mothers and children, and about the child's later development—however naturally or even rightly it might have arisen—is bound to affect a worker's judgment and capacity to help the families. Fortunately this is now realized, and various research projects are under way to help fill in this gap.

This question of long-term after-care indeed needs consideration, but since any extension of case-work would require further funds, it again raises the question of why, in a field so responsive to the personal approach, voluntary societies that are so experienced and so well equipped to give help should be so disastrously short of funds. Apart from a few large organizations such as Dr Barnardo's, they are almost without financial resources. The drying up of voluntary funds is general in nearly all fields of social work, but in this field it is particularly acute, since much of the work is done by the most penurious body of all, the Church. Nor is it easy, when funds are required, to publicize the needs of a group of mothers who value their privacy so much.

Nevertheless a great deal has been achieved in spite of these difficulties. Happily there is a very close relationship between the Ministry of Health, which is very deeply concerned with the welfare of illegitimate children and their mothers, and the N.C.U.M.C., the co-ordinating body for voluntary work among them, and much has been achieved by their steady co-operation. It is a field in which co-operation between statutory and voluntary bodies has to be close, for the needs of illegitimate children are acute enough to require public action and yet individual cases vary so much that something more sensitive than general legislation is often needed to deal with them.

CHAPTER 9

TWO MOTHERS TELL THEIR STORIES

We would have liked to include in this study enough stories of individual unmarried mothers to give some portrait of their diversity and of some of the characteristics most common among them. But it was a condition of the research that lies behind this book, a condition self-imposed and also naturally insisted upon by the case-workers who generously helped to provide the material, that privacy should be scrupulously respected and no story used that could possibly be identified with any particular person.

In view of this we confine ourselves to two stories, told by unmarried mothers in their own words. One is by a girl who had a child by a coloured man, and the other is about a small boy whose mother and grandmother were both unmarried. In each instance the child's illegitimacy has been complicated by a second factor—racial problems in one case, a family history of nervous illness in the other—and is to that extent not wholly typical. But these two mothers have unselfishly recorded their experiences in the hope that they may be of value; and both have faced, with great courage, a long succession of problems which a mother who keeps her child with her must be prepared to face.

SANDRA'S MOTHER

When I knew that I was to have a baby I was filled with mixed feelings. The father of my child was an African, therefore I knew that besides being an unmarried mother I should have to face also the snubs and cruelty of the colour prejudice.

I went into hospital with a slipped disc and stayed until I was four months pregnant. The Lady Almoner did her best to comfort me and took me to Coram Street, where Miss Granger filled me with hope when she told me about the Mother and Baby Homes in various parts of England.

When I returned to the hospital, the local Welfare Worker came to see me and told me she would try to get me into one. I went to a convalescent home for a month and when I returned I went straight to a Mother and Baby Home near London.

It was then February and I expected my baby in April.

We were asked to have a certain amount of articles for ourselves and our expected children. I had most of these articles thanks to my mother's kindness and I had knitted a great deal during my stay in hospital.

I had very little money and had to claim National Assistance and when I had paid for my board and lodging which, I may add, was remarkably inexpensive, I was left with five shillings pocket money.

The girls at the Home varied a great deal in both age and education. I myself am fortunate in having been well educated and I have had nursing training, though I did not finish my full course.

We did the housework for the Home during the morning and were free during the afternoon and evenings.

I have never been a very religious person though I do believe in God and I have never favoured being subjected to religion. Every morning and evening we went into the chapel for prayers which seemed to me long and tedious. We had sinned perhaps in the eyes of God, but was there any need to fling it in our faces twice a day?

The vicar came every Friday evening and he certainly tried to fight shy of our condition. He never once tried to preach to us about ourselves but of other people for whom we might have pity instead of our merely being filled with self-pity.

All women, whether married or not, are inclined to behave rather differently from their usual selves when motherhood is approaching and we were no exceptions.

My own child insisted on being a month late and I could not stand it any longer. I saw other girls go to hospital before me, and I felt a sort of jealousy. I was quite unnecessarily rude to the Superintendent of the Home and she was very patient with me. I flew into rages and refused to co-operate in any way, however, I soon calmed down and apologized.

When I felt the first sign of labour, I was overjoyed. At last, I thought, I should see my little son or daughter, and again I should have someone I could love who would not run away. All through the ten months I had wondered not only whether it would be a boy or a girl, but what colour 'it' would be. Coloured children are so varied. The girls used to say 'I bet it will be coal-black', and I tried in vain to tell them that not even pure Africans were 'coal-black'.

When at last Sandra was born I was so happy. She was sweet and did not look at all like a new-born baby, which was of course probably due to her post-maturity.

I was happy during my fourteen days in hospital and I did not have to tell many lies to the other women. They just assumed that my husband was in Africa.

The day came when I was to return to the Home, just as proudly as all the other girls.

Usually one of the other girls came to the hospital in a taxi, but as it was a Sunday the nurse came. Imagine my misery when instead of being able to carry my baby home myself, my little girl was snatched from the Ward Sister's arms and I had to sit and look on during our drive home.

As soon as we reached the Home she was again whisked away and put into the nursery where she screamed for about two hours without stopping.

'What a temper your daughter has' I was told, and only I knew it was not temper but utter misery. I experienced it myself.

We had lunch and during the meal I hardly spoke.

'What was it like?' 'Did you have any stitches?' Question after question was fired at me by the expectant mothers and the mothers tried to compare their confinements with mine, but having experienced such blood-curdling tales of stitches and such like on my arrival at the Home, and after having seen a sixteen-year-old girl go to the hospital with terrible fears, I was determined to say nothing except a few words of encouragement, and I must say that quite a few fears were dispersed in this way. Ever after that, when I heard mothers telling gory details to the others I tried to change the subject.

Sandra had been a great difficulty in hospital as she refused to breast-feed. I discovered later that she was tongue-tied, but I always remember one evening in the nursery at the Mother and Baby Home.

All the other babies had taken their feeds in the given half-hour for feeding, top and tailing etc. and were tucked up in their cots, but Sandra was trying hard to suck and was just getting nowhere. The nurse came in and said I was to put her upstairs and let her go hungry. I wrapped her up and took her upstairs with tears streaming down my face. I could not bear to think of her being hungry, and I was miserable. I put her in her cot and howled.

The nurse came in and took me downstairs to the staff room. 'Don't cry, dear,' she said. 'I know it seems unfair, but Miss ——— has made the rule that all babies must be in bed by half-past six and I shall get into trouble if they are not.'

I understood and told her that Sandra could not suck properly so the next day she was test weighed and it was proved that she only took about half an ounce in about half an hour. She was given a supplementary bottle and my mind was at rest.

This was not by any means the end of her continuous crying. Day and night she screamed. I had no sleep; I lay awake rocking the cot and when I did drop off I woke in a panic, after dreaming that I had fallen asleep and dropped her on the floor.

During the day all the babies were put in their old shabby prams —minus handles, wheels, etc. and left to sleep until lunch time.

In the afternoons one of the mothers was 'on Nursery'. We took it in turns to look after all the babies and change them when necessary. The 'Nursery Girl' invariably came to me and said 'Your child is a ——— nuisance' in very pretty language. I was in despair knowing that I was helpless.

One visiting day my mother came and, of course, I took her to see Sandra in the garden; later I was told that the girls were *not* to take visitors to see their babies without permission.

All these little rules and regulations seemed so unfair, after all they were our babies.

I never intended to have my baby adopted. I was determined to keep her and keep her well.

I discussed the matter with my Welfare Worker who told me about a Hostel for Mothers and Children. After a short discussion I decided that I should like to go to this London Hostel so we made an appointment for an interview with the Warden.

My Welfare Worker and I went to London on the day of the interview; we arranged that the nurse should look after Sandra for the day as she was then on a bottle.

It was a nice break from the usual routine to go back to London though only for the day.

I liked the look of the two huge houses with their lovely lawns behind. The babies were all in the front garden in their prams and cots either sleeping or gurgling happily. I spotted a little coloured boy and went straight to him.

The Warden came out. She took us to her cosy panelled office where I noticed a television set. She saw me looking at it and said that the girls watched it in the evenings. They had seen the Coronation sitting on cushions and chairs, all tightly packed into the small room!

We were shown over the Hostel and I liked the airy night nurseries and the cosy looking bedrooms for two or three girls. The sitting-room was large with plenty of easy chairs and a gramophone and a piano.

We had lunch and then went back to the office to arrange when I should go there.

The Warden told me to try and get a job which paid not less than £5 a week. My Welfare Worker and I left and as she had an engagement she suggested that I should go to the Labour Exchange and see about a job.

I went to Great Marlborough Street Exchange and asked about a job as a Saleswoman. I found one I liked and after a few preliminary phone calls I went for an interview at once.

I got the job and arranged to start after a fortnight. I did not tell them I was an unmarried mother. In some cases the employer is sympathetic, in others he is unreasonable, therefore I decided not to mention the fact.

I returned to the Home and told everyone what I thought of the Hostel; the girls who were keeping their babies decided they too would go there.

The fortnight passed quickly and I was allowed more freedom. I saw many sights which upset me. Why is it not possible to take a girl's child away at birth if she does not wish to keep it? Whatever her feelings are before her unwanted child is born, those feelings change once she has seen the little helpless creature which she has produced. I only saw one girl who was not affected in this way, and she was rather a senseless child who thought of nothing but getting back to her American airman! She had things made so easy for her that I feel she will be in the same position again before long.

My grandmother came to fetch me when I left the Home, she had never seen Sandra before and she held her in her arms and said

'Oh, poor little darling.' I looked at Sandra's large black eyes gazing at my grandmother and thought 'Why is she a poor little darling? I will give her all I can and try to make her feel she is not different.'

We arrived at the hostel about four o'clock. The Warden and the sister greeted us and I took Sandra to the nursery. It was a very hot day and she had not slept during the whole journey. She just screamed at the top of her voice and even refused a drink of orange juice.

I went to my room and unpacked. There were two other beds in the room and I wondered what their occupants would be like. I had a bath, it was wonderful to have a bath at any time, instead of having a rota on which we were listed for two a week as at the other Home. Expectant mothers do need a bath a day, but of course there was only one bathroom.

I wandered into the sitting-room and out on to the verandah. By that time the girls had started to return from work. A short plump girl came up to me and introduced herself. I naturally asked her what the hostel was like. She merely said 'You'll find out for yourself, but don't trust anyone, not even your best friend.' I was puzzled, but I found out what she meant at a later date! There was dinner and then short prayers in the chapel.

I must say here that religion was never inflicted on us as at the Mother and Baby Home. We had prayers every evening and chapel on Fridays but if we did not wish to attend church on Sundays we need not. I know most of the homes and hostels are run by the Church, and I appreciate it, but I honestly think that if people are forced to do something, they are immediately turned against it.

Every new girl was interviewed by the vicar, a youngish man who helped us a great deal with our problems.

It was wonderful to have a good night's sleep. The babies stayed in their nurseries with the night nurse to attend to them. The doctor came every Monday to see the children and attended to everything urgent. It was discovered that Sandra's restlessness and constant crying was due to the unsuitability of National Dried Milk, and she was tried with various mixtures until a suitable one was found. This relieved my mind a good deal, I know these baby foods are expensive and that one takes advantage of the cheap milk for babies, but if only the Home had tried a few different foods, all our worries would have been over.

I went to work with a clear mind and I enjoyed it.

We had one late pass a week until eleven o'clock and I went to visit a friend who I now hope to marry at a future date.

While we were out we had to ask another girl to feed our babies and put them to bed. This usually presented a difficulty to me as a few of the girls did not want to touch Sandra although she was a great favourite of the nurses and Warden. At last I made a friend, an Irish girl whose baby's father was Indian. She always looked after Sandra and she loved her.

After I had been at the hostel a short while I began to realize that unless our own and our babies' belongings were well hidden away they began to disappear. Each baby had a 'locker' by its cot, but unfortunately this did not lock. Powder, nighties, combs, etc. disappeared and only once did we discover a lost article in another girl's locker. When anything was missing two of us were allowed to search the nurseries. I definitely think there should be a locker system so that we should not lose so much, after all, we can ill afford it. At that hostel I lost an almost new coat of my own, a baby's nightie, a pair of shoes and a purse with all my money for the week in it.

At the week-ends we could have visitors or take the babies away, it was wonderful. At the Mother and Baby Home we could never go out with the babies unless we went on the common opposite the house and even then we felt rather ashamed of the prams.

Nearly everyone at the hostel had her own pram, and my Welfare Worker got a grant from Dr. Barnardo's Homes for my pram which I bought from a girl who was leaving.

On Sunday evenings we had a sandwich supper after which we had a meeting to discuss different things which had happened during the week and to tell us what week-end work we had, but it usually turned into a free-for-all with everyone being catty about someone else. This I think was wrong and I was horrified that the Warden of such a place should allow this. She seemed to have definite favourites with whom she took sides against a less fortunate person. I then realized what the girl had meant on my first day, she always seemed to be one of the down-trodden!

I had a wonderful twenty-first birthday in the September. I had a cake and stayed out until midnight on my late pass. The cook always made the birthday and christening cakes and decorated them beautifully. I could not have had a happier time in my own home.

One day while I was at work I received a message from a woman I had known in a city in the South-west of England. She offered me a job in a nursing home of hers just outside the town and I could take Sandra. I discussed it with the Warden who thought it was a good idea as jobs with babies were few and far between. I accepted and went there in November. I felt a kind of regret at leaving the friends I had made and the babies of whom I had grown fond. The Warden had announced that she herself was leaving shortly and I knew that things would not go quite so smoothly for a few girls. I must admit that in spite of her little faults (which, after all, we all possess) she was ideal for the job. She had been married and had a daughter of nineteen. She had actually experienced the same anxieties as we had with her own child, and she understood our feelings. She did her best to treat us like normal people to prepare the way for our future. We could go to her with our problems and go away with easy minds.

We went to our new home one cold November morning and arrived at lunchtime. I felt rather worried when I saw that the enormous house had hardly any furniture in it and that I had nowhere to put my own or Sandra's clothes.

The owner told me that the first patient would arrive in a couple of days. What she did not tell me was that I was entirely unaided and I was nurse, cook, cleaner and mother all rolled into one, with very little time to be a good mother, or in fact a good anything. She did not pay her bills very promptly and therefore during the snow we were left without coal and with very little food. Sandra developed bronchitis while cutting teeth and was confined to her bedroom. She was wonderful and so placid. I had to face the complaints of the patients and I was almost at breaking point. Suddenly we were told that we were moving out next day and I felt on the verge of suicide. All sorts of thoughts flashed through my mind. 'Where could we go?' 'Would Sandra be taken away because I couldn't afford to keep her?' I felt ill with cold, worry, and I had no one to turn to. I had not asked for help from anyone all along, but in despair I got in touch with some good friends of mine nearby for whom I had worked as Nanny three years before. They knew about Sandra and had known her father. They said they would like me to come back and work for them as housekeeper but could not afford to pay me a great deal. I didn't care, I was overjoyed. At last Sandra and I were wanted by somebody and I wouldn't have to part with her.

So now at last we are settled. Sandra is just over a year old, walking like any other child and saying 'Dad Dad', 'Mum Mum' and other baby words even though she does not know who 'Dad Dad' is. She is happy all day and I really think she is no different from any other child. I have had very little help from her birth until the present time. I want her to be well educated because I think that coloured people can be respected as much as any one else as long as they can behave properly in an educated society. It is a pity that some sort of financial help cannot be given to unmarried mothers if they have very little money when their children reach school age because this is when it is needed most.

Perhaps it would be easier if you could discriminate between the girls who want to keep their babies and bring them up to be better people then they are themselves, and the girls who want their babies for a short while before they tire of them like a child with a new toy. These are the girls who need your help and will be grateful for it without taking advantage of your kindness; the other girls will be like the sixteen-year-old girl I mentioned earlier, and let the same thing occur again because the path was made so smooth for them the first time.

If a girl in my position can get herself a residential job where there are already children in the family she will find that her own child is happier. There are three here and I know Sandra is happy; she can stand the roughest of play and she revels in it.

One thing I find is that some people profess to sympathize with the unmarried mother, as did the woman I worked for, whilst really they think they can get cheap labour by employing her as nobody else will do so, and she will jump at the chance, whatever the work, especially if her child is coloured like mine.

IAN'S MOTHER

My story begins long before my birth. It has its roots in the upbringing of my grandfather. I am told that all our troubles originate from the fact that my maternal great-grandparents were cousins, but I have more recently been informed that can have nothing to do with it unless some peculiar family circumstances or atmosphere resulted. They were considered to be gentlefolk and people of some considerable wealth but their two surviving children both grew up to be eccentrics. The youngest son was my grandfather. He was a rebel from the start. He refused to follow the calling chosen for him by his parents but went into an engineering works as an apprentice and worked his way up. However, he always fell out with his bosses (he worked in the West Riding) and never considered them to pay him a wage fit for such work as his! This resulted in an early retirement when he proceeded to live on the earnings of his three daughters. As a result of this all three were kept in strict retirement, when not working, and not allowed any 'followers'. On the surface the idea was that no one was good enough for them but we can see through that. His wife was a Saint but like many others so named was much too meek and mild for her bullying husband. His temper was terrible and my aunt often speaks of times when he would throw a boiled egg down the wallpaper because it wasn't cooked to his liking, and all his children grew up in great fear of him. My mother was the youngest and the favourite. It is rather striking that she should be the one to go 'off the course'. At the age of 21 she became the mother of an illegitimate daughter, myself, and subsequently gradually deteriorated mentally until, when I was 4 years old she was certified insane and removed to a Mental Hospital. My only memories of her are of times of stress when she would either be quarrelling with my aunt (they were always enemies due to the jealousy of my aunt) or times when she would threaten to take her life and people would chase her to take possession of the carving knife or other weapon.

I was subsequently brought up by my grandmother. I had another aunt who took in dressmaking at home but she was always very sensitive—used to rush away weeping when my grandfather spoke to her—and finally when I was 11 years old joined my mother and died in the same Hospital from pneumonia. I slept with that aunt and watched her mind slowly disintegrate. The day she was taken away I went off to the Grammar School knowing I should never see her again altho' no one had told me.

That was my early background. I was said to be an able child at school. I know I read fluently at the age of 4. I was also very musical and had the musician's highly strung temperament. As I grew older I was involved in so many emotional tangles and stresses that it is no wonder I could not concentrate on my work. I matriculated with some measure of success at 16 but by that time something of great moment had come to pass which put an end to any further scholastic advance. I had for some time realized that I could not be my grandmother's child altho' I always called her mother and I had often asked my late aunt how it was that though we had the same mother we were not sisters! Of course I had no reply. When I was fifteen my grandmother died after a long illness. The doctor said she was just worn out. My grandfather blamed me often—saying that she had always had to bother with me. While I was clearing out a drawer after her death I found the papers relating to my birth. I discovered that I was, as I had feared, the daughter of Margaret in hospital, who had always seemed to me so ugly and noisy and had tried to cut her throat in the kitchen. I had been taken to visit her in hospital and had been scared by the other patients and refused to go again. I had no pleasant associations with my mother. It was a desperate blow to me and it seemed to me terrible that my father had not wanted to marry her and so had not wanted me either. He may have been already married but that did not occur to me at the time.

I knew that to go to a University one had to supply a birth certificate so from that moment determined that I must leave school—I could not go to a University and have to produce evidence of my shame. I can still see the words 'illegitimate female child' on the documents whatever they were—I suppose they were an affiliation order or appertaining thereto. I didn't stop to read it all, but I remember standing in front of a long mirror and repeating these words over and over again with a nasty hollow feeling inside. It struck me that that was why I had so few friends at the Grammar School because I had heard that another girl from my village had been telling 'horrid tales' about me and I supposed that that was what the 'tales' were all about. My only living blood relations were my aunt with whom I am living at the time of writing this, and my grandfather. As the two were enemies, I stayed on alone with my grandfather for two years, i.e. until the age of seventeen. We lived on his old-age pension, ate sparingly and apart from help from a woman friend of my grandfather who came in very occasionally to help I did the housework at night. My grandfather would not burn gas so I had to do my homework by oil lamp. As I could not concentrate while he was there I used to begin after he had gone to bed and sit up until one or two a.m.

Such was the state of affairs that I felt I had to get away from home. The more my Headmaster tried to persuade me to stay and take a University Scholarship the more I told him that I couldn't work properly and should have to leave. At last he agreed on condition that I did not become a Children's Nurse which was what I wanted. I imagined that I should never marry as no man would want an illegitimate person (!) and so I must find fulfilment in caring for other people's children. In the end I went as a probationer in a large Children's Hospital near London. I liked my work there but was not very popular with the Home Sisters because I was so quiet and morose off duty. They made my life very hard and I was terribly lonely as all my friends left within the first six months or so and I knew no one in the vicinity.

Early in the war I sank into deep melancholia and was sent to a doctor who advised an immediate change. I wrote and asked the remaining aunt (with whom I am living now) if I might stay awhile with them. I went, but was told that 'if I was going like my mother and other aunt' she couldn't do with me—she had had enough with the others. Next day she had found me a post as Nurse-companion to a child in Leeds. From there I joined up.

How I loved my life in the W.A.A.F. for the first year! It was a release from all the tensions of my previous life. I had lots of friends who knew nothing about me and didn't want to know. I was a number, a cog in a wheel. I was happy for the first time. I did well at my job and my happiness lasted until I fell in love for the first time at 20. We were very much in love and ecstatically happy until I had to take him home! I had a few men-friends after that but the association always ceased before I had to go into details of my family!

In 1944 I went abroad—volunteered—and was sent to Egypt. I didn't take to the life out there—it was too artificial and I felt alone in a crowd. The only person who attracted me out there was David—and he was married. I didn't know this until I had been out with him several times—until I had known him about 3 months, in fact, and then someone who was jealous of him told me I was wasting my time on him. Of course it was the usual story of the wife not living with him since the conception of their third and last child, then aged 9. Of course, I said I couldn't go on seeing him and was very angry that he hadn't told me. He said he thought I knew! I was desperately in love with him and equally unhappy. However, my release number came up and I decided we should have to break it up and so I came home. While waiting for the boat we were informed that the crew (Polish) had mutinied and we were given a 48-hour pass until she was re-manned. Of course I went straight back to David and we had a celebration after which our son was conceived.

I came back to England that Christmas and knew on arrival that I was probably pregnant. I spent a week or two with my aunt and then told them I was going to get a job in London. I told David: he said he would not desert me and sent me a 'fat' cheque. I spent a horrible few weeks in a hostel, living on my gratuity and savings and then one day I bumped into a man I had known in Egypt. He immediately got me a job in a Government Department where he had influence. I didn't want to take it as I knew I was pregnant and didn't know how they'd take it when I left to have a baby! However, fate took a hand and I went into office life. I loved it and made wonderful friends—while all went well, that is. I told the woman in charge of the office—I will call her Doris—that I was going to have a baby. Her husband was abroad in the Army and she said that for the last month or so I could go to her flat—but she would have to ask the landlady. The landlady objected.

I wrote to the National Council for the Unmarried Mother and Her Child, and said I wanted to make arrangements where to have my baby and told them I planned to have it adopted. They put me in touch with a Moral Welfare Worker who, I must say, didn't appear to be able to help me. She said I'd better book a bed but what was to become of me before or after she didn't know. They were 'fully booked' at that particular Moral Welfare Home, but would I consider going to work as a domestic in a Nursing Home, having the child there and working afterwards until something else came along? I said any port in a storm! I left it to her for the time being but things were none too rosy in that direction.

In the meantime the head of my department found out my condition—I asked my friend to tell him—and on my return from the clinic one day he greeted me with open arms saying he was glad I had gone to them and hoped I would go back after the adoption of the child. He immediately went to arrange for me to have leave of absence for the birth. He was wonderful—as were all the people there.

I must tell you before it escapes my memory that Doris knew someone there who knew of someone who could arrange an 'operation' for removal of unwanted foetus. I will call this acquaintance of Doris's W——. W—— said she wouldn't do anything unless Doris gave her my name and address but she did know of someone in the West End who would perform such an operation costing £60-£100 according to the Nursing Home. Knowing the tongue of W——, Doris refused the information and in any case I shrank from such an operation. I was glad later on seeing the victim of one!

I was during this time living in a bed-sitting-room in North London. I looked after myself well—took in all my vitamins—and always prepared myself substantial meals. Sometimes at week-ends I would picnic in the woods and then I would think perhaps I ought to keep my baby and have fun like these other parents did. All the same I thought it impossible. In any case I would never bring a child to suffer in the way I had suffered. If he or she were adopted, he or she would never be any wiser, but would have the joy and security of two real parents like those other children in the wood. So I knitted one pram set, bought one dress and three nightgowns—to hand over to adopters.

On the day of the great Victory Parade my landlady told me I should have to get out as my condition was now obvious. I spent all my lunch hours searching out a room and some time in the evening if I wasn't too exhausted—all to no avail. By the time I got there they were all taken. No one knew of a single empty room and just as I was thinking I should have to sleep in the woods my landlady said I could stay on longer as she was going away and didn't want to leave the house with strangers. I then had word from a Moral Welfare Home for Unmarried Mothers (I prefer the name 'hostel' and will give it that name in future) that I could go to them. So on August 3rd (baby was expected in September) I was duly admitted and what a relief! That hostel was like a harbour after a stormy sea. I worked in the laundry until the week before the baby was due, but I suffered from blood pressure, and so was removed to the kitchen. I was so glad of that hostel that I would not like to criticise it for the world. But I wish these places could be put on a basis whereby they could always get fully qualified and suitable staffs. Or even be sure of a full staff and not have to make do with anybody who will take the job.

It seems to me that here is a great work to make a home for these girls who have gone through so much. Just a little kindness and encouragement will go such a long way at a time like that. Also is it necessary for the Superintendents to be so hard and impersonal—and yet so kind when one has left the precincts? Surely it is not essential to discipline that we should all be treated like naughty children all the time. However, for the most part, we were a happy and jolly crowd—apart from the mothers whose babies were to go to adopters. Some of these took it valiantly—others were distressing to behold. I shall never forget Jean whose red dress was perpetually sodden with milk and tears.

After my son was born I returned to the hostel and was told by the Outdoor Worker who had promised so much that 'Now my troubles were over!' They were just beginning.

After my 8 weeks I had to find a job. I couldn't go out, and never saw a newspaper—in any case was completely drained of initiative! Outdoor Worker said no job going so how about putting Ian into a Home until I 'turned round'? Said O.K. and had Ian vaccinated ready. Doctor said 'Don't part with him', so decided not to. Glad after when Home in question was closed down! Took only job known of—with Mrs B———, large woman who spent time in 'good works'—signing cheques, sitting on committees and doling out Welfare foods in clinics. 10-roomed house, all cooking, cleaning, shopping—in fact all duties bar weekly wash. This I coped with and my 8-week old son, starting after his 6 a.m. feed and finishing in time for the 10 p.m. feed.

Breakfasts were taken in bed every morning at 7.15 a.m. I had to send home for plimsolls as I hadn't to make any noise. 'Madam' complained that my 'clicking' on of electric fires gave her a headache and I must do it more quietly. She nearly shot out of bed when I drew back the curtains! Then I was nearly always rung for during breakfast as the toast was usually too thin or too thick—likewise

P

the porridge. I never had time to eat more than a mouthful per meal myself.

Dinner had to be on the hot plate ready to serve at 6.45 prompt and must be 'fresh from pan'. This necessitated my putting down Ian two or three times during feed to see to vegetables or pudding. Then I had to don white coat ready to 'wait'. Clearing and washing up and washing nappies, etc. took me until 10 p.m. Whole house was 'gone through' daily; one afternoon I cleaned silver, another scrubbed all scrubbable floors, remaining afternoons, ironed or shopped. I had Sunday afternoon free and Wednesday half-day. I had 25s. per week. This household employed a series of girls with babies from same Hostel. Fortunately Mr. B―― has retired and they have left the neighbourhood.

Mr B―― said when I got settled in he would teach me a spot of valeting for himself and son! My milk went, but Mrs B―― said good job—that baby took too much out of me. By Christmas, thoroughly worn out—I went to sleep in the bath three nights running, and couldn't go upstairs upright. I had to crawl up on all fours. Shall never forget mahogany dining-table which had to be cleaned with wash leather and elbow grease nightly—after being covered with gravy, water, syrup from preserved ginger, etc. etc. Nor shall I forget Mrs B――'s cigarette ends all round the bath—in fact all round the house!

I rang up the office; they said they had my job if I wanted it. Found foster-mother and went back to job—meant to find flat and have baby home within 6 months. David, back from Egypt, said would furnish it for me but didn't help to find!

After 8 months foster-mother belligerent! Said take baby or I must adopt him. Took him away to only job then available—in H.Q. of Mission (also training school for Parochial Workers). Promised well—flatlet at top of 91 stairs—but hadn't bargained for 'miserable' cook and no other staff worth speaking of. Still more worn out after wear and tear of stairs, seeing to Ian—cleaning my daily quota of 4 rooms, stairs (brass rods), vegetable cleaning and assisting cook, laying tables, waiting, washing up and assisting with shopping combined with Ian's afternoon walk. Due to cook's temperament soon I was only remaining 'staff'. Friend of ex-foster-mother had mentioned a job going in Scotland. Clinic doctor said that Ian needed fresh air and I knew I couldn't face up to present life long, so packed up and went to Scotland. At first in 'green pastures'. Huge house being converted into guest house —hens, ducks, geese, Shetland ponies, sheep, cats and dogs. Everything for a happy small boy! Person owning all these a psychopathic case. Took to me until 'adopted parents' became friendly with me. Jealousy stepped in. She had a fixation on 'mother'. (Slept with her while father had own wing in house). Mother was forbidden to speak to me and I was banished to kitchen quarters. Cooked for and waited on staff of two Dutch girl guides, two men and self. Very peculiar existence. Besides household duties had care of aviary. Most of staff had been sacked for fictitious reasons. Dish of cold boiled rice was missing from pantry—self accused and banished to another part of house. Bedroom running with damp, festooned with webs. Bed slept in by recently sacked handyman! Quite bare except for bed and cot. Lived in suitcases. Accused of stealing canned foods and potato chipping machine! Sent out to cottage on mountain side and old woman and foster-child from South of England installed in same cottage to look after Ian. Registered foster-mother with doctor's reference—yet I have never seen such cruelty to children. Ian left alone in cot most of day while she took other child out.

Applied to Ministry of Education (had applied for teaching whilst doing War Service and had afterwards informed them that as I was having a child I couldn't pursue the matter further—but had been interviewed). Said if I could have child provided for would they let application stand?

By this time, geese, sheep, one of the ponies, and most of the birds of the aviary had all died, and from lack of guests, and from indiscriminate spending, the family was bankrupt. The Dutch girls went back to Holland and eventually the foster-mother left the district The 'queer type' had in the meantime taken twins (five-months old) for adoption from a Salvation Army Home. Whether the adoption went through I cannot say, but it oughtn't even to have been considered. I think the family are now in Canada.

Mrs H———, mother of queer type, said she would see Ian was O.K. while I did the one-year emergency training, then 'in go'. Ministry of Education wrote asking would I explain how it was that although I was unmarried I had a child. I did so at great length. Was given place in college without further interview. Could not leave child with that foster-mother as every evening he would cry on my return from work, practically all night on, and I could see he was very unhappy and insecure with her. In any case I did not like or trust her. Came home to arrange for him to go into Nursery while I was in college. When I went for Ian he was a little pale wraith. The registrar, a woman, responsible for supervision of foster-children informed me that Ian was grossly neglected and she would have had to have removed him had I not arrived to fetch him.

Went to S.S.A.F.A. Said would try to help but representative nearest college would have to do it. Couldn't get Ian in anywhere except County Council residential Nursery. Awful place—children filthy—ill-clad—ate from filthy bare tables—probationers scandalous in 'curlers' and slippers—children took off their clothes to mop up pools on floor, etc. etc. etc. However, Ian reasonably healthy except for epidemics and ringworm. My college year over Nursery wouldn't keep Ian until I found rooms—said if I didn't fetch him by a certain date would remove him to Cottage Homes in other part of county. Didn't want this. Was advised to go out as 'Mrs'. Mistake as I couldn't stand the deceit. Everyone asked how long I had been a widow—how did it come about?—etc. etc. Dreadfully unhappy—large class of 49. Landlady objected to Ian's eczema (brought this with him from Nursery). Went to London to try and find rooms or/and job. No resident jobs going. Walked London by day, slept in hotels by night for a fortnight. Nothing doing.

Forces Help Society refused aid as I had no Service papers with me—could not suggest help from other source. Said S.S.A.F.A. couldn't deal with me without Service Release Book! L.C.C. would not help as I hadn't been resident long enough in London. Old contacts knew of nothing. Was complete outcast. None would deal with me. Church Army cried out 'full up'. On the streets!

Sent telegram to aunt saying coming to them temporarily. Was met by aunt who was pleased. Uncle with weak heart found Ian great comfort and I was able to run to phone doctor when heart attacks came on. So it was a good thing I had come and I was very welcome. Took teaching job and became 'Miss' again to own great relief. Ian happy. Eczema cleared up, grew much bigger and stronger. Now at seven he is a beautiful boy and very clever. He is very tall and strong and knows I am not married. He is, however, being subjected to a certain amount of curiosity regarding the whereabouts of his grandmother and is not happy at school where the headmistress (he is in her class) is a peculiar character. I am still unhappy because I cannot bear my aunt but I am afraid to move again. I find my work very tiring and life at the moment is overwhelming.

If I were to go through the same thing again *I would not keep my baby*. I think girls should not be encouraged to keep them unless the 'encouragers' can see a way of settling her with a right and proper milieu where she and her baby can find happiness and security. My child's home is full of tensions and cross-purposes. My aunt is perpetually at him—never leaves him alone. What sort of a man, and more important, husband and father will he grow up to be?

PART III

CITIZENS OF THE FUTURE

CHAPTER 10

THE INFLUENCE OF SOCIAL POLICIES ON THE CHILDREN'S FATE

THE OLD-FASHIONED PUNITIVE ATTITUDE

One must recognize that the fate of illegitimate children is not just a matter of chance, and that it does not always represent the free choice of the parents. What happens to the children is partly moulded by social policies—either deliberately, or as the consequence of indirectly related policies.

Illegitimate births have occurred ever since marriage laws were made, but there is reason to believe that they were once less common in England than they are today, and also much less of a problem. In medieval villages many children were certainly conceived before marriage, but as often as not the parents were neighbours and fellow villagers, and could marry before the child's birth. If they could not there was still no great social problem: the manor absorbed and provided for its children as its future labour force, irrespective of their birth, or unwanted babies were left on the doorstep of the nearest convent.

These 'bastard children' did not become a major social problem until the sixteenth century, when the religious houses, which had cared for the foundlings, were despoiled of their wealth by Henry VIII, and the parishes, forced to look after their own poor, strongly objected to assuming the additional responsibility for providing for the unwanted babies of those they loosely described—with a surprising failure to understand the human complexity of this problem—as 'idle beggars and vagrants'.

The question now touched the ordinary man's pocket, and so gave rise in 1576 to some very sour legislation, 'concerning bastards begotten and born out of lawful matrimony (an offence against God's and Man's laws) the said bastards being now left to be kept at the charges of the Parish where they were born, to the great burden of the same parish and in defraud of the relief of the impotent and aged true poor of the same parish, and to the evil example and encouragement of the lewd life . . .'

In the Act of 1601, two years before the death of Elizabeth I, previous measures to solve the twofold problem of helpless destitution and wilful vagrancy were codified.[1] Workhouses were set up, and a poor rate established in every parish, whose duty it was to appoint an overseer to levy the rate, to relieve the distresses of those prevented from working by age or infirmity, to provide work for those able and ready to do it, and to punish those who preferred to remain 'idle and disorderly'. Those who could find no work or refused to work were consigned to the Bridewell, the house of correction, half prison and half workhouse.

This Act of 1601, the basis of all English poor-law legislation, certainly reduced unemployment, vagrancy and helpless destitution, yet it seems to have done little to check illegitimacy. Sterner measures were taken. In 1610 it was enacted by James I that 'every lewd woman who shall have a bastard which may be chargeable to the parish shall be committed to the House of Correction for one year'. A woman who had a second illegitimate child was imprisoned for life unless she found sureties for her good behaviour, and as those prepared to hazard their money in this way were far from numerous, she usually abandoned or murdered her child. In consequence infanticide became so common that King James concluded that he must take further action.

'Whereas', ran the Act of 1624, 'many lewd women that have been delivered of bastard children, to avoid their shame and escape punishment, do secretly bury or conceal the death of their children, and after, if the child be found dead, the said women do allege that the child was born dead, whereas it falleth out . . . that the said children were murdered by the said women, their lewd mothers', the concealment of the death of an extra-marital child was to be read as evidence of murder by the mother, unless she could bring witnesses to prove that it was actually born dead.

If the parish authorities succeeded in capturing them, the fathers of illegitimate children were also punished. In 1626 a man 'was committed to the Middlesex House of Correction to be there flogged and there detained until it shall appear to the Court that the female bastard begotten by him of the body of Anne M. is dead'.

---

[1] Much of the material that follows is drawn from Mary Hopkirk's *Nobody Wanted Sam*.

A law enacted in the eighteenth century, which gave a putative father the choice of supporting the child (which many were unable to do), going to prison or marrying the girl, became a crying scandal. Parson Woodforde, while holding a curacy in Somerset, recorded in his diary in 1768:

'I married Tom Burge of Ansford to Charity Andrews of Castle Cary by Licence this morning. The Parish of Cary made him marry her and he came handbolted to Church for fear of running away.'

During that century our social attitude to the problem was still punitive. A mother who had an illegitimate child was made to do public penance. In Scotland she and the child's father were summoned before the kirk sessions, admonished, rebuked and fined for their iniquity; in England she had to face being arrayed in a white sheet and forced to confess her sins openly before the assembled congregation. To avoid such an experience it sometimes seemed worth while to murder the baby.

Even in the nineteenth century, when public penance had gone out of fashion, the economic difficulty of rearing an out-of-wedlock baby remained an incitement to murder. In the days before birth control (which may be roughly dated from 1870) the natural baby ran a high risk, for even legitimate babies were exposed. In the 1820's it was not uncommon to find their bodies in public places. John Stuart Mill, as a young clerk at India House, 'walking early every morning from Kensington to the City by Kensington Park and the Green Park to enjoy the trees and grass . . . more than once found and several times witnessed the finding of murdered infants',[1] and as late as 1870 the tiny bodies of two hundred and seventy-six babies, most of them less than a week old, were discovered in London alone. For generations, living babies were left on private doorsteps or at the gates of foundling hospitals. In Italy even today they are silently handed over at the turnstiles of convents.

Until 1845 legislation concerning illegitimacy formed part of the poor law, power of enforcement being vested in the parish, but by the Bastardy Act of that year, the mother of the illegitimate child could take civil action against the father by summoning him to petty sessions. By the Bastardy Laws Amendment Act of 1872, followed by that of 1873, justices were empowered to order parents who abandoned illegitimate children to make payment to the parish for their maintenance. These payments, however, were expressly

[1] *Amberley Papers*, letter from John Robertson, written in 1873.

described as 'for the punishment of the mother and reputed father of such bastard child'. No mention was made, as Dr Pinchbeck points out in *Social Attitudes to the Problem of Illegitimacy*, 'of the welfare of the child, and it is clear that the main concern of parliament was not an enlightened social purpose of enabling the child to be reared in the best possible manner, but the relief of public expenditure and punishment of those responsible for bringing these children into the world'. The law remained punitive, its purpose to protect society against the illegitimate child and its parents, not to protect the illegitimate child against society. The child had no legal rights at all. It was not regarded as related to its mother and had no claim on her: it was *filius nullius*.

'The duty recognized by the state', writes Grace Abbott, 'was the one of preventing or reducing illegitimacy and the dependency that it created. Under the double standard of morals public opinion held the mother to be the offender, and the question was assumed to be how women could be kept from transgressing the moral and statutory law. The early legislation was not based on any scientific study of the causes of these extra-matrimonial relations even so far as the women were concerned. Such a study we now know would have involved consideration of such personal factors in the mothers as feeble-mindedness, ignorance of the biological facts of life, high sexual suggestibility, lack of industrial proficiency and of personal development. It would have revealed the influence of family standards and ideals, poverty in the home, and immoral and unsympathetic parents. Education, early employment and the type of employment, would have been discovered to be present in the chain of causes that led to this deviation from the legal and social standard. The presence of a socially inferior race, the position of women and the community attitude towards pre-marital relationships, especially after betrothal, would also have been found to influence the illegitimacy rate of a nation. Any consideration of these causes indicates how futile punishment of the mother would be in most cases and that, no matter what policy of prevention the state adopted, there would be children born out of wedlock whose needs and rights the state should consider. Enlightened selfishness as well as sympathy for the innocent victims required a programme for the care of the children. But reliance was placed on deterrence. Harsh punishments for the mother and denial of legal rights to the children were relied upon to reduce illegitimacy. To protect the victims of these illegal relationships would, it was believed, increase the number of illegitimate children.'[1]

THE POLICY OF HELPING MOTHER AND CHILD TO REMAIN TOGETHER

Towards the end of the Victorian Age a different idea arose in England, that of 'helping an illegitimate child by helping his mother and enabling them to remain together'.[2] Josephine Butler was the pioneer of this new approach: when she began her work, an unmarried mother had still to choose whether to surrender (or murder) her baby or to live with it in the workhouse, but by the end of her intensive life (she died in 1906) a strong Moral Welfare movement had developed in the Church of England whose declared aim was, and remains to this day, to do everything possible to enable unmarried mothers who are capable of it to keep their children if they wish to do so.

Josephine Butler's outlook proved extremely influential and gradually gained general currency. As early as 1918 the Local Government Board, moved by the high death rate among illegitimate infants, gave it limited recognition:

'The health of infants and young children who lack the support of a father often needs special attention and it is on all grounds desirable that the mother and child should be kept together in such cases, especially during the first year.'[3]

This policy was firmly endorsed in the Ministry of Health Circular No. 2866, paragraph 5 (see page 178). Although this circular was issued under the stress of war, when it was important to avoid placing an overwhelming burden upon the local authorities or voluntary bodies, its basic principle—of keeping mother and child together in every suitable case—was by then well established.

At the conference on 'Homes and Hostels of the Future' arranged by the N.C.U.M.C. in 1945, Dr Dorothy Taylor, of the Ministry of Health, showed how far some circles were pressing this policy.

'In August of this year,' she said, 'I wrote to twenty-three Medical Officers of Health of different types of areas all over the

---

[1] Grace Abbott, *The Child and the State*, vol. 2, pp. 493-4 (Chicago, 1938).
[2] Barbara Reeve and Ena Steel, *Moral Welfare*, chapter 7, *Social Case-Work in Great Britain*.
[3] Circular to the Maternity and Child Welfare Act, 1918, quoted by W. M. Frazer and C. O. Stallybrass in *Textbook of Public Health* (1946).

country to ask them to let me have the benefit of their experience . . . I emphasized the fact that in the Ministry we are anxious to pursue a policy which would enable the mother to keep her child with her . . . From the replies . . . of a total of 7,541 illegitimate births in selected County Boroughs and County Councils, 81 per cent of the babies remained with their mothers . . . We must aim to improve on that figure.'

Recently the wisdom of this policy—and especially of such a general 'blanket' policy as this might seem to imply—has been questioned. Helena Deutsch pleaded for moderation.

'We must admit that our psychologic understanding is still very incomplete; we never know how a decision that seems wise and in harmony with reality at the beginning will work out later.

'A good solution should take both aspects into consideration—adjustment to outside reality, and understanding of the psychic factors.

'One should not try to adjust the woman to reality by making her yield to outside compulsion and renounce the child. Nor should one insist on the ideology of happiness through motherhood if the woman is incapable of such realization under the given conditions.'[1]

Dr Bowlby went farther, pointing to American research studies that suggested that a high proportion of unmarried mothers are psychologically disturbed women, often from broken homes, who may be unfitted to give a child the emotional stability it needs, and that to leave them to struggle alone with the child's upbringing or to return it to the grandparents' home—commonly the source of the mother's own emotional difficulties—may perpetuate a vicious circle. 'As a result of data such as these, progressive policy in the U.S.A. in regard to illegitimate children has changed abruptly in the last ten years and far more adoptions are being arranged.'[2]

The working party set up by the N.C.U.M.C. to study this and other questions reported in 1953 that no conclusion that amounted to a change of policy had been reached. It was felt that too little was yet known about the development of illegitimate children in this country, whether they stay with their mothers or not. Stress was laid, however, on the importance of assessing rightly the mother's real attitude to her child before a decision was taken.

---

[1] Helena Deutsch, *The Psychology of Women*, vol. 2, pp. 345-6 (1947).
[2] *Maternal Care and Mental Health*, p. 99.

The suggestion had been mooted that mothers tended to fall into three groups—a small one who rejected their children emotionally, perhaps because of the unhappy sordid experience that led to their conception, or because they interfered with the mothers' desire for pleasure; a larger one who were ambivalent in their feeling; and others whose attitude to their children was constructive and loving, as possibly their relationship with the fathers had been. One suggestion quoted by the working party in its report was to the effect that, while it would seem wrong to encourage the first group to keep their children, and with the second the decision might be difficult, the last should probably be given all help and encouragement, if it was financially possible, to keep their babies with them. The most important conclusion reached at that stage, however, was that research into the development of illegitimate children was quite essential. On a small scale, relating so far only to the children's early years, it has now begun.

But supposing the child remains with its mother, the circumstances in which it does so may still be varied. In some countries strong religious and social pressure is brought to bear on prospective parents to marry 'for the child's sake'. Such forced marriages occur in this country also, both before and after the child's birth, and unless the parents love one another, can bring unhappiness to everyone concerned, while a panic 'cover-up' marriage to another man may work out quite disastrously. It is important, therefore, to realize that it is no part of the Church of England's policy, as expressed through the Moral Welfare movement, to encourage men and women to make unloving marriages, for 'a marriage that takes place merely to hide the illegitimacy of a child is no solution for either of the partners concerned'.[1]

EFFECT OF THE DIVORCE LAWS

A very large number of children live with their parents as members of unofficial families. This solution cannot be welcomed by either Church or State. It is, however, undoubtedly the product of a social policy: the grounds for divorce are strictly limited in this country, but in almost every unofficial family one or other of the parents is married to some other person, and many have sought,

---

[1] Barbara Reeve and Ena Steel, *Moral Welfare*, p. 155, *Social Case-Work in Great Britain*.

but cannot obtain, a divorce. Nor is it only that the grounds for divorce are limited. The process is slow; the cost was so high until recently that few working people could afford it; and a husband or wife is entitled to refuse, even after years of separation, to set a marriage partner free. Human nature being what it is, some men and women revolt at what they feel to be fetters; they come to regard their marriage as the dry bones of marriage—in A. P. Herbert's phrase, as 'holy deadlock'. They may fall in love again and long to remarry; they may still even hope for or expect to obtain a divorce. But perhaps the new lovers have sexual relations and then discover that a child is on the way. They set up house together, planning to marry 'as soon as the divorce comes through'. The situation drags on: a child is born, another is expected. Finally, some years later, in another district, one may meet a quiet and most respectable-seeming couple, a Mr and 'Mrs' Brown, who have a thriving family and do not excite the curiosity of their neighbours at all, unless by their reticence about the past. Like thousands of other unofficial families they have faded quietly into the landscape and have taken on the protective coloration of marriage, without ever having been through a marriage ceremony.

These unofficial unions can be found at every social level and at very different moral levels. A professional man, whose wife has for years been in a mental hospital, may fall in love with another woman, but the law will not grant him a divorce; a working woman who has left a bullying husband may find a man she can love and who will help to support her children; a roaming husband whose wife 'does not understand him' may have a casual affair, fall in love, find the girl is expecting a child and decide to set up a new household; or a feckless, unstable woman, who has long ago left her husband, sets up house for a few months with this man or with that, adding new unwanted children to her family year after year, perhaps each with a different father. For her no social policy can be held responsible, except the lack of policy that lets problem families recur.

Divorce could be made easier for a few of these men and women, but any change in the law may set up incidentally another new series of problems. Laws are based upon compromise and when a new one is framed, a price has to be paid. One may only have shifted the burden from one set of children's shoulders to another. As *Sweden* has found to its cost, the children of divorced parents

THE INFLUENCE OF SOCIAL POLICIES

may suffer as much as the illegitimate. But laws are framed by society—that is, in the end, by ourselves. We can be careful to choose policies that entail the minimum price in human suffering, and ensure that as little as possible of it falls upon children; and since we ourselves make the policies, any children who suffer through them, do so on our responsibility and can claim our full attention.

POSSIBILITY OF ADOPTION

The development of legal means of adoption has made life happier for a great many illegitimate children. Adoption became legal in 1926, and since then a number of steps have been taken to make its operation more effective. The chances that a child who is adopted will be placed in a suitable home, young enough to make it feel it belongs there, are yearly increasing and any woman who has an illegitimate child is nowadays fully aware that there is—or, at any rate, may be—this alternative for her baby. Yet only about one in five of these mothers parts with her child to adopters (a question we shall return to later in the next chapter). One would like to know whether this is the 'natural' number of women who would—or should—part with their babies, or whether it too is influenced by social policies. Certainly a number of women cannot face the financial and social difficulties that are likely to confront them at present if they keep their babies with them. On the other hand, there are certainly others who would not be brave enough—or, it may be, rash enough—to keep them were it not that Mother and Baby Homes tend to urge them to stay with the children and make no final decision until the babies are a few weeks old: by then, especially if they have also breast-fed them, a tie may have been created between mother and baby that is extremely hard to break. Quite apart from the question as to whether or not the mothers can bring up their children successfully, one should recognize that there are some who would not attempt it but for the support of a widespread feeling that it is somehow their duty to do so.

In the important study, made in Toronto in 1943,[1] of the history and adjustment of illegitimate children aged fourteen and fifteen who had remained with their mothers and relatives, the research

---

[1] See page 120 and A CANADIAN STUDY OF TEEN-AGE CHILDREN, chapter 13.

workers concluded that the policies of the social agencies were apt to be too rigid.

'Obviously not all unmarried mothers will fit into any one pattern, yet an attempt was made over the years to force them to do so . . . Some agencies, for example, insisted upon mothers remaining with their children for at least the first few months, hoping that the affection which would be stimulated during that period of care would result in the mothers finding a means of keeping their children. Agencies have advocated mothers keeping their babies on the grounds that the children would be a stabilizing influence if the mothers were forced to take responsibility for them . . .

'Analysis of the agencies' records and the material secured from the interviews suggest that these blanket policies and attitudes had over-influenced the mothers in their decision to retain custody of their children. The records show that many of the mothers who had cared for their babies during the greatest period of dependency found it impossible to release them, even when they knew that the future offered little opportunity for satisfactory living for themselves or little chance for normal growth for their children . . .'

One of the larger agencies had the slogan, 'A mother has a right to her child and the child a right to his mother.' On this the research workers commented, 'Whether the "right" would benefit either seemed to be a matter of no importance.' Quite a number of the mothers in the study had needed help in *releasing* their children, rather than encouragement to keep them.

'While one might be guided and helped to keep her child, another might be equally well guided if she were helped to release it. While it is not the caseworker's role to tell the mother what she should do, she should be able to show the mother the probable result of her decision.'

In many ways, then, our social attitudes, and the outlook of social agencies, affects the fate of the babies. Still more, of course, has it been affected by the magnificent work of the Maternity and Child Welfare Departments, to whom many children owe the simple fact that they have survived their childhood at all.

CHAPTER 11

WHAT HAPPENS TO THE CHILDREN AS THEY GROW UP?

FOLLOW-UP SURVEYS

As yet it is not possible to state with any confidence what happens to illegitimate children as they grow up. To give even a broad picture of their fate is difficult, since extremely few studies have been made, and in this country even those have been confined to the first five years at most of the children's lives. As far as the facts are concerned one can put together a few fragments of the portrait.

National figures show that of every hundred illegitimate children three die before they are a year old, and something over twenty are at some stage adopted (by someone other than their parents). The experience of certain counties and boroughs seems to suggest that round about three out of every hundred natural children may be in public care. Surveys in several areas indicate that, at least in the cities, a third or more of the illegitimate children may grow up in unofficial families. Quite a high proportion of mothers later marry the natural fathers or some other man, and most, though not all, of these evidently keep their children with them. Of the relatively small number left, most of the children live with their grandparents, with or without their mothers, and a few—a precarious and therefore extremely important few—grow up with mothers who are living on their own.

The evidence for this is set out later in this and the following chapters and is drawn chiefly from the following sources, which will be quoted in greater detail:

1. Manchester: Survey of circumstances of illegitimate children after five years. Covers four hundred and twenty-seven children born in 1933. Published in the annual report, 1938, of the Medical Officer of Health. (See page 51).
2. Midboro: Survey of circumstances of illegitimate children

after five years. Covers two hundred and sixty-eight children born in 1949. Published in the *Medical Officer*, 14th December 1956: *Follow-up of Illegitimate Children* (See page 53).

3. Newcastle-upon-Tyne: Survey of circumstances of illegitimate children to the end of their first year. Covers a majority of the sixty-seven children born in May and June 1947. Published in *A Thousand Familes in Newcastle-upon-Tyne*. Sir James Spence et alii. (See page 69).

4. Survey of circumstances of illegitimate children after three years. Covers one hundred and eighty children born in various areas in 1952. Published in *Moral Welfare*, January 1957: *What Happens Afterwards?* (See page 115).

5. Registrar-General's *Statistical Review of England and Wales*, 1950, *et seq.* (for figures relating to infant deaths and to adoptions).

6. Home Office: *Children in the Care of Local Authorities in England and Wales* in November 1953, November 1954 and March 1956 (H.M.S.O., Commands 9145, 9488 and 9881).

7. Figures furnished by various Children's Departments in relation to children in public care.

Certain other surveys are quoted, but 1 to 4 listed here have the advantage that all the children studied were at least a year old and, within each study, were all of about the same age.

Before looking in detail at the various circumstances in which the children grow up it may be worth while to summarize the findings of two of the surveys, which are relatively recent and cover all the illegitimate children, born in a single year or selected months of one year, who could be traced in two cities.

Midboro

At the end of five years the circumstances were known of 86 per cent of the illegitimate children born in 1949 (two hundred and forty-five of the two hundred and eighty-four births registered). In the words of the Medical Officer of Health:

'Very broadly . . . for every 100 illegitimate children whose records are available, approximately 30 of the mothers are at the end of five years married and 40 are cohabiting. Practically all these mothers keep their children, which settle happily. Of the other 30, that is, those who are neither married nor cohabiting, about half, that is, 15, part with their child, mainly by adoption. The other 15 keep the child.'

This analysis omits the 14 per cent of children whose circumstances were not known. Expressed in relation to the *total* number of illegitimate births registered in the city in that year, the figures would read:

	% (approx.)
Dead	2.5
Adopted	11.0
Living with mother	64.0
Living with other relatives (usually grandparents)	3.5
Living with foster-parents	1.5
Living in institutions	3.5
Not known	14.0
TOTAL	100.0

It is important to note that over 80 per cent of all those children whose fate was known were living with two 'parents'—either with their own natural parents who had married or were cohabiting, or with their mother and another man she had married, or with adoptive parents. In addition, about another 10 per cent (twenty-five children) lived with the mother's family and, where the grandfather was a member of the household, no doubt had in him some kind of father substitute. A further few, about 1.5 per cent, had foster-parents. Thus only a tiny number (certainly under 10 per cent)—those living with their mothers alone or placed in institutions—had, at the time the study was made, only one parent figure or none in their lives.

Newcastle-upon-Tyne

At the end of a year, seven children had died and eighteen had left the city, and in some cases the history of these was not known to the end of their first year, but:

'No less than 27 of the remaining 55 infants we knew lived with both parents as members of unofficial families. In 6 other cases the parents were married after the birth of the child, and in the seventh the mother married another man. Seventeen infants were accepted into the mother's family and looked after by the grandparents, and in 3 further cases the maternal grandmother was dead but the father of the child was living with the mother's family, usually as a lodger. In only 3 cases did the mother appear to live alone at the time of delivery . . . Most of the illegitimate children entered a family circle, either that of the parents (34) or that of the mother's family (17) or that of the adopted parents (12).'

After this general introduction we may look in turn at each of the main family patterns in which illegitimate children grow up. But first there are those who do not live long.

DEATH IN INFANCY

Many natural children do not survive their infancy. In 1950 about 1,400 died before they were a year old, nearly four out of every hundred children; in 1955 about three in every hundred. Most of them die before they are a month old, and about a third on the same day that they are born.

The neo-natal deaths are often the result of a premature birth, and that in its turn can be due to the fact that the mother did not seek ante-natal care in time or, owing to poverty, did not feed herself properly or worked too long or too hard during her pregnancy.

Forty years ago, however, the hazards of being an illegitimate child were much greater. Not three, but more than eighteen illegitimate children out of every hundred died in infancy, their chance of survival being only about half that of a legitimate baby. Today their risk of dying in the first year is still higher than among other children: in England and Wales (1955) by only 26 per cent, but in Scotland (1954) by 70 per cent.

Below are the figures (per thousand live births) of children dying in infancy in England and Wales:

	1918	1950	1955
Legitimate	91	29	23
Illegitimate	196	39	29

A very great improvement in ante-natal and post-natal care in the whole community has begun to reach the illegitimate child, though still slowly in Scotland.

There may always be some slight difference between the infant mortality rates of legitimate and illegitimate children, since more natural than legitimate children are first babies and the risk is rather higher with first births. One may expect a difference, too, so long as illegitimacy and poverty, poverty and poor health, are associated. But in recent years some districts, through careful and vigilant case-work, have sometimes succeeded in bringing the illegitimate infant mortality rate lower than the legitimate: the gap is narrowing and could still be narrowed.

Death, however, is only one of the many hazards. It was noticed in the *Newcastle-upon-Tyne* survey that the accident rate among illegitimate children was 18 per cent as against 5 per cent among the legitimate, and since it has long been accepted that the infant mortality rate is a sensitive index of children's general health, natural children are evidently still of poorer health than the rest of the community.

CHILDREN WHOSE MOTHERS MARRY AFTER THEIR BIRTH

A number of women marry soon after the child's birth or within the next few years. In *Midboro*, of the single women who bore children in 1949, one hundred and five whose children were still living and had not been adopted were traced after five years. Of these 21 per cent (twenty-two) had married the father and another 21 per cent some other man. In *Manchester*, of the unmarried mothers who bore children in 1933, roughly 8 per cent (forty-four out of the three hundred and seventy-six who could be traced) married the child's father within five years of the birth, and 7 per cent a man other than the father. The high proportion in Midboro, whose survey refers to a period sixteen years later than Manchester's, may be related to the fact that divorce is now commoner and less expensive. In the Moral Welfare survey of a group of children born in 1952—a survey confined to those in touch with the Moral Welfare workers —17 per cent of the unmarried mothers (twenty-seven out of one hundred and sixty-one) married the child's father within three years, and 21 per cent some other man.

Where the Mother Marries the Child's Father
Where the mother marries the father after the birth of the child it is usually because one or other has been waiting for a divorce to come through. (Now and again the story may be different: the man may not be prepared to marry until he is sure it is 'necessary' or until he has seen the child and satisfied himself that he is the father;

or again, after seeing the child he may come to care for it). Once they marry, these parents normally make a home for the child, and so far as is known—no special studies have been made—the children of such marriages normally settle down happily. There is no reason why they should not do so if the marriage itself is a happy one.

By the Legitimacy Act of 1926, a child was legitimated by the marriage of its parents, but only if there was no bar to marriage at the time of the birth. Commonly there was a bar: one or other of the parents was married to someone else. In that case the law stood firm: the child could not be legitimated. Since the passing of the Legitimacy Act of 1959, the position has been very much better. Now every child whose parents subsequently marry one another can be legitimated (unless complications arise over such matters as the father's country of domicile) and most of the child's legal difficulties are removed. It is tempting to believe that they have all been removed, but that is by no means the case. Legitimation is not legitimacy; it is only a half-way house. A legitimated child has rights similar in certain stated respects to a legitimate child; not in all. In especial, while its inheritance rights are greater than those of an illegitimate child, they are less than those of a legitimate one. Nor is legitimation, under these two Acts, made retrospective to the child's birth: it dates only from the marriage.

The 1959 Act also provides that a child of a void marriage, e.g. a bigamous one, may in most cases be treated as legitimate if either or both of the parents reasonably believed the marriage to be valid at the time of the act of intercourse resulting in its birth; and provisions are made for children born out of wedlock whose parents later contract an invalid marriage believed by one or both to be valid.

Where the Mother Marries Another Man
Sometimes the mother marries another man as a quick 'cover-up' marriage or, more often, a few years later. The younger she is when the child is born the better her chances of marrying. Whether the marriage provides a home for the child depends very much upon circumstances. Some men will make it clear from the start that they will marry the girl only if she parts with her child to her parents or to adopters. Others may be attracted to her just because they admire her courage in facing up to difficulties and her qualities as a mother: they may grow as fond of the child as if it were their own. A marriage of this kind—between, as it were, three people—may

prove a very happy one. But in many cases the man's feeling is divided—at first he may be ready enough to offer the child a home, but as soon as he has children of his own, or strains are felt in the marriage, the illegitimate child becomes a pawn in the marital struggle: the father attacks, the mother defends the child. Or perhaps the mother rejects it because it seems to be the source of the difficulties in her marriage and transfers her affection to her new children. In either event the illegitimate child's position is unenviable.

Difficulties can arise, even more seriously, when a married woman has a child by someone other than her husband and her husband offers to take the baby home. This quite often leads to an unhappy situation for the child, and social workers sometimes feel bound to advise the woman to have the child adopted from babyhood.

Children whose mothers marry another man after their births are not thereby legitimated, and even if the neighbours assume that the child is legitimate, its legal position remains insecure. It is usually advisable for the mother and her husband to adopt the child jointly. It will then have the same surname as any child of the marriage, its new father will have the same legal obligation to maintain it as he has towards his other children (a point that could become important if ever the marriage broke up) and it will inherit from him if he dies intestate.

Lately there have been about three thousand such joint adoptions every year, as compared with not much more than a hundred joint adoptions of children by their natural parents—which proves incidentally that not less than 10 per cent, and presumably more, of all mothers of illegitimate children do later marry some other man.

The Moral Welfare survey comments on these marriages that 'most of the husbands are willing to accept the child', and it emerged from the *Midboro* follow-up that, at the end of five years, three-quarters of the women who had been single at the child's birth but later married the natural father or another man, still had the children with them. But neither study comments upon how these children developed.

CHILDREN OF UNOFFICIAL FAMILIES

A surprisingly large proportion of all illegitimate children grow up with both their parents as members of unofficial families.

In the *Midboro* follow-up it was found that at the time of conception about half of the two hundred and sixty-five mothers in the study has been living with the putative fathers (see page 68). At the end of five years, of the two hundred and two whose marital circumstances were known, eighty-nine (44 per cent) were still doing so. Nearly all of them had kept their children. Of the two hundred and sixty-eight children in the study, information was available five years later about two hundred and thirty-eight, of whom eighty-one (30 per cent) were living with cohabiting parents. The discrepancy between these figures arises from the fact that more tended to be known about the children than the parents.

In *Newcastle-upon-Tyne* twenty-seven of the sixty-seven children studied were living as members of unofficial families at the end of a year—that is, just half of the fifty-five children who could still be traced.

Other figures quoted in chapter 2 suggest that around a third of the parents of illegitimate children—at least in the larger towns —may be cohabiting, and it may be presumed that in most, at any rate, of these cases their children are living with them. How does this work out from the children's point of view? The Medical Officer of Health for *Midboro* wrote:

'For every 100 [illegitimate] children born whose records are available, approximately 30 of the mothers are at the end of five years married and 40 are cohabiting. Practically all these mothers keep their children, who settle happily.'

In *Newcastle-upon-Tyne* the general picture of the environment of illegitimate children was less happy; an assessment of the stability of fifty-four families, in half of which the parents were cohabiting, led to the conclusion:

'In no less than 32 of them the environment was unstable and unsatisfactory—far more than the expected number.'

'The standards in [the] family circle, however, varied widely and the children received very different degrees of care and protection. Many families obviously led stable and happy lives, and these were largely unofficial families where the parents were living together, one or both being married or separated from their legal wife or husband.'

The following comment by a health visitor on one family of this kind is typical of a great many, but not all, that have been read in the course of our research:

'Mother a sensible good type. They appear to be a happy couple and do their best for the children. Children's welfare excellent.'

In the *Midboro* survey made when the children were of varying ages from a few weeks to a year old, the health visitors reported on the physical welfare of the children of ninety-three mothers who were cohabiting stably as follows:

	%
Excellent	19
Good	26
Adequate	44
Fair	3
Poor or bad	8
TOTAL	100

Valerie Hughes commented: 'In view of the many disabilities under which the non-legal family labours, particularly over housing, the fact that 90% of the parents who were cohabiting were looking after their children adequately, and frequently excellently, is worth remarking. In several cases the mother was making very remarkable efforts in conditions which would defeat many women, and in the absence of comparable data about married parents, it is difficult to know to what extent the figure of 10% for neglected children is significant.'

Describing the emotional hazards of different forms of care, Dr Christine Cooper instanced the child who is cared for by its mother and father in an unofficial family group, and commented:

'In many cases this works well, and is probably the best solution if the mother can cope with running a home. Nevertheless, the situation can give rise to insecurity and anxiety for the children, especially when the union is an unstable one.'[1]

Although such evidence as we possess at present about the children of these unions is, on the whole, surprisingly encouraging, many of the families must live under a constant strain. Strains, of course, tend to arise in any family that has a secret to hide; generally the truth must be concealed from the neighbours, who can be cruel if they find out, and often the children themselves are uncomfortably aware that some secret is being kept from them. Some families, to conceal their position, move to another district, which

---

[1] Christine Cooper, *The Illegitimate Child* (*Practitioner*, April 1955), reprinted as a booklet by N.C.U.M.C.

means that in times of crisis they may be far away from the friends and relatives to whom they would have turned for help. If the union should break down, the family is in a much less favourable position than a legal family: the mother cannot claim maintenance for herself at all, and for the children only if she has, or can obtain, an affiliation order.

Yet on the evidence a majority of these unions do prove remarkably stable, and where they do break down it quite often proves to be because the children were not all by the same father. In the *Midboro* follow-up, as well as the 44 per cent of parents who were living together stably, there were some, but relatively few, women—another 7.5 per cent—who lived with men who only supported them intermittently, or with whom the relationship had already come to an end.

It would be interesting to know whether it is in any way significant that the number of children received into public care as the immediate result of the break-up of an unofficial family is, in *London* at any rate, fairly small. Of 3,092 natural children who were in the care of the L.C.C.'s Children's Department in 1953, only 2.6 per cent were received into care for that immediate reason. It may have been a contributory cause in a greater number of cases, since the separation of such parents could well lie behind a series of troubles that would lead only later to a child being received into care, and the L.C.C. gave only the main precipitating cause. But as it stands, the figure may possibly be interesting and worth pressing to the rough conclusion: *if* as is quite approximately estimated on page 243, something like 3 per cent of illegitimate children are in public care, and *if* less than 3 per cent of *these* were received into care owing to the break-up of a liaison, then only about one child in ten thousand is received into care for that immediate reason. Inasmuch as a high proportion of all parents of illegitimate children seem to be cohabiting, this may be an interesting sidelight on the stability of unofficial families, or it may be of no significance, concerned as the L.C.C. figure was with only precipitating causes.

However, all the evidence seems to suggest that cohabitations where there are children tend in the main to be remarkably stable, perhaps because the men and women face the difficulties of such a relationship with deliberation and realism, or because they are generally older and more experienced, and do not face this path unless they are unquestionably devoted to each other. This might also explain why so many of their children seem, on the slight information we have, to be settling happily.

WHEN THE FATHER SEEKS CUSTODY

Fathers living in stable cohabitation have in practice a real relationship with their children, but under the law, the natural father has no automatic right of access to his child, no voice in its upbringing.

In general, that an illegitimate child whose parents live apart should not be in touch with its father seems to be right—to have half a father can be more disturbing than to have none—and in the ordinary way the father is unlikely to wish to have the child. But this is not always so. The joint committee appointed by the British Medical Association and the Magistrates' Association reported as follows:

'There are some cases where the father has consistently done his best for his illegitimate child and sometimes these children are received by the wives of the fathers into their own families. This is frequently to the child's advantage . . .We feel strongly . . . that the father of an illegitimate child should, like the mother, be empowered to apply to a court for custody. Courts should be permitted to make such an order in cases where the father has done his best to maintain the child. We consider that the knowledge that the father can apply to the court for custody, and the thought that this action might be taken if the child is neglected, might well stimulate some mothers of illegitimate children to take better care of their children.'

The legal sub-committee of the N.C.U.M.C. recommended in its report that 'if the father applied for custody of guardianship of the child, either at the time of making the order or subsequently, it should be within the jurisdiction of the Court where it seemed desirable in the child's interest to grant him custody and control'.

The question particularly arises where the mother proves herself an unsuitable person to have care of the child, or is unable to care for it, and the father has proved his affection and ability to accept responsibility. An instance was quoted in the Press in 1957. Believing her to be his legal wife, a man lived for a number of years with a woman who had two or three children by him. Then suddenly she left him, taking the children with her. On tracing her he found that, having fallen ill, she had been unable to look after the children, who had been placed for the time being in a local authority Home. The mother refused to meet him, and when he endeavoured to remove the children from the Home he learnt for the first time that, contrary to his belief, his wife's previous marriage had not been dissolved. Consequently, since his own marriage with her had been bigamous, he had no right over the children, the eldest of whom sent him a pathetic letter, asking him to bring her home. He had a home ready for them, but the mother refused her consent, and he was told that in law he could do nothing about it.

The Legitimacy Act of 1959 would now, by section two, have allowed these children to be treated as legitimate.

Section three of the same Act allows the father or the mother of an illegitimate child to be granted a court order for its custody, or for access to it, though there must be a special application to the court for this purpose. This new legislation is of historic importance, since it gives the father rights that he has not possessed in this country. It remains to be seen, however, how the courts will interpret their powers and how often or in what type of circumstances they will consider themselves justified in granting custody to a father.

CHILDREN BROUGHT UP IN THE GRANDPARENTS' HOME

Quite a number of children grow up in their grandparents' home, at least for a part of their childhood, or live with other relatives. It is usually the mother's parents who heroically assume this burden.

In *Newcastle-upon-Tyne* most of the natural children who were not adopted during their first year, or whose parents were not cohabiting, lived with their grandparents: about 50 per cent lived with cohabiting or married parents and about another 25 per cent in the grandparents' home. In *Midboro* 'an important factor in keeping the children was the attitude of the grandparents. If they accepted the child and were prepared to offer a home to the mother and child, then there was a good chance that the mother would keep him'; and a majority of the mothers who at the end of five years were neither married nor cohabiting and who had kept their children (twenty out of thirty-two) were living with their parents. Many of them were going out to work by day in factories or shops, leaving their children in the grandmothers' care. Another group of ten mothers, however, who had been living with the grandparents, had, by the end of the study, all but given up the care of the child, often because they had married and left home. 'Most of these children settled well, sometimes calling the grandparents "mother and father". The households, except two which seemed unsuitable, seemed to be happy and secure, although they seldom contained other children.'

In *Manchester*, of the four hundred and twenty-seven children who could be traced in 1938, when they were about five years old, ninety (21 per cent) had been absorbed into the maternal grandparents' family, and three (less than 1 per cent) lived with other relatives. The Manchester Medical Officer of Health expressed the view that 'on the whole, the circumstances of the children living with two parents or as part of the grandmother's family, did not differ from that of legitimate children . . . The child living with two parents usually had a brother or a sister, and therefore some sort of family life, and the one living as part of the grandmother's family was regarded as the youngest member, with the real mother as an older sister, the child addressing her by her christian name.'

Social workers often regard a return to the grandparents' home as the best solution in an imperfect world, the only one that may offer a child without a father, at least until the grandparents' death, complete economic stability and a more or less complete and stable family background. Paragraph 5 (*a*) of the Ministry of Health's Circular No. 2866 urged welfare workers: 'Wherever possible to persuade the girl to make known her circumstances to her parents and, if the home is likely to be a satisfactory one, to persuade the grandparents to make a home for the little one.' But lately the wisdom of this policy has been questioned. In her article in the *Practitioner*, Dr Christine Cooper wrote that it 'may provide the child with a satisfactory home, but in some cases he is over-protected or rejected by his mother, grandparents or others in the family who may have mixed feelings about his existence. Not infrequently he grows up believing his grandparents to be his parents and sometimes thinks his mother is his sister, which may have serious consequences when the truth is revealed, as it inevitably is.'

Ian's mother, who told her story in chapter 9, had that very bitter experience. We have a vivid memory also of an evening spent in a working-class family where the grandmother had the effective care of her illegitimate grandson. The small boy was three years old; he was playing with an eighteen-year-old uncle, whom he obviously delighted in and no doubt regarded for the time being as his 'father'. The grandmother, a powerful, kindly woman, remarked:

'We all spoil him outrageously! We want to make up to him for everything he has missed.'

The boy's mother, a sad-looking girl of twenty, was standing outside the group.

'She's going out to a dance,' said the grandmother. 'We want her to have some happiness while she is still young, and to make herself new friends.'

The girl was the one person looking out of place in that picture: a mother and yet not a mother. The grandmother was usurping her natural role, and the girl only earned the child's living. It was a loving family doing its best for the child, yet there was something unnatural about it. Perhaps this can hardly be avoided.

It seems to be a usual solution in rural communities and may perhaps work best in them where, after the first shock, the situation is usually accepted pretty naturally. Dr Leontine Young urges, however, that if a girl returns to her own home with the baby, it 'is almost certainly doomed to failure unless a girl's family and community can honestly accept both her and the child without shock, critical judgment, or recrimination'.

'Otherwise', she continues, 'there are almost insuperable obstacles to their finding a secure and unbiased place for themselves. In addition, many of these girls come from severely neurotic homes and their return with the baby is tantamount to a sentence of future damage and unhappiness for both. In many cases acute rivalry develops between the girl and her mother for possession of the child, who becomes in effect a pawn between the two. Often the girl becomes more of a sister than a mother to her child and may ultimately leave the home, bequeathing him entirely to her mother. When that mother is a dominating, possessive woman the child suffers inevitable personality damage which is augmented by the fact that he has no clearly established place of his own either in the home or the community. Rarely is the fact of his illegitimacy permanently forgotten.'[1]

There is further evidence on these lines in the *Toronto* study. Of the ninety-two teen-agers studied, as many as forty-three (about 47 per cent) were found to be showing signs of maladjustment and this was clearly related to their experiences.

The Toronto research workers reported that the social agencies 'have encouraged the mothers' parents and relatives to provide homes for the children, and have defended this procedure on the grounds that the children would be assured of affection if left within their family group'. There was little evidence that the agencies had helped the mothers or their relatives to realize all that was involved for themselves and the children in the decision to retain custody, and too little thought was given to the question of whether the grandparents could provide a happy or normal home for the child.

'The need for caseworkers knowing more about the homes of the mothers' parents before the children were placed in them was made evident by the study . . . The records indicated, in many instances, that the relationships which existed between the mothers and their parents were unhappy, and had given the mothers little opportunity of normal development during their growing years. In spite of this, their parents, simply because they were the parents, were regarded as suitable people to provide homes for their children.'

The study showed that in some cases the presence of the babies in the home was simply one more cause for dispute between the mother and her parents, and although more than half of the children spent some period or other in the grandparents' or other relatives' home, the necessity for constant change of placement 'showed that these homes did not offer any degree of permanence'. Moreover, in only a few cases was there evidence that the families had been given any preparation for the reception of the children or any knowledge of the difficulties that they would inevitably encounter over later years.

Referring to this study Dr Bowlby writes that in a number of cases 'the mother's parents had been forced, urged or encouraged to provide homes, despite the relationship between the mother and her parents having for long been unhappy, with the result that the baby became the cause of yet further friction'.

'Naturally', he continues, 'there were cases where the arrangement of the mother or her parents looking after the baby had

[1] *Out of Wedlock*, p. 152.

worked well, but this seemed to have occurred only when the mother was stable, had good relations with her parents, and was fond of the baby and his father—not a very frequent set of circumstances.'[1]

It seems that in returning a child to the home where its mother grew up disturbed emotionally, one risks the perpetuation of a social process whereby 'one generation of deprived children provides the parents of the next generation of deprived children'.

But it would be unkind, as well as unjust, to leave this as the last word upon the grandparents' role. In personal care and in money, they often contribute more to the child than its own father may ever do, and this without a shadow of legal obligation. The desire to help their child and grandchild often leads middle-aged and elderly couples, at a time of life when they might expect to take things more easily, even when they have retired and have few financial resources for themselves, to take on the great burden of making a home for their grandchild, conceived so unexpectedly and in such unhappy circumstances.

CHILDREN LIVING WITH SOLITARY MOTHERS

Not very many mothers keep their children if they can neither return home to the grandparents nor set up a household with the child's father. The number is uncertain.

In *Manchester* in 1938 about 12 per cent of the five-year-olds were living with solitary mothers in this fashion. They are described as 'living rather precariously with mothers who were either widows or single girls living alone in receipt of Public Assistance, or were single girls living on their own earnings, the child being looked after by a landlady while mother went to work'. The Health Department was not happy about these children, whom it described as the group that gave cause for most anxiety.

'This type frequently changed her lodgings for various reasons and was difficult to trace. These children lived in insecure unsatisfactory surroundings, cared for by a variety of different people during the mother's absences, and the health visitors experienced great difficulty in maintaining an adequate supervision.'

In the *Newcastle-upon-Tyne* survey there were few women in this position. 'In only 3 cases did the mother appear to live alone at the time of delivery. Our experience ... conflicts with the common

---

[1] *Maternal Care and Mental Health*, p. 98.

WHAT HAPPENS TO THE CHILDREN?

view that unmarried mothers live alone in a single room or flat, or that they are friendless in this situation.' The survey, however, covered only sixty-seven families.

The numbers were also small in *Midboro*. At the end of five years barely 4 per cent (nine) of the women who could be traced were living on their own and had kept their children. Four of these mothers were in lodgings, two in residential domestic service, and three, who had previously been married, had homes of their own.

On the other hand, in a survey made in *Kent* at the end of 1946, of nine hundred and ninety illegitimate children of varying ages under five who were living in private households, as many as 28 per cent were living with solitary mothers—a few, but only a few, attending day nurseries.[1]

What the proportion may be elsewhere in England we do not know; but supposing it is even as low as 4 per cent, this might still represent well over 1,000 children growing up in this fashion every year or, in relation to the half million natural-born children in this country under school-leaving age, something like 20,000 children.

The number is, however, not so important. What *is* important is the acute problem these families raise. Social workers are constantly faced with the questions: Can these mothers look after their children properly? How are they to manage? Can the child hope to have a settled home? How often, after a few years, will the whole scheme break down and the mother abandon the child, leaving it with foster-parents or finally in public care?

Dr Christine Cooper describes the life of many of these children.

'The child is cared for in constantly changing circumstances, being moved about among relatives and friends, taken round to different lodgings by the mother, or put in and out of day or residential nurseries. He often has periods in the care of the local authority's Children's Department, and finally may be removed from his mother's care to an institution or foster home. Here his behaviour is usually difficult or delinquent, and this may result in further changes of care. This unfortunate fate is suffered by many illegitimate children and there is an urgent need for steps to be taken to prevent such treatment. The mother is usually vacillating in her attitude to the child, being alternately over-protective and

---

[1] Dr Anna G. Gardiner, in *Journal of the Medical Women's Federation*, reprinted by N.C.U.M.C. in a booklet entitled *Discussion of Illegitimacy*.

neglectful. He is unable to attach himself permanently to his mother or reliable substitute, and develops into the affectionless, delinquent adolescent who, as Bowlby has pointed out, only too often produces illegitimate children himself and the cycle is repeated.'[1]

She suggests in the same article that to some extent this unhappy picture is the result of the social policies discussed earlier in the previous chapter.

'In this country it is the general policy to encourage mothers to keep their illegitimate babies except in special circumstances. In most cases it is considered wise for them to remain with their babies and breast-feed them for at least six weeks, and not until after this period is it thought possible that a wise decision can be made with regard to the future care of the child. This is true in some cases, but one has only to look into the histories of countless children in residential nurseries and children's homes, to see how bad for many children are these two policies. Many mothers are over-influenced to keep their children, to whom at first they become extremely attached. Caring for a new-born baby, however, in the calm of a Mother and Baby Home is a very different thing from managing to support and provide emotional outlets single-handed for a difficult older child or adolescent. When breakdowns occur during these stages the child's early experiences may have produced such a disturbed personality that nothing can now rectify it.'

A number of unhappy stories of this kind are told in the next chapter.

Dr M. M. Methven also writes in the *Discussion of Illegitimacy*:

'The single illegitimate child who remains in the care of his mother is very liable to suffer, broadly speaking, either from over-protection or rejection. In the first case the mother values her offspring disproportionately because of a lack of alternative emotional satisfactions in her life, and in the second case the mother resents the impediment to her freedom of action and yet refuses (for neurotic reasons) to give up her right to bring up her own child . . . Often these children are moved from home to home . . . They move in most cases not to a normal home but to another makeshift—sleeping with mother but spending all their day in a nursery (often from a very early age); . . . unofficially "boarded

[1] *The Illegitimate Child.*

WHAT HAPPENS TO THE CHILDREN? 261

out" with foster-parents who accept the responsibility for a variety of reasons and who discharge it in a variety of ways . . . Even where the mother finds a satisfactory job where she can have her child with her, it is difficult for her to supply the attention of both a father and mother and often life is unnecessarily complicated by her inevitable reaction to the opinions (expressed or latent) of her relatives and friends . . . It is obvious that only an intelligent and well-balanced woman is likely to be able to cope with this situation satisfactorily, so that the child can develop normally—and while such a woman may, she is not likely to, become the mother of an illegitimate child.'

In the same discussion Dr Doris Odlum argued: 'For the few who really want to keep the baby with them the way is very hard. Both financially and socially the odds are heavily against them and only rarely do they succeed.'

What actual evidence have we as to their success or failure? Unfortunately still too little. The claim made by Dr Dorothy Taylor that among a total of 7,541 children about whom information had been furnished to the Ministry of Health, about 81 per cent had remained with their mothers, referred mainly to their infancy. Dr Fenton commented on this at the same conference:

'I am always disturbed in my own mind that one is able to keep track of these children up to the age of two or three, but after that it is very often not easy to find out what has happened.'

Without a single study of the fate or development of any group of illegitimate children in this country after the age of five, we have to depend on the general experience and impressions of individual social workers. Dr Taylor herself quoted the experience of one Medical Officer of Health to this effect—'a mother who keeps her child with her has, by the time the child is five, (*a*) returned to her parents, (*b*) married, or (*c*) had the child adopted . . . Few girls continue to accept full responsibility for the child after it has reached the age of five.'

Summarizing the *Toronto* study, Dr Bowlby writes that of the ninety-two children, 'only 25 had remained with the same family group since birth, though a further 19 had accompanied their mothers through a variety of changing circumstances. The remaining 48 (52%) had changed their mother-figures—usually two, three or more times.'

CHILDREN PLACED WITH FOSTER-PARENTS

Some mothers place their babies with foster-parents soon after birth, while they are looking around for a room to which they can take the child, and a job where they can earn enough to support it. They think of the foster-placement as a temporary plan, but the months go by, the mother still hopes to have her child home 'one day', but finds no way of doing so. The foster-placement spins itself out indefinitely, yet she will not face the thought of parting with the child permanently to adopters. Or if she never really cared for the baby or finds the foster fees too much of a strain, she calls less, finally disappears, and may be found to have deserted her child entirely, abandoning it to strangers. Or, a year or two later, she may marry and suddenly swoop down and carry away a puzzled child who has meanwhile settled very happily with its foster-parents. No one can prevent her from doing this, but it is a rare mother who can frankly recognize when she is condemning her baby to a life without roots, or is realistic enough to let the foster-parents adopt it. Even after years of neglecting the child, she may attempt in court at the last minute to prevent its legal adoption. But who is it who has a 'right'—a mother to her child or the growing child to security?

Foster-parents, who must love and yet be ready to give up the child, need to be mature, stable and understanding people—'parents' who can accept and even welcome the mother's role in the child's life, share it ungrudgingly with the mother, never criticize her in its presence, but help it to grow up with affection and understanding for her, as well as for its foster-home. It may still be hard for some children to grow up without conflicts. Sometimes they turn to their foster-parents as to a refuge from the confusion of life with their mother, or if they are taken away, try desperately to get back to the foster-home.

It is quite possible that large numbers of natural children spend some part of their childhood with foster-parents, but at any one time the number seems to be small. The Moral Welfare study found only 4 per cent (seven out of a hundred and eighty) in foster-parents' care at the end of three years. The *Midboro* follow-up found only 1.7 per cent (four out of two hundred and thirty-nine) being fostered at the end of the fifth year, while in the *Kent* study, less than 4 per cent (thirty-seven out of nine hundred and ninety) were living with foster-parents.

A description of the conditions, however, in which some are fostered—in Dr Bowlby's words, a 'very disturbing account of the hazardous and ever-changing lives of foster-children'—was given by the Medical Officer of Health for *Willesden* in 1939.

'The majority of foster-children are illegitimate. Their mothers are frequently in employment and may work up to a month before confinement. During this last month when they are not employed they must keep themselves and make some provision for the child. They are generally confined in hospital. At the end of ten days or a fortnight they are discharged. They have no money left. They have nowhere to go. They are handicapped by the child. It is important that they get work at once. What often happens seems to be that such a mother finds some woman who, perhaps out of kindness or perhaps in hope of money later on, takes the child whilst the mother is searching for work. The child may be well cared for or not, but in any case the mother probably in the circumstances does not enquire too closely. She is glad to get anybody to take her child. If she gets work and pays the woman it may be that the child stays on for a time but if the payments are small and irregular the child may be passed from one woman to another, finding no stability in life at all.'[1]

There are, of course, many other children most carefully placed in selected and approved foster-homes by Children's Departments or children's societies. That is a different matter. The tendency for the voluntary societies to board children out is increasing. The foster-parents are sometimes even relatives, who are ready to offer the child a good and loving home but have to ask for some financial help. The 'Auxiliary Boarding-Out' scheme of Dr Barnardo's and the similar scheme of the Church of England Children's Society, which enable suitable mothers to 'foster' their own children, may prove a very great benefit to the children. A young girl who takes her baby back to her parents' home and goes out to work to support it may earn very little, which often results in strains cropping up between her and her parents. Even a small foster fee can completely transform the picture: the mother regains her self-respect, the

---

[1] Annual Health Report for Borough of Willesden, 1939, quoted by Bowlby in *Maternal Care and Mental Health*, p. 96.

grandparents relax and are more tolerant towards her, and the child grows up free of strain, secure and happy among its own relatives. The society keeps tactfully in touch with the mother to watch over the child's progress. This is an imaginative scheme that may grow considerably.

CHILDREN IN THE CARE OF THE VOLUNTARY SOCIETIES

Unfortunately no one knows how many illegitimate children are in the temporary or long-term care of the large voluntary societies that run Homes for children; but the following details are available:

Dr Barnardo's Homes: An average of about 250 illegitimate children are admitted annually.

Church of England Children's Society: Has in its care, in Homes, special schools, etc., approximately 4,500 children. Of the 1,196 taken into care during 1957, 803 (about 67 per cent) were illegitimate.

National Children's Home and Orphanage: Of the 603 children received into care during 1957, 240 were illegitimate.

These societies still have to place some children in relatively large institutions, though several also create smaller homes for them if they can—houses for about sixteen children at a time, with a house-mother and perhaps a house-father, and a more intimate homelike atmosphere. In these 'cottage homes' the child can find a mother substitute, but only if the same house-mother stays on throughout the child's residence.

If the precise number of natural children in the care of these societies is not known, several surveys show the number who were in 'institutional' care of any kind at a given date, some of them with voluntary societies and others in local authority Homes. In *Midboro* about 4 per cent (ten out of two hundred and thirty-nine) were in 'institutions' at the age of five; in the Moral Welfare study as many as 11 per cent (nineteen out of a hundred and eighty) were in 'institutions' when they were about three years old, but covering as it did only women known to the Moral Welfare workers, this study included a relatively large number of younger women, and of those who had experienced difficulties, or who were not cohabiting. In the *Manchester* survey only one child out of the four hundred and twenty-seven five-year-olds traced was in an 'institution'—a tribute to the solidarity of Lancashire family life as well as to the city's case-work.

CHILDREN WHO ARE ADOPTED

Inasmuch as the natural child does not count in law as a member of either its father's or its mother's family, who have no responsibility towards it, the death of the mother can disrupt the child's life even more seriously than if it were legitimate. If the mother has not appointed a guardian, the child may be bandied about from one unwilling relative to another, or pass into the care of the Children's Department to be placed with foster-parents. Even if the mother appoints a guardian, the father is free to contest this in court and if it is held to be in the child's interest, he may be given custody, or appointed co-guardian, on the mother's death.

The child's position is legally safeguarded only if its mother or one of her family adopts it, since this gives it a real relationship in law with her relatives, who then acquire normal responsibilities towards the child; it also enables the child to inherit from its mother, in common with her legitimate children, if she should die without leaving any valid will. By the Adoption Act of 1950, an adopted child inherits on intestacy from the adopter, and is treated for this purpose as a child of the adopter and not of its natural parents; though these provisions do not apply in *Scotland*.

About every fifth illegitimate child is adopted—by someone, that is, other than its own parents. Since the difficulties facing a mother who keeps her baby are so great, the reader may wonder why the number is not larger. But the decision rests with the mothers and they choose to keep their babies. Many of the children live already with both natural parents, either in unofficial families or with parents who have married, and for these the question of parting with the child to adopters probably rarely arises.

Social workers have reacted against the extreme cruelty with which, until late in the last century, mother and child were separated, and most of those who work amongst unmarried mothers take the view that it is better and more natural for the mother and child to stay together, where they can reasonably do so. They recognize that adoption might offer more economic security, but they hesitate to sever the natural bond and, faced with the choice between advising such ruthless surgery and encouraging the mother and child to stay together, most of them would prefer to choose the gentler course.

Too little, indeed, is even known about the later effects of adoption upon children. Adoption is still very recent and the adoption societies, feeling bound to protect the privacy of adopters, refused until very recently to open their doors to research. As Mary Ellison put it, 'a large number of adopters, although grateful for the help they have received, prefer to fade out of the picture once the legal process has ended. For this reason it is impossible to collect reliable statistics of adoption success or failure.'[1] It was only within the last few years that Margaret Kornitzer was able, with their agreement, to attempt the first pioneering study, a follow-up made with the help of adoptive parents who volunteered to co-operate.[2] But until much further study has been made, and similar research work is undertaken into the later development of natural children who stay with their mothers, no one can say whether, by and large, children are happier with adoptive parents or with their mothers, or which conditions indicate or favour adoption.

Adoption may offer a child very great benefits, but one must not idealize it. Only a quarter of the adoption orders made concern adoptions arranged by societies registered for the purpose or by local authorities. There are still many 'under the counter' or 'fish queue' adoptions arranged casually by mothers who want to get rid of their babies, and many thousands made by well-meaning or irresponsible third parties who may be more interested in satisfying adoptive mothers than in the babies' welfare. Much has been done in the last few years to control and regulate adoption, but it remains a most difficult task, with a great many loopholes: the courts and Children's Departments can usually combine to prevent unsuitable adoption orders from being made, but they cannot prevent bad placements from being made by a mother initially, and until 1959 they are often unable to remove a child from a home considered unsuitable, even if the order were refused. The societies registered for adoption also work under difficulties: they are not allowed to make any charge at all for their services, so some are

---

[1] Mary Ellison, *The Adopted Child*, p. 79 (1958).
[2] See *Research Project* by Margaret Kornitzer, published in the report of the Residential Conference of Societies Registered for Adoption, July 1955. Miss Kornitzer has also written a more comprehensive book, *Child Adoption in the Modern World* (Putnam, 1952).

still hampered by lack of funds and have sometimes to make use of relatively inexperienced helpers.

As for the mothers' reaction at handing over their children even to a registered adoption society, some are still disconcerted by the rule of most societies—though it may be a wise provision—that the mother and adoptive parents should not meet one another. Some mothers who love their children, but doubt whether they should keep them, not unnaturally hesitate to send their babies off like parcels into the unknown, fearing that the child might be unloved or unhappy.

There is no doubt, of course, that in a great many cases the adoption of an illegitimate baby offers it security, love and the welcome of a warm, wide, family circle—benefits that it might never experience in other circumstances. But one must not be blind to the fact that no one can be *sure* that it will do this. Adoption is an art that our society is only beginning to learn. No one can yet speak with confidence about how it is working, or how it compares, say, with a reasonably loving unmarried mother keeping her baby, until very much further research has been undertaken.

These are some of the difficulties. Another is the possessive but irresponsible parent. The law in the past regarded children somewhat as chattels belonging to their parents and at their free disposal, and to some extent still does so. A mother may mishandle or neglect her child for years, leaving it with foster-parents and never visiting it, or moving it from one temporary home to another, yet if it comes to a question of adoption she may refuse to give her consent. A provision was included in the Adoption Act, 1950, that her consent might be waived if she withheld it 'unreasonably', but courts were chary of overruling a mother's wishes. Parental 'rights' tended to dominate over parental duties. There are painfully vivid stories of mothers who stood irresponsibly in the way of adoption.[1] The Adoption Act, 1958, by providing explicitly that a court may dispense with a mother's consent if she has abandoned, neglected or persistently ill-treated the child, or cannot be found or is incapable of giving consent or is withholding her consent unreasonably, now gives the courts a chance of meeting this problem.

Since the difficulties an unmarried mother must face if she keeps her baby, the unsettled life that the child may have and the difficult emotional problems, above all the lack of certainty that the out-

[1] *The Adopted Child*, pp. 74-7.

come will be happy, have been constantly stressed, it is only fair to say also that some adopted children—and no one knows how many—at present face similar difficulties. Possibly adoption could ensure a happy future for more babies than at present, but it remains for adopters or adoption societies to prove this by encouraging detailed studies of the outcome of adoptions; and if other workers believe that a baby is happier with its mother, they too should establish this through detailed studies.

Few decisions ever face a mother that are harder than this one: is it her duty to keep or to part with her child? For her the decision is painful; for the child it may be crucial. When an unmarried woman finds that she is expecting a baby, there may be nothing to guide her at first but her own panic. 'Most unmarried mothers,' an experienced worker has commented, 'start by having a panic wish to have the child adopted.' A check has been made in one Mother and Baby Home; at least 90 per cent of the mothers at first wanted their babies adopted, but after the babies were born, two-thirds of the mothers changed their minds.

In the end, about one mother in five parts with her baby to adopters. In 1950, for example, some 35,000 illegitimate children were born; in 1957, about 34,500. In each of these years more than 10,000 natural children were adopted; they account for about 80 per cent of all adoption orders. About 3,000 of these natural children remain with their own parents: adopted by their mother or father, or both of them together, but more often by the mother and another man she has since married. About 7,000 a year are adopted by strangers, friends, or other relatives. In relation to the numbers born that represents 20 per cent of all natural children, though the real proportion may be slightly lower, since children are adopted at various ages and a few years ago the number born was higher.

About two-thirds of these adoption orders (65 per cent in 1950) are granted to strangers to the child or to persons unrelated within the meaning of the Adoption Act. Of this group of adoptions, a quarter are completed before the children are six months old, more than half before they are nine months old, and a majority—two-thirds—before they are a year old.[1] Since the child must be in the continuous care of the adoptive parents for at least three months before an adoption order is granted, this means that at

[1] See Table 15.

least a quarter and probably more of them were in their new homes before they were three months old, and probably well over half before the age of six months. This does not fulfil Dr Bowlby's ideal that the child should be placed for adoption 'soon after birth', that 'the first two months should become the rule',[1] that it should be, as Miss Kornitzer says, 'as early as possible in life',[2] for well over 2,000 natural children a year are adopted by families unrelated to them at ages above a year old; some seven hundred are five years old or more, and certainly many of these were not placed in infancy.

The N.C.U.M.C. and the Church of England Moral Welfare Council, however, hold that it is better that no decision—and therefore, as far as possible, no placement—should be made before a child is at least six weeks old, in case the mother should come to regret too hasty a decision. They hold that, on balance, far more harm is being done at present by hasty and reckless placements, or by unscrupulous or thoughtless people separating mother and child before the mother is even in a proper state of health to make a wise decision, than by these later placements. To place a child with foster-parents at birth with a view to adoption is, in their view, contrary to the spirit of the Adoption Act, which lays down that consent to adoption may not be given until a baby is six weeks old. Many unmarried mothers are too unhappy and disturbed during pregnancy for their maternal feelings to awake until after the birth, but when they see and feed the child they may begin to realize how deeply they could care for it. Moral Welfare workers point out that a mother who has parted with her baby hurriedly or even from necessity may even grieve so much afterwards that she has a second illegitimate baby. One young mother, for instance, whose parents refused to let her bring the child home, parted with it to adopters, but two years later came back to the worker with a second child, declaring that she would never have had it if the first had not been adopted. Such cases are said—we have no evidence on this point—to occur not infrequently, and even if some of these mothers are really deeply disturbed women impelled by unconscious motives to repeat a pattern, it is clearly important in general for a mother to feel that she has reached a decision of such importance

---

[1] *Maternal Care and Mental Health*, pp. 101 and 103.
[2] *Child Adoption in the Modern World*, p. 30.

without external pressure, freely, realistically and responsibly. For this, time may be necessary.

On this question of time, however, Dr Bowlby and some *Scandinavian* social workers incline to disagree with the commonly held English opinion. Dr Bowlby affirms that 'if the mother has sought care reasonably early it should be possible for the experienced case-worker to help her reach a realistic decision either before the baby is born or soon after, since most of the factors which matter (e.g. stability of personality, realism towards the problem and attitude towards the putative father) will be evident in her life before the birth of the baby. If all of these are adverse the baby's birth will not change them, and the likelihood is small of the mother making a success of looking after the child.'[1] A number of social workers, in *Scandinavia* particularly, consider that it is cruel to ask a mother to see and breast-feed a baby and then to part with it; many unmarried mothers feel the same. It also raises the issue as to how far a grieving mother in a state of emotional upset really benefits a baby, even in the first weeks. Certainly once a mother has fed her baby the scales begin to be weighted against her parting with it.

About 5 per cent of adopted natural children are taken into the care of relatives—grandparents, uncles, aunts. The child may have lived with them for years before any application for an adoption order is made, but when it begins to attend school or the mother leaves home to marry another man, adoption is sometimes recognized as an advantage: the child gains a clean birth certificate, the same surname as other members of the family and the full financial security of a child of the family. Six out of ten of such children are adopted before the age of five, though less than a quarter before they are a year old. Something like five hundred adoptions of this kind take place every year, and it would be of interest to know the stories that lie behind them: whether the grandparents are simply regularizing a long-standing position, or if some of these children have been deserted by their mothers after an attempt to keep them.

Turning to the cases where a mother adopts her own child, it is interesting to see that the number of single women who do so is still very small—fifty-nine in 1950, eighty-six in 1957—in spite of the fact that it is quite commonly advised by social workers.

---

[1] *Maternal Care and Mental Health*, p. 102.

A Roman Catholic mother, who was unmarried, explained her reluctance to adopt her own son on the grounds that 'it would feel unnatural, like rejecting him'. But possibly a more usual reason is that the women do not appreciate the advantages of a legal fiction—this one is not without awkwardness—and find that for most purposes the shortened form of birth certificate meets their needs. Some women, however, do change their names by deed poll, pose as widows and adopt their babies.

Before the passing of the Legitimacy Act, 1959, when the parents married after the child's birth, they sometimes adopted it jointly, but not many did so: in 1950 one hundred and seventeen; in 1957 one hundred and ten. The majority of these occurred around the time when the child entered school and required a birth certificate. The number remained small, despite the fact that if there was an obstacle to the parents' marriage at its birth, it could never be legitimated and might well come to need the legal protection that adoption gave it. The 1959 Act rendered this step, in the ordinary case, unnecessary.

The natural father plays a very small part in adoptions: in 1950, besides the joint adoptions mentioned above, there were twenty-five cases of the putative father adopting his child by himself, and about forty cases of his doing so jointly with the woman to whom he was married when the child was born. This represents less than 2 per cent of the adoptions of illegitimate children; and about six out of every thousand natural fathers.

It is the mother who later marries another man who is most anxious to adopt her child. She is afraid that her illegitimate child may be at a disadvantage compared with the children of the marriage, and hopes that her husband, by joining in the adoption, will accept it as a full member of the family. There are about three thousand adoptions of this kind every year, and in nine cases out of ten the child is already three years of age or over.

What is it in practice that decides a mother to keep her child or part with it? In the view of the Medical Officer of Health for *Midboro*, the attitude of the maternal grandparents is often decisive. In the follow-up survey there were forty-six cases in which children were placed for adoption or lived with foster-parents or in an institution. Nineteen of these mothers parted with their children because they were unable to provide a home; five because they did not wish to cause suffering to their families; four because they could not afford to keep the child. On the other hand there were twelve women who clearly had no interest in their babies, three who had married since the child's birth and found that their husbands did not want the child in their homes, and two—not a large number, but worth noting—who felt that adoption was in the child's best interest.

There is no doubt that some unmarried mothers part with their children *because* they love them: they want the child to have a normal, secure and happy family life, with two parents. The letter of one girl of twenty is characteristic:

'The heart-breaking part of it all is parting with my small daughter, but I am putting her happiness and welfare before my own. I am sure it would be selfish to keep her, and so I am trying to make myself think of our parting as part of the price I must pay for having been so stupid.'

Some of those who part with their babies are, of course, quite young girls. A mother aged fourteen or fifteen may sometimes, with her parents' help, keep her own baby and bring it up, but not very often. Even is she is in her teens, her own lack of earning power or her parents' persistence may persuade her to part with it: they may hope that she will forget the whole interlude, or they may be too poor to help her, or fear scandal. A girl of fifteen had a baby by a sixteen-year-old boy. The case-worker described the parents as 'very nice children'. They were deeply in love but clearly too young to marry, so the baby was adopted and the girl returned to her parents.

A disturbing point emerged from the *Midboro* survey. When the teen-agers had a relatively normal home, the baby was commonly adopted. But twelve had either lost their parents or had no stable home because their parents were separated. Most of these girls, one might have supposed, would find it almost impossible to give their baby a normal upbringing. But only three parted with them: the other nine clung to their babies, possibly sometimes feeling, as one mother expressed it, that it was the only thing that 'belonged to her' in an empty, friendless world. A Children's Department may do its best to dissuade such a girl from trying to keep her baby, but prove unsuccessful. Of the sixteen-year-old girl mentioned on page 116, the social worker reported:

'I would never have tried to persuade her to keep her baby and the authorities advised us on no account to let her get fond of it, since it ought to be adopted at the first possible moment. But she never even considered parting with it.'

COLOURED CHILDREN

The tacit policy of the N.C.U.M.C. and the Church of England Moral Welfare Council seems to be that the less the children of coloured fathers are treated as a special group, the less they will become one. Even during the war the numbers were not very large, running into only a few hundreds; but they create a special problem, for it is often very difficult to find anyone who will adopt a coloured child.[1] If they do not remain with their mothers, these children tend to become the spoilt darlings of residential nurseries. If one goes into any Home for unmarried mothers or any institution for children, one is liable to be greeted by the radiant smile of a thoroughly happy, dark-skinned baby whose future is very uncertain.

Recently the large number of immigrants from the *West Indies* has complicated the problem. In the Caribbeans it is the usual thing for children to be born to unmarried couples. If a woman from those islands bears an illegitimate child in Great Britain, she often does so with no sense of guilt, her problems being chiefly practical ones: to find lodgings or money or somewhere to go to have the baby. These mothers generally love and manage to keep their children.

CHILDREN OF MENTALLY DEFECTIVE MOTHERS

A far more difficult problem is posed by illegitimate children born to mentally defective mothers. The number of such births is rather smaller than is generally imagined (see MENTAL LEVEL, p. 62). In London, between 1951 and 1953, of the 10,500 mothers of illegitimate children, only thirty-five (0.3 per cent) were mentally defective. But since it has been estimated that there are in the care of local authorities all over the country three or four thousand of these children,[2] it is an obviously urgent question what pro-

---

[1] Though when the *Scottish Daily Express* ran an article in June 1957 on the difficulty of finding an adoptive home for one two-year-old coloured child, the response was overwhelming; within a week there were one hundred and fifty applications from adopters.

[2] County of Devon Children's Committee, *The Illegitimate Children of Mental Defectives*, 1953.

portion may be expected to be defective or retarded themselves, and how they should be brought up.

The old supposition was that a mental defective's child ran a high risk of inheriting the defect. Early studies pointed to groups of children with defective parents of whom 40, 60 or even 70 per cent were growing up to be seriously retarded or defective themselves.[1] But in these early studies intelligence tests on both parents and children were rarely used, the meaning of 'mental defect' was not always defined, and it seems likely that some of the early research workers failed to distinguish between the effects of inheritance and environment. Many defective children in the past grew up either in old-fashioned institutions or with families incapable of giving them a normal upbringing and who were given little help. It is known now how easily a child starved of the right stimulus, or of proper care and affection, may grow up to be mentally retarded. The results of modern research, and of more understanding care, have thus led to an entirely different view.

The new approach is expressed in an important study made in 1957 by the clinical psychologist of the Fountain Hospital at *Tooting*.[2] In a survey of one hundred and fifty children born to seventy-three women who had been certified as feeble-minded, only four of the children were found to be educationally subnormal, and it was suggested that even those might be functioning at a low level because of adverse upbringing. The children's average I.Q. was 91.3. Those of them who had been brought up by their own mothers, discharged mental defectives, did not seem to be unduly depressed in intelligence, as *their* average score was 98.7.

Professor Penrose, the greatest living authority on the subject, has gone so far as to state:

'Personally I do not believe that there is any truth in the idea that deterioration of the population will occur if high-grade defectives are allowed to breed naturally.

'However, judged from the point of view of the child, the conditions of health and nutrition depend upon the mother a great deal and I think that each case must be judged upon its merits as a medical rather than an eugenic problem.'[3]

---

[1] Some are quoted in the report of the Departmental Committee on Sterilization (H.M.S.O., 1934).
[2] M. W. G. Brandon, *The Intellectual and Social Status of Children of Mental Defectives* (*Journal of Mental Science*, October 1957).
[3] Quoted by Brandon in his article.

This, of course, has implications of the highest importance. If the fears still so strongly held by many social workers and members of the public that a defective's child is likely to 'inherit' the defect are unfounded, then there is no reason why the fostering or adoption of a defective's child should be delayed until the child's normality has been established. It can be settled early into its final home, with immense gain to the child.

At present, however, this point of view is unfamiliar, and further research will probably have to be done before it finds acceptance among those who are primarily responsible for the children. The second and more immediate question is how the children should be brought up. There are several schools of thought. The children are usually born to high-grade mental defectives who are living in the community either on licence or as unnotified defectives. Some local authorities will certify women of sub-normal intelligence if they become pregnant, even if until their pregnancy they had been living at home and working: it is convenient administratively, since it enables the local authority to segregate them. The children are then normally parted from their mothers and brought up in institutions, though the mothers themselves may later return to normal life and sometimes even have further children.

Unfortunately a child deprived of affection in this way may *become* mentally backward. It has been suggested that if suitable hostels were provided where selected mothers could keep their children with them—under supervision and with highly skilled help from women trained in the care of children—some of these children would experience a love and family life that is otherwise denied to them. A defective mother can sometimes be very good to a young child and deeply devoted to it: at that age it does not pose her complicated intellectual problems! Some may lose their affection for the baby once it has left the dependent stage of infancy, but even a year or so of affection may be better for a child than none, and there may be responsible relatives ready to help. Even an experimental hostel of this kind, skilfully run, might lead to deeper knowledge of how to help these families.

Alternatively, the child may be placed with a loving foster-parent and, if this works out happily, may sometimes later be adopted into the family. In the *Devon* survey it was shown that as many as 60 per cent of West of England children were successfully boarded out, a few of the best adjusted had been adopted, but less than one in four was seen regularly by its mother, and less than one in ten had any substantial hope of going home to her.

That defectives' children can often be adopted with success and prove of normal intelligence has been established. The *Iowa* Child Welfare Research Station published in 1948 a study of two groups of adopted children whose mothers were mentally retarded.[1] The conclusion of this research was that 'children of mothers with low intelligence or from fathers with low occupational status or from a combination of both, placed in adoptive homes in infancy, attain a mental level which equals or exceeds that of the population as a whole' and that 'the frequency with which cases showing mental retardation appear is no greater than might be expected from a random sampling of the population as a whole'. One group of eighty-seven children, mostly illegitimate, whose mothers had I.Q.s of 75 or less, were placed in an orphanage before they were six months old and with adoptive parents before they were two years of age. Their mean I.Q. at about the age of five was 105.5. Fifteen of them ranked above 120, and only four below 80. A group of thirty-one adopted children who might have been suspected of a 'poor intellectual inheritance' on both sides of the family, since the mothers were intellectually retarded and the fathers unskilled or relatively unskilled labourers, scored at the same age a mean I.Q. of 104.

It seems, then, that much re-thinking is necessary on this whole subject. The old genetic fears may be ill-founded. Early fostering or adoption may be safer than is still generally supposed. Some mothers and children might be happier kept together. The chance of the children growing up normal and happy, given a suitable environment or the right skilled help by case-workers in the early stages, is far higher than has been imagined. This does not mean that the problem is not one to which much thought and skill and loving care must always be devoted, but at last, in this generation, there seem to be grounds for hope.

---

[1] Harold M. Skeels and Irene Harms, *Children with Inferior Social Histories, Their Mental Development in Adoptive Homes* (*Journal of Genetic Psychology*, 1948).

CHAPTER 12

CHILDREN IN PUBLIC CARE

A GENERAL SURVEY

A large number of natural children spend some part of their childhood in public care as 'children deprived of normal home life'. They come into care for a variety of reasons. There are those whose deprivation is only temporary: the mother may be in hospital or in prison or have been evicted from her lodgings. The 'long-stay' cases—those remaining in care for six months or longer and sometimes up to the age of eighteen—fall into three main groups:

1. Those who have no homes because their parents have died or deserted them or are destitute or incapacitated. They are taken into the care of the local authority (the Children's Department) under Section 1 of the Children Act, 1948 and, if later the Department resolves to assume full parental responsibility, under Section 2.

2. Those who are removed from their homes either because of their own misbehaviour or because their home conditions so seriously endanger their moral and physical development that it would not be right for them to remain in them. They are committed by the juvenile court to the care of the local authority (the Children's Department), the first under 'fit person' orders: offenders; the second under 'fit person' orders: non-offenders.

3. Those who have some mental or physical handicap of their own that calls for institutional care. They are the primary responsibility of the Health Department and are generally supervised by that Department or the Education Department, or maintained by Regional Hospital Boards. If they are received into the care of the Children's Department, it is for a reason other than their handicap.

'Short-stay' cases form only a small proportion of the children in care, though the aggregate number who have passed in and out of care in that way may be large. Of all the children in care in 1950, only 6 per cent were short-stay cases. In *Liverpool* in April 1955 there were three hundred and ninety natural children in long-term care to only ten short-stay cases; in *Birmingham* in November 1954 there were five hundred and thirty-eight children in 'medium or long-term' care to nine short-stay; and in *London* in November 1953, 2,948 long-term to one hundred and forty-four short-stay. Nor is the proportion of natural children among those entering short-term care higher than among those in long-term: in *Devon* in 1953 it was 40 per cent in both cases, and in *London* at November of that year they formed 36 per cent of the long-stay cases and 30 per cent of the short-stay.

At that time—the end of November 1953—there were in all 65,309 children in the care of Children's Departments in England and Wales, including 19,059 affected by 'fit person' orders. They were either boarded out, placed in local authority Children's Homes, residential nurseries, etc., or accommodated in voluntary Homes at public expense. In 1959 the number was 61,580. These totals did not include those in the care of Health Departments, in approved schools or living in voluntary Homes or boarded out by the societies.

Many of those in the care of the Children's Departments were legitimate, and the proportion of natural children among them is unknown. However, the table on page 280 may give us a hint. A group of counties and boroughs contribute their figures to it, and though they show wide variations, the average proportion of natural children among those in care is about 33 per cent. This, on a nation-wide basis, would mean that around 20,000 natural children were in care at the end of 1953. This figure is a rough estimate and must be taken as that in building up this picture of the children in care, for though the table includes figures from cities and agricultural counties with a wide range of size and of illegitimacy rates, it is not fully representative.

A great burden of expense falls on the local authorities through these illegitimate children needing care, and a great expenditure of time, trouble, understanding, and willingness to take on the problems of distressed or difficult people. (It should always be remembered with gratitude for how long some of these burdens lay on the pioneers in this field of service, such as Dr Barnardo's and the Church of England Children's Society, and how much they still carry). In financial terms alone it costs about £5 million a year to maintain 20,000 children in care, this being a third of the total annual cost to the ratepayers of running the Children's Departments in this country, which rose from about £14 million in the year 1953-4 to an estimated cost of over £15 million in the year 1956-7. To board one child out in 1953 cost the Children's Departments an average of £1 8s. 10d. a week; to maintain one in a local authority Home, anything from £3 2s. to £9 13s. 1d.—an average of £5 5s. 1d. a week. For 1956-7 the estimated cost of boarding a child out was £1 12s. 10½d. a week, and the estimated cost of maintaining a child in a local authority Home was £6 13s. 8d. apart from administrative charges.

Much of this expenditure is inevitable. There will always be illegitimate children, and always among them some who will need costly public help—for instance the imbecile child and the greatly disturbed older child. But how far the cost could be cut down by changes of policy—changes that on their own merits have much to commend them in question of adoption and of help to mothers in their own homes—deserves consideration.

A great deal of suffering falls on these illegitimate children who have no home, or whose homes break up or fail them. To be deserted, or to have one's mother disappear through death or insanity or imprisonment, may be agony to a child who has no other stable background. Some, who have natural strength of character and who are fortunate in those who befriend them and in the age at which this break-up happens to them, recover their balance; some do not.

These 20,000 or so children in care are not the only children who are temporarily or permanently away from their mothers. There are many thousands who are either handicapped children supervised by Health Departments, children certified as defectives living in institutions maintained by Regional Hospital Boards, or living in approved schools, or placed out in their own Homes or foster-homes by societies such as Dr Barnardo's and the various church societies—only a proportion of whom have been placed in their care by the Children's Departments. Many of these children have not wholly lost touch with their mothers, though they spend much of their childhood parted from them.

Our rough figure of 20,000, then, represents much personal suffering and a great national burden—and yet, surprisingly, the proportion of all illegitimate children who are in the care of the Children's Department is not large, possibly only about 3 per cent;

NATURAL CHILDREN IN PUBLIC CARE

	Number of natural children in care at 30.11.1953[1]	Total number of children in care at 30.11.1953[1]	% of children in care at 30.11.1953[1] who were illegitimate	Illegitimate % of live births, 1953	Total number of children per 1,000 under age of 18 in care at 30.11.1953
	(1)	(2)	(3)	(4)	(5)
ADMINISTRATIVE COUNTIES					
Cardiganshire	35	121	29.0	3.3	9.5
Carmarthenshire	71	220	32.3	3.3	5.3
Glamorganshire	157	1033	15.2	3.0	5.1
Gloucestershire	192	533	37.8	5.5	4.4
Soke of Peterborough	22	74	30.0	6.2	4.5
Radnorshire	17	42	40.0	3.5	7.9
Somerset	225	647	34.8	3.7	5.2
Wiltshire	225	614	36.6	5.3	6.0
BOROUGHS					
Bath	34	134	25.3	4.1	7.3
Birmingham[2]	538	1338	40.0	5.6	4.8
Blackpool	43	138	31.0	8.3	4.9

Brighton[3]	85	266	32.0	8.0	7.8
Leeds[4]	243	691	34.0	6.7	5.5
Leicester	163	513	31.8	5.7	6.9
Liverpool[5]	400	1624	24.6	5.4	7.4
London	3092	8719	36.0	4.8[6]	13.0
Merthyr Tydfil	26	103	25.2	3.4	6.5
Newport, Mon.	45	190	23.7	4.7	6.7
Nottingham[4]	132	562	23.5	7.2	7.2
Oxford	89	205	43.4	7.8	8.2
Swansea	53	238	23.0	3.9	5.8
TOTAL	5887	18005	Average 32.7	5.2	Average 6.7
England and Wales		65309		4.7	6.2

[1] But see footnotes 2–6.
[2] Columns 1–3 show the position at 30.11.1956.
[3] Columns 1–3 show the position in May 1956.
[4] Columns 1–3 show the position at 31.3.1955.
[5] Columns 1–3 show the position at 21.4.1955.
[6] Average for 1936–53, the years in which these children were born.

for 20,000 is only 3.3 per cent of the 600,000 or so illegitimate children who were born in the preceding eighteen years and were still alive at the end of 1953.[1] This is partly because so many natural children grow up in far more normal home surroundings than one is apt to recollect—many with adoptive parents, many more with a mother and father who are cohabiting stably without marriage, and some with parents who have since married one another. Few of these children are seriously at risk.

However, the risk of becoming a deprived child is very much greater for the natural child than for the legitimate. Of every thousand children under the age of eighteen at the end of 1953, six were in care.[2] Of these six, four on our reckoning may have been legitimate and two illegitimate; but of every thousand in that age group, sixty were born illegitimate, so two out of that illegitimate sixty (3.3 per cent) were in care, but only four out of the nine hundred and forty legitimate children—or 0.5 per cent. Thus, if our figure of 20,000 was roughly accurate, the risk of becoming a 'deprived child', and thus of passing into the care of the Children's Departments, was six or seven times as great for a natural as for a legitimate child.

But this is only a portrait of the cumulative total in public care at a given date, the end of 1953, and it may well give a false impression of the proportion of natural children still entering care. The years 1936 to 1953 from which those children were drawn cover the difficult war years in which many were illegitimately born who could never hope for a normal family life—some of the children fathered by coloured and Dominions servicemen or by foreigners; conceived by girls who had little or no further contact with the child's father because he went overseas or died. It also includes an unhappy legacy from the old days before the Children's Departments came into being (1947), and before the Curtis report (1945), Dr Bowlby's *Maternal Care and Mental Health* (1952) and other studies had made people as aware as they are today of children's need for stable relationships: when to separate a child from his

---

[1] 668,209 illegitimate children were born alive in the eighteen years 1936 to 1953 inclusive; something over 40,000 of these died before the age of one and some further probably smaller number must have died between the ages of one and eighteen.

[2] In 1954 the proportion in England and Wales was 5.5 per cent, though in London it was as high as 11.5 per cent and in Bournemouth and Hastings 9.5 per cent and 9.2 per cent respectively.

family or known friends and put him in an institution might still have been considered by some officials the only practical way of solving a child's troubles.

It is therefore relevant to ask whether the picture has since changed. Some of the cities contributing figures to the table on page 280 have gone out of their way to point out that such a change has in fact taken place. In *Birmingham* the proportion of children in care at the end of 1953 who were illegitimate was 40 per cent, but among the 1954 admissions, only 25 per cent. In *Leicester* natural children formed 32 per cent of the total number in care at the end of 1953, but in the year 1st April 1954 to 31st March 1955 the Children's Department admitted only 22 per cent. In *Nottingham* the parallel figures for those in care were 23.5 per cent at 31st March 1955, but only 14.5 per cent of the admissions in the twelve preceding months. It is now, of course, the policy of all Children's Departments and the effective practice of the best of them to do everything possible to avoid the unnecessary break-up of family life. So far as natural children are concerned, this is becoming easier because a single woman can now earn much better wages, and because the help given to an unmarried mother over the birth and in resettlement afterwards has become far more effective. The increase since the war in the proportion of natural children who are adopted may also have eased the local authorities' burden.

Even if the proportion is falling, it remains high. This is not, of course, an experience unique to Britain. As Dr Pinchbeck has pointed out, although reliable statistics are hard to come by, 'in Finland, of the children taken into care in 1946, either as delinquent or deprived children, 46.9% were illegitimate; in Sweden a quarter of all children taken into care in 1950 were illegitimate'.[1] *Sweden's* figure is almost exactly the same as the one *Birmingham* and *Leicester* have quoted for 1954, and *Finland's* wartime experience under occupation was far more difficult than our own, and left a greater legacy of unwanted children.

Perhaps some people reading the term 'in care' may picture these children living an institutional life or at best in that once 'modern' substitute for the large institution, the 'cottage home' such as Dr Barnardo's, for example, did so much to develop. Many children, though fewer each year, do still live an institutional life, though the tendency is now for these children to be placed in smaller and

[1] *Social Attitudes to the Problem of Illegitimacy* (1954).

more nearly homelike institutions where their emotional as well as their physical needs can be met, so far as the present shortage of capital and of suitable staff allows; and increasingly those living in institutions are the ones who, owing to some physical or mental handicap, do genuinely require institutional care or who, owing to emotional maladjustment, cannot fit into a foster-home. The large institution, however well run, can rarely give a child the continuity of mothering it needs, and the modern movement is all away from institutional life and towards the creation of an environment for the child as near as possible to that of a real home—placing the child with good foster-parents, sometimes its own relatives. If the mother cannot keep the child, the hope is often that this foster-home will develop in time into a *de facto* and finally into a legal adoption. Of *all* children in the care of local authorities in England and Wales in 1952-3, under 45 per cent were in local authority Homes, and 12 per cent in voluntary Homes. The proportion of those boarded out with private families has steadily risen: 35 per cent in 1949, 42 per cent in 1953 and 47 per cent in 1959.

REASONS WHY CHILDREN COME INTO CARE

After this general survey we can come to the individual child. What are the actual crises and what the underlying reasons that bring any natural child into public care? In this country illegitimate children are not received automatically into public care, or, for reason of the illegitimate birth alone, made subject to official guardianship, as they are in, for example, *Western Germany, Austria, Sweden, Denmark, Finland, Minnesota* and *Switzerland*. There must be some real reason other than the child's illegitimacy, some real proof of actual and acute deprivation, before the Children's Department is free to take action. One should look therefore for the immediate precipitating cause that led the Children's Department, or those with whom the child was living, to take action, and usually also for some deeper underlying difficulty or difficulties, that led to the breakdown.

Since they form the hard core of the problem, we shall consider here chiefly the illegitimate children who enter long-term care, and two groups in especial: those who were in care of the *London* County Council Children's Department in November 1953 and those who entered the care of the County of *Devon* Children's

Committee in 1951 and 1952—two authorities with a deservedly high reputation for their handling of children's problems.

As a 'normal' background to our more specialized study, it may be useful to discover first what reasons bring any children, whether legitimate or illegitimate, into care. In analysing the reasons that brought two groups of children into long-term public care, David Donnison comments:

'It is remarkable how small a part is played by disease and accident in the break-up of these families; where they occurred there were usually many signs that the children had already been neglected for other reasons. Bad health was seldom the chief reason for the break-up; but it was often a secondary factor. It looks as if the ordinary family, with the help of its relatives and neighbours, usually survives such disasters. The family with fewer ties of affection and fewer friends to support it does not.'[1]

In this sentence David Donnison has possibly placed his finger on the chief reason why so many illegitimate children are in care. Unless adopted early in life, the child of an unmarried mother who is not cohabiting stably and who has not married after the child's birth often lacks just that circle of affectionate and responsible relatives and friends that surround the luckier legitimate child. He has only half as many relatives—his mother's family—and these grandparents and aunts are often less willing to help just because of the social stigma attaching to his illegitimacy; they have, in any case, no legal obligation towards him. And if his mother's family has rejected her, she has almost certainly left home and so is away from the home-based circle of friends who might have helped her.

A second reason why so many natural children need care is that so many (perhaps 10 per cent) are born into problem families. Their birth is just one more sign of the families' failure to cope with life. Poverty, bad health and housing, low-grade mentality, emotional instability, social irresponsibility, the feeling of failure, the sense of being looked down on by neighbours—all these things interact and set up a vicious circle.

Does the large number of natural children in care perhaps need no further explanation? That question remains to be examined in the following pages.

The Children's Department of *London* County Council has analysed the immediate precipitating reasons that led to 3,092

[1] David Donnison, *The Neglected Child and the Social Services* (1954).

natural children being in their care at 30th November 1953. The ages of these children were:

	%
Below school age	31.5
Aged about 5 to 9	29.5
Aged about 10 to 14	26.1
Aged about 15 and over	12.9
TOTAL	100.0

The immediate precipitating reasons why they were received into care are given as follows:

WHY IN CARE	NUMBER OF CHILDREN
Abandoned, deserted or lost	801
Long-term infirmity of parent or guardian	448
Homeless (not evicted)	381
'Fit person' orders: non-offenders	378
No parent or guardian	152
Temporary illness of parent or guardian (not confinement)	97
Separation of cohabiting parents	81
'Fit person' orders: offenders	70
Homeless (evicted from National Assistance accommodation)	54
Homeless (evicted)	41
Confinement of mother or guardian	39
Separation of married parents	25
Licensed from approved schools and in care	6
Other reasons	519
TOTAL	3092

The number in the category of 'abandoned, deserted or lost' is exceedingly high. This includes, however, children whose mothers placed them with foster-parents but after a time ceased to keep up their payments; the foster-parents therefore applied to the local authority for help. If it is clear that the mother has, say, deserted the child, the Children's Department may receive it into care but continue to board it with the same foster-parents, paying them a foster fee. The child may therefore remain in the same foster-home unaware that it is 'in care' and little affected by it. This use by the Children's Departments of their powers is important and is further discussed below.

It should also be noted that those removed from their homes

as beyond parental control ('Fit person' orders: offenders) were very much smaller in number than those received into care because of detrimental home conditions ('Fit person' orders: non-offenders).

London's experience cannot, however, be assumed to be typical. The number of natural children in care there is out of all proportion to the number of London-born natural children. To London come unmarried mothers from all over Great Britain and from *Northern Ireland* and *Eire*, seeking the anonymity of a great city. Here many of the children of mixed parentage are born. Some girls come to London in their pregnancy. Others include those restless, adventure-seeking young women, unsatisfied or unhappy in their own homes, who, finding themselves adrift in a large city away from their friends and families, crave affection and excitement and soon become pregnant. Probably an even larger number come to London looking for work or help with an illegitimate child, or a mixed family, already on their hands. London's social services have to carry not only London's own serious social problems but also many more wished on them by a large and feckless floating population.

A smaller but more intimate picture of natural children in care is given by the study of the illegitimate children who entered the care of the County of *Devon* Children's Committee during 1951 and 1952—sixty-one children from forty-eight families. To enable this study to be made, the Children's Officer, Mr Kenneth Brill, kindly co-opted the present writer temporarily on to his staff, giving her access to the files. Sometimes these could be discussed with the staff to fill in the picture of the child's background, but the writer had not the advantage of knowing the families personally, nor were the social workers who knew them best always available. The study therefore remains to that extent a superficial one, pointing to the need for deeper studies from within Children's Departments themselves.

In this authority the illegitimacy rate was about average—4.9 per cent in 1952—and the number of children under the age of eighteen in public care again about average—5.7 in 1,000 (1953). But it is a rural area, chiefly agricultural, where a considerable goodwill evidently can be and most certainly is tapped in the neighbourhood in seeking happy foster-homes where the children can be placed. In seeking solutions to the children's problems this Department has an ingenuity and determination that amounts almost to genius and so this study can indeed be said to be one of that 'hard core' of illegitimacy that most stubbornly resists solution.

The following table sets out the main precipitating reasons for the children being received into care, and the ages at which this occurred.

Only forty-eight families are represented because quite often several children from one family entered care. The ten neglected children, for instance, came from only four homes, and the eight evicted mothers came from four families who had between them twenty-three children, some of them legitimate.

It is striking that of the children who came into care, very few were only children—only fourteen out of sixty-one. Eight of these had mentally defective mothers, one mother was insane, two were dead, and three of the children had been born to girls of fourteen or fifteen—so young that they could not have been expected to care for a child. No child who came into care was the only child of a mentally normal girl of sixteen or over.

All of the children belonged to families of two to seven children, and half to families of four or more. This too fits into the general pattern of problem families, which tend to be families of over the average size. The more children one has, the harder it is to cope successfully.

Only five of the forty-eight mothers had been recently cohabiting with anyone when the child came into care, and in none of these cases was any breakdown of the cohabitation responsible for the child's difficulties, which arose directly from the parents' character: their extremely low mental or moral level. Three of the children had a mother who cohabited with various men and persistently neglected the children; one had a promiscuous mother of low mentality who had already been in prison with one of her lovers for neglecting her other children; another was abandoned by cohabiting parents, later imprisoned for neglect, who refused to have him back after he was discharged from hospital. In the one other case, the father was in prison, the mother expecting a new confinement, the child was placed with foster-parents and the mother then disappeared. The personality of the parents, not the breakdown of the cohabitation as such, brought these children into care.

Among our forty-eight families, eleven mothers were mentally defective and one insane; several others were seriously unbalanced mentally. Most of the rest seemed to belong to the general run of

IMMEDIATE REASON	0-6 months	7-12 months	1-3 years	4-5 years	6-10 years	11 years upwards	TOTAL Children	TOTAL Families
Mother ill (dying)			1		2		3	1
Mother insane					1		1	1
Mother mentally defective	7	3					10	10
Mother's new confinement				1	1		2	2
Financial aid sought by person looking after child[1]	1	1	1	1	2	2	8	8
Mother had deserted		2	1	1	1		5	4
Mother evicted				4	4		8	4
Neglect by mother or cohabiting parents (usually N.S.P.C.C. prosecution)		1	2	3	4		10	4
Child in moral danger				1	1		2	2
Child beyond control					1	6	7	7
Very young mother taken into care during pregnancy	2		1				3	3
Adoption sought			1				1	1
Failed adoption						1	1	1
TOTAL	10	7	7	11	17	9	61	48

[1] In this instance the table shows why the person who had charge of the child applied to the department and not why the child was received into care. In most of these cases the mother had died or deserted some time before.

'socially defective' or problem families so well known to the authorities: to the worst type of neglectful parents, quite often with many children, usually poor, often poorly housed, evicted or homeless, usually irresponsible, occasionally promiscuous. At least twenty of the 'parents'—mothers, putative fathers or acting fathers —had prison sentences behind them, sometimes for child neglect. Indeed, the child's illegitimacy often seems to be only one incident in the family's general career of 'social ineffectiveness'. Apart from the large mentally defective group, the mothers of natural children in care differ little, if at all, from the married women who have children in care. Nineteen of the families in this survey, covering thirty—or almost half—of the children, can be described as problem families.

The children who entered care because their mothers had deserted or been evicted were almost always the children of problem families. It is rarely a case of simple failure to pay rent. Quite often what lay behind these stories was an unhappy marriage to someone who was not the children's own father.

Wendy, Mary and June, for instance, were the illegitimate children of a woman who had since married and had two children by her husband. It was not a happy marriage, and divorce proceedings were pending. The husband refused to take responsibility for any of the children except his own. The mother and all five children therefore left him, leaving their home but unable to afford other accommodation. The mother refused Part III accommodation. Dr Barnardo's at first paid her a boarding-out grant to help her keep the children with her, but they finally had to go into a Children's Home until the N.S.P.C.C. could find them somewhere to live. All five were in care for a while until in the end the legitimate—only the legitimate—children were taken home by the father. Where a mother has both legitimate and illegitimate children, all may suffer but particularly the illegitimate.

Another story is also characteristic. Harry was boarded out as a baby and his mother disappeared soon after. Later she reappeared, but the father was now in prison, and as she was expecting another baby, she did not want Harry home. Harry was therefore received into care, which gave the foster-parents some financial security, and eight months later, his parents having married, he was taken home. He was then fifteen months old.

Four families, including ten illegitimate children, were received into care when the parents were prosecuted for neglect. The four Jackson children came in and out of care several times when they were small. Their mother was mentally unstable and had been a voluntary patient at a mental hospital: there was talk of her being sterilized. She had seven illegitimate children: three by an Italian, who were now in various Children's Homes in Scotland; one by an unknown man; and three by the man with whom she had recently been cohabiting and whom she had now married. Several were received into care for a couple of weeks while the youngest child was being born and again briefly a year later while the husband was ill. A few months afterwards they had to leave their cottage. The mother refused Part III accommodation, so two of the children were taken into a Children's Home and two placed with foster-parents. They were being rehoused, but the mother was on probation and would remain under supervision for several years.

A married woman of forty had two illegitimate children by a soldier with whom she had been cohabiting and then another by a sailor. She had always neglected the children but the first opportunity for prosecuting her did not come until the last cohabitation came to an end and she first began leaving the children alone in the house while she went in pursuit of various men. All three children were received into care.

It has been estimated that at least one family in every hundred is a socially defective or problem family. In *The Neglected Child and His Family*,[1] for example, there is quoted an estimate of over 1 per cent in *Herefordshire*, nearly 2 per cent in *Glossop* and a claim from *Rotherham* that 5 per cent of all its school-children came from problem families. How many of these families included natural children we unfortunately do not know.

It is clear enough that the problem-family background rather than the children's illegitimacy as such—either directly or indirectly—was what brought most of the children in the *Devon* study into care. If one adds to these thirty another dozen whose mothers were defective, insane or mentally unstable, two-thirds of the sixty-one are accounted for.

And what of the others? They fall into two groups. The first consists of those who were received into care as 'beyond control' —a tragic group, since they entered care so late—ranging from ten

[1] Women's Group on Public Welfare, *The Neglected Child and His Family* (1948).

to fourteen years of age—and much damage had already been done. These seven children had had a varied history, but often their trouble was that they never knew to whom they really 'belonged', being passed from pillar to post, from one foster-home to another, throughout their childhood. The second group is of those eight who were officially 'in care' but in fact living with foster-parents receiving a boarding-out allowance.

A few stories of the first group will show what kind of childhood led to their becoming 'beyond control' and how often frequent changes of home were a factor.

Paul was referred to by the Child Guidance Clinic as a 'failed adoption' when he was twelve. His mother had placed him in a foster-home soon after his birth, but he had had to be evacuated during the war to a Waifs and Strays nursery. At four and a half he was so high-spirited and naughty that he was removed to a Hostel for observation. The educational psychologist recommended a private billet and, at the age of seven, Paul was placed with his future adopters. He was already wild but was legally adopted. Nine months later he was referred to the Psychiatric Clinic. He had become defiant the day after the adoption order was made, stole, was difficult and cunning at school and brought his adoptive mother to the edge of a nervous breakdown. In the next two and a half years he had seven different homes, returning from time to time to the Hostel, sometimes at his own request. His adoptive mother had meanwhile died and the Children's Department took responsibility for him under a 'fit person' order.

Jonathan was received into care when he was eleven, after being placed on probation for theft. He had an unstable mother, and little relationship with his stepfather, whom he did not like. He kept asking after his own father and often ran away to his grandparents. The Children's Department finally took him away from his parents at his own request and found him a home with relatives.

Several other children were received into care after a series of thefts had showed up their insecurity. Charles, for instance, was thirteen at the time. Nothing was known of his mother, either by the boy himself or apparently by anyone else, and he had been with foster-parents as long as he could remember. Outbreaks of theft—sixpences, half-crowns—and also of bed-wetting began when he was told that he was not his foster-mother's own son. He was placed in a Home, but continued to steal, so was removed to another. At the time of the study he spent his holidays with his foster-parents, but the Probationer Officer urged that he should make his main home elsewhere. He was a child of low I.Q. (65), though with such a history it is hard to say how much of this was due to emotional disturbance.

Of the eight children in the second group, five had had a more or less undisturbed childhood. Four of them had been only two or three weeks old when they were placed and had stayed with the same foster-parents ever since. In one case the mother ceased payment when the child was four months old, another at nine months when she went to gaol, a third stopped payment when a new baby was expected, and a fourth when the child was twenty months old. In each of these cases one would like to know whether the mother might not have reached a different decision earlier and perhaps placed the child from the first with adopters if she had had the right skilled advice at the time of its birth. The mother's part in the arrangement broke down so early that one is tempted to think that it might have been foreseen: either her inadequate personality or feeling for the child or her sheer poverty led to the breakdown, and these facts might have been clear to the social worker by the time the child was born. However, in these cases they had good foster-parents and perhaps little damage was done.

The two children who had lost their mothers were received into care, following many changes of home, well after their mothers' deaths. There were relatives who were willing to help but could not do so without financial assistance. The boarding-out allowance paid to them therefore acted in effect much as would a guardian's allowance (not normally payable if only the mother has died), though it was more generous in scale. One of these children had been dragged hither and thither in his lifetime, living with his mother and her latest lover, and attending nine different schools. After his mother's death he went to stay with his grandfather and pleaded to remain there. The boarding-out allowance made this possible. The other child lost his mother when he was five, and in the next year had six different homes among friends and relatives, finally settling down with an aunt and uncle who were willing to give him a home now that his mother was dead and a small income was guaranteed to them.

These, then, were the main reasons why this group of sixty-one children entered care: thirty of them belonged to problem families;

twelve had defective, insane or mentally unstable mothers; seven were beyond control after a long history of unhappiness and insecurity; eight were received into care after the mother's death or desertion, to enable their foster-parents to keep them. It may prove to be a fairly typical picture of why natural children are received into care, though that question could not be answered without much further research.

Bournemouth Children's Department points out that 10 per cent of *all* the children received into its care during the year ended 31st March 1955 were natural children—mostly the babies of literally unmarried mothers—received into care 'purely because, as a result of their illegitimacy, their mothers had no accommodation in which they could look after them themselves'. In the *Devon* survey more than half the children would have been received into care even if they had been legitimate, and this was usually because their parents were, by personal endowment or cumulative misfortune, unable to manage a family. There were only five cases in which illegitimacy played a direct decisive part: the boy who became disturbed when he learned that he was not his foster-parents' son; the stepfather who refused to look after his wife's illegitimate daughters; a married woman who parted with a child to foster-parents and was later unable to keep up her payments because her husband did not know of the child's existence; a mother who parted with her child when she married another man and found herself expecting a new baby at a time when he was unemployed; and a woman who found she could not afford to keep two illegitimate children.

Here, too, one wonders whether a more considered decision when the child was born might not have led the mothers to place their children from the beginning with adopters. Clearly many of the mothers in this chapter who tried to keep their children were so sorely lacking in the qualities needed—affection and responsibility, mental stability, health and fair earning power—that perhaps they should have been advised at a very early stage to seek adopters and not to try to bring the children up themselves.

CHAPTER 13

THE CHILDREN'S DEVELOPMENT

THE HOME BACKGROUND

Since no study has been made in England of any group of natural children above the age of five, it is impossible to say how their development compares with that of legitimate children.

The *Midboro* study of five-year-olds did not suggest that there was any particular cause for anxiety. In the great majority of cases the children's homes appeared to those engaged in the research to be financially and emotionally secure, and the physical and mental development of the children and quality of their general care seemed satisfactory. The report even concluded that 'in the great majority of cases' there was 'no emotional problem in the home', though one may doubt how far the health visitors were in a position to assess this. There were only ten cases, fewer than 4 per cent, in which the children's environment was regarded as being 'emotionally insecure, due to an unsettled home background' and five where the children's physical development was below normal. But it is doubtful whether this Midboro study can be taken as typical.

The general impression one derives from the *Newcastle-upon-Tyne* study is quite different. At the end of the first year of the children's lives:

'Altogether we were able to make an assessment of the stability of 54 families, and in no less than 32 of them we considered the environment unstable and unsatisfactory—far more than the expected number. At least 10 of these families were grouped as "problem families" of the type which gives rise to many of the most insoluble social difficulties of a large city. Also, as one might expect in such families, there were many examples of failure of the mother to cope with the situation and in not more than one half could we say that she was really giving a satisfactory standard of care to the child. Twelve out of 56 families lived in conditions of statutory overcrowding and 14 in houses not accepted as fit for habitation. Thus an illegitimate infant runs a far greater risk than a legitimate infant of living in a home where the maternal capacity, the family stability, and the physical environment and housing conditions are all variable.'[1]

This is, certainly, an assessment of the children's early environment and not of their development, but the Moral Welfare study of three-year-old children with whom these agencies were in touch is also disquieting.

'The case-workers assessed whether the home background was emotionally secure. Of the 79 children in the care of relatives or of single mothers still living singly, the home background was said to be unsatisfactory for about a third. In some cases there were quarrels or rivalry over the upbringing of the child between the mother and the grandmother, who often had the care of the child during the day when the mother was at work. In other cases the mother was backward or unbalanced, lazy or promiscuous. Some mothers frequently changed their work and their lodgings, their home background having little stability. Also in about one-third of such cases the mother's financial position was considered by the case-workers to be insecure.'[2]

ILLEGITIMACY AS A CAUSE OF JUVENILE DELINQUENCY

There is a fair amount of evidence that a number of illegitimate children do suffer severe emotional damage that results in anti-social behaviour. During evidence given before a Select Committee appointed in 1852 to inquire into the treatment of 'criminal and destitute juveniles', Matthew Davenport Hill, the Recorder of *Birmingham*, remarked that 'the testimony of inspectors of prisons and of gaolers, and the chaplains of gaols, is uniform to the fact that illegitimate children form a very large class of juvenile criminals'. Although the position has much improved since his day, three studies confirm that the proportion of illegitimate children among young delinquents is still high enough to be disquieting.[3]

Cyril Burt took in his study two hundred consecutive cases of juvenile delinquency in *London*, and found that 7.6 per cent of the

[1] *A Thousand Families in Newcastle-upon-Tyne.*
[2] *What Happens Afterwards?* (*Moral Welfare*, January 1957).
[3] Cyril Burt, *The Young Delinquent* (1935).
  A. M. Carr-Saunders, H. Mannheim and E. C. Rhodes, *Young Offenders* (1942).
  Hermann Mannheim, *Juvenile Delinquency in an English Middletown* (1948).

delinquents, as against 0.7 per cent of his control group, were of illegitimate birth—although only some 4 per cent of the births registered in London were illegitimate. The proportion of illegitimate children was particularly high among the girls, 9.5 per cent as against 6.5 per cent among the boys. Mental complexes about their birth or parentage were a contributory cause of delinquency among 4.9 per cent of the boys and 10.9 per cent of the girls.

In *Young Offenders*, a study of about a thousand delinquent *London* boys, it was also found that only 0.8 per cent of the control group were described an illegitimate, but 3.7 per cent of the delinquents. This is not a large figure, but that it may be significant is confirmed by studies in a group of provincial cities—*Manchester, Leeds, Sheffield, Hull, Nottingham, Cardiff*—where the percentage of children of illegitimate birth among delinquents was found to be twice as high as in control groups: for the cities taken together, 5.1 per cent as against 2.5 per cent. These figures have, however, to be read with a certain reserve since both in *London* and the provinces the proportion of illegitimate children in the studies, and particularly in the control groups, was noticeably smaller than in the population at large.

Hermann Mannheim noted among the findings of his study that 'the percentage of illegitimate children is fairly high' among boys placed on probation—over 7 per cent among those placed on probation between 1933 and the outbreak of war, and nearly 10 per cent in a wartime group. He also referred to the figures quoted in *Young Offenders*, adding evidence from studies made in *Bradford, Lincoln* and *Portsmouth*. He was cautious about drawing conclusions, since he regarded the existing material as not sufficiently comprehensive, but he noted as 'surely a significant factor' that, from such incomplete pre-war and wartime records as were available—records admittedly too incomplete for proper statistical analysis—as many as 25 per cent of girls placed on probation were illegitimate as against 7 to 8 per cent of boys.

Dr Stott, in his study for the Carnegie United Kingdom Trust, lists 'the broken home, illegitimacy and step-parentage' as 'social factors which predispose to delinquency'.[1] He includes some full-length studies of illegitimate boys who grew up emotionally disturbed, aware that they are not wanted in their homes and

---

[1] D. H. Stott, *Delinquency and Human Nature* (1950).

becoming in some cases bitterly anti-social upon the discovery of their illegitimacy.

EFFECTS ON CHILD OF MOTHER'S DISTURBED PREGNANCY

Recently Dr Stott has reopened another aspect of the subject. His studies of mentally defective and scholastically backward children suggest that a certain type of disturbed behaviour may derive from neural damage suffered by the foetus during pregnancy.[1] An instance given is that of the timid, 'unforthcoming' backward child who may, given enough encouragement, prove to have normal energy and capacity for affection, but who is by temperament pathologically unassertive. It appears that this is closely associated with stress, sometimes physical and sometimes emotional, suffered by the mother during the latter part of her pregnancy. Other striking findings, supported by the work of other research workers, have been the close and apparently causal association between ill-health and other forms of stress suffered by the mother during her pregnancy, especially during the early months, and many cases of mental retardation, juvenile ill-health and even some congenital malformations.[2]

This research is in too early a stage for its final implications to be assessed, but it will be remembered how unexpected was the association found between German measles in an expectant mother and mental defect in her child, and it is of obvious importance that other possible types and sources of injury should be re-investigated with an open mind.

SOME CLINICAL STUDIES

A tragic source of material about the maladjustment of illegitimate children is found in the records of Child Guidance Clinics throughout the country. Although we are far from having reached a point where referrals to Child Guidance Clinics are any true measure of the extent of psychological ill-health among these or any other group of children, one may learn from these records some of the

---

[1] D. H. Stott, *Evidence of Pre-Natal Impairment of Temperament in Mentally Retarded Children* (*Vita Humana*, 1959).

[2] D. H. Stott, *Physical and Mental Handicaps Following a Disturbed Pregnancy* (*Lancet*, 18th May 1957).

emotional hazards of illegitimacy and how children can suffer, directly or indirectly, from their birth status.

Looking at random through a group of cases one comes upon a nine-year-old referred to the clinic by the juvenile court as 'beyond control'. He had attacked his mother with a saw and had been making preposterous demands of her practically at the point of a gun. He was the illegitimate child of a married woman, he was unwanted and, in her innermost feelings, his mother had rejected him. But she felt so acutely guilty about this that she had tried to make up for it by spoiling him: by now she no longer had the strength to say 'No' to any of his demands. The boy loved and hated her, and the conflict showed in his wild behaviour—yet it may well have been that when he was most cruel to her it was to test, to prove her love.

In contrast to this passionate boy, one comes upon a small girl with 'that curious lack of expression which one finds so often in children who were rejected in infancy'. She had been moved several times in her childhood and had never been able to develop any loyalties. She had been adopted at the age of four and a half after her mother's death, but had no affection at all for her adoptive parents who, in their distress, brought her to the psychiatrist.

Then there is the seven-year-old boy who burst into wild rages when he was mildly teased at school. He felt odd man out at home, partly because he had a different name from his stepbrothers. The psychiatrist advised his stepfather to adopt him and give him the family surname.

But there is also the child who *was* adopted but learnt this only when she was twelve years old and was overcome with grief. The father she had always thought her own had recently died, and to learn that she had never been his child was the final blow. When she was brought to the psychiatrist she said she was not a 'real' child, so she was sure nobody could love her. She felt desperately isolated.

There is a violent five-year-old who bit and scratched: she had sensed her mother's guilt feelings towards her and played upon them. She had a grudge against her mother for not having given her a father. 'Why,' she demanded, 'haven't I got a daddy like other children? Where do they get them from? Why don't *you* go out and get me one too?'

A mother's feelings of guilt towards an illegitimate child often have an ill effect. Her guilt may seem to be the natural result of having a child out of wedlock, but be morbid in origin and degree. A small boy, who had lived with a beloved grandmother until she died, was taken home by his mother at the age of three in almost impossible circumstances: she had married a man who did not know of the child's birth and very much resented this unexpected stepson. The psychiatrist suggested that the boy might be happier in a foster-home, but the mother's guilt feelings were too strong for her to part with him. 'It would make me happy if he were taken away and I mustn't be happy. I don't deserve to be.'

Unless helped by the clinics in good time, many of these children may never grow up to have normal relationships. Their feeling towards other boys and girls of the opposite sex is disturbed by guilt, their fears a reflection of their mothers' fears that they too will one day 'get into trouble'. Some of the mothers, disappointed and isolated by unhappy experiences, or afraid of gossip, or often enough simply too over-tired and over-pressed to have any social life, keep themselves to themselves and discourage even the child from making normal friendships. Or the child itself, moved from one family to another, may be uncertain to whom it belongs and never learn to give anyone its trust.

From these clinical studies, with their deep understanding of what a child may suffer, one realizes vividly how closely a child's happiness is bound up, after all, with his mother's. The facile assumption that the unmarried mother should 'suffer for her mistakes' has a flaw. During the child's infancy, while the mother is struggling through her own griefs and difficulties, the child is taking in his first vital impressions of the world. The mother's attitude at that time may influence the child far more profoundly than her outlook later, when she wins through, perhaps, to a measure of inner peace. Her basic strength and security in those early years, her love and enjoyment of the child, her happiness in the world they share, might have led him to feel that the world is good and friendly, so that he would become outgoing, make friends easily, be stable enough to take knocks and disappointments—because he is emotionally secure. But if, during his infancy, the mother is working through a host of emotional difficulties, at times loving her child with a possessive passion, over-protecting and spoiling him, at other times rejecting him as the source of her own unhappiness, as the person who stands between her and her hopes of a normal life, he may grow up feeling that the world is as unreliable as his mother; the emotional wear and tear of those early years may permanently hamper him. If the child feels her habitual disapproval and irritation, perhaps derived from her own fears and guilt, he may come to think that the world is hostile and unloving. It is *not* enough that the mother may grow out of her emotional disturbances and leave them behind, for by then the child's personality may already have been seriously damaged. This is what society risks when it urges mother and child to stay together, but lets her task become almost intolerably difficult. If the mother feels herself to be an outcast and over-pressed beyond endurance, how likely is the child to feel relaxed, secure, accepted and socially approved?

The presence or absence of a father figure in the child's life, and the mother's attitude to the father, may also be of vital importance. Through a father's attitude to him a boy learns to accept and look up to authority, or resent it and rebel; he learns to respect his own manhood through loving his father.

A child normally has a wide family circle who may be very important to him: brothers and sisters, aunts and cousins, grandparents, to whom he can turn when others of the family have no time for him or are intolerant. An illegitimate child may be cut off from all of these, or feel insecure and uneasy in his relationship with them.

The records of Child Guidance Clinics in this country are rich in proof of these things, and full of pictures of how illegitimate children suffer through our blunders. But the clinics treat only the misfits; there is still little picture of how illegitimate children fare as a whole. No study has been made of the later development of an entire group of children, from which one might learn which environment, by and large, is the most favourable for illegitimate children: whether they develop most happily with their mothers or adopted by strangers, brought up in the grandparents' home, or with a family circle of stepbrothers and stepsisters. For the most important—indeed almost the only—study to date of the later development of illegitimate children one must turn to a piece of research published in *Canada*.

A CANADIAN STUDY OF TEEN-AGE CHILDREN[1]

This valuable piece of work, already referred to in these pages, covered ninety-two children—forty-nine boys and forty-three girls—aged fourteen and fifteen and born in *Toronto* in 1925-6. It was based on interviews with the mothers and other persons who had had the children in their homes. Few of the children were seen personally, for fear of arousing their anxiety or the mothers' opposition, but additional information was secured from schools and social agencies. It should be noted that the children were still young and that some were only just beginning to question or understand the implications of their social status.

The Parents
Half of the mothers were mentally sub-normal.[2] Of those whose home conditions during their growing years were known, forty out of fifty-seven came from homes broken by death, separation or discord. Most of the fathers were men of small means. Comparatively little was known of them, since the agencies' main interest in them had been in their ability to pay towards the children's support.

The Children
Forty-nine of the children seemed to be happy and well adjusted; forty-three (some 47 per cent) were presenting problems. Outstanding behaviour problems had brought over fifty to the particular attention of school authorities and other bodies; four had been brought before the juvenile court. Delinquency among the boys (seventeen cases) took the form of stealing, perpetual truancy, being members of gangs, bullying, defiance, excessive lying. In the girls (only four cases) the problems were chiefly late hours, running away (followed in one case by pregnancy), truancy and stealing.

Other commoner symptoms of maladjustment were anxiety, and the inability to make friends. Nearly three-fifths of the children

---

[1] *A Study of the Adjustment of Teen-Age Children born out of Wedlock who remained in the Custody of their Mothers or Relatives*, made in 1943 by the Unmarried Parenthood Committee of the Welfare Council of Toronto and District.

[2] The term 'sub-normal' is not defined in the Canadian study. Nowadays it would be used only of those with an I.Q. of 80 or less.

were said to make lasting friendships, but the remainder seemed incapable of it, or made their friends among those of bad repute. They bullied other children, assumed a superior attitude or withdrew from contact. The attitude in the home had sometimes made it difficult for these children. Nearly a third had lived with people who showed them little affection, and it was small wonder that they had not learnt themselves to extend friendship and trust. Others had been over-protected by anxious mothers and discouraged from making friends.

'She is my companion,' said one mother. 'We are just like a couple of sisters. She would rather be with me. She never goes out with girls or boys.'

An anxiety that they should not make friends with children of the opposite sex was often shown. Some boys and girls had had the fact of their illegitimacy thrown in their faces by children of the neighbourhood and feared further hostility. But lack of security *within* their family group seemed to be the main reason why they were unable to make good friendships.

A number of reasons for poor adjustment or difficult behaviour were evident. Three-fifths of the children who were presenting personality or behaviour problems were those living with persons of sub-normal mentality. Indeed, one must allow for the influence of this factor throughout the study, for less than two-fifths of those living with sub-normal mothers (half of the mothers in the study) or relatives made a satisfactory adjustment, while as many as three-quarters of those who grew up with persons of normal mentality seemed to be quite well adjusted.

The children's own mental equipment was sometimes a factor. Of forty-one children tested, fourteen had I.Q.s below 80, and of the other fifty-one, fourteen were estimated to be sub-normal. The children of normal mentality made a decidedly better adjustment; over two-thirds adjusted well, as against one-third in the sub-normal group.

An important factor was that many of the children had lived unsettled lives. Only about a quarter of them remained with the same family group from birth to the age of fourteen or fifteen; and of sixty-seven who had changed home, only nineteen remained with their mothers throughout. Thirteen children moved only once, but twenty-six changed home twice, twelve three times, and sixteen four times or more. One child was moved nine times between birth and the age of two and a half years.

Constant movement gave these children little opportunity to establish good family relationships, yet the change of home itself was not the only cause of the children's poor adjustment: some of them had not been wanted in any home since their birth and a number had been moved 'from families to whom they thought they belonged and by whom they were loved, into other families who had no desire to have them'. Sometimes parents or relatives grew tired of giving them care or, irritated by what they regarded as the mother's irresponsibility, told her to take the child elsewhere; the mothers, on their side, resentful of the attitude of their families and constant reminders of their past behaviour, left home taking their children with them.

In several cases the death or inability of relatives to keep them led not only to the children being uprooted from their homes but also to their becoming aware for the first time of their illegitimacy. The mother's inability to give an adequate explanation as to why she had not previously kept the child with her was sometimes a difficulty. Children who had been properly prepared and given an explanation they could accept did not appear to be upset by changes in placement, but those who were unconvinced by the explanations grown-ups gave them, often became uncertain and insecure in their family group.

Broadly the children who had not settled in one home before the age of three showed more problems than those who were established earlier. Of fifty-five settled by the age of three or younger, only eighteen showed signs of maladjustment, but of nineteen who had not settled till the age of seven, all but three presented problems.

It was found that children who had been told quietly and objectively about their illegitimate birth by persons whom they loved and trusted—it did not matter so much by whom—and children who seemed not to know of it at all, settled better than those left in uncertainty or who had discovered the truth in an unhappy way. It emerged that only one in seven had been told of their illegitimacy without their parents or relatives contradicting it, although nearly half had some knowledge of their status. The others were believed, by relatives, not to know of their illegitimacy, though sometimes this may be doubted, since relatives were apt to be slow to realize how much a child suspected. A number of boys and girls were clearly suffering from their mothers' evasiveness and hesitancy about telling them the truth. The mothers tended to put it off, fearing that it would spoil their relationship, or fearing to face their own deep feelings of guilt towards the child. But the children often had doubts and anxieties raised in their minds by remarks made in their presence by relatives and friends visiting their homes, and by the sudden silences or change of conversation that followed. One girl from an otherwise happy home who suspected that there was something strange about her birth but was constantly fobbed off by a mother who still felt guilty towards her, exclaimed passionately when she was about fourteen:

'If I ever find out that you have not told me the truth after I have asked you so many times, I will run away and you will never see me again!'

This child was devoted to her stepfather and happy in school: her insecurity arose directly from her mother's denials of the truth. Probably she would have accepted knowledge of her birth status more easily than any more uncertainty. Another mother remarked of her son:

'He used to ask me about his father, but I always put him off. He hasn't asked me lately, so I imagine he has forgotten.'

One cannot but wonder whether he had.

A girl, who was getting beyond control, and going around with a rough gang, settled down quietly after she was told the truth plainly and sympathetically. The mother explained how her own wildness when she was young had led to their having to do without the companionship of the girl's father, but that the girl had come by her brains honestly, as her father was a very clever man. 'She is rather proud of him, although she has never seen him.' Another was told the facts by a neighbour and then heard them hotly denied by her mother.

'Of course,' said the mother afterwards, 'I told her it wasn't true. . . . She is difficult enough now. Goodness knows what she would be like if she knew the real facts.'

When the mothers were afraid of telling the truth or unable to do so calmly, there was often someone else in the child's circle sufficiently loved and trusted to do so. One grandmother gave a straightforward explanation to a girl of twelve which seems if anything to have deepened the girl's affection for her mother. One of the boys, soon after learning that he was illegitimate, came across the word 'bastard' in a book he was reading and asked its meaning. The aunt who had brought him up explained and the boy said, 'Like me?' She answered in the affirmative. He showed no anxiety, even if it bothered him, and as he continued to ask questions openly, it was hoped that he would come to accept the facts without too much hurt. When he was still small a case-worker had told his aunt that he might ask many questions about his parents when he was older. 'She told me never to lie to him, but to give him in a quiet, kindly way as little or as much information as I thought he could understand.' The prescription had evidently worked, for the boy's manner was friendly and easy and there was every indication that his relationships were normal.

Some of the children had suffered in their relationship with stepbrothers and stepsisters in the home. This usually seems to have been the fault of adults. Some illegitimate children were over-protected by their mothers, making the others feel that favouritism was being shown; or where the mother was not over-possessive, she or the stepfather might reject the child and compare it unfavourably with the other members of the family.

'Why does Dad always pick on me?' said one lad to his mother. 'The others can get away with anything.'

There was not enough information to show how far the different types of family set-up influenced the children's development. About half of those who lived with their grandparents and mother settled well, though half did not; half of those who lived alone with the mothers adjusted happily, the other half did not; about half of those who lived with mothers who had married another man, settled well, about a half did not; the same was true where the mother had married the natural father, and so on. The twelve who lived with mothers who were cohabiting, living in 'common law union', with the fathers or other men, did not seem a very happy group. With few exceptions, the women came from homes with good standards and seemed to feel insecure or guilty, distressed by the way they were living or had lived ('I lived a perpetual lie until we were married') and this affected the children. Besides, a number of the unions proved unstable. Most of the children living with their grandparents alone settled well.

But the child's development depended less upon the nature of the family make-up than upon its personal security in the home.

'Children, in order to develop normally,' ran the report, 'must have a sense of belonging and of really being wanted and loved by their family group. Perhaps one of the most outstanding points which was revealed from the study was in this connection. Nearly two-thirds of these children are living in homes where they are really wanted and the children themselves appear to have affection for the people with whom they are placed. A few of these adults have been over-protective and others have little conception of how to guide wisely, but at least they have given the children a feeling of being loved. Nearly two-thirds of these children are well adjusted. In contrast with this situation, the children who are living with people who have no affection for them, show an unhappy picture. Of 29 children who are living in these homes, there is not one child who is well adjusted.'

Failure of the Social Agencies
As we have mentioned, the research workers concluded from the study that the social agencies had often failed to give the mothers the help they required. The research workers believed, for example, that if the mothers had been 'sufficiently released from their guilt feeling', seven of them, who had made poor adjustment and whose children had suffered in consequence, might never have attempted to keep their babies. Eight of the mothers actually stated in the interview that if they had had the opportunity to make another decision, they would not have kept their children and the interviewers suspected that the number of those who had privately come to this conclusion was higher. The need for continued supervision was stressed, so that mothers and relatives who found their plans working unsatisfactorily could be shown some other way of meeting their problems.

It was considered that the social agencies lost contact too early. In more than a third of the cases it had ended before the child was a year old, and in nearly two-thirds before it was three. Slightly over two-thirds of the forty-three who had made a poor adjustment belonged to families where contact with the social agencies had ceased when the child was under three. If the mother married or took the baby back to her parents' home the agencies were apt to record that 'the family is now able to manage without further assistance', but events proved that this was anything but an accurate statement, for, ran the research workers' report, 'neither of these solutions necessarily offered security to either mother or child'.

The mother still had many adjustments to make, for some of which her imagination had not been in the least prepared, and had also to help the child to overcome many problems arising from its illegitimate birth. Many mothers needed guidance in answering their children's questions, or were in need of financial or vocational help. While many of the problems that developed later might have been met and overcome if skilled service had been given in the early months or years, the need for continued supervision in many cases was also evident. The mothers were shy about asking for help and in some cases the attitude of the agencies had made them withdraw from contact. In particular, too little understanding was shown of the problems of mothers who were cohabiting with the children's fathers. Some method of arranging follow-up visits to the mother at varying periods seemed to be needed, since the women, although anxious and unable to handle their problems, were hesitant about applying for help and guidance.

A more careful approach, it was felt, should be made to the fathers. A better understanding of their point of view might have helped some of the mothers to be more realistic, and an objective approach by social workers that stimulated a man's interest in his child and aroused his goodwill would be more likely to bring results than the hard, impersonal 'hand of the law'.

A CHALLENGE TO RESEARCH

There is always a danger in drawing upon studies, however fine their quality, that were made in another country. More than once in this book we have drawn attention to studies that have included, in particular, a much higher percentage of unstable or mentally defective mothers than one might expect to find in England. Dr Leontine Young, writing of her studies in the *United States*, notes that the proportion of neurotic women in them may be higher than one might find in some European countries. But in the absence of English studies, it is inevitable that these should be quoted, if only as a challenge to research. The issues they raise for both mother and children are too important to be met with the weak defence of ignorance.

There is, in any case, too much evidence to show that children in this country suffer as a result of their illegitimacy. It is not even necessary for it to be manifested in anti-social behaviour or in obvious clinical symptoms, for it to be real. A boy may come to the edge of marriage and then find that his fiancée's people will not accept him because he was born illegitimate; a girl may feel ready to marry anyone at all who will forgive her the stigma of illegitimate birth. We have mentioned the old people who did not like to apply for pensions for fear of revealing their illegitimacy—so much and so long had they suffered. Those who assume that it is only the old who suffer in this way, and that children are no longer shunned for being illegitimate, should have to see a boy as he turns to his mother when he is taunted by the neighbours' veiled questions, imploring her to arm him with some story to account for his father's absence.

That boy is a citizen of the future. Will he grow into a worthy one? Will he be given a chance? Will the way soon be made clear for the legislative reforms that are so urgently needed? It is to be hoped so. Every year another 30,000 illegitimate boys and girls are born in England and Wales alone, and the half million below school-leaving age cannot be left waiting indefinitely for the generosity, the justice and affection that they must have if they are to grow up into the sound and happy people it is within them to become.

PART IV
THE DEVELOPMENT OF A NEW APPROACH

CHAPTER 14

LEGISLATIVE REFORMS IN OTHER COUNTRIES

From a comparison of individual laws abroad with those of this country it will be seen that in certain parts of the world a new approach towards illegitimacy has been developing. The old punitive attitude, common to most countries, has been found increasingly unworkable. Not only did it fail to prevent illegitimacy; it also caused untold suffering to the children as innocent victims of their parents' mistakes and produced in their disturbed personalities a new and formidable set of social problems. A generation of disinherited children does not add to the well-being of a country.

But every nation, when it has found itself pressed to the edge of reform or a basic revision of its philosophy, has been faced with the same question: if, for the sake of the children, conditions are made easier for unmarried families, will there not be a great increase in illegitimacy? Will not the very basis of family life be undermined? And is education enough? Must there not also be some penalty *after* the event if illegitimacy is to be kept to a minimum?

It is interesting to see what the experience of other countries has shown, what experiments have been made, and how far they have stood up to the test of time. There have been four major attempts to give natural children full equality before the law. Each was made when Europe was in the throes of major social ferment: the first in *France*, during the revolutionary upheaval of 1789-95; the second and third, in *Norway* and *Russia* respectively, during the Great War of 1914-18; while the latest is now taking place behind the Iron Curtain, in the countries occupied by the Russians in World War II. The Norwegian reforms, however, are different in character from the others; they were not the result of any sudden upheaval but, rather, express the gathered force of two great allied movements—the women's and labour movements—that had been developing in that country over many years.

THE FRENCH INHERITANCE LAW AND ITS AFTERMATH

Four years after the outbreak of the Revolution, the French brought in an inheritance law that imposed perfect equality upon the natural heirs, legitimate and illegitimate—though, as some restraint upon the far-reaching effects of such a change, the principle was introduced at the same time that 'la recherche de la paternité est interdite'. No court proceedings could be taken to establish paternity; recognition could only be voluntary.

The inheritance law did not survive the First Republic, but unfortunately the second principle was adopted into the Code Napoléon (promulgated in 1804) and survived to make havoc of the French bastardy laws—and indeed of the other countries where the Code was introduced—to as late as 1912. Even today the French ruling is that paternity out of wedlock may be declared by a court only in the case of abduction, rape, notorious cohabitation or in certain narrowly defined cases of seduction, such as those made under written promise of marriage. Otherwise it is permitted only where the father has acknowledged or maintained the child. Thus, in the normal case, where a man simply seduces a girl without promise of marriage, or where either of them is already married, the child has no claim, even to maintenance, upon its father. A similar stand is taken by several other countries that adopted the Code Napoléon.

Thus the short-lived inheritance law had in the end the very opposite effect from the one the reformers had intended. Coming too early in history, before the mind of the nation was ripe for it, it provoked a reaction from which many of the countries that adopted the Code have not yet recovered. More than a hundred and twenty years were to pass before radical ideas bore fruit again—and then not in France.

French law does, however, incorporate one principle of great advantage to natural children: that of the *acknowledged child*. A natural child not born of adultery or incest may be acknowledged voluntarily by its father, and if this is done in due form it establishes civil ties between them. The father has the same duties of parenthood or guardianship as he would towards a legitimate child. If he is the first to acknowledge the child, or does so at the same time as the mother, he is given the full parental authority. There is no parallel to this in Great Britain, although it has now long been possible in number of European countries—for example, in *Italy*, *Spain*, *Portugal* and, in a somewhat different form, the *Netherlands* and *Scandinavia*. The acknowledged child has, under French law, the right to its father's name. it may inherit from him, though not from the grandparents, and if it is co-heir with legitimate children it is entitled to half the share due to a legitimate child. This last provision is found also in Spain and Italy. In France an unacknowledged child whose paternity has been declared by a court may not ordinarily inherit, although if it is the child of adultery or incest it may claim maintenance.

A NEW PHILOSOPHY IN SCANDINAVIA: THE CASTBERG LAWS

Norway[1]
Early in the twentieth century, a powerful movement grew up in *Norway* for the betterment of the legal, social and economic position of natural children. As in England, the automatic effect of placing the entire burden of a child's care upon the mother was to throw most of these children upon poor relief. A decree introduced in the eighteenth century placed some responsibility at least upon the father (half the amount the poor-law officials considered necessary to support the child up to its tenth year), but this contribution had more the character of compensation to the mother than an economic right for the child. Various minor improvements were made during the nineteenth century and, as early as the 1880's, two bills designed to give children equal inheritance rights with the children of marriage were introduced. The Government felt, however, that the occasion was inopportune for pressing them and that society was not yet prepared to accept such extreme measures, although it was admitted that conditions in respect to illegitimate children were unsatisfactory and had been so for years.

At the beginning of the twentieth century various developments occurred that caused a change in the public outlook. First, pressure for radical reform grew up inside the labour movement. A draft bill, passed in 1901 by the annual convention of the Norwegian labour federation, was presented to the Government with a resolu-

---

[1] Sources for this section, other than those quoted in the text, are Grace Abbott's *The Child and the State* (Chicago, 1938), and various reports published in Norwegian by the Social Department in Oslo in 1951.

tion declaring 'that the woman in the relations which are the basis for this law is more disadvantageously situated than the man and that she and the child need greater protection and a more liberal and secure economic support . . .'

'The sorrow and misfortune,' the resolution continued, 'which result from the relations dealt with in this legislation most frequently strike upon the women and children of the poorer classes. For these reasons as well as for the sake of common justice and humanity, organized labour demands the reform of this legislation.'

The principles of reform insisted upon in the resolution were that: (1) it was the duty of the father to give equal support to both his legitimate and illegitimate children; (2) as regards succession, the illegitimate child should inherit in the father's line equally with a legitimate child and should have an equal right to the father's name; (3) all expenses for the support and education of the illegitimate child should be upon the father; (4) the mother should be entitled to a contribution 'as compensation for her loss of earning capacity resulting from the pregnancy and the child's care'; (5) contributions to the mother during pregnancy and at the time of confinement should be assessed upon the father before the birth took place; (6) contributions should be levied and collected without claim or demand from the mother and by the proper public authorities who should employ process to enforce their collection; (7) more stringent penalties should be invoked for failure on the father's part to meet his obligations to the mother and the child; (8) society should improve and make more stringent the supervision exercised over neglected children.

These remarkable proposals—for in 1901 they were the first to have been brought forward anywhere in the world—did not lead to any immediate Government action, except that a questionnaire was sent out to the local authorities, county councils, courts, magistrates and others, to ascertain their views. A further bill was introduced in the 1904-5 session and a further important series in 1909, but again no action was taken, although the replies to the questionnaire had shown a preponderance of opinion in favour of inheritance rights. A Government inquiry into the living conditions of illegitimate children was, however, initiated in 1906-7, and brought to light very disquieting facts.

Meanwhile the movement for women's emancipation was developing fast, a generation earlier in Norway than in England.

After the first demands for economic independence and political equality had been satisfied, attention was turned to the sphere of responsibilities, particularly the safeguarding of motherhood.

Behind each of these movements stood a remarkable man: Councillor of State Johan Castberg, who in 1908 was raised to be Minister of Justice. To him, more than to anyone else, society and natural children all over the world owe a deep debt of gratitude for bringing the fresh air of a new philosophy into the problem of illegitimacy and for pressing through, even at that early date, legislation that has been the inspiration of all the Scandinavian countries and is still reaching out to influence the rest of the world.

The Norwegian Storting of 1912 was composed of one hundred and twenty-three members, about a hundred of whom were elected on a more or less radical reform policy, so the work of Castberg and his friends could at last bear fruit. The Social Department, founded in 1913, of which Castberg soon became head, laid before the Storting a series of important bills. In 1915 the Children's Rights Laws were approved by the Crown. They were based on the principles laid down in the resolution of the labour federation in 1901 and in draft bills repeatedly laid before the Government in the intervening years.

The Children's Rights Laws, generally known as the 'Castberg Laws', today govern the position of natural children in Norway; various amendments have not altered their spirit. Castberg himself describes their main principles thus:[1]

'The Norwegian Children's Rights Laws are a result of [the] development of the women's movement. This is the new principle, which is dimly discerned behind the chief provisions of the law. It was this principle also which aroused the most violent opposition and at the same time received the most sympathetic support. On one side the old domination of man with his contempt for "natural" motherhood; on the other side the respect for and protection of motherhood for its own sake. This principle was embodied in the law by "the establishment of the equal responsibility and duty of the father and the mother towards the child; the equal right of the child towards its father and mother; the duty of the father to take care of the child's mother before, during and after her confinement; the right of the child to be brought up according to the

---

[1] Johan Castberg, *The Children's Rights Laws and Maternity Insurance in Norway* (*Journal of the Society of Comparative Legislation*, John Murray, 1916).

father's social position, if the father should be the more well-to-do of the parents; and last but not least, the duty of society to try to establish paternity in all cases, this being an absolute contrast to the code Napoléon: *La recherche de la paternite est interdite*" ...

'The first paragraph of the fundamental law [relating to the status of illegitimate children] contains the principle inspiring the whole legislation. It is the following:

"A child whose parents have not entered into marriage with each other has—subject to exceptions otherwise established by legislation—the same legal position in regard to its father as to its mother."

'In immediate connexion with this law are:

(*a*) the enactment that whichever of the parents has the care of the child shall provide for it as if it were legitimately born . . .; and

(*b*) the inheritance law, according to which the child also has the right to inherit from its father and his relatives . . . as if it were a child born in marriage.

'In discussing the purposes of the bill the Social Department says that Norwegian legislation is still based on the outrageous and unnatural fiction that an illegitimate child has only a mother —that legally it has no father. This applies even if the identity of the father is beyond any doubt. The law also in this case deprives the child of the right of a child to have a father, who is practically only placed in an economic relation to his child. The child is excluded from his family, from his name, and from his inheritance. The father is in regard to his child a stranger, the child is repudiated and disowned. This is not based on moral reasons, nor is it enacted out of regard to the marriage, as the illegitimate child has all the claims of a child to its mother. She must work for the child and bring it up, the child has the legal right to her family name, and the child inherits from her and all her relatives in the same way as a child born in marriage.

'The disproportion between the responsibility placed upon the man and the woman is the more outrageous as it is due to legislation in which women have had no share, legislation exclusively by men. It is not only a wrong done to the mother and the child, but a demoralizing institution, as it frees the man from his natural responsibility and thereby tempts him to recklessness in giving life to a human being instead of regarding it as one of the most serious responsibilities in a man's life. It breaks down man's respect for women, brutalizes his view of the relation between parents, and between parents and children, and in this way repudiates what is the ethical basis of marriage.

'At the same time this legalized irresponsibility of the man, his legally protected anonymity, exposes the child to want and disgrace, and contributes to the feeling of these children of being singled out and disowned, and causes so many of them to go down in the struggle for life.

'The increasing social sense of justice, and especially the citizenship of women with rights and duties towards society, has little by little raised a demand for an alteration in this unfair distribution of the responsibility of man and woman. In most countries one can see a strong movement in the direction of improving the legal position of the child born out of marriage and of increasing the duties of the father. Moreover, in other countries besides Norway, the view is now being pressed forward that the present arrangement is a repudiation of the demand for civil equality and for the equal rights and duties of man and of woman.

'The new legislation attempts to make up for the wrong towards mother and child imposed by the previous law. It seeks to remove the injustice of visiting society's disapproval of the illegitimate relation between the parents on the child. It aims at establishing the paternity and increasing the feeling of responsibility of the father towards mother and child. It aims at crushing the system of concealment and lies in which paternity now is allowed to be shrouded, and which is in itself an offence to wifehood and to marriage. It enforces the duty of the man to take care of the woman who is with child by him. It is based on the fundamental principle of strengthening society by protecting motherhood and by allowing the child to be provided for and to have its rights both to its father and to its mother.'

On the right to inherit, Castberg has this to say:

'As to the special question of the full right to inherit both from the father and from the father's relatives, this demand has already taken hold of the people's sense of justice. This was shown in 1904, when the Government laid this question before all the county councils both in the country and in the towns. Most of them recommended that the rights of inheritance should be given. This was shown still more distinctly by the attitude to this question of the different parties in the Storting. The contest was not fought on the question for or against the right of inheritance of these unhappy children, but only as to what extent it should be applied . . .

'Both the department's proposal and its advocates in the Storting emphasized the point that the chief end in sight was not simply that the child should obtain the economic advantage which this right of inheritance might sometimes secure for it—in most cases the inheritance would be nothing or next to nothing. It was a demand for justice which they wanted to grant—a demand that the child should have an equal claim before the law to its father and to its mother, subject only to the exceptions bound up with natural causes, and with the actual state of conditions, that the parents do not live together. These exceptions are on one side the mother's preferential right to have the child with her, on the other the legitimate children's allodial right (*odelsret*) to the family's land property, and the preferential right of the eldest legitimate child to take possession of his father's estate or farm on a cheap valuation . . .

'Another point was strongly put forward by the promoters of the bill. The right of inheritance would in many cases make it difficult for the father to conceal the existence of the child. They said in the debate: the father will from the first know that his child will come forward at the moment of his death and claim his inheritance. It is right that he should have prepared his family for this eventuality, that he should not be enabled to conceal the existence of his own child from those nearest to him. It was the cowardice, the untruthfulness and the irresponsibility of such concealment which the bill intended to demolish . . .

'It was not . . . the economic side of the question which was urged by the opponents of the bill when they pleaded consideration for the wives as an argument against the bill. They depicted in strong colours the sorrow and shame of the wives and the legitimate children when at the death of the husband and father the illegitimate child came forward with a claim of inheritance on the division of the property—they would then first be aware of the existence of the child In their anxiety they went so far as to say that such a surprise would become common in the so-called "better" homes, as if these homes would be filled with illegitimate children if this law was put into force!

'Now—apart from this exaggeration—it must be agreed that the sorrow and disgrace are more due to the actual existence of this child and to the lies and concealment about it, than to the fact that its existence is at last revealed to the man's family. The Children's Rights Laws aim expressly at preventing the claim to inheritance from an illegitimate child coming as a surprise to the man's family after his death. A man owes it to his wife to tell her the truth. It is the lie which is degrading, injurious to marriage and offensive to the wife and her children.

'But further, if the illegitimate child is legally entitled to know who are its parents, and if society is of opinion that this is a matter of justice to the child, it cannot be deprived of this right for the reason that it brings distress to the father's family. The father cannot for this reason be freed from his responsibility. If a man steals or commits another criminal action no one demands that he shall be free from punishment or responsibility because it will bring sorrow or disgrace to his family. Still less can this be argued when it implies an injustice to an innocent child.'

Castberg further supports his argument for enforcing the acknowledgment of paternity by citing the ineffectiveness of the mothers in standing up for their own and the children's rights, and the reluctance of magistrates to support them.

'Only 40 per cent of the mothers claim the alimony, and only 25 per cent of the claims for confinement expenses are decided by the magistrates. The mothers shrink from making their claims for fear of offending the father of the child.'

An important part of the law dealt with the establishment of paternity.

'Every birth is to be notified (by the midwife and doctor, as well as by the woman herself), and it is the duty of the mother to give the name of the father. She may do this before her confinement. As soon as this information has been given, the magistrate has to draw up a document imposing the necessary contributions for child and mother on the father named by her. This document is forwarded to the father. If he denies that he is the father of the child, he must within a certain period appeal to the judge and ask for an action to be laid against the mother. This is done by the administration without any expense to either of them. The whole procedure is in this way independent of the demand of the mother . . .

'If . . . the question of paternity must be decided by a Court, the law, as will be seen, proceeds very cautiously. It is only where there is no uncertainty that the Court gives its decision on the paternity.' The law in that case gave the child the choice between taking its father's name or its mother's. 'If the mother, e.g. has a bad reputation, a presumption will arise which will generally exclude a decision of paternity, even if cohabitation within the natural span of time is proved. The father will then only be sentenced to pay contributions, and the child will not obtain the right to inherit from him or to take his name . . .

'The preceding paragraphs clearly indicate the attitude of recent legislation towards the unmarried mother, as emphasizing the fact that the State's chief concern consists in the welfare of the illegitimate child as such. Most of the legislation referred to is seeking to help the mother, if by so doing it helps the child. There is thus an absence of the retributive element in the State's attitude, and a frank acknowledgment that the situation exists and that nothing should interfere with the State's interests in the child who is to be a future citizen. Obviously this conflicts with that type of public opinion which is fearful that by helping the child it will remove from the mother a stigma which now operates in a preventive manner, and that there will be a resulting increase of illegitimacy. That there may be such a close bond between the mother and her child that nothing can be done for the one without influencing the other, is true, but that the State should take a hand in handicapping the child because of its mother's misdeeds is an argument which few would uphold.'

To sum up: Norwegian law has since 1915 placed the responsibility for establishing paternity on the shoulders of the State, and therefore requires the mother to report the facts about paternity to the local authorities. If the child's paternity has been established, whether by its father's voluntary or tacit acknowledgment or by decision of a court, it can claim inheritance to his estate and has, subject to the preferential rights already referred to, the same rights of succession as his legitimate issue. Under a recently enacted law, should the father be dead or unknown, the child is entitled to fifty kroner (about fifty shillings) a month from the Children's Security Funds.

Sweden and Denmark
The Castberg Laws have had a deep influence upon the growth of

child welfare and maternity legislation in other Scandinavian countries.

Sweden has incorporated the principle that it is the duty of the mother to name the father, and the guardians appointed to oversee the welfare of the natural child and others without a male breadwinner have a duty to 'ensure that the parentage of the child, if illegitimate, is established and that the child will receive maintenance contributions'. This and a somewhat parallel scheme in *Denmark* actually go farther than the Norwegian provisions, since they introduce official guardianship for natural children. In *Sweden* a Royal Commission has recently presented a proposal that an illegitimate should inherit on equal terms with legitimate children.

In *Denmark* a child whose paternity has been established does inherit on equal terms with legitimate children. In the event of the death of a 'possible father', liable only for maintenance contributions, any amount due or overdue at that time is paid out of his estate. If, on the other hand, the child has been receiving maintenance advances through the local authority, these are continued after the father's death.

Paternity or maintenance obligation is established in as many as 95 per cent of all cases in *Denmark*. In *Sweden*, where there is no such category as 'possible father', the paternity of about 81 per cent of all natural children under the age of eighteen in 1950 has been ascertained.

Implications of the Castberg Laws

The fear expressed by the opponents of the new legislation that it might result in an increase in illegitimacy proved unfounded. In 1915, the year of its introduction, illegitimate children represented about 7 per cent of all children born alive in *Norway*. Since that date the proportion has dropped steadily, except in the war years, and in 1956 was only 3.5 per cent.[1] In *Sweden*, where much more far-reaching economic aid has been offered by the State since the 1930's, the rate has dropped from 15 per cent in 1915 and 16 per cent in the late 1920's to 10.2 per cent in 1956. So striking are these and other figures that the 1958 edition of the *Encyclopædia Britannica* has offered these more humane policies its indirect blessing: 'The policies regarding illegitimate children have been especially liberal in the Scandinavian countries, and studies

[1] For comparative figures see Tables 1 and 2.

conducted in these countries produced no evidence that such a liberal policy promoted illegitimacy.'

Although all arguments may seem weak ranged against Castberg's ethical passion, the time may not yet seem ripe in Britain for stripping away all our national reticences and forcing illegitimacy into the open air. That time must come, but a small population such as Norway's can more quickly achieve a frank and open attitude of mind than a complex industrial society such as our own. At present it is even doubtful if the child would always gain from knowing who its father was, any more than an adopted child would always gain from knowing the identity of its real mother. These are difficult decisions and must vary from case to case. Whatever decision is taken will be painful for the child.

Unfortunately, hardly any reform or social change can ever be achieved without the sacrifice of some other value: society itself is based upon compromise and still more, the delicate machinery of law. Though Castberg's laws may not solve all our problems, they throw out to us a necessary challenge and indicate the general *moral* direction in which we should move.

THE PLACE OF A NATURAL CHILD IN A COMMUNIST SOCIETY

U.S.S.R.

Czarist *Russia*—like eighteenth-century England—savagely penalized illegitimate children for their parents' errors. Russian literature gives a vivid picture of the fate of thousands of homeless and abandoned waifs who picked up a precarious living on their own account as thieves and toughs in the cities. But within less than two months of the establishment of Soviet power, there was a strong reaction and the very concept of illegitimacy was swept away—to such effect that in a recent Russian dictionary the word 'illegitimate' was defined as 'a term used in capitalist countries'. The family was to be based primarily on descent rather than marriage, and the decree of December 1917, as codified on 17th October 1918, affirms:

'Actual descent is regarded as the basis of the family, without any difference between relationships established by legal or religious marriage or outside marriage.'

This law has sometimes been read as a general invitation to practise free love, and indeed in the early aftermath of the revolution there was such a movement in certain circles, but its prime purpose and effect were quite different. An attempt was being made to separate the question of marriage from the question of responsibility for the family. Registration of marriage actually became compulsory—though not effective—at the same date. In Russia, as in many countries containing large and remote agricultural areas, there has long existed a tradition, unrecognized by law, of stable unions unregistered by Church or State. Such a tradition existed in *Scotland* until the 'Gretna Green' form of marriage was abolished in 1940, but there, if the couple concerned had made a public declaration of their intention to live together, the union was recognized in common law and the children regarded as legitimate. In Czarist Russia the children of such unions were bastards and consequently hundreds of thousands of children were growing up without adequate protection. Whatever, then, we may think of the new conception of 'marriage' later introduced in the U.S.S.R. (and it is clear, from the debates that took place when a new Family Code was under consideration,[1] that many of the peasant delegates disapproved of them roundly), this new definition did a great deal to safeguard the children born of such unions, to protect their legal and economic status and to save them from ignominy. In the early period the number of such unions increased for a while—in 1923 one marriage in twenty was unregistered—so such safeguards were particularly necessary.

Under the 1918 legislation the establishment of paternity was a fairly simple matter: the unmarried mother notified the local registrar's office of the father's name; the registrar would serve notice on the man and if he did not reply within a fortnight he would be assumed to be the father (a system that provoked a good deal of mirth among the delegates at a later meeting of the Soviet: 'What happens, comrades, if I am in the Far East and unable to send in my protest? They will go and marry me off without my knowledge and with a baby on top of it all'). If there had been several men all could be made liable to pay. With paternity established, the woman could demand support from the putative father during and immediately after her pregnancy; the father had the full paternal obligation for the maintenance and supervision of his child. ('If

---

[1] Discussions on the Draft of the 1926 Family Code, quoted by Dr Rudolf Schlesinger in *The Family in the U.S.S.R.* (1949), where all these matters are considered more fully.

you like tobogganing,' as a delegate said, 'you must like pulling your sledge uphill.') In its turn the child could inherit from its father, though not from his relatives.

A new Family Code of 1926 reaffirmed the principle that: 'The mutual rights of children are based on consanguinity. Children whose parents are not married possess the same rights as children born in wedlock.' Various alterations were made, however, in the law regarding the establishment of paternity. Only one man might be named as responsible. ('What are we to do,' asked a delegate, 'when other children point their fingers at the child of a *de facto* marriage and tease him with having several fathers? What kind of an education would that produce, comrades?') The defendant was given a month's notice before becoming 'father by default' and might contest the claim, while paying alimony, at any time during the following year. The onus of disproof, however, remained on the man.

The essential spirit behind the 1918 and 1926 legislation was that 'the child of an unmarried mother has equal rights and status with children born in wedlock and suffers no obloquy because of its birth . . .What is essential is that the innocent child shall not suffer and that the moral indignation which is felt at the behaviour of lax or irresponsible people shall not make the child a victim.'[1]

The U.S.S.R. deserves great credit for being among the first countries in the world to *try* to embody this philosophy in its legislation. But, as Russia herself has found, it is difficult to achieve: a child may be secured from public ignominy, but giving it a right to a father does not necessarily give it a father or make it feel less inferior on this account, and to secure a father is not necessarily to secure maintenance from him. If it is difficult in the British Isles to trace putative fathers who move from place to place to avoid their obligations, it must be almost impossible in a country as vast as Russia. There are mass movements of population, and added to these came the mass movements of soldiers during World War II.

In the 1940's there was a sudden shift of policy in the U.S.S.R. One factor in it may have been the impossibility—perhaps even, in Russian eyes, the undesirability—of seeking to make these wartime soldiers shoulder the responsibility for their irregular behaviour. But the primary reason was a comprehensive new population policy:

---

[1] Beatrice King, *Marriage, Morals and the Soviet Family* (*Anglo-Soviet Journal*, vol. V, No. 3, 1944).

there was felt to be a crying need to replace the millions of men the country had lost during the war and to do so in spite of the overwhelming preponderance of women of marriageable age over men.

First, in 1943, the right of natural children to inherit from their fathers was withdrawn. Then in 1944 all paternity suits were forbidden and the father ceased to have any responsibility—financial or otherwise—towards his natural child. Under a decree of 8th July 1944, described as 'for the protection of motherhood and childhood', steps were taken 'to abolish the existing rights of a mother to appeal to the court with a demand for the establishment of paternity and obtaining alimony for the support of a child born of a person with whom she is not living in registered marriage'. In place of the father, the State assumed entire financial responsibility for the support and upbringing of children of unmarried mothers. The special payments to these women corresponded with the alimony they would have received from the child's father had he been earning the average wage of a skilled worker in the village or a semi-skilled worker in the town, with, of course, the big difference that the State would make punctual payment. In that, by the same decree, a tax was imposed on bachelors, many putative fathers continued to pay an indirect subsidy.

The allowances, payable until children reached the age of twelve, were on a fairly generous scale—one hundred roubles a month for one child, one hundred and fifty for two children, and two hundred for three or more children. Unmarried mothers with three or more children were also entitled to the allowances paid to all mothers of large families, varying from eighty to three hundred roubles a month, according to the number of children, but payable only from the child's second to fifth birthdays. Mothers of large families were also promised lump-sum payments of several thousand roubles on the birth of their later children, and those with five, seven or ten children were offered respectively, Motherhood Medals, Orders of Motherhood Glory and the title of Heroine Mother, whether married or not.

In the currency reforms of 1947 the allowances to unmarried mothers were halved, the sum payable being then scarcely enough to take more than a fraction of the burden off the mother's shoulders. Taking the purchasing power of the rouble in 1947 as, very roughly, between fivepence and sixpence, the allowance for the first natural child was about £1 to £1 5s. a month, for two children about

£1 10s. to £2 and for three or more about £2 to £2 10s. So that—except that there was an allowance for the first child—a Russian woman received no more than an unmarried mother in Great Britain, who, under the Family Allowances Act of 1945, could claim £2 for four weeks for two children, £3 12s. for three, £5 12s. for four, and so on, increasing steadily with each child born. To press the matter to the extreme, the mother in Great Britain with eight illegitimate children under school-leaving age could claim £15 12s. every four weeks for their support, whereas a Russian mother could claim less than £10 a month and some of that only until the children reached the age of five.

Although such close comparisons between the value of allowances paid in one country and another are not really possible, especially in view of the much lower standard of living in U.S.S.R., the point is worth making in case the reader is tempted to think that the Russian allowances might have a greater effect on the illegitimacy rate in the country than is really probable. The introduction of family allowances in Great Britain did not have that effect; they coincided with a drop in the number of illegitimate births (see Table 4). Again, the removal of any social stigma from illegitimacy in National Socialist *Germany* caused no increase in the illegitimacy rate, which, if the figures are reliable, dropped sharply under Hitler, thus: 1926-30, 12.2 per cent; 1931-5, 10 per cent; 1936-9, 7.8 per cent (see Table 1). This may have been due to the facilitation of early marriage, the special marriage subsidies and full employment, but it occurred in spite of official encouragement of bastardy by the offer of generous bonuses to unmarried women willing to assist the Fatherland by bearing children. The number of women who would deliberately choose to have an extra-marital child, even with the inducement of allowances, would probably be fairly small at any time. In our view, it is not such minor advantages or disabilities that chiefly affect a country's illegitimacy rate, but the state of public opinion.

Since 1954 there has been a public campaign in the U.S.S.R. for the revision of the law.[1] There seems to be little support for a continuation of the 1944 legislation. Many think that the abolition of the father's responsibility was a mistake. Even in the U.S.S.R., it seems, children are suffering real hardship at school because their birth

---

[1] Rudolf Schlesinger, *Proposed Changes in Family Law* (*Soviet Studies*, April 1957).

certificates, with an empty space where the father's name should be, betray their illegitimacy, and moral stigma does still attach to this. The tightening up of divorce since 1944 has led to the establishment of unofficial families—as in the West—and so to an increase in the number of births out of wedlock. The problem of 'illegitimacy' is not, it seems, to be solved as easily as was once hoped.

Nevertheless the U.S.S.R. should be remembered for its contribution from 1917 onwards towards the welfare of the natural child, for its attempt to remove the stigma from the child itself, to achieve for it equality before the law, and to ease the difficulty of the mother during pregnancy and lactation by such measures as labour laws to safeguard her from losing her job, to control her hours of work and to enable her to feed her baby in free periods provided during a working day, as also in the provision of crèches and nurseries.

Eastern Europe[1]

Since 1944 each of the People's Republics of Eastern Europe has adopted the basic concept of the Russian decree that all children are equal before the law.

Bulgaria. The distinction between marital and out-of-wedlock children was abolished in principle in 1944. Article 76 of the Constitution of 1947 reads: 'Marriage and the family are under State protection. Only a civil marriage performed by the competent organs is legally valid. Children born out of wedlock have equal rights with the issue of lawful marriage.'

Rumania. Article 26 of the Draft Constitution of 1948 provided that 'parents have the same obligation towards their children born without wedlock as to those born from wedlock'. This article did not appear in the later Draft Constitution of 1952, which provided instead (Article 83) that 'the State protects marriage and the family, and defends the interests of mother and child. The State grants aid to mothers of large families and unmarried mothers, maternity leave with full pay, and provides maternity homes, crèches and day nurseries'.

---

[1] This section is based on information collected in 1954 and does not claim to be complete or up-to-date.

Poland. Under the Constitution 'a child born out of wedlock suffers no loss of rights'. Paternity, which can be established either by acknowledgment or in the course of legal proceedings, gives the father of the child of an unmarried mother the same duties towards it as the father who is, or was, the mother's husband.

Hungary. The description 'illegitimate' was abolished in an Act of 1946 that laid down that children born in and out of wedlock have equal legal status. The child born out of wedlock belongs not only to the mother and her family but also to the father and his family (which goes farther than the U.S.S.R.'s legislation) and consequently is a legal hereditary successor and has the right to bear the father's name. Alimony is the same for out-of-wedlock children as for the children of divorced or separated parents, and amounts to a minimum of 20 per cent of the father's income.

Jugoslavia. The Law on Parents' and Children's Relationships has 'rejected the legal discrimination affecting children born out of marriage' and what an official bulletin describes as the 'decadent prejudice about the reduced worthiness' of such children, and has sanctioned, in this province of family law, their equality with those born in marraige. The child is regarded as fully related to both its father and mother, but not to its parents' next of kin, which would, it is argued, 'be conducive to the weakening of marriage and family'. Children whose parents were betrothed but whose father died before the marriage was concluded may be treated as legitimate.

Czechoslovakia. The Constitution of 1948 provides that 'the rights of a child shall not be prejudiced by virtue of its origin', and by an Act of the same year out-of-wedlock children were given equal rights with the children of marriage.

Eastern Germany.[1] The Constitution of 1949 provides: 'Illegitimacy should in no way prejudice the rights of the child and its parents. Any laws providing otherwise are herewith repealed.' The child receives the mother's name, but has the same claim for maintenance against the father and his relatives—and against the mother and her relatives—as a child of marriage. It has, however, no duty of maintenance towards the father in its turn, and the

---

[1] This section gives the position up to August 1958.

father is allowed only such personal access to it as the mother permits.

The entire parental care falls upon the mother, who is also the child's legal representative. The child no longer comes under the automatic supervision and guardianship of the Youth Board, as in pre-war Germany or in Western Germany today. Only with regard to the child's claim against its father are certain safeguards made: the regional Department for Aid to Youth, and not the mother, is the trustee in this sphere, though the trusteeship may be terminated at the mother's request if the well-being of the child admits it, or at the Department's own decision when the goal of the trusteeship is achieved. If, however, the child is not under its mother's parental care, the Department becomes its guardian.

As regards the father's responsibility for maintenance, the amount required from him is calculated according to the position of both parents, thus varying according to his means. Cases were quoted in *Neue Justiz*[1] in 1953 of fathers paying twenty-five, thirty-five or even forty-eight marks monthly. An instance of twenty-five marks was evidently regarded as low and therefore raised by court order.

Since 1954 a most interesting debate has been going on in Eastern Germany in connexion with the draft of a new Family Law Book, which, at the time of writing, has not yet been enacted. The general principle laid down is that 'out-of-wedlock' children have in relationship to their parents and their parents' relatives the legal status of children born of marriage', though it is added: 'In so far as the following proposals include modifications of the general rule, they are made necessary by the fact that the parents are not bound together by marriage.'

Under the draft 'the father of the child born out of wedlock is deemed to be the man who had sexual relations with the woman during the period of conception. Intercourse that clearly did not lead to the conception is not taken into account.' Eastern Germany is thus proposing to adopt substantially the same position as the Scandinavian countries, avoiding both the concept of 'many fathers' and the rule in Great Britain that if the woman had several lovers at the period of conception, no man can be regarded as the father. The evidence of blood tests and anthropological tests (see page 138) is admissible.

---

[1] Journal of law and jurisprudence, published by the Ministry of Justice etc., Eastern Germany.

The child is the legal heir of his mother and of any of her relatives, as if a child of marriage, and if he is a minor or incapable of work at the death of his father, or of a relative of the father who is liable for his maintenance, he inherits like a child of marriage. In this the draft differs from the law of most of the People's Republics, where a natural child has full rights of inheritance from his father.

These rather fragmentary extracts from Eastern European drafts and decrees show at least that there is a general movement towards a radical improvement in the natural child's position, though it is taking a number of different forms. It does not follow that the economic or social position of such children in those countries is yet any better than, or even necessarily as good as, in some of the relatively well-to-do countries of Western Europe which have a much longer history of social legislation. One must not expect too much in so short a time, or hope for too mature a wisdom among those who legislate during a period of revolution. There are at present two views—held, broadly, by West and East German officials—as to whether natural children in Eastern Germany may not for the time being have suffered as much in practice from their removal from the guardianship of the Youth Board as they have gained from their new legal status. Yet, in the more backward States of Eastern Europe, where, for so many citizens, the lights have been going out, it does seem that a light of some kind has been lit for natural children that may in time to come bring new security to thousands of them.

And in *England?* Fortunately we are not in the throes of revolution, so we can face these questions more quietly, building up gradually and soberly towards a new approach, as the Norwegians did in the early years of this century. Our solution is not likely to be as radical as the French or Eastern European; nor, perhaps, will it ever contain all the radical elements of the Scandinavian. We like to give more freedom of choice to the citizen—even to as difficult a citizen as the unmarried mother. But embedded in the Castberg and other laws are many hints and ideas that we could well ponder, and that might, if we wish, bear new and good fruit in our own country.

CHAPTER 15

THE STATE AS GUARDIAN

As an alternative to giving illegitimate children equality before the law, or as a safeguard where it is attempted, a number of countries have developed far-reaching schemes of State guardianship for all illegitimate children, designed to give that somewhat handicapped group more careful protection. These schemes take many forms, and since they raise important principles in the handling of illegitimate families, some account of them is necessary.

THE GERMAN SCHEME

The idea that all illegitimate children should be placed under professional guardianship was first developed in *Germany* over sixty years ago, and it is in *Western Germany* that it is still found in its mostly highly developed form. The scheme was based on the theory that an illegitimate child would find itself at a disadvantage if it were treated in the same way as other children: it had no legal father, many of the mothers had proved incompetent at handling their children's affairs, some were irresponsible, and many had evaded the duty of claiming financial help from the putative father.

Under the German Family Law of 1896 parental authority over illegitimate children was divided between the mother and a guardian, and since 1924 that guardian has been the State. The scheme involves three main principles: (*a*) parental authority passes to the official guardian, who thus has considerably greater authority over the child than its own mother; (*b*) it is the duty of the guardian to protect the child's financial interests and (*c*) to ensure its general physical and moral well-being.

From the child's birth the Jugendamt (Youth Board), which is the child welfare office of the district, accepts what might be called a paternal role. The real father is held to have no legal relationship with the child, although he has the first duty to maintain it. The mother has normally the privilege and duty of looking after her child from day to day, and in many matters—such as deciding where it should live and how it should be educated—she normally has the initiative; but unless a judge takes special action to transfer the guardianship to her, she has not full parental authority. Until the child is twenty-one the Jugendamt as guardian must advise and help her and protect the child's interests. The Jugendamt, not the mother, administers the child's financial affairs and is its representative in law: it has both the knowledge and the necessary means for protecting the child morally, financially and legally, even if need be against its mother, and it has the power to intervene at once if the ward's welfare seems to be in danger. The guardian's functions are in practice generally discharged by individual officers of the Jugendamt whose personal relationship to the child is as firmly established as that of an ordinary guardian.[1]

Given extreme care in the appointment of qualified officials and a very high standard of training in social matters—and in this Germany was for many years ahead of most European countries—these powers have certainly given to the local authority an enviable opportunity to do 'preventive' social work: to intervene, that is to say, *before* a child is psychologically injured, *before* the wrong decisions are taken.

Germany was prepared to pay a certain price to achieve this. Clearly such rights can be exercised within a family only at the price of depriving a mother of certain of her own natural rights and of her full natural status as a citizen. We in this country might be reluctant to see any reform that detracted from a mother's personal responsibility for her child unless she had—in some way other than becoming an unmarried mother—already proved her incapacity. A simple official distinction that brands married mothers *per se* as capable and unmarried mothers *per se* as incapable might seem wrong in both fact and principle. To deprive a competent older woman, for example, of the full management of her child, and to do this automatically from the moment of her child's birth, irrespective of any actual evidence that she has neglected it or is incapable of bringing it up alone, would be regarded in some countries as an unwarranted interference with civil liberties. Many social workers might argue, also, that by taking away the mother's sense of responsibility, one may deprive her of her strongest incentive to grow up into a responsible parent: she may need advice and guidance

---

[1] League of Nations Child Welfare Committee, *The Official Guardianship of Illegitimate Children*, 1932.

but, they would say, it should normally be given with the knowledge that the full responsibility and privileges of parenthood rest with *her*.

Two points of view are possible here and both are widely held. In the view of West German officials the scheme has worked extremely well, and still meets with little criticism or opposition from the mothers. Of five hundred mothers whose opinion was invited during a survey in 1954-5, 80 per cent were in favour of the continuance of official guardianship. On the other hand, *Eastern Germany*, in its socialist movement for the equality of women, has jettisoned the entire scheme. (After all, no one has ever suggested that a widower, a man, required State supervision!) On rather different grounds *English* social workers have been chary of proposing the introduction of State guardianship, many of them believing that it would involve too great an interference with the freedom of the individual or that, however great an advance it may have represented sixty years ago, it no longer accords with modern ideas. An English children's officer might deeply envy the power of early intervention it would give him, yet feel that the power given was too wide and too automatic, and the group of children over whom it was exercised selected in rather an arbitrary way.

SCANDINAVIAN SCHEMES

It is from the German scheme that the *Swedish* and *Danish* schemes derive, though each places a rather different emphasis upon these various aspects of the guardian's work. These are the two countries that give the most generous aid to the illegitimate family, and their official guardianship schemes are far-reaching.

In *Sweden* a child welfare guardian is appointed for every child born out of wedlock, just as it is in special cases for those whose parents are separated or divorced.[1] But this official guardian in no way relieves the mother of her natural duties or takes her place as the child's representative. As far as possible he must co-operate with the mother, who remains the child's real guardian in the eyes of the law. If a case occurs in which the interests of the child require the official guardian to take the child's side against the mother, only then, in the last resort, if she has proved incompetent to look after the child, may she be deprived of her legal guardianship.

[1] Chapter 8 of *Parent's Code* of 1949.

Sweden has thus considerably modified the first of the three German principles. The other two it retains: it is the guardian's duty not only to safeguard the child's financial interests if the mother needs assistance but also to help her generally with advice and counsel. In *Stockholm* these functions are exercised by women social workers employed by the municipality, who visit every illegitimate child as often as necessary, in the ordinary case perhaps four or five times a year. Many carry an exceedingly high case-load, say some four hundred children, of whom about half may be illegitimate. Visits are made, however, even where unmarried parents are cohabiting, since it is felt that a crisis might arise suddenly if the *ménage* came to an end. In the countryside, where the population is widely scattered, a volunteer, such as a teacher, often has to take over the guardian's duties—a solution regarded as less satisfactory. The general intention is to change over to women social workers when and where it proves possible.

If a Swedish woman is receiving advances of alimony or other help from the public purse the child welfare guardians make it their task to see that the money is spent in the child's interests. It is clear that when there is this skilled but friendly supervision the State can much better afford to be generous towards the women.

Finland has somewhat similar provisions for the automatic supervision of all illegitimate children up to the age of seventeen.

In *Denmark* a rather different scheme is in operation, depending less upon the use of trained social workers and more upon enrolling selected citizens to supervise various categories of children who require special protection. The scheme is not restricted to illegitimate children; it includes all foster-children under fourteen years of age, those placed with daily minders, or those whose parents are on poor relief or receiving other communal help: but children born out of wedlock are subject to supervision until they are seven years old or, if their home circumstances seem to warrant it, until the end of their fourteenth year. During infancy—that is, until they are one year old—they must so far as possible be supervised by women with special knowledge of infant care. In *Copenhagen* the health visitors, trained nurses, perform the task until the child is two years old. From then up to the age of seven both boys and girls are to be supervised by a woman; from seven to fourteen both men and women are employed. Although this work falls officially upon the Child Care Committee, most of it is in fact delegated to ordinary citizens selected for their experience and understanding of children and their capacity for public service; relatively few are trained social workers. The task of 'inspector', as it is called, is a public duty that one cannot refuse to undertake, and is unpaid. Only if it proves impossible to enrol a sufficient number of suitable inspectors on this basis may permission be granted for paid workers to be employed.

In 1951 a good third of all the children under supervision were illegitimate. Originally the work was focused chiefly on the children's physical well-being, but it is now more widely interpreted. It is considered important to find inspectors who will be able to make a tactful and intimate contact with the child and its parents, and even advise in difficulties that require a skilled understanding of the child's emotional life. Since such people are very hard to find there are at present in Denmark, as in England, two schools of thought: those who would like to see more of the work delegated to trained health visitors, with their high professional standards, and those who feel that, with the great advances in the present generation in the understanding of children's psychological needs, neither the health visitor nor the average inspector has an adequate social training and that the whole scheme, however enlightened in its day, may now be open in some respects to the charge of amateurism.

Nevertheless, the inspectors fulfil certain very important tasks. For example, if it transpires that endeavours are being made to remove a supervised child from a good foster home, the Child Care Committee—to whom the inspector will refer—may rule that it must not be removed without the Committee's consent. Experience has shown that it is particularly unfortunate for a child to change foster-homes frequently, and in this way a move can be prevented before harm is done.

Another important Danish organization, the Maternity Aid Institutions, is available to help and advise unmarried mothers. These centres, now established all over the country, began as a voluntary effort, but since 1939 have been taken over by the State. They are staffed by doctors, lawyers, psychiatrists and social workers, and offer personal, legal and social help and advice, if necessary even economic aid, to pregnant women, married or unmarried, and to the mothers of families. They are empowered to help the women in a wide variety of ways: they act as a focal point for the distribution of welfare foods; provide layettes; arrange for domestic help during the period of confinement; procure places where an expectant mother can stay during pregnancy or go with her child after its birth; help in appropriate ways to find foster-homes or arrange adoptions; offer courses in child care; and even, in suitable cases, give a mother generous economic help while she qualifies to earn her child's living. This last function is regarded as an important one. The Maternity Aid Institution in *Copenhagen*, for example, provides a number of modern flats where unmarried mothers may live with their children and be maintained financially while they take a professional or apprentice training in whatever work will best fit them to act as the children's breadwinners. This help may be made available to a mother for as long as two years: women have been trained as shorthand typists, kindergarten teachers, dieticians, etc.

It is within this imaginative and human organization that the various legal questions are also first dealt with. It is the task of the Maternity Aid Institution to get in touch with the child's father and to obtain maintenance from him. Every unmarried pregnant woman is therefore advised to notify the centre by the end of the sixth month of her pregnancy, so that a financial agreement with the father can be negotiated. If a satisfactory arrangement can be made it is registered with the magistrates' court: if the father refuses to pay, a court order may be necessary. Should the father then default, advances of alimony are made through the court, but only under safeguards: the Child Care Committee has the right to order that the money is spent in a certain way and if these directions are not complied with or conditions otherwise make it necessary, the Child Care Committee may arrange to draw the advance itself and apply it for the benefit of the child, or give it to the mother only in small instalments. These various services ensure that an unmarried mother receives the aid or counsel she requires, and where financial assistance is given her, they provide a convenient means of keeping in touch.

The work of the Maternity Aid Institutions has become famous beyond the borders of Denmark and, since the war, *Finland* has developed a somewhat parallel organization in its Social Consulting Bureaux.

Provisions for the automatic official guardianship of all illegitimate children, based somewhat more closely on the German model, also exist in *Switzerland* and *Austria*. The Swiss appoint a curator who safeguards the child's financial interests and is then replaced by a guardian, unless the guardianship board prefers to place the child under the parental authority of its mother or father.

In *Norway* intervention by the State between an illegitimate child and its parents is on a much more limited scale than in either Sweden or Denmark. In most cases it is deliberately restricted to a single task: identifying the child's father and obtaining from him due maintenance for mother and child. There is no general scheme for official guardianship over all natural children. Parental authority normally remains with the mother, or whichever parent has the custody of the child, and the Child Welfare Committee appoints a legal guardian only where this seems to be specifically necessary: if the child is neglected or does not live with its parents; if the mother is under age or asks for a guardian to be appointed; or if the child's interests otherwise seem to require it. Such a guardian is, in Norway, usually a private individual who must 'see that the child is cared for properly and in a responsible manner, and that the parents perform their duty' and in particular that 'the father's contribution actually be paid',[1] but they are only appointed in a small minority of cases.

As soon, however, as an illegitimate child is born (or earlier if its mother gives notice of her pregnancy), an officer of the law known as the Bailiff of Alimony, who is responsible for handling the financial claims of all broken families against the fathers, must get into touch with the mother. If she has not already notified him, the doctor or midwife will have done so. In *Oslo* a special office handles all these claims. The Bailiff of Alimony, who is a lawyer and an experienced social worker, has the help of a married woman social worker. She visits the mother in hospital or in her own home, enquires into the family's financial circumstances and the identity of the child's father, then reports back to the Bailiff, who himself contacts the father and tries to arrive at a satisfactory financial agreement with him. Since this can be registered with the courts and have all the force of law, a court case is necessary only if no satisfactory agreement can be obtained. This arrangement—the division of work between a man and a woman, each of whom can, if it seems advisable, interview clients of the same sex, and the store of legal knowledge and experience in social work that they share

[1] *Guidance for Guardians*, April 1915.

between them—has proved a particularly happy one. Although it is officially designed only to safeguard the child's financial interests, the skill that the workers bring to bear inevitably leads them to be consulted on innumerable personal matters covering the whole scope of the child's and the mother's, sometimes even the father's, welfare. In the countryside it is often necessary for the work of the Bailiff to be undertaken by the rural policeman, which, as in Sweden, is usually a much less satisfactory arrangement.

Norwegian social workers tend to regard the Swedish and West German schemes of automatic official guardianship as unwarranted interference by officialdom into family life. They prefer their own system, whereby a mother, automatically in touch with the authorities over the child's financial affairs, can seek advice of her own accord: she is free to take it or leave it, but it is gladly and skilfully given.

And *English* social workers? We would probably prefer a system under which the parents' contact with the authorities was less automatic even than it is in Norway, but we could surely do worse than offer to unmarried parents a continuing service that was as sensitive in spirit and of as high professional skill.

PART V

THE SUMMING UP

CHAPTER 16

SOME QUESTIONS AND CONCLUSIONS

WHY IS THE ILLEGITIMACY RATE SO HIGH?

Many countries have lower rates than ours. In the Netherlands in 1950 it was 1.5 per cent, whilst the lowest ever reached in England and Wales was 3.9 per cent in the early years of this century. In 1958 it stood at 4.9 per cent, 36,174 live births.

Why are there still so many? There are several ways of answering this question, each leading to a different facet of the truth.

It can be said, for example, that natural births occur on their present alarming scale because extra-marital relationships are so widespread. No one knows how widespread they are, nor is the illegitimacy rate any index—for contraception, abortion and 'cover-up' marriages all affect the number of children born illegitimate—but that they are common is clear. In a stabler and simpler society, many of them would lead to marriage. We have seen that a great number of the births are the result of population shifts—through war or immigration or the growth of towns—or the individual moving about of men and women in search of jobs or training or adventure, on holiday or short assignments, or sometimes in work such as lorry driving or commercial travelling that keeps them on the move. These people are often lonely and rootless. Brief affairs flare up. Without enough affection and knowledge of each other to make them want to marry, and without the social and family pressure that would persuade them to in a settled community, they drift apart. The illegitimate children resulting are in a sense part of the price paid for industrial mobility and for the social and political upheavals of our time.

Again, it can be argued that illegitimacy is a by-product of Christianity, the price that civilization pays for setting its sights so high. Christianity sets a high value on the family and the personal standards that guard it. The family was orginally the condition of survival for the young and the very old; it remains incomparably the best nursery for children, perhaps the greatest source of human happiness, and at its best the nearest approach to living in love. But the family, though generally tough, can break with the strain. It is not surprising that society—aiming at a Christian ideal but not charitable enough itself to be called Christian—has often been savage to those who have endangered it. Extra-marital intercourse, abortion and easy divorce each threaten something essential in the family relationship—the unanxious trust, the welcome to children, the willingness to face problems and difficulties for the sake of something too good to lose. Although it is a sub-Christian impulse that wishes to strike at and punish the children that are born in breach of the ideal of monogamy, or even their parents, it occurs because it is a natural human impulse to wish to punish in others the tendencies that we deny or repress in ourselves. This is largely a sub-conscious impulse, but that makes it only harder to control. One does not wish to see others 'getting away with' behaviour one has not permitted to oneself. The placing of a whole category of children in a lower status than those born of marriage has followed from this impulse. As long as we remain in our present no man's land between the Stone Age and the Kingdom of Heaven this impulse, and this problem, will remain.

HOW CAN THE RATE BE REDUCED?

A question that must be in many minds is whether the present large number of illegitimate births is in any sense inevitable or whether social action could be taken to reduce it. It might well seem that social effort and public money would be better expended on trying to reduce the number than on devising makeshift arrangements to safeguard the children after they have been born. The number could certainly be reduced, and quickly, at a social cost that would be generally regarded as intolerable—or it could be gradually lessened by gentler methods. They are worth discussing.

Penalizing the Parents

In the past, society has relied chiefly on deterrents. It was argued that if life were made sufficiently difficult and unpleasant for the mother, fewer women would risk having illegitimate children. Fewer, perhaps, did, but many continued to have them. Men and women in love live too strongly in the present to be deterred simply by a negative system of penalties, unless these are so ruthless as to be intolerable in a Christain society. Their chief effect was to create a mental climate in which there was little chance that illegitimate children would grow up healthy, happy or balanced people.

It is true that one must rely on the force of public opinion to help limit the number of illegitimate births—otherwise, as in the *West Indies* today and part of *South America*, a majority of children may be born illegitimate. But there is no need for it to be punitive, negative, unloving in character. Stoning or imprisoning women, exposing the babies, imposing fines or treating the women as tribal outcasts; in general, ensuring the parents' or children's unhappiness—all these sub-Christian methods have been tried, and illegitimacy has continued to flourish.

Forced Marriage
A pregnant girl could be forced or persuaded into marriage with her lover, whenever he could be traced and both were free to marry. This might not reduce the illegitimacy rate very much—in *Midboro* only about a third of the parents whose civil status was known were both legally free to marry and for some of these marriage was impracticable—but it would do something. It would certainly produce unhappy marriages. They would be unhappy for the parents and the children, would often lead to separation or other love affairs and so to the birth of new illegitimate children and the setting up of more 'unofficial families'. The illegitimacy rate would probably be reduced a little on balance, but at a cost.

Early Marriage
Unmarried motherhood—though not, to the same extent, illegitimacy—could be almost eliminated if all girls were married at puberty and divorce forbidden—or, failing any such impractical policy, if early marriages were encouraged by social and economic pressure. But the current experience is that early marriage is usually unwise. Of those made by girls below the age of twenty, a quarter already end in divorce, so many more, one must assume, lead to unhappiness or separations. It is not certain, either, that under present conditions in this country the number of illegitimate births would fall so very greatly if marriage took place earlier: it might lead to fewer births among unmarried women but more among faithless wives. Although, in *Midboro*, 60 per cent of the

mothers were unmarried, 26.3 per cent were married and another 11.5 per cent had been married at some time—37.8 per cent of the total. Socially this could become a more serious problem than that of the unstable or carefree adolescent.

Legalized Abortion
Abortion might be legalized, and performed under the Health Service for all who asked for it. In that event, very many of the children now conceived would never be born. One cannot say how many. Illegal abortion is very widespread. It was estimated in 1939 that there were something like 44,000 to 60,000 cases in the country every year, and that as many as 6 to 8 per cent of all pregnancies were being illegally terminated.[1] Many of these were legitimate pregnancies, but there was evidence enough that many unmarried women were resorting to abortion. Yet the fact remains that those who continue to become unmarried mothers include a number who, though they have conceived by mistake, deliberately decide to bear their children. With a mixture of maternal and moral feelings or natural fear, many have an aversion to the idea of abortion, which, apart from the moral issue, is not a safe and easy operation, even in skilled hands; the dangers of physical and mental shock are considerable. Some women, too, long deeply for a child, whether they have to bring it up alone or can do so with the father. Others have self-punishing personalities; others are thoughtless. If abortion were legalized a number of these would still continue to bear their children. Illegitimacy would be reduced, but would not cease to exist.

Easier Divorce
Divorce could be made easier, so that more of the parents who now set up unofficial families could marry and have legitimate children instead. It is quite possible that this would do more than any other single factor to reduce the illegitimacy rate. Of the *Midboro* parents whose marital status was known, 69 per cent were barred by an existing marriage—often in reality a long-standing separation—from marrying one another. It is impossible to say how many would have married had they been free to do so: probably the third who were stably cohabiting and a number of others. The illegitimacy rate could very likely be reduced in this way, by a stroke

[1] *Report of the Inter-Departmental Committee on Abortion* (H.M.S.O., 1939).

of the pen, to under 3 per cent of all live births.

If, however, divorce were made easier or allowed at the instance of one partner, whatever the other wished, the stability of many marriages would be undermined and the happiness of many other children—the existing and future children of marriage—imperilled. Nearly every marriage has at least some moment of stress when for a brief while the partners rely almost solely on their vow and intention of permanence and society's insistence that marriage should endure. Many good marriages would founder in the absence of this support.

So here society has constantly to weigh up anew the difficult and delicately balanced choice between two sets of needs.

Birth Control

What effect would a wider knowledge and practice of birth control have upon the illegitimate birth rate? Here opinion is sharply divided. There is first the vital question as to how far it is desirable to instruct adolescents and the unmarried in the use of birth control, but even if one sets this aside for the moment and considers only the more limited question of how far it would lead to a reduction in the number of illegitimate births, there are two opinions.

'Extra-marital intercourse,' declares Professor Crew, 'always has been, is, and will continue to be, exceedingly common. There seems to be no social force capable of checking it.'[1]

He stresses that the illegitimacy rate is an index of the ignorance concerning contraception that prevails among individuals, and that this is society's direct responsibility.

'Society condemns and punishes abortion, infanticide and illegitimacy, but takes no steps to encourage the production of safe contraceptives in sufficient numbers and to instruct young women in their use.'[2]

The logic of this view is supported by *Sweden's* experience. The growth of sex education in that country since the 1930's, and the deliberate spread of knowledge about more effective methods of birth control, brought about quite a sharp fall in the number of illegitimate births. Between 1930 and 1950 the rate fell from 16.0 per cent to 9.5 per cent, and this in spite of the far-reaching measures taken during the same years to make life economically easier for

---

[1] *Measurements of the Public Health*, p. 77.
[2] *Ibid.*, p. 66.

unmarried mothers and their children. Fewer girls entered marriage pregnant, which was attributed by Alva Myrdal 'exclusively' to birth control.[1] Those who bore illegitimate children increasingly tended to be quite young women and girls, which seemed to mean that it was 'more directly related to ignorance'. This, pitiable in itself, might 'seem to be amenable to intentional social change in the form of sex education'.

What reason is there to believe that it might have the same effect in *England*? Some, at any rate. After 1870, when the growth in the practice of birth control first began to affect our birth rate, there was a sharp decline in the proportion of unmarried women who became pregnant and a fall from about 6 to 4 per cent in the illegitimacy rate. On the other hand, although proof in such matters is extremely hard to obtain, it is generally believed that since World War I there has been some increase in extra-marital relationships, and—whatever the reason may be—the illegitimacy rate is now around 5 per cent. But the important point here is probably that our illegitimate birth rate is very much lower than Sweden's and so is at least rather nearer to its irreducible minimum.

A higher proportion of those who have illegitimate children in England may be women who would be unlikely, even with instruction, to practise birth control effectively. Many social workers with much experience among unmarried mothers take that view. Their argument runs as follows. A small but steady number of unmarried mothers are seriously below average mentally; it would be useless to attempt to teach them birth control by present methods, which require foresight and a minimum skill. Some unmarried mothers are neurotic and would probably take no steps to safeguard themselves. Helena Deutsch wrote of one woman:

'She became pregnant repeatedly, and a strict taboo against birth control ruled over her conceptions and pregnancies. Hers were compulsive pregnancies.'[2]

That may be an extreme case, but social workers often have to deal with women not unlike her. If such a woman is advised to use contraceptives she may be deeply shocked: it is of the essence of her moral alibi that she is helpless, that 'something comes over her' and it 'just happens'. To use contraceptives would imply that she knew what she was doing! And this point of view is not confined

---

[1] *Nation and Family*, p. 47.
[2] *The Psychology of Women*, vol. 2, p. 313.

SOME QUESTIONS AND CONCLUSIONS

to the neurotic. There are many women impulsive and impatient by nature and averse to all forms of planning. It would seem to some of them rather calculated and cold-blooded—and would they be so exceptional in feeling this?—to go to a tryst ready provided with contraceptives, or even entirely determined to say 'No'. There are some whose pregnancy seems to be a reaction against too planned and disciplined a life—the middle-aged nurse or schoolmistress may sometimes be in this category, and the girl of rather rigid personality who is so deeply shocked by her own actions. Those who conceive extra-maritally always include a large proportion of those who dislike planning, who do not stop to think or, if they do think, do not worry. A knowledge of birth control would not, by itself, help them.

One must acknowledge that there may in the future be forms of contraception that will better suit their temperament. Research workers have for long been trying to develop a pill that would give twenty-four hours' immunity from conception, and some doctors have even suggested that in our Brave New World there may one day be a contraceptive with which every girl will be automatically fitted at puberty and will remove only when she wishes to conceive. If that day comes, illegitimacy will be outmoded, though there may, of course, be other, larger problems.

A difficulty in assessing how effective, even from the purely practical angle, wider education in birth control might be, is that no one knows how many people in this country have extra-marital relationships, or how many of these already practise birth control. It may be a high proportion. Among the married the practice of contraception has increased very greatly over the last fifty years. In a survey of some 11,000 married women made by the Population Investigation Committee in 1946-7, it emerged that only 15 per cent of those who married in 1900-10 had ever practised any form of it, but as many as 66 per cent of those who married in 1935-9.[1] The present number may well be higher.

But that survey also proved that a knowledge of contraception was no general panacea. Almost a quarter of the children born to those married women who normally practised birth control were 'unwanted'. Contraceptive appliances sometimes failed; more often the marriage partners failed to use them! The unmarried—

[1] Papers of the Royal Commission on Population, Vol. 1: *Family Limitation* (H.M.S.O., 1949).

or at any rate, unmarried girls and women—have more reason to be careful, but there is no reason to suppose that they are.

One must remember, too, that a number of potential unmarried mothers are Roman Catholic. Even if they have moved so far from their Church's point of view as to have an extra-marital relationship, they often have an almost instinctive aversion to the use of contraceptives. If it seems contradictory that they should keep a minor rule of the Church while breaking a greater, it is understandable. Human nature is like that, and the teaching that contraceptives are 'unnatural' at a higher moral level blends easily enough with the reversion to a 'natural' irresponsible life at a lower, even if it ends with natural children.

If we turn to the ethics of teaching birth control to the unmarried, there is again a division of opinion and some of it goes very deep. There would be general agreement that to instruct the young who are simply 'out for a good time' in the bare principles of contraception apart from any teaching of values would be inviting trouble. Most social workers would feel considerable hesitation at any general educational programme that at all risked giving adolescents—at an age, and perhaps in a period of history, when sexual curiosity is at its height—any further inducement to enter pre-marital relationships; and the belief that they could be undertaken with little risk of conception would certainly act, for some boys and girls, as a turning point, as it does for some older women.

A number of social workers, including perhaps a majority of Church workers, would go farther than this, and would never—or practically never—be willing to refer an unmarried person to a doctor or clinic for advice on contraception. They feel that to do so would not only involve them in a very heavy and uncertain responsibility but would also seem to imply that the Church or society condoned sex relationships outside marriage. Christians, they would argue, must be single-minded and take a clear stand—not only in their own lives but also in the advice they are prepared to give.

Other case-workers, and many in the medical field, take the view that if one wishes to help a person one must start by accepting that person as he or she is. If the gap between the social worker's own ethic and that of the person she is trying to help can be bridged in time to avoid the risk of an extra-marital pregnancy, that may be the ideal. If in the event it cannot, it may be wiser and rather more realistic to offer that person instruction in birth control. If it is withheld, children may suffer. Those who take this view would instance certain unofficial families living in very poor financial circumstances. A woman may not be prepared to leave a married man with whom she is living: if she did so, she would be depriving her children of their home and father. He, on the other hand, has two families to maintain: his non-legal and his legal one. A social worker may be faced with the choice of leaving such a woman to bring more unwanted children into that insecurity and drag down farther the living standards of two families, or of referring her for advice over contraception. Again, a younger girl may have conceived a child by her 'fiancé', a married man waiting for a divorce, and thereafter be determined to live with him until they marry. It may depend upon the social worker whether this young couple conceive more children outside marriage or are told how to avoid them.

These are always difficult questions, and social workers answer them differently. Moral Welfare workers are in a particularly difficult position here because, through their untiring work, they have won a position that gives them a responsibility towards many women who do not and never will share their religious or moral point of view. This may require of a social worker an almost superhuman degree of understanding and detachment. It is not made easier by the fact that whether or not a woman should be offered this instruction is so closely bound up with her individual personality that the decision—either way—may have a vital effect upon her.

The Long-Term Solution
One thing would help, slowly but surely, to reduce the rate. If the young experience deep love in their own homes, they are more likely to value marriage, far less likely to wander around seeking love wherever they can get it without knowing what it is. But until they have that experience, we must accept the fact that something perhaps not far short of our present rate is unavoidable, and be prepared to treat the mothers and children with humanity.

WISE TREATMENT OF MOTHER AND CHILD

There is, of course, a tension between the two needs: to safeguard society against irresponsible parents; and to safeguard the child's future by alleviating the mother's difficulties and distresses during its formative years and thereby enable it to grow up emotionally balanced and secure.

Changes of policy could have a considerable effect. There will always be some children who stay with their mothers and some who are adopted, so the best possible provisions are necessary to deal with either contingency. One day, with new knowledge, social workers will be better able to assess an individual woman's capacity for motherhood in these difficult conditions; financial help will be more readily available for those who need it; far more will be known about the comparative development in health and happiness of children who remain with their mothers or who are adopted. Then the time will come to think out policies afresh.

The danger is that the less one knows about illegitimacy, the more one tends to have strong feelings. There is need for continued research. At present we work in the dark, guided by a mixture of instinct and experience, and by a very slowly growing understanding.

BIBLIOGRAPHY

Sources quoted or referred to in the text are indicated by an asterisk.

BRITISH ISLES

*ABORTION, INTERDEPARTMENTAL COMMITTEE ON. *Report.* H.M.S.O. (1939).

ANDERSON, E. W., HAMILTON, M. W. and KENNA, J. C. Psychiatric, Social and Psychological Aspects of Illegitimate Pregnancy in Girls under 16 years. *Psychiatria et Neurologia*, No. 133 (Basle).

ASHLEY, ANNE. *Another Man's Child.* Scottish Council for the Unmarried Mother and Her Child (1945).
Illegitimate Children and Their Parents in Scotland. Scottish Council for the Unmarried Mother and Her Child (1955).

*BEVERIDGE, SIR WILLIAM. *Social Insurance and Allied Services.* H.M.S.O. (1942).

*BOWLBY, JOHN. *Maternal Care and Mental Health.* World Health Organization, Geneva. H.M.S.O. (1952).

BOWLEY, AGATHA. The Unmarried Mother and Her Child. *Fortnightly* (June 1950).

*BRANDON, M. W. G. The Intellectual and Social Status of Children of Mental Defectives. *Journal of Mental Science*, Vol. 103, No. 433 (October 1957).

*BRITISH MEDICAL ASSOCIATION and MAGISTRATES' ASSOCIATION. *The Law in Relation to the Illegitimate Child.* British Medical Association (1952).

*BURT, CYRIL. *The Young Delinquent.* University of London Press (1925).

CARE OF CHILDREN COMMITTEE. *Report.* H.M.S.O. (1946).

*CARR-SAUNDERS, A. M., MANNHEIM, H. and RHODES, E. C. *Young Offenders.* Cambridge University Press (1942).

*CHESSER, EUSTACE. *The Unwanted Child.* Richard Cowan (1947).

*COOPER, CHRISTINE. The Illegitimate Child. *Practitioner* (April 1955), reprinted as a booklet by N.C.U.M.C.

*CREW, F. A. E. *Measurements of the Public Health.* Oliver & Boyd (1948).

*DEUTSCH, HELENA. *The Psychology of Women.* Research Books Ltd (1947).

*DEVON, COUNTY OF, CHILDREN'S COMMITTEE. *The Illegitimate Children of Mental Defectives* (1953).

*DONNISON, DAVID. *The Neglected Child and the Social Services.* Manchester University Press (1954).

*DONNISON, DAVID and STEWART, MARY. *The Child and the Social Services.* Fabian Society (1958).

*ELLISON, MARY. *The Adopted Child*. Gollancz (1958).
Encyclopædia Britannica, 11th, 13th, 14th and 1958 editions. Illegitimacy.

*FISHER, LETTICE. *Twenty-One Years and After*, 1918-1946, 2nd edition (1946) of a short history of the work of the N.C.U.M.C., first published by the N.C.U.M.C. in 1939.
*FITZGERALD, HILDE. *Illegitimacy and War*, chapters 3 and 4, *History of the Second World War: Studies in the Social Services*. H.M.S.O. (1954).
*FRAZER, W. M. and STALLYBRASS, C. O. *Textbook of Public Health*. Livingstone (1946).
*FREEMAN, T. W. *Ireland*. Methuen (1950).

*GARDINER, ANNA G. See N.C.U.M.C., *Discussion of Illegitimacy*.
*GENERAL REGISTER OFFICE. *Annual Reports of Births, Deaths and Marriages*, 1842 to 1920.
Statistical Reviews of England and Wales, 1921 to 1956.
Census, 1951, *Great Britain*. One per cent sample tables, 1952.
Classification of Occupations, 1950.
GLOVER, EDWARD. *The Psycho-Pathology of Prostitution*. Institute for the Scientific Treatment of Delinquency (1945).
*GORER, GEOFFREY. *Exploring British Character*. Cresset Press (1955).
*GREENLAND, CYRIL. Some Ecological Aspects of Unmarried Parenthood. *Lancet* (19th January 1957).
Unmarried Parenthood: I. Unmarried Mothers. *Medical Officer* (9th May 1958).
Unmarried Parenthood: II. Putative Fathers. *Medical Officer* (16th May 1958).
Illegitimacy, a series of four articles. *Scotsman* (26th-29th January 1960).

HALL, M. PENELOPE. *The Social Services of Modern England*. Routledge & Kegan Paul (1952).
HALSBURY, LORD. *Encyclopaedia of the Laws of England*, Vol. 3, 1953 edition. Butterworth.
*HEALTH, MINISTRY OF. *Annual Reports*.
Circular No. 2866. 16th November 1943.
*HOME OFFICE. *Annual Reports*.
Children in the Care of Local Authorities in England and Wales in November 1954. H.M.S.O. Command 9488.
Children in the Care of Local Authorities in England and Wales in March 1956. H.M.S.O., Command 9881.
*HOPKIN, W. A. B. and HAJNAL, J. Analysis of the Births in England, 1939. *Population Studies* (September 1947).
*HOPKIRK, MARY. *Nobody Wanted Sam*. John Murray (1949).

JEGER, LENA M. *Illegitimate Children and Their Parents*. N.C.U.M.C. (1951).
'J.F.J.' The Legitimacy Act, 1959. *Solicitors' Journal* (25th September 1959).

BIBLIOGRAPHY

*JORDAN, G. W. and FISHER, E. M. *Self-Portrait of Youth.* Heinemann (1955).
*JOY, CELIA M. Illegitimate Children and Their Parents—A Survey of Case Work for 1952. *Moral Welfare* (January 1954).
*KORNITZER, MARGARET. *Child Adoption in the Modern World.* Putnam (1952).
Research Project, paper published in the report of the Residential Conference of Societies Registered for Adoption, July 1955.

*MACDONALD, E. K. Follow-up of Illegitimate Children. *Medical Officer* (14th December 1956).
*MANCHESTER, MEDICAL OFFICER OF HEALTH FOR. *Annual Report*, 1938.
*MANNHEIM, HERMANN. *Juvenile Delinquency in an English Middletown.* Routledge (1948). SEE ALSO UNDER CARR-SAUNDERS.
MENTAL DEFICIENCY COMMITTEE, REPORT OF, (Wood Report), H.M.S.O., 1929.
MORAL WELFARE COUNCIL. What Happens Afterwards—A Survey of Unmarried Mothers and Their Children after Three Years. *Moral Welfare* (January 1957).

*NATIONAL ASSISTANCE BOARD. *Annual Reports.*
National Assistance (Determination of Need) Regulations, 1948. H.M.S.O., Statutory Instrument 1948, No. 1344.
*NATIONAL COUNCIL FOR THE UNMARRIED MOTHER AND HER CHILD. *Annual Reports.*
Discussion of Illegitimacy, 1947.
Homes and Hostels of the Future, 1945.
Schemes for Homes and Hostels, 1946.
SEE ALSO UNDER COOPER, FISHER, JEGER.

*PINCHBECK, IVY. Social Attitudes to the Problem of Illegitimacy. *British Journal of Sociology* (December 1954).
*POLITICAL AND ECONOMIC PLANNING (P.E.P.). The Unmarried Mother. *Planning*, No. 255 (1946).
*POPULATION INVESTIGATION COMMITTEE and ROYAL COLLEGE OF OBSTETRICIANS AND GYNAECOLOGISTS. *Maternity in Great Britain.* Oxford University Press (1948).
*POPULATION, ROYAL COMMISSION ON. *Report.* H.M.S.O. (1949).
Papers: Vol. I. *Family Limitation.* H.M.S.O. (1949). Vol. II. *Reports and Selected Papers of the Statistics Committee.* H.M.S.O. (1950).
*RACE, R. R. and SANGER, R. *Blood Groups in Man*, 3rd ed. (Blackwell, 1958).

*REES, ALWYN D. *Life in a Welsh Countryside.* University of Wales Press (1950).
*REEVE, BARBARA and STEEL, ENA. *Moral Welfare*, chapter 7, *Social Case-Work in Great Britain*, edited by Cherry Morris. Faber & Faber (1950).
*REGISTRAR-GENERAL FOR ENGLAND AND WALES. *See* GENERAL REGISTER OFFICE.
*REGISTRAR-GENERAL FOR SCOTLAND. *Annual Reports.*

*ROWNTREE, B. S. and LAVERS, G. R. *English Life and Leisure.* Longmans (1951).
SCOTT, EILEEN M., THOMSON, A. M., ILLSLEY, R. and BILES, MARION E. A Psychological Investigation of Primagravidae. *Journal of Obstetrics and Gynaecology of the British Empire* (June and August 1956).
*SPENCE, SIR JAMES et alii. *A Thousand Families in Newcastle-upon-Tyne.* Oxford University Press (1954).
*STERILIZATION, DEPARTMENTAL COMMITTEE ON. *Report.* H.M.S.O. (1934).
*STEVENSON, A. C. *Recent Advances in Social Medicine.* Churchill (1950).
*STONE'S JUSTICES' MANUAL, 1954.
*STOTT, D. H. *Delinquency and Human Nature.* Carnegie United Kingdom Trust (1950).
Saving Children from Delinquency. University of London Press (1952).
Unsettled Children and Their Families. University of London Press (1956).
Bristol Social Adjustment Guides and Manual. University of London Press (1956-8).
Physical and Mental Handicaps following a Disturbed Pregnancy. *Lancet* (18th May 1957).
Evidence for Pre-Natal Impairment of Temperament in Mentally Retarded Children. *Vita Humana* (September 1959).
*SUTHERLAND, HALLIDAY. *Irish Journey.* Geoffrey Bles (1956).

*THOMPSON, BARBARA. Social Study of Illegitimate Maternities. *British Journal of Social and Preventive Medicine* (April 1956).

WILKINSON, G. S. *Affiliation Law and Practice.* Solicitors' Law Stationery Society Ltd. (1958).
Changes in the Law Relating to Illegitimate Children. *Justice of the Peace and Local Government Review* (31st October 1959).
*WILLESDEN, BOROUGH OF. *Annual Report,* 1939.
*WITTKOWER, E. D. The Psychological Aspects of Venereal Diseases *British Journal of Venereal Diseases* (June 1948).
*WOMEN'S GROUP ON PUBLIC WELFARE. *The Neglected Child and His Family.* Oxford University Press (1948).

UNITED STATES

*ABBOTT, GRACE. *The Child and the State,* Vol. II, Part III: *The Child of Unmarried Parents.* University of Chicago Press (1938).

KAMMERER, P. G. *The Unmarried Mother.* William Heinemann (Medical Books) Ltd (1918).

*KINSEY, A. C. *Sexual Behaviour in the Human Male.* Saunders (1948).
Sexual Behaviour in the Human Female. Saunders (1953).

*MORLOCK, MAUD. *The Fathers of Children Born Out of Wedlock.* U.S. Children's Bureau, Social Security Administration, Department of Health, Education and Welfare (1939).

Determination and Establishment of Paternity. U.S. Children's Bureau, Social Security Administration, Department of Health, Education and Welfare (1940).

REIDER, NORMAN. The Unmarried Father. *American Journal of Orthopsychiatry*, XVIII.

*SHAPIRO, SAM. *Illegitimate Births*, 1938-47. American Office of Vital Statistics (1950).

*SKEELS, HAROLD M. and HARMS, IRENE (Iowa Child Welfare Research Station). Children with Inferior Social Histories, Their Mental Development in Adoptive Homes. *Journal of Genetic Psychology* (1948).

VINCENT CLARKE, The Unwed Mother and Sampling Bias. *American Sociological Review* (1954).

*YOUNG, LEONTINE. Personality Patterns in Unmarried Mothers. *Family Journal of Casework*, Family Service Association of America (New York, 1945).
Out of Wedlock. McGraw Hill Publishing Co. (1954).

CANADA

*UNMARRIED PARENTHOOD COMMITTEE OF THE WELFARE COUNCIL OF TORONTO AND DISTRICT. *A Study of the Adjustment of Teen-Age Children born out of Wedlock who remained in the Custody of their Mothers or Relatives* (Toronto 1943).

SCANDINAVIA

*NELSON, GEORGE R. (editor). *Freedom and Welfare, Social Patterns in the Northern Countries of Europe.* Ministries of Social Affairs of Denmark, Finland, Iceland, Norway, Sweden (1953).

DENMARK

DANISH MOTHERS' AID CENTRE. *Review of their History and Activities.* Danish Institute (Copenhagen, 1957).

*DANSKE KVINDERS NATIONALRAD og DANSK KVINDESAMFUND (DANISH WOMEN'S NATIONAL COUNCIL AND DANISH WOMEN'S SOCIETY). *Den Enlige Moder* ('The Solitary Mother'). Det Danske Forlag (Copenhagen, 1953).

HORSTEN, HOLGER. *Børneforsorgen i Danmark* ('Child Care in Denmark'). Nyt Nordisk Forlag, Arnold Busck (Copenhagen, 1953).

NORWAY

CASTBERG, JOHAN. The Children's Rights Laws and Maternity Insurance in Norway. *Journal of the Society of Comparative Legislation*, John Murray (1916).

TABLE 2a COUNTRIES

ILLEGITIMATE PERCENTAGE OF ALL LIVE

	1900	1938	1939	1940	1941	1942	1943	1944	1945	1946	1947
BRITISH ISLES											
England and Wales	4.0	4.2	4.2	4.3	5.4	5.6	6.4	7.3	9.3	6.6	5.3
England	4.0	4.3	4.2	4.3	5.4	5.7	6.5	7.4	9.4	6.6	5.3
Wales	3.8	3.9	3.7	3.8	4.5	4.7	5.4	6.4	7.9	5.6	4.3
North Wales	6.0	5.3	—	—	—	—	—	10.3	—	—	—
South Wales	3.3	3.4	—	—	—	—	7.0	—	—	—	—
Scotland	6.5	6.1	6.0	5.9	6.6	7.1	7.6	7.9	8.6	6.6	5.6
Northern Ireland	2.7	4.5	4.7	4.6	4.8	4.9	5.5	5.6	5.4	4.4	3.8
Irish Free State—Eire [a]		3.3	3.2	3.2	3.5	3.7	3.8	3.9	3.9	3.9	3.4
WESTERN EUROPE AND GREECE											
Austria	—	20.9	16.2	13.8	13.2	14.2	16.0	20.3	25.5	24.5	20.2
Belgium	7.4	2.5	2.4	3.1	3.0	2.4	2.6	3.4	4.2	3.8	3.1
Denmark	9.6	9.0	8.7	8.8	8.6	8.5	8.9	9.2	9.9	7.9	8.0
Finland	6.3	6.6	7.7	9.3	6.0	6.9	6.4	7.4	7.0	6.0	5.6
France	8.8	6.3	6.3	7.1	8.1	7.7	7.9	9.4	10.5	8.7	7.6
Germany [a]	8.7	7.7	7.8[b]	—	—	—	—	—	—	—	—
Western Germany	—	—	—	—	—	—	—	—	—	16.4	11.9
Greece	—	1.4	1.4	—	—	—	—	—	—	—	—
Iceland [a]	16.5	23.7	23.7	25.6	24.3	24.6	25.1	25.4	24.0	25.9	25.6
Italy	5.9	4.1	4.1	3.8	3.9	3.8	3.8	4.6	5.2	3.8	3.7
Netherlands	2.6	1.4	1.3	1.4	1.7	1.7	1.8	2.0	3.5	2.5	1.9
Norway	7.3	6.0	6.2	6.4	6.9	7.3	7.5	7.3	7.4	5.8	5.3
Portugal	11.6	15.6	15.7	15.7	15.1	14.1	13.4	13.0	12.6	12.3	12.1
Spain [d]	4.4	—	—	—	4.8	5.4	5.9	6.2	6.3	6.2	5.5
Sweden	11.4	12.7	12.4	11.8	10.9	9.2	8.8	9.0	9.6	9.3	9.4
Switzerland	4.5	3.5	3.5	3.8	3.8	3.4	3.2	3.2	3.5	3.4	3.5
EASTERN EUROPE											
Bulgaria	—	2.9	3.1	3.1	3.0	—	—	2.4	—	—	—
Czechoslovakia	—	7.8	7.7	6.3	5.5	5.1	4.4	4.6	9.9[e]	8.9	8.5
Esthonia	—	8.4	—	—	—	—	—	—	—	—	—
Hungary	9.4	8.4	8.7	8.5	8.6	—	—	—	—	8.1	—
Jugoslavia	—	4.8	4.8	—	—	—	—	—	—	—	—
Latvia [f]											
Lithuania	—	6.7	6.1	—	—	—	—	—	—	—	—
Poland	6.1	—	—	—	—	—	—	—	—	—	—
Rumania	—	9.3	9.2	9.2[h]	—	8.2	—	—	—	—	11.9
Russia	2.5[i]	—	—	—	—	—	—	—	—	—	—

[a] Includes still births.
[b] Excludes natural children of servicemen killed in action. No figures available for 1940-5.
[c] No figures kept for Greece as a whole from 1939 to 1955. Figures for 1950 and 1955 refer only to Athens-Piraeus. Figures for 1956 and 1957 refer to the whole of Greece.
[d] No figures kept for 1938-40.
[e] From 1945 the Czech figures include the Sudetan area.
[f] The only available figure is 4.6 for 1922.
[g] Nil in law, but 6.6 in fact. May include still births.
[h] January to August 1940.
[i] 1902.

BIBLIOGRAPHY

JUGOSLAVIA

New Jugoslav Law on Parents and Children, bulletin on Legislation in Jugoslavia issued by Association of Jurists of the P.P.R. of Jugoslavia (Belgrade, 1951).

U.S.S.R.

*KING, BEATRICE, Marriage, Morals and the Soviet Family. *Anglo-Soviet Journal*, Vol. V, No. 3 (1944).

*SCHLESINGER, RUDOLF. *The Family in the U.S.S.R.* Routledge & Kegan Paul (1949).
Proposed Changes in Soviet Family Law. *Soviet Studies* (April 1957).

SVERDLOV, G. M. Legal Rights of the Soviet Family. *Soviet News* (London, 1945).

WOMEN'S BRITISH-SOVIET COMMITTEE. *New Soviet Law on Mothers and Children, Marriage and Divorce*. London Caledonian Press (1944).

INTERNATIONAL

*BUREAU MUNICIPAL DE STATISTIQUE D'AMSTERDAM. *Vital Statistics for Important Towns of the World*, 1880-1909 (1911).

*LEAGUE OF NATIONS
CHILD WELFARE COMMITTEE OF THE ADVISORY COMMISSION FOR THE PROTECTION AND WELFARE OF CHILDREN AND YOUNG PERSONS. *Annual Reports.*
Study of the Position of the Illegitimate Child, 1929.
Official Guardianship of Illegitimate Children, 1932.
ADVISORY COMMITTEE ON SOCIAL QUESTIONS (formerly ADVISORY COMMISSION FOR THE PROTECTION AND WELFARE OF CHILDREN AND YOUNG PERSONS). *Study of the Legal Position of the Illegitimate Child*, 1939.

UNITED NATIONS
ECONOMIC AND SOCIAL COUNCIL, COMMISSION ON THE STATUS OF WOMEN. *Status of Women in Family Law*, 1952.
Parental Rights and Duties, 1953.
Report of the Committee of Experts on the Recognition and Enforcement Abroad of Maintenance Obligations, 1952 etc.

ACTS, ENGLAND AND WALES

Adoption Acts, 1950 and 1958.
Affiliation Orders Act, 1914.
Affiliation Act, 1952.
Affiliation Proceedings Act, 1957.
Bastardy Acts, 1845 and 1923.
Bastardy Laws Amendment Acts, 1872 and 1873.
Births and Deaths Registration Act, 1953.

Children Acts, 1948 and 1958.
Children and Young Persons Act, 1933.
Family Allowances Acts, 1945 and 1959.
Legitimacy Acts, 1926 and 1959.
Magistrates' Courts Act, 1952.
Maintenance Orders Acts, 1950 and 1958.
Married Women (Maintenance) Act, 1949.
Maternity and Child Welfare Act, 1918.
Matrimonial Causes Act, 1948.
National Assistance Act, 1948.
National Insurance Acts, 1946 and 1951.
Nursery and Child-Minders Regulation Act, 1948.
Poor Law Acts.
Population (Statistics) Act, 1938.
Visiting Services Act, 1954.

APPENDIX OF TABLES

TABLE 1   COUNTRIES OF THE WORLD

ILLEGITIMATE PERCENTAGE OF ALL LIVE BIRTHS AS REGISTERED, 1876-1950

EUROPE	1876-80	1881-5	1886-90	1891-5	'96-1900	1901-5	1906-10	1911-15	1916-20	1921-5	1926-30	1931-5	1936-40	1941-5	1946-50
England and Wales	4.7	4.8	4.6	4.2	4.1	3.9	4.0	4.3	5.5	4.3	4.5	4.3	4.6	5.2	5.5
Scotland	8.5	8.3	8.1	7.4	6.8	6.4	7.1	7.2	7.6	6.8	7.3	6.9	6.1	7.6	5.7
Ireland	2.4	2.7	2.8	3.6	3.6	2.6	2.6	2.9	3.2	—	—	—	—	—	3.8
Northern Ireland	—	—	—	—	—	—	—	—	—	4.3	4.7	5.0	4.6	5.2	3.8
Irish Free State—Eire	—	—	—	—	—	—	—	—	—	2.6	3.0	3.4	3.2	3.8	3.2
Austria	13.8	14.5	14.7	14.6	14.1	12.8	12.2	23.6a	24.5b	21.0c	25.6	26.5	18.6	17.8	20.6
Belgium	7.4	8.2	8.7	8.8	8.0	6.8	6.3	6.4d	6.9e	5.6	4.4	3.3	2.5f	3.1	3.0
Bulgaria	—	—	—	—	—	0.4	—	—	1.2e	1.2g	—	2.3	2.9	—	—
Czechoslovakia	—	—	—	—	—	—	—	—	10.1e	10.0	10.7	10.9	8.7	5.9h	—
Denmark	10.1	10.0	9.5	9.4	9.6	10.1	11.0	11.4	11.3	10.6	10.9	10.0	8.7	9.0	7.7
Esthonia	—	—	—	—	—	—	6.1i	—	—	7.4j	8.5	9.9	9.1k	—	—
Finland	7.3	7.0	6.5	6.5	6.6	6.5	7.0	7.8	8.1	8.8	8.1	7.7	7.5	6.7	5.6
France	7.2	7.8	8.3	8.7	8.8	8.8	8.9	8.7	12.0l	8.7	8.4	7.5	6.6	8.7	7.5
Germany	8.7	9.2	9.2	9.1	9.0	8.4	8.8	9.0c	11.7c	10.8c	12.2c	10.0c	7.8cdm	—	—
Western Germany	—	—	—	—	—	—	—	—	—	—	—	—	—	—	11.5c
Greece	—	—	—	—	—	—	—	—	—	1.2	1.3	1.3	1.3f	—	—
Hungary	7.3	7.9	8.2	8.5	9.0	9.4	9.4	9.2	9.8	9.6	9.3	9.3	8.5	—	—
Iceland	22.6c	20.2	20.4	17.7	15.5	13.9	13.0	13.2	13.1	13.3	14.4	18.4	23.3	24.7	26.2
Italy	7.2	7.6	7.4	6.9	6.2	5.7c	5.2c	4.8c	4.8c	4.0c	5.1c	5.1c	5.1c	4.3	3.6
Jugoslavia	—	—	—	—	—	—	—	—	—	4.9n	4.7	5.2	5.0o	—	—
Latvia	—	—	—	—	—	—	—	—	—	4.6p	—	—	—	—	—
Lithuania	—	—	—	—	—	—	—	—	—	5.0	4.9	7.2	7.0	—	—
Luxembourg	—	—	—	—	—	4.1	5.1	6.5	5.8	4.5	4.9	4.0	3.2	5.0	4.4
Netherlands	3.1	3.0	3.2	3.1	2.7	2.3	2.1	2.1	2.2	1.9	1.8	1.7	1.4	2.1	1.8
Norway	8.4	8.1	7.5	7.1	7.4	7.0	6.6	7.0	7.0	6.9	7.0	7.0	6.3	7.3	4.8
Poland	—	—	—	—	6.1q	—	—	—	3.1r / 8.4s	7.5t	5.9u	6.0v	—	—	—
Portugal	—	—	—	—	—	—	—	—	—	—	—	—	—	—	—
Rumania	2.8	2.7	12.3	12.2	12.1	11.6	10.2	12.7	13.0	12.6	14.3	14.8	15.6	13.6	12.0
Russia	—	—	2.7	2.7	2.7	—	9.0w	7.9	9.0	9.8	9.1	10.5	—	—	—
Spain	—	—	—	—	4.9	4.4	4.6	4.8	5.8	6.0	6.1	—x	—x	—x	—
Sweden	10.0	10.2	10.3	10.5	11.3	11.9	13.5	15.4	14.5	14.9	16.0	15.3	12.6	9.5	9.3
Switzerland	4.7	4.8	4.7	4.6	4.5	4.3	4.5	4.7	4.5	3.7	4.1	4.1	3.7	3.4	3.6

AFRICA														
Union of South Africa sa	—ab	—	—	—	—	—	—	—	2.2	2.3	2.6	2.6	2.3	2.2	1.6
AMERICA														
NORTH AMERICA														
Canada	—	—	—	—	—	—	—	—	—	—	3.0	3.6	3.9	4.1	4.0
United States	—	—	—	—	—	—	—	—	2.2sc	2.6	3.1	4.0	4.1	4.0	4.0
CENTRAL AMERICA														
Panama	—	—	—	—	—	68.7ad	—	—	68.9	70.6	71.0ae	69.9af	61.8	66.6ag	—
Salvador	—	—	—	—	—	—	—	—	—	59.0	—	—	—	—	—
SOUTH AMERICA														
Argentina	—	—	—	—	—	—	—	—	—	—	—	—	—	27.2ah	—
Chile	—	—	—	—	—	35.1	—	37.5	38.3	36.2	33.5	29.8	27.6	23.7	21.0
Paraguay	—	—	—	—	—	—	37.0	—	—	70.3	—	—	—	—	—
Uruguay	—	—	—	—	—	—	—	—	—	28.8	—	—	—	—	—
WEST INDIES														
Jamaica	—	—	—	—	—	64.5	62.4	65.3	69.2	71.6	72.1	71.8	70.8	69.5	68.6
AUSTRALASIA														
Australia	4.2ai	3.9	4.6aj	5.0	5.9	6.0	6.1	5.5	5.0	4.7	4.7	4.7	4.2	4.2	4.0
New Zealand	2.3	2.9	3.2	3.8	4.4	4.5	4.5	4.3	4.5	4.5	5.1	4.7	4.3	4.7	4.0

a 1914-15.
b Without the Bundesland Burgenland.
c Includes still births.
d 1911-13.
e 1919-20.
f 1936-9.
g 1921-4.
h Reflects territorial changes.
i 1905-9.
j 1922-5.
k 1936-8.
l 1914-19.
m Excludes natural children of servicemen killed in action.
n 1924-5.
o 1936-9.
p 1922.
q 1900.
r 1918.
s 1920.
t 1921.
u 1927, 1929-30.
v 1931-2.
w 1907-10.
x No figures kept for 1931-40.
sa Births of European race only.
ab Figures available only from 1913.
sc 1917-20. United States figures are estimated only, as not every State records them.
ad 1908-10.
ae 1926, 1928-30.
af 1931-3, 1935.
ag 1943.
ah Territory of Formosa, N.E. Argentina, 67.6, 1941-5.
ai New South Wales, Victoria and Queensland.
aj Excludes Western Australia.

TABLE 2a COUNTRIES

ILLEGITIMATE PERCENTAGE OF ALL LIVE

	1900	1938	1939	1940	1941	1942	1943	1944	1945	1946	1947
BRITISH ISLES											
England and Wales	4.0	4.2	4.2	4.3	5.4	5.6	6.4	7.3	9.3	6.6	5.3
England	4.0	4.3	4.2	4.3	5.4	5.7	6.5	7.4	9.4	6.6	5.3
Wales	3.8	3.9	3.7	3.8	4.5	4.7	5.4	6.4	7.9	5.6	4.3
North Wales	6.0	5.3	—	—	—	—	—	10.3	—	—	—
South Wales	3.3	3.4	—	—	—	—	7.0	—	—	—	—
Scotland	6.5	6.1	6.0	5.9	6.6	7.1	7.6	7.9	8.6	6.6	5.6
Northern Ireland	2.7	4.5	4.7	4.6	4.8	4.9	5.5	5.6	5.4	4.4	3.8
Irish Free State—Eire [a]		3.3	3.2	3.2	3.5	3.7	3.8	3.9	3.9	3.9	3.4
WESTERN EUROPE AND GREECE											
Austria	—	20.9	16.2	13.8	13.2	14.2	16.0	20.3	25.5	24.5	20.2
Belgium	7.4	2.5	2.4	3.1	3.0	2.4	2.6	3.4	4.2	3.8	3.1
Denmark	9.6	9.0	8.7	8.8	8.6	8.5	8.9	9.2	9.9	7.9	8.0
Finland	6.3	6.6	7.7	9.3	6.0	6.9	6.4	7.4	7.0	6.0	5.6
France	8.8	6.3	6.3	7.1	8.1	7.7	7.9	9.4	10.5	8.7	7.6
Germany [a]	8.7	7.7	7.8[b]	—	—	—	—	—	—	—	—
Western Germany	—	—	—	—	—	—	—	—	—	16.4	11.9
Greece	—	1.4	1.4	—	—	—	—	—	—	—	—
Iceland [a]	16.5	23.7	23.7	25.6	24.3	24.6	25.1	25.4	24.0	25.9	25.6
Italy	5.9	4.1	4.1	3.8	3.9	3.8	3.8	4.6	5.2	3.8	3.7
Netherlands	2.6	1.4	1.3	1.4	1.7	1.7	1.8	2.0	3.5	2.5	1.9
Norway	7.3	6.0	6.2	6.4	6.9	7.3	7.5	7.3	7.4	5.8	5.3
Portugal	11.6	15.6	15.7	15.7	15.1	14.1	13.4	13.0	12.6	12.3	12.1
Spain [d]	4.4	—	—	—	4.8	5.4	5.9	6.2	6.3	6.2	5.5
Sweden	11.4	12.7	12.4	11.8	10.9	9.2	8.8	9.0	9.6	9.3	9.4
Switzerland	4.5	3.5	3.5	3.8	3.8	3.4	3.2	3.2	3.5	3.4	3.5
EASTERN EUROPE											
Bulgaria	—	2.9	3.1	3.1	3.0	—	—	2.4	—	—	—
Czechoslovakia	—	7.8	7.7	6.3	5.5	5.1	4.4	4.6	9.9[e]	8.9	8.5
Esthonia	—	8.4	—	—	—	—	—	—	—	—	—
Hungary	9.4	8.4	8.7	8.5	8.6	—	—	—	—	8.1	—
Jugoslavia	—	4.8	4.8	—	—	—	—	—	—	—	—
Latvia [f]	—	—	—	—	—	—	—	—	—	—	—
Lithuania	—	6.7	6.1	—	—	—	—	—	—	—	—
Poland	6.1	—	—	—	—	—	—	—	—	—	—
Rumania	—	9.3	9.2	9.2[h]	—	8.2	—	—	—	—	11.9
Russia	2.5[i]	—	—	—	—	—	—	—	—	—	—

[a] Includes still births.
[b] Excludes natural children of servicemen killed in action. No figures available for 1940-5.
[c] No figures kept for Greece as a whole from 1939 to 1955.
Figures for 1950 and 1955 refer only to Athens-Piraeus. Figures for 1956 and 1957 refer to the whole of Greece.
[d] No figures kept for 1938-40.
[e] From 1945 the Czech figures include the Sudetan area.
[f] The only available figure is 4.6 for 1922.
[g] Nil in law, but 6.6 in fact. May include still births.
[h] January to August 1940.
[i] 1902.

OF EUROPE

BIRTHS AS REGISTERED, 1900, 1938-57

1948	1949	1950	1951	1952	1953	1954	1955	1956	1957	
5.4	5.1	5.1	4.8	4.8	4.7	4.7	4.7	4.8	4.8	England and Wales
5.4	5.1	5.1	4.9	4.9	4.8	4.8	4.7	4.9	4.9	England
4.3	3.9	4.1	3.8	3.9	4.0	3.5	3.5	3.5	3.4	Wales
—	—	5.2	—	—	—	—	—	—	—	North Wales
—	—	3.6	—	—	—	—	—	—	—	South Wales
5.8	5.5	5.2	5.1	4.8	4.6	4.5	4.3	4.2	4.1	Scotland
3.6	3.7	3.4	3.1	3.3	2.8	2.9	2.4	2.7	2.4	Northern Ireland
3.3	3.1	2.5	2.5	2.5	2.1	2.1	2.0	1.9	1.7	Irish Free State—Eire
19.1	20.7	18.3	17.8	16.5	15.9	15.5	14.4	13.5	13.3	Austria
3.1	2.6	2.6	2.3	2.3	2.2	2.1	2.1	2.1	2.0	Belgium
7.7	7.4	7.4	7.0	6.7	6.8	6.7	6.6	6.8	6.9	Denmark
5.6	5.5	5.2	4.9	4.7	4.5	4.4	4.2	4.2	4.3	Finland
7.2	7.0	7.0	6.8	6.8	6.7	6.4	6.3	6.3	6.2	France
—	—	—	—	—	—	—	—	—	—	Germany
10.2	9.3	9.6	9.5	8.9	8.6	8.3	7.7	7.3	7.7	Western Germany
—	—	3.1c	—	—	—	—	1.5c	1.4	1.5	Greece
26.6	25.2	27.9	27.5	25.2	25.4	27.6	26.5	25.2	24.9	Iceland
3.5	3.4	3.4	3.9	3.4	3.3	3.2	3.1	3.0	2.8	Italy
1.7	1.6	1.5	1.4	1.4	1.3	1.3	1.2	1.2	1.2	Netherlands
4.9	4.0	4.1	4.0	3.7	3.6	3.5	3.4	3.5	3.7	Norway
11.8	11.8	11.8	11.6	11.5	11.2	10.9	11.0	10.6	10.5	Portugal
5.7	5.7	5.2	5.2	5.1	4.8	4.6	4.2	3.8	3.8	Spain
9.3	9.2	9.5	10.1	10.0	9.8	9.8	9.9	10.2	10.1	Sweden
3.7	3.6	3.8	3.5	3.5	3.6	3.7	3.6	3.7	3.8	Switzerland
—	—	—	—	—	—	—	—	—	—	Bulgaria
7.6	6.6	—	—	—	—	—	—	—	—	Czechoslovakia
—	—	—	—	—	—	—	—	—	—	Esthonia
—	—	—	—	—	—	—	—	—	—	Hungary
—	—	—	—	—	—	—	—	—	—	Jugoslavia
—	—	—	—	—	—	—	—	—	—	Latvia
—	—	—	—	—	—	—	—	—	—	Lithuania
—	—	g	—	—	—	—	—	—	—	Poland
—	—	—	—	—	—	—	—	—	—	Rumania
—	—	—	—	—	—	—	—	—	—	Russia

TABLE 2b COUNTRIES OUT

ILLEGITIMATE PERCENTAGE OF ALL LIVE

(The figures for 1933 were compiled by the League
Other figures are drawn from the *Encyclopaedia*

	1900	1933	1938	1939	1940	1941	1942	1943	1944	1945	1946
ASIA											
Japan	8.8	—	—	—	—	—	—	—	—	—	—
AFRICA											
Algeria, European	—	7.4	—	—	—	—	—	—	—	—	—
Algeria, Mohammedan	—	0.7	—	—	—	—	—	—	—	—	—
Union of South Africa ab	—c	2.7	2.3	2.3	2.2	2.2	2.2	2.3	2.1	2.2	1.9
AMERICA											
NORTH AMERICA											
Canada	—	3.8	4.2	4.0	3.9	4.0	4.1	4.0	4.2	4.5	4.1
United States d	—	4.0e	4.1	4.2	4.0	4.1	3.7	3.6	4.0	4.6	3.9
Hawaii	—	—	—	—	—	—	—	—	—	7.5	—
Cuba (1929) White	—	12.4	—	—	—	—	—	—	—	—	—
Cuba (1929) Coloured	—	49.2	—	—	—	—	—	—	—	—	—
Mexico	—	—	—	—	—	—	—	—	—	27.3	—
CENTRAL AMERICA											
Costa Rica a	—	22.5 (1931)	—	—	—	—	—	—	—	—	—
Guatemala a	—	52.5 (1928)	—	—	—	—	—	—	76.1	—	—
Nicaragua	—	—	—	—	—	—	—	—	—	63.9	—
Panama a	—	70.5	—	—	—	—	66.3	—	—	—	—
Salvador a	—	59.9	—	—	—	—	—	—	—	—	—
SOUTH AMERICA											
Argentina	—	25.8	—	—	—	—	—	—	—	—	—
Bolivia	—	—	—	—	—	—	—	—	—	—	—
Brazil	—	—	—	—	—	—	—	—	—	—	—
Chile	—	31.7 (1929)	—	—	—	—	—	—	—	—	—
Columbia a	—	28.0	—	—	—	—	—	—	—	—	—
Ecuador	—	—	—	—	—	—	—	—	—	—	—
Paraguay a	—	66.5	—	—	—	—	—	—	—	—	56.6
Peru	—	—	—	—	—	25.8	—	—	—	—	—
Uruguay a	—	28.6	—	—	—	—	—	—	—	—	—
Venezuela a	—	59.5	—	—	—	—	—	—	—	—	—
WEST INDIES											
Barbados	—	—	—	—	—	—	—	—	—	—	—
Bermuda	—	—	—	—	—	—	—	—	—	—	—
Dominican Republic	—	—	—	—	—	—	—	—	—	—	—
Jamaica	—	—	—	—	—	—	—	—	—	—	—
Trinidad and Tobago	—	—	—	—	—	—	—	—	—	—	—
Windward Is. (St. Vincent)	—	—	—	—	—	—	—	—	—	—	—
AUSTRALASIA											
Australia a	6.2	4.7	4.2	4.1	3.8	3.8	3.9	4.4	4.5	4.5	4.3
New Zealand	4.6	4.6	4.3	3.9	3.9	3.6	4.0	4.8	6.0	4.9	4.4

a Includes still births.
b Births of European race only.
c 2.2 in 1913, the first year for which figures are available.
d Estimated figures, as not every State records them.

SIDE EUROPE
BIRTHS AS REGISTERED, 1900, 1933, 1938-57

of Nations Advisory Committee on Social Questions.
Britannica, national statistical year books, etc.)

1947	1948	1949	1950	1951	1952	1953	1954	1955	1956	1957	
3.8	3.2	2.7	2.5	2.2	2.0	1.9	1.7	1.7	1.6	1.5	Japan
—	—	—	—	—	5.6	—	—	—	—	—	Algeria
—	—	—	—	—	1.5	—	—	—	—	—	
1.5	1.5	1.7	1.6	1.6	1.7	1.5	1.3	1.2	1.5	1.7	Union of South Africa
4.0	4.3	3.9	3.9	3.8	3.8	3.8	3.9	3.8	3.9	4.0	Canada
3.7	3.9	4.0	4.3e	3.9e	3.9e	4.1e	4.4e	4.5e	4.6e	4.7e	United States
—	—	—	—	—	—	—	—	—	—	—	Hawaii
—	—	—	—	—	—	—	—	—	—	—	Cuba
—	—	—	—	—	—	—	—	—	—	—	Mexico
—	—	—	—	—	24.2	—	—	—	—	—	Costa Rica
—	—	—	—	—	—	—	—	—	—	—	Guatemala
—	—	—	—	—	—	—	—	—	—	—	Nicaragua
—	—	—	—	—	—	—	—	—	—	—	Panama
—	—	55.6	—	—	—	—	—	—	—	—	Salvador
—	26.6	—	—	—	—	—	—	—	—	—	Argentina
28.4	—	—	—	—	—	—	—	—	—	—	Bolivia
—	—	—	—	—	—	—	—	—	—	—	Brazil
—	—	—	19.7	—	—	—	—	—	—	—	Chile
—	—	—	—	—	26.5	—	—	—	—	—	Colombia
34.8	—	—	—	—	—	—	—	—	—	—	Ecuador
—	—	—	—	—	—	—	—	—	—	—	Paraguay
—	—	—	—	25.8	—	—	—	—	—	—	Peru
—	—	—	—	—	—	—	—	—	—	—	Uruguay
—	—	—	—	58.2	—	—	—	—	—	—	Venezuela
—	—	—	—	—	—	—	—	61.5	—	—	Barbados
—	—	—	—	—	30.6	—	—	—	—	—	Bermuda
—	—	—	58.6	—	—	—	—	—	—	—	Dominican Republic
—	—	—	—	—	—	70.9	—	—	—	—	Jamaica
—	—	—	—	—	—	—	50.3	—	—	—	Trinidad and Tobago
—	—	—	—	—	—	—	76.6a	—	—	—	Windward Is. (St. Vincent)
4.0	4.0	4.1	3.8	3.8	3.9	4.0	4.0	4.1	4.2	4.2	Australia
3.8	3.8	3.8	4.0	4.3	4.5	4.3	4.3	4.5	4.6	4.9	New Zealand

e		White	Coloured
	1933	2.1	15.6
	1950	1.7	18.0
	1951	1.6	18.3
	1952	1.6	18.3
	1953	1.7	19.1
	1954	1.8	19.8
	1955	1.9	20.2
	1956	1.9	20.4
	1957	2.0	20.7

TABLE 3   TOWNS OF THE WORLD

ILLEGITIMATE PERCENTAGE OF ALL LIVE BIRTHS AS REGISTERED, 1880, 1900, 1950

	1880	1900	1950
Aberdeen	10.7	8.1	5.3
Adelaide	—	7.2 (1908)	3.1
Amsterdam	6.0	5.3	3.9
Athens-Piraeus	—	—	3.1
Auckland	—	8.3	7.2
Barcelona	8.4	7.1	6.4
Basle	11.4	10.2	6.9
Belfast	3.7	3.3	2.9
Berlin	13.4	14.9	16.4
Berne	12.4	6.9 (1901)	6.0
Birmingham	4.3	4.0	5.5
Bordeaux	—	26.5	13.5
Breslau	15.5	16.7	—
Brighton	7.6	5.3	8.9
Brisbane	7.9[a]	16.1[a]	5.5
Bristol	3.9[b]	2.5	4.3
Brussels	28.0	25.3	12.0
Bucarest	22.9	15.0	—
Buenos Aires	—	12.6 (1910)	11.2 (1947)
Cardiff	2.7	2.5	4.8
Cologne	—	—	14.5
Copenhagen	19.1	24.5	11.4[c]
Danzig	16.3	11.9	—
Detroit	—	—	(1947) 3.6
Dover	3.8	4.2	7.2
Dresden	18.1	20.0	—
Dublin	1.0	3.0	1.8
Dumfries	14.2	12.3	6.5
Dundee	10.4	8.8	6.6
Dunedin, N.Z.	—	6.3	4.5
Edinburgh	7.8	7.9	5.3
Essen	2.7	3.4	7.5
Florence	18.0	16.0	6.4
Frankfurt-on-Main	9.9	12.5	14.8
Genoa	10.2	12.5	5.4
Glasgow	7.7	6.5	5.5
Hamburg	9.2	12.4	10.6
Helsinki	16.2	15.6	7.1
Innsbruck	14.5 (1881)	12.6	21.3
Inverness	7.3	6.3	7.6
Johannesburg			
European	—	—	—
Coloured	—	—	21.6
Kingston, Jamaica	—	—	64.5
Leeds	5.4	6.1	6.8
Leipzig	16.0	18.0	—
Leningrad	27.2 (1881)	23.5	—
Lisbon	—	34.6	19.7
Liverpool	4.7	6.0	6.0

	1880	1900	1950		1880	1900	1950
London	3.9	3.6	7.0	Plymouth	3.4	3.1	7.6
Lwow (Lemberg)	43.9 (1881)	35.0	—	Prague	47.0	31.7	—
Lyons	21.0 (1881)	22.5	—	Quebec	—	—	4.8
Madrid	—	21.9	7.7	Reykjavik	—	17.5 (1920)	27.6
Manchester	3.3	3.4	7.3	Riga	6.4 (1881)	6.5	—
Marseilles	—	16.6	9.0[d]	Rome	21.0	17.8	7.0
Melbourne	7.5	9.1	3.8	Rotterdam	5.8	4.4	2.4
Milan	11.5	9.9	6.8	Salzburg	36.7 (1881)	30.0	22.0
Montreal	—	—	7.5	Santiago, Chile	—	—	19.1
Moscow	43.2	27.3	—	Sheffield	5.5	4.9	3.8
Munchen (Munich)	28.2	25.8	20.5	Stirling	6.4[a]	6.7[a]	6.4
Naples	8.5	10.6	5.8	Stockholm	30.2	31.2	10.5
Newcastle-upon-Tyne	5.3	3.8	4.5	Sydney	6.7	10.1	4.4
New York	—	1.9	—[e]	Tokyo	—	10.3	3.6
Oslo	13.0	14.3	4.1	Toronto	—	4.7	5.4
Ottawa	—	—	3.6	Turin	15.3	13.2	4.6
Paris	25.5	26.8	16.6	Venice	17.4	12.1	5.2
Perth, Australia	6.7	8.9	3.3[f]	Vienna	44.4	31.8	15.5
Perth, Scotland	8.8	7.2	6.7	Warsaw	19.8	10.3	—
Philadelphia	—	— (1947)	5.6[g]	Washington	—	—	(1947) 9.4[h]
				Wellington, N.Z.	—	10.9	5.9
				Zurich	9.0	11.7	7.5

a For Registration District.
b With Barton Regis.
c Births only to women resident in Copenhagen.
d Approximately.
e No data. 7.7 (estimated) for 1958.
f Metropolitan area, including the city of Fremantle.
g White 1.7; coloured 22.1.
h White 3.3; coloured 20.7.

Many of the figures for 1880 and some for 1900 are drawn from *Vital Statistics for Important Towns of the World, 1880–1909*, published in 1911 by the Bureau Municipal de Statistique d' Amsterdam.

TABLE 4
ENGLAND AND WALES
ILLEGITIMATE PERCENTAGE OF ALL LIVE BIRTHS AS REGISTERED
1842-1958

Year	%	Year	%	Year	%	Year	%
		1870	5.6	1900	4.0	1930	4.6
		1871	5.6	1901	3.9	1931	4.4
1842	6.7	1872	5.4	1902	3.9	1932	4.4
1843	—	1873	5.2	1903	3.9	1933	4.4
1844	—	1874	5.0	1904	4.0	1934	4.3
1845	7.0	1875	4.8	1905	4.0	1935	4.2
1846	6.7	1876	4.7	1906	4.0	1936	4.1
1847	6.7	1877	4.7	1907	3.9	1937	4.2
1848	6.5	1878	4.7	1908	4.0	1938	4.2
1849	6.8	1879	4.8	1909	4.1	1939	4.2
1850	6.8	1880	4.8	1910	4.1	1940	4.3
1851	6.8	1881	4.9	1911	4.3	1941	5.4
1852	6.8	1882	4.9	1912	4.3	1942	5.6
1853	6.5	1883	4.8	1913	4.3	1943	6.4
1854	6.4	1884	4.7	1914	4.2	1944	7.3
1855	6.4	1885	4.8	1915	4.4	1945	9.3
1856	6.5	1886	4.7	1916	4.8	1946	6.6
1857	6.5	1887	4.8	1917	5.6	1947	5.3
1858	6.6	1888	4.6	1918	6.3	1948	5.4
1859	6.5	1889	4.6	1919	6.0	1949	5.1
1860	6.4	1890	4.6	1920	4.7	1950	5.1
1861	6.3	1891	4.2	1921	4.5	1951	4.8
1862	6.3	1892	4.2	1922	4.4	1952	4.8
1863	6.5	1893	4.2	1923	4.2	1953	4.7
1864	6.4	1894	4.3	1924	4.2	1954	4.7
1865	6.2	1895	4.2	1925	4.1	1955	4.7
1866	6.0	1896	4.2	1926	4.3	1956	4.8
1867	5.9	1897	4.2	1927	4.4	1957	4.8
1868	5.9	1898	4.2	1928	4.5	1958	4.9
1869	5.8	1899	4.0	1929	4.6		

TABLE 5
ENGLAND AND WALES
NUMBERS OF ILLEGITIMATE BIRTHS
1851-1958

1851-1860	423,171
1861-1870	457,006
1871-1880	427,198
1881-1890	419,122
1891-1900	381,802
1901-1910	370,418
1911-1920	389,765
1921-1930	310,775
1931-1940	259,213
1941-1950	444,080

Year	Number	Year	Number	Year	Number
1915	36,245	1930	29,682	1945	63,420
1916	37,689	1931	28,086	1946	53,919
1917	37,157	1932	27,011	1947	46,603
1918	41,452	1933	25,408	1948	41,574
1919	41,876	1934	25,785	1949	36,907
1920	44,947	1935	25,106	1950	35,250
1921	38,618	1936	24,895	1951	32,771
1922	34,138	1937	25,341	1952	32,549
1923	31,522	1938	26,379	1953	32,503
1924	30,296	1939	25,570	1954	31,609
1925	28,896	1940	25,633	1955	31,145
1926	29,591	1941	31,058	1956	33,534
1927	29,023	1942	36,467	1957	34,562
1928	29,702	1943	43,709	1958	36,174
1929	29,307	1944	55,173		

TABLE 6

COUNTIES OF ENGLAND AND WALES

ILLEGITIMATE PERCENTAGE OF ALL LIVE BIRTHS AS REGISTERED
1842, 1850, 1900, 1938, 1945, 1950, 1957

	1842	1850	1900	1938	1945	1950	1957
ENGLAND AND WALES	6.7	6.8	4.0	4.2	9.3	5.1	4.8
LONDON	3.2	4.1	3.6	6.3	11.3	7.0	8.9
Bedfordshire	7.7	8.0	5.0	3.9	8.9	5.4	4.8
Berkshire	7.3	7.9	4.7	4.3	13.0	5.9	5.3
Buckinghamshire	7.3	7.4	4.2	3.7	9.1	4.4	4.1
Cambridgeshire	7.2	7.5	4.5	4.2	13.5	5.1	4.2
Cheshire	9.4	8.3	4.1	3.2	8.7	4.5	3.6
Cornwall	4.2	6.0	5.1	4.6	11.8	5.2	4.1
Cumberland	11.4	10.1	6.0	4.8	9.5	4.2	3.9
Derbyshire	8.1	8.3	4.0	3.4	7.9	4.3	4.0
Devonshire	5.1	5.3	3.6	4.8	12.8	5.8	4.8
Dorset	6.7	7.1	3.9	4.9	13.4	5.7	4.4
Durham	5.6	6.6	3.3	3.5	6.9	3.8	3.2
Ely, Isle of	—	—	—	4.9	11.6	6.2	5.5
Essex	5.3	6.3	2.7	3.3	7.9	4.1	3.9
Gloucestershire	6.1	5.6	3.6	3.6	9.7	4.7	4.7
Hampshire	6.4	6.4	4.0	4.9	11.9	6.0	5.4
Herefordshire	10.6	11.0	6.0	7.0	12.7	6.7	4.8
Hertfordshire	7.0	7.8	4.0	3.3	8.6	4.0	3.3
Huntingdonshire	5.1	5.3	5.3	5.9	12.2	6.7	3.8
Kent	6.3	5.7	4.0	4.1	8.4	4.9	4.3
Lancashire	8.7	7.5	3.8	4.1	8.9	5.2	5.0
Leicestershire	7.2	8.7	3.9	3.8	10.8	4.8	4.6
Lincolnshire	6.3	7.3	5.5	5.5	10.6	6.0	4.7
Middlesex	3.4	4.2	2.9	4.0	7.0	4.5	5.0
Norfolk	9.9	10.7	6.1	4.5	14.9	5.7	5.2
Northamptonshire	6.4	6.1	3.7	3.6	10.6	4.8	4.7
Northumberland	6.8	7.7	4.1	4.0	7.6	4.1	3.9
Nottinghamshire	9.9	9.4	5.0	4.6	10.0	5.6	5.4
Oxfordshire	7.5	7.6	5.0	5.1	12.7	5.2	5.7
Peterborough, Soke of	—	—	—	5.0	13.2	7.1	5.0
Rutland	6.8	4.5	3.9	5.2	10.6	3.9	4.2
Shropshire	9.3	9.5	6.2	4.7	11.0	5.8	3.9
Somerset	6.2	6.3	3.6	3.4	10.6	4.2	3.9
Staffordshire	7.4	6.2	3.7	2.9	6.7	4.0	3.7

TABLE 6—*Continued*

	1842	1850	1900	1938	1945	1950	1957
Suffolk	8.1	8.4	5.6	—	—	—	—
West	—	—	—	3.4	16.1	5.6	5.8
East	—	—	—	4.6	13.5	5.2	4.4
Surrey	3.5	4.7	3.9	4.1	9.2	4.3	4.1
Sussex	6.8	6.6	5.1	—	—	—	—
West	—	—	—	5.8	11.7	5.8	5.5
East	—	—	—	6.3	13.5	7.0	3.9
Warwickshire	5.1	5.7	3.3	3.8	8.8	5.5	5.7
Westmorland	9.3	9.0	6.7	4.6	10.7	5.1	4.7
Wight, Isle of	—	—	—	5.1	10.1	5.1	4.0
Wiltshire	7.3	7.2	4.0	4.0	13.3	4.9	4.3
Worcestershire	6.2	6.8	3.7	3.5	8.5	4.5	3.6
Yorkshire							
East Riding	6.9	7.0	5.0	5.7	11.3	5.8	4.9
West Riding	7.1	6.9	4.3	4.2	8.3	5.2	4.6
North Riding	8.9	8.6	5.1	4.7	9.2	5.4	4.7
WALES	6.8	7.0	3.8	3.9	7.9	4.1	3.4
North	7.5	7.6	6.0	5.3	10.3	4.1	—
South	6.9	7.3	3.3	3.4	7.0	3.6	—
Monmouthshire	4.6	5.0	3.2	3.8	7.2	3.3	3.0
Anglesey	—	—	—	7.3	12.1	7.0	5.5
Brecknockshire	—	—	—	7.2	9.2	3.4	3.1
Caernarvonshire	—	—	—	6.0	9.6	5.2	5.2
Cardiganshire	—	—	—	6.9	10.1	3.5	3.2
Carmarthenshire	—	—	—	3.4	7.0	3.5	3.2
Denbighshire	—	—	—	4.4	11.2	5.1	4.0
Flintshire	—	—	—	3.5	9.1	4.5	3.3
Glamorganshire	—	—	—	3.1	6.8	3.8	3.4
Merionethshire	—	—	—	6.6	12.0	10.2	5.3
Montgomeryshire	—	—	—	6.3	13.2	6.5	3.3
Pembrokeshire	—	—	—	5.4	9.0	4.6	2.5
Radnorshire	—	—	—	5.8	6.3	3.3	3.2

TABLE 7 TOWNS OF ENGLAND AND WALES

ILLEGITIMATE PERCENTAGE OF ALL LIVE BIRTHS AS REGISTERED, 1950, 1957

	1950	1957
NATIONAL AVERAGE	5.1	4.8
LARGE TOWNS	5.3	5.7
SMALL TOWNS	4.5	3.9
RURAL AREAS	4.7	3.7

Number of illegitimate births, if less than 50, shown in brackets.

Town	1950	1957	Town	1950	1957
Acton	5.0	6.7	Cambridge	5.6	5.1
Barking	2.5 (30)	4.0 (37)	Canterbury	7.0	4.1 (31)
Barnsley	5.5	3.1 (41)	Cardiff	4.8	5.0
Barrow-in-Furness	4.7	4.2 (41)	Carlisle	5.0	4.8
Bath	4.5	4.3 (48)	Cheltenham	7.2	7.8
Beckenham	2.8 (26)	3.0 (28)	Chester	7.5	4.6 (45)
Bedford	6.9	6.0	Chesterfield	4.0	3.8 (37)
Bexley	4.7	2.7 (33)	Chislehurst and Sidcup	3.2	2.8 (34)
Birkenhead	5.9	4.3	Colchester	4.9	5.2 (40)
Birmingham	5.5	6.9	Coventry	6.3	5.3
Blackburn	5.2	4.2	Crosby	3.6	3.9 (34)
Blackpool	6.2	6.8	Croydon	5.1	5.4
Blyth	4.2 (28)	4.5 (28)	Dagenham	4.2	3.3 (38)
Bognor Regis	7.8 (24)	4.7 (15)	Darlington	6.0	4.1 (47)
Bolton	4.2	5.1	Derby	6.5	5.7
Bootle	4.3	3.3	Dewsbury	5.8	4.3
Bournemouth	8.0	8.7	Doncaster	6.1	6.4 (40)
Bradford	6.9	6.9	Dorking	6.9 (22)	5.0 (14)
Brentford and Chiswick	5.2 (47)	6.9	Dover	7.2 (44)	4.2 (25)
Brighton	8.9	7.4	Ealing	4.8	4.9
Bristol	4.3	4.6	Eastbourne	7.9	5.1 (30)
Burnley	6.8	5.2	East Ham	3.7	3.8
Burton-on-Trent	5.8	3.8 (34)	Edmonton	4.4	3.6 (45)
Bury	6.1	6.4	Enfield	3.8	4.2

	1950	1957			1950	1957	
Exeter	5.5	5.5		Liverpool	6.0	5.3	
Finchley	3.7	4.3	(36)	London	7.0	8.9	
Folkestone	6.1	6.1	(43)	Lowestoft	6.4	3.7	(23)
Gateshead	3.5	4.0		Luton	5.3	4.8	
Gillingham, Kent	4.6	4.8	(47)	Maidenhead	7.7	7.9	(45)
Gloucester	5.6	6.2		Maidstone	6.0	5.0	(35)
Gravesend	3.2	4.4	(25)	Manchester	7.3	8.2	(47)
Grimsby	7.3	5.3		Margate	8.1	10.1	
Halifax	7.2	6.9		Merthyr Tydfil	3.4	3.2	(44)
Harrogate	6.9	6.3	(45)	Middlesbrough	7.2	5.5	(36)
Harrow	3.3	4.2		Mitcham	4.2	3.8	(38)
Hastings	8.2	6.3	(47)	Morecambe and Heysham	8.0	3.7	(33)
Hayes and Harlington	3.5	2.3	(36)	Newcastle-under-Lyme	4.5	3.2	
Hendon	7.0	4.4		Newcastle-upon-Tyne	4.5	5.0	
Hereford	4.9	3.4	(27)	Newport, Mon.	2.9	2.8	(46)
Heston and Isleworth	3.9	4.0	(20)	New Windsor	9.1	6.7	(35)
Hornchurch	3.4	1.7		Northampton	5.9	6.6	(26)
Hornsey	4.8	6.2	(36)	Norwich	5.8	5.7	
Hove	8.0	6.7		Nottingham	7.2	8.3	
Huddersfield	5.5	5.7		Oldham	5.1	6.0	
Hull	5.8	5.8		Oxford	6.0	7.8	
Huyton with Roby	3.8	4.3	(40)	Penzance	8.0	4.4	(23)
Ilford	3.0	2.7		Peterborough	7.3	5.0	(11)
Ipswich	5.0	7.1		Plymouth	7.6	5.3	
Kidderminster	6.9	4.6	(41)	Poole	5.4	5.6	
King's Lynn	8.0	8.4	(36)	Portsmouth	6.6	6.6	
Kingston-upon-Thames	3.4	7.5	(17)	Preston	5.8	6.4	
Lancaster	5.6	7.2	(41)	Ramsgate	6.1	8.1	(44)
Leamington Spa	7.8	7.8	(43)	Reading	6.4	6.3	(33)
Leeds	6.8	6.4	(45)	Rhondda	3.6	3.0	
Leicester	5.9	6.7		Richmond, Surrey	6.5	5.6	(49)
Leyton	3.5	4.3		Rochdale	6.5	5.3	(41)
Lincoln	7.2	5.8		Romford	4.5	3.1	(33)

	1950		1957			1950		1957	
Rotherham	3.7		3.4		Swindon	4.5		4.7	
Rugby	4.1	(30)	3.6	(27)	Thurrock	3.9		4.1	
Ruislip-Northwood	4.1	(38)	4.5	(46)	Tottenham	5.0		6.5	
St. Helens	4.1		2.8		Twickenham	4.7		4.8	
Salford	7.2		6.0		Tynemouth	4.5		4.3	
Salisbury	7.3	(38)	5.2	(30)	Uxbridge	4.0	(47)	3.9	(41)
Scarborough	7.5	(47)	4.3		Wallasey	6.0		4.4	
Scunthorpe	5.2	(47)	3.9	(45)	Walsall	5.0		4.8	
Sheffield	3.8		3.8		Walthamstow	3.8		4.4	
Shrewsbury	4.3[a]		3.8	(28)	Warrington	6.5	(32)	4.6	
Slough	4.6	(29)	4.8		Wembley	2.8		3.3	
Smethwick	3.1	(48)	5.8		West Bromwich	3.7	(44)	4.2	(48)
Southampton	6.9	(37)	6.3		West Ham	4.7		5.1	
Southend-on-Sea	4.9		6.0		West Hartlepool	5.7		4.8	
Southport	6.4		6.5		Weston-super-Mare	5.8	(31)	4.8	(35)
South Shields	4.5		3.3		Weymouth and Melcombe Regis	7.3	(39)	3.2	(19)
Stockport	5.3		4.0		Widnes	4.7		4.2	
Stockton-on-Tees	4.0		3.7		Wigan	2.6	(36)	1.9	(23)
Stoke-on-Trent	4.5		3.6		Willesden	6.0		11.4	
Stretford	6.1		6.5		Wolverhampton	5.2		6.5	
Sunderland	4.2		3.6	(26)	Worcester	5.0		3.3	(32)
Surbiton	4.6	(39)	3.4		Worthing	6.4	(45)	5.0	(34)
Swansea	3.1		3.4		York	5.7		4.7	

[a] 7.6 in 1948.

TABLE 8a
LONDON

ILLEGITIMATE PERCENTAGE OF ALL LIVE BIRTHS AS REGISTERED
1842, 1900

Number of illegitimate births, if less than 50, shown in brackets.

1842		1900	
City of London	0.6	Stepney	0.6 (11)
Rotherhithe	1.3	Holborn	1.3
St. Luke	1.7	Bethnal Green	1.3
Hackney	1.8	Woolwich	1.4
Strand	1.9	Mile End Old Town	1.6
Poplar	2.0	St. Olave, Southwark	1.7
Bethnal Green	2.1	St. George in the East	2.1 (45)
Islington	2.2	Poplar	2.2
St. Saviour; St. Olave	2.2	St. Saviour, Southwark	2.3
Bermondsey	2.3	Greenwich	2.4
St. George, Southwark	2.5	Hampstead	2.5 (40)
Stepney	2.6	Whitechapel	2.7
St. George in the East	2.7	Islington	2.8
Shoreditch	2.7	Camberwell	2.8
Clerkenwell	2.7	Shoreditch	3.1
Lambeth	2.8	Wandsworth	3.2
Greenwich	2.8	Lewisham	3.3
Holborn	2.9		
Newington	3.1		
St. George, Hanover Sq.	3.1		
LONDON	3.2	LONDON	3.6
Kensington and Chelsea	3.4	Fulham	4.2
Camberwell	3.4	Chelsea	4.3
St. Giles	3.5	City of London	4.3 (17)
Pancras	3.5	Pancras	4.5
Westminster	4.1	Strand	4.5 (16)
Whitechapel	4.1	Paddington	4.6
St. Martin in the Fields	4.6	St. George, Hanover Sq.	4.6
Marylebone	6.9	Kensington	4.7
St. James, Westminster	9.3	Westminster	4.7 (31)
		St. Giles	4.8 (49)
		Hackney	4.9
		Lambeth	5.1
		Marylebone	17.7[a]

[a] Parish of St. Mary, 38.6; rest of Marylebone, 5.4.

TABLE 8b
LONDON

ILLEGITIMATE PERCENTAGE OF ALL LIVE BIRTHS AS REGISTERED, 1938, 1950, 1957

Number of illegitimate births, if less than 50, shown in brackets

1938		1950		1957	
Poplar	2.1 (42)	City of London	2.7 (1)	Woolwich	4.2
Bermondsey	2.4 (35)	Poplar	3.4 (42)	Bermondsey	4.8 (45)
Bethnal Green	3.4 (45)	Bermondsey	3.6 (42)	Lewisham	4.8
Deptford	3.5 (49)	Stoke Newington	3.7 (32)	Poplar	5.1
Woolwich	3.5	Deptford	4.0	Deptford	5.8
Lewisham	3.6	Lewisham	4.2	Bethnal Green	6.1 (49)
Greenwich	3.8	Greenwich	4.3	Greenwich	6.1
Battersea	4.2	Woolwich	4.4	City of London	6.2 (2)
Camberwell	4.2	Hackney	4.6	Southwark	6.3
Hackney	4.2	Battersea	5.4	Shoreditch	6.6 (49)
Shoreditch	4.4	Bethnal Green	5.6	Camberwell	7.0
Stepney	4.5	Wandsworth	5.7	Wandsworth	7.6
Southwark	5.2	Chelsea	6.2	Battersea	7.9
Stoke Newington	5.2 (36)	Finsbury	6.4 (40)	St. Marylebone	8.0
Finsbury	5.3 (39)	Camberwell	6.8	Finsbury	8.1
Wandsworth	5.7	Hammersmith	6.8	Hackney	8.8
Islington	6.2				
LONDON	6.3	LONDON	7.0	LONDON	8.9
Lambeth	6.9	Stepney	7.1	Stoke Newington	9.0
Fulham	7.0	Shoreditch	7.2	Fulham	9.3
Hammersmith	8.5	Islington	7.3	Stepney	9.3
Chelsea	9.6	Fulham	7.5	Hampstead	9.5
Kensington	10.1	Lambeth	8.3	Islington	9.8
St. Pancras	11.7	Southwark	8.3	Holborn	10.3 (26)
Hampstead	12.0	Hampstead	9.4	Westminster	10.4
St. Marylebone	12.1	Holborn	10.0 (30)	St. Pancras	10.9
Paddington	14.2	Kensington	10.1	Hammersmith	11.1
Westminster	14.5 (37)	Paddington	10.2	Lambeth	12.1
Holborn	14.8 (9)	Westminster	10.5	Kensington	12.8
City of London	15.5	St. Pancras	10.8	Chelsea	14.1
		St. Marylebone	12.7	Paddington	16.2

TABLE 9a

ENGLAND AND WALES

AGES OF MOTHERS OF ILLEGITIMATE AND LEGITIMATE CHILDREN

1950

Age	ILLEGITIMATE CHILDREN Number	%	LEGITIMATE CHILDREN %
13	6		
14	38		
15	174		
16	455		0.06[a]
17	1,036		0.4
18	1,533		1.1
19	2,085		2.3
Under 20	5,327	15.1	3.8
20	2,257		3.5
21	2,111		4.9
22	1,995		5.7
23	1,960		6.3
24	1,861		6.9
20–24	10,184	28.9	27.3
25–29	8,676	24.6	33.2
30–34	5,595	15.9	19.9
35–39	3,861	11.0	11.9
40–44	1,316	3.7	3.5
45–49	104	0.3	} 0.2
50 and over	3	0.001[a]	
Not stated	184	0.5	0.2
Total	35,250	100.0	100.0

[a] All figures but these two are here taken to the first decimal point only, which accounts for certain discrepancies in the totals.

TABLE 9b
ENGLAND AND WALES
AGES OF MOTHERS AT ILLEGITIMATE AND LEGITIMATE MATERNITIES [a]
1957

Age	ILLEGITIMATE MATERNITIES Number	%	LEGITIMATE MATERNITIES %
12	2		
13	9		
14	45	0.1	
15	241	0.7	
16	627	1.8	0.1
17	1,337	3.8	0.6
18	2,114	6.0	1.5
19	2,512	7.1	2.8
Under 20	6,887	19.6	5.0
20	2,514	7.2	4.1
21	2,318	6.6	5.4
22	2,110	6.0	6.2
23	1,882	5.3	6.6
24	1,760	5.0	6.9
20-24	10,584	30.2	29.2
25-29	7,157	20.4	32.3
30-34	5,357	15.3	20.1
35-39	3,771	10.7	10.4
40-44	1,240	3.5	2.8
45-49	101	0.3	} 0.2
50 and over	1	0.003[b]	
Total	35,098	100.0	100.0

[a] Table AA, Registrar-General's *Statistical Review of England and Wales*, Part II, Civil, 1957. Note that 'maternities' not 'births' are referred to, i.e. still births are included and multiple births—twins etc.—are counted as a single maternity.

[b] All figures but this one are taken to the first decimal point only, which accounts for certain apparent discrepancies in the totals.

TABLE 10
ENGLAND AND WALES [a, b]
ILLEGITIMATE AND PRE-MARITALLY CONCEIVED LEGITIMATE MATERNITIES
1938-56

YEAR	ILLEGITIMATE MATERNITIES	PRE-MARITALLY CONCEIVED LEGITIMATE MATERNITIES	TOTAL MATERNITIES CONCEIVED OUT OF WEDLOCK		% OF IRREGULARLY CONCEIVED MATERNITIES REGULARIZED BY MARRIAGE OF PARENTS BEFORE BIRTH OF CHILD
			NUMBERS	% OF ALL MATERNITIES	
1	2	3	4	5	6
1938	27,440	64,530	91,970	14.4	70.2
1939	26,569	60,346	86,915	13.8	69.4
1940	26,574	56,644	83,218	13.7	68.1
1941	32,179	43,362	75,541	12.7	57.4
1942	37,597	40,705	78,302	11.8	52.0
1943	44,881	37,271	82,152	11.8	45.4
1944	56,477	37,746	94,223	12.3	40.1
1945	64,743	38,176	102,919	14.9	37.1
1940-5	262,451	253,904	516,355	12.9	49.2
1946	55,138	43,488	98,626	11.8	44.1
1947	47,491	59,633	107,124	12.0	55.7
1948	42,402	62,304	104,706	13.4	59.5
1949	37,554	59,185	96,739	13.1	61.2
1950	35,816	54,188	90,004	12.8	60.2
1946-50	218,401	278,798	497,199	12.6	56.1
1951	33,444	50,477	83,921	12.3	60.1
1952	33,088	50,740[b]	83,828	12.3	60.5
1953	33,083	50,266	83,349	12.1	60.3
1954	32,128	50,901	83,029	12.2	61.3
1955	31,649	50,638	82,287	12.2	61.5
1956	34,113	54,895	89,008	12.6	61.7

[a] Table L, Registrar-General's *Statistical Review of England and Wales*, Text, Civil for the five years 1946-50. Note that 'maternities' not 'births' are referred to, i.e. still births are included and multiple births—twins etc.—are counted as a single maternity.
[b] From 1952 onwards the figures relate only to women married once only and are drawn from Table XI, *Statistical Review*, Part III, Commentary, 1956.

TABLE 11

ENGLAND AND WALES [a, b, e]

THE FIRST-BORN CHILD OF MARRIAGE
1938-57

YEAR	TOTAL NUMBER OF FIRST LEGITIMATE MATERNITIES	NUMBER IN WHICH CHILD WAS CONCEIVED BEFORE MARRIAGE	% OF BRIDES PREGNANT BEFORE MARRIAGE [c]
1938			22.5[d]
1939	254,841	57,895	22.7
1940	255,439	55,612	21.8
1941	247,342	41,645	16.8
1942	284,198	39,213	13.8
1943	294,571	36,433	12.3
1944	287,468	36,905	12.8
1945	252,644	37,287	14.8
1946	331,869	42,579	12.8
1947	380,603	58,558	15.4
1948	314,198	61,050	19.4
1949	285,982	57,914	20.3
1950	261,347	53,374	20.4
1951	251,542	49,774	19.8
1952[e]	247,352	50,090	20.3
1953	251,487	49,564	19.7
1954	248,169	50,160	20.2
1955	247,177	49,952	20.2
1956	263,611	54,140	20.5
1957	272,569	55,497	20.4

a Table QQ, Registrar-General's *Statistical Review of England and Wales*, Part II, Civil for the years 1938-51. The figures have reference to the first legitimate maternity of the present marriage.

b In Scotland the percentage of first births taking place within 8½ months of the date of the present marriage was 20.2 in 1950 and 18.2 in 1954. In 1953, 21 per cent had been married for less than 9 months. There is little difference here from the English figures.

c The phrase 'percentage of brides', although in common currency as a shorthand term, is not strictly accurate, nor is it used by the Registrar-General. One important group is here excluded—women who have no children of their marriage—so the one-in-five proportion is of those who do in fact have children.

d Figures available only for last six months of 1938, when this information first became available.

e Table LL of Part II, Civil for the years 1952-7. The figures for these years have reference only to the first legitimate maternity to women married once only.

TABLE 12
ENGLAND AND WALES [a]

PERCENTAGE OF MATERNITIES IRREGULARLY CONCEIVED AMONG MOTHERS OF DIFFERENT AGES 1950

AGE OF MOTHERS AT MATERNITY	% OF LEGITIMATE MATERNITIES IN WHICH CHILD WAS CONCEIVED BEFORE MARRIAGE	FIRST MATERNITIES % OF ALL FIRST MATERNITIES IN WHICH CHILD WAS IRREGULARLY CONCEIVED	% OF MOTHERS CONCEIVING IRREGULARLY WHO MARRIED BEFORE CHILD'S BIRTH	% IN WHICH CHILD WAS BORN ILLEGITIMATE	ALL MATERNITIES % OF LEGITIMATE MATERNITIES IN WHICH CHILD WAS CONCEIVED BEFORE MARRIAGE	PERCENTAGE CONCEIVED IRREGULARLY
16	1	2[b]	3[b]	4	5	6
17	97	98	47	51	46	98
18	88	91	68	28	60	88
19	76	81	77	17	57	74
20	57	63	77	12	42	54
21	42			9	29	38
22	30			6	20	26
23	21			5	13	18
24	16			4	9	13
Under 20	13			4	6	10
20-24	67	74	73	17	48	65
25-29	24			5	14	19
30 and over	9			4	4	7
All ages	9			4	2	6
	20			5	8	13

[a] Adapted from Tables AA, OO, QQ(a), Registrar-General's *Statistical Review of England and Wales*, Part II, Civil, 1950
[b] Columns 2 and 3 are confined to women aged 16 to 19, since at these ages it is probable that almost all illegitimate children born were first-born children: these columns therefore refer to illegitimate children as well as those pre-maritally conceived.

TABLE 13

ENGLAND AND WALES [a]

AGE DISTRIBUTION OF MOTHERS
1950

AGE OF MOTHERS AT MATERNITY	IRREGULARLY CONCEIVED MATERNITIES			REGULARLY CONCEIVED MATERNITIES	
	% OF CHILDREN ILLEGITIMATE	% OF CHILDREN LEGITIMATE BUT PRE-MARITALLY CONCEIVED	TOGETHER	% OF ALL MATERNITIES	% OF FIRST MATERNITIES OF PRESENT MARRIAGE
	1	2	3	4	5
Under 20	15	28	23	4	9
20–24	29	49	41	27	42
25–29	25	15	19	33	31
30–34	16	5	9	20	12
35–39	11	2	6	12	5
40 and over	4	1	2	4	1
	100	100	100	100	100
Average age	26¾	22	22½	28	25
Peak age	20	20	20	24	22

[a] Adapted from Tables AA, QQ(a), Registrar-General's *Statistical Review of England and Wales*, Part II, Civil, 1950.

TABLE 14
STANDARD REGIONS OF ENGLAND AND WALES [a]
CHILDREN CONCEIVED OUT OF MARRIAGE, 1950

REGION	% OF BRIDES PREGNANT AT MARRIAGE	% OF ALL LIVE-BORN CHILDREN		
		CONCEIVED BEFORE MARRIAGE	BORN ILLEGITIMATE	TOGETHER
	1	2	3	4
North	22.3	8.5	4.2	12.7
East and West Riding	22.8	8.7	5.2	13.9
North-West	23.0	8.7	5.1	13.8
North Midlands	22.9	8.6	5.2	13.8
Midlands	22.5	8.5	4.9	13.4
East	18.9	7.1	5.0	12.1
London and South-East	15.5	6.1	5.4	11.5
South	18.6	7.0	5.6	12.6
South-West	19.2	7.2	5.0	12.2
'North' Wales (see Note b)	25.7	9.6	5.2	14.8
'South' Wales (see Note b)	23.0	8.7	3.6	12.3
ENGLAND AND WALES	20.4	7.6	4.8	12.3

[a] Adapted from Tables RR, PP and p. 10 of E, Registrar-General's *Statistical Review of England and Wales*, Part II, Civil, 1950.
[b] These are the 'Standard Regions' used by the Registrar-General, i.e.:

North: Cumberland, Durham, Northumberland, Westmorland, North Riding.
North-West: Cheshire, Lancashire, part of Derbyshire.
North Midlands: part of Derbyshire, Leicestershire, Lincolnshire, Northants, Nottinghamshire, Soke of Peterborough, Rutland.
Midlands: Herefordshire, Shropshire, Staffordshire, Warwickshire, Worcestershire.
East: Bedfordshire, Cambridgeshire, Ely, Huntingdonshire, Norfolk, Suffolk, part of Essex and of Hertfordshire.
London and South-East: London Admin. County, Middlesex, Surrey, Sussex, Kent, part of Essex and of Hertfordshire.
South: Berkshire, Buckinghamshire, Dorset, Oxfordshire, Hampshire, Isle of Wight.
South-West: Cornwall, Devon, Gloucestershire, Somerset, Wiltshire.
Wales 2 (chiefly North Wales): Anglesey, Caernarvonshire, Cardiganshire, Denbighshire, Flintshire, Merionethshire, Montgomeryshire, Pembrokeshire, Radnorshire.
Wales 1 (most of South Wales): Brecknockshire, Carmarthenshire, Glamorganshire, Monmouthshire.

TABLE 15   ENGLAND

AGES OF ILLEGITIMATE CHILDREN AT

AGE AT ADOPTION	1 BY THE CHILD'S MOTHER c		2 BY THE MOTHER ALONE		3 BY THE MOTHER AND THE NATURAL FATHER, WHOM SHE HAS MARRIED SINCE THE BIRTH		4 BY THE MOTHER AND HER HUSBAND (A MAN OTHER THAN THE NATURAL FATHER)d	
	Number	%	Number	%	Number	%	Number	%
1950								
Under 6 months	19		2		2		15	
6-8 months	14		5		3		6	
9-11 months	29		1		1		27	
Under 1 year	62	2.0	8	13.6	6	5.1	48	1.7
12-17 months	73		3		6		64	
18-23 months	81		4		7		70	
Over 1 year and under 2 years	154	5.0	7	11.9	13	11.1	134	4.6
2 years	176	5.7	3	5.1	10	8.6	163	5.6
3-4 years	879	28.6	13	22.0	29	24.8	837	28.8
5-9 years	1,355	44.0	17	28.8	33	28.2	1,305	45.0
10-14 years	273	8.9	6	10.1	17	14.5	250	8.6
15-20 years	179	5.7	5	8.5	9	7.7	165	5.7
3 or over	2,686	87.3	41	69.4	88	75.3	2,557	88.1
Total all ages	3,078	29.5	59	0.6	117	1.1	2,902	27.8
1957								
Under 6 months								
6-8 months								
9-11 months								
Under 1 year								
Total all ages	3,382	31.0	86	0.8	110	1.0	3,186	29.1

a   Adapted from Tables T4 (1950) and T5 (1957), Registrar-General's *Statistical Review of England and Wales*, Part II, Civil. Each percentage is rounded off to the nearest decimal point, which accounts for the occasional apparent discrepancies in addition.
b   The child must have been placed with the adopter at least 3 months before the ages shown.
c   Age 3 or over, adopted by own mother, 65.1 per cent, i.e. 2,686 (col. 1) out of 4,129 (col. 9).
d   Usually a man she has married since the child's birth. A man to whom she was married at its birth would be regarded in law as its father, even if the woman registered it as another man's, unless her husband took active steps to bastardize it, and it is unlikely that he would then later wish to adopt it.

AND WALES

ADOPTION AND WHO ADOPTED THEM [a, b]

5 BY THE NATURAL FATHER (WITHOUT CHILD'S MOTHER)[e]		6 BY OTHER RELATIVE		7 BY NO RELATIVE [f, g]		8 BY OTHER THAN MOTHER		9 TOTAL	
Number	%	Number	%	Number	%	Number	%	Number	%
				1950					
2		39		1,659	24.3	1,700	23.1	1,719	16.5
2		44		1,932	28.3	1,978	26.9	1,992	19.1
2		27		903	13.2	932	12.6	961	9.2
6	9.2	110	23.7	4,494	65.8	4,610	62.6	4,672	44.8
6		32		636	9.3	674	9.2	747	7.1
2		20		250	3.7	272	3.7	353	3.7
8	12.3	52	11.2	886	13.0[h]	946	12.9	1,100	10.5
7	10.8	35	7.5	322	4.7	346	4.9	540	5.2
13	20.0	82	17.6	437	6.4	532	7.2	1,411	13.5
19	29.1	127	27.3	433	6.3	579	7.9	1,934	18.5
10	15.4	42	9.0	139	2.0	191	2.6	464	4.4
2	3.1	17	3.7	122	1.8	141	1.9	320	3.1
44	67.6	268	57.6	1,131	16.5	1,443	19.6	4,129	39.5
65	0.6	465	4.5	6,833	65.4	7,363	70.5	10,441	100.0
				1957					
								2,295	21.0
								2,337	21.3
								754	6.9
								5,386	49.3
32	0.3	539	4.9	6,960	63.8	7,531	69.0	10,913	100.0

			%
e	By natural father alone	25	0.2
	By natural father and his wife (not child's mother)	40	0.4
	By natural father and his wife (child's mother)	117	1.1
		182	1.7

f Within the meaning of the Adoption Act.
g Under 1 year, by no relative, 96.2 per cent of the illegitimate children that were adopted.
   Under 2 years, by no relative, 93.2 per cent of the illegitimate children that were adopted.
   Under 3 years, by no relative, 90.3 per cent of the illegitimate children that were adopted.
h Under 2 years, 78.8 per cent.

INDEX

Abbott, Grace, 236-7, 315, 356
Aberdeen, 62, 64, 83-4, 89
Abortion, 11, 36, 82, 98, 105-6, 107, 343, 346, 353
Adoption. *See under* Children
Affiliation, 11, 49, 114, 115, 122, 126-56, 161, 165, 180, 186, 359
    Act (1952), 128, 140, 141, 359
    Proceedings Act (1957), 133, 359
    State guarantees, 148-50, 161
Alberta, 130, 135
Algeria, 34, 37
Allowances, 124, 128, 139, 151, 157-75, 286, 289, 290, 293, 328
    boarding-out (foster fees), 139, 204-5, 279, 286, 289, 290, 293
    child's special, 165
    family, 151, 158, 159-63, 168, 328
    guardian's, 164-5, 293
    maternity, 158-9
    See also Grants; National Assistance
Anglesey, 44
Anthropological tests, 138, 331
Argentina, 34, 37
Australia, 22, 34, 77
Austria, 21, 37, 38, 124, 137, 138, 155, 284, 339

Barbados, 34
Barnardo's Homes, Dr, 205, 206, 209, 217, 263, 264, 278, 279, 283, 290.
Bastardy Act (1845), 180, 235, 359
    Laws Amendment Acts (1872 and 1873), 11, 135, 180, 235, 359
    Act (1923), 180, 359
Bavaria, 38
Bedfordshire, 42
Belgium, 21, 38, 45
Benefits. *See* Allowances
Bermuda, 34
Beveridge, Lord, 158, 160, 168, 169, 353

Bexley, 47
Binder, Prof. Hans, 8, 56, 77, 93, 98-108, 358
Birmingham, 44, 47, 69, 179, 204, 278, 280, 283, 296
Birth certificates, 76, 181, 221, 270, 271, 328-9
    control, 23, 29, 36, 39, 41, 59, 82, 96, 235, 347-51
    registration, 31, 35-7, 44, 59, 66, 76, 181, 271
Births and Deaths Registration Act (1955), 181, 359
Blood tests, 137-8, 331
Bolivia, 34
Bolton, Mrs Frances, 29
Bournemouth, 47, 282, 294
Bowlby, Dr John, 13, 95, 108, 238, 257, 261-2, 263, 269, 270, 282, 353
Bradford, 48, 297
Brandon, M. W. G., 274, 353
Brighton, 47, 281
Brill, Kenneth, 8, 287
British Columbia, 135
British Journal of Social and Preventive Medicine, 62
British Medical Association, 130-1, 135, 138, 152, 253, 353
British Medical Journal, 137
Brittany, 41
Brussels, 45
Budapest, 45
Bulgaria, 38, 43, 329
Burt, Cyril, 296, 353
Butler, Josephine, 176, 183, 237
    Memorial House, 183-4
Buttle Trust, 207

Canada, 22, 34, 35, 95, 124, 135, 136, 140, 152, 301-9
Cardiff, 41, 44, 45, 47, 297
Cardiganshire, 280
Carmarthenshire, 280
Carnegie United Kingdom Trust, 297
Carr-Saunders, A. M., 296, 353

Case-work, 52, 92-4, 120, 156, 177, 178, 181-2, 183, 184-9, 190, 201, 202, 208-10, 242, 247, 257, 270, 276, 296, 306, 307, 336, 340, 350-1
Castberg, Johan, 122, 176, 317-22, 357
Chesser, Dr Eustace, 128, 353
Child Guidance Clinics, 12, 292, 298-301

CHILDREN

accident rate, 247
adoption, 36, 40, 63, 75, 79, 92, 93, 106, 107, 114, 116, 117, 118, 127-8, 165, 179, 185, 186, 207, 214, 224, 225, 229, 238, 241-2, 243, 245, 249, 262, 265-73, 276, 282, 283, 284, 285, 289, 292, 293, 294
after-care, 197-8, 201, 207-10, 307-9
boarded out. See Allowances, boarding out; foster homes
coloured, 211-19, 273, 282
custody, 11, 253-4, 257
death in infancy, 12, 35, 123, 243, 245, 246-7, 282
delinquency, 12, 260, 287, 289, 291-2, 296-8, 299, 302
development, 12, 91, 93, 209, 239, 249, 277, 295-309, 352
education and schooling, 113, 139, 159, 163, 164, 166, 167, 205, 207, 219, 270, 316
first-born, 73-5, 76-8, 159, 160, 246-7, 288
in foster-homes, 93, 106, 118, 157, 198-9, 204-5, 245, 259, 260-1, 262-4, 271, 275, 279, 284, 286, 288, 291, 292, 293
follow-up research, 12-13, 51, 53, 189, 243-309
guardianship, 98, 164-5, 253, 265, 293, 323, 331-2, 333-40
health and welfare, 12, 64, 119, 123, 157, 163, 164, 236, 237, 246, 274, 285
home environment, 12, 91, 93, 244-6, 248-9, 256-64, 265-7, 277, 279, 282, 285, 287, 295-6, 301, 306-7
infanticide, 35, 234, 235, 237

inheritance. See under ILLEGITIMACY
legitimation, 30-1, 65-7, 79-80, 81, 248, 249, 254, 271
living with parents cohabiting without marriage, 11, 36, 67-72, 74, 91, 126, 185, 239-40, 244-5, 249-53, 282, 288, 306, 351
living with solitary mothers, 68, 72-3, 106, 113-229, 237-9, 245, 258-62, 294
maintenance, 11, 122-56, 159, 163, 165, 167, 235-6, 252, 316, 317-32
maladjustment, 12, 257, 284, 298-301, 302-3, 307
mental defectives, 274-6, 279
of mental defectives, 62-3, 273-6, 288, 308
premature births, 123, 246
in problem families, 240, 285, 288, 290, 291
in public care, 12, 243, 252, 277-94
social policies, influence of, 11, 169, 233-42
status, 11, 122, 236-7, 248, 313-23, 327-32
Children Act (1948), 277, 360
Children's Departments, 12, 13, 204, 244, 263, 266, 272, 277, 278, 279, 282, 283, 284, 286, 287, 292
Chile, 34
Christianity. See Religion
Church Army, 207, 228
Church of England, 237, 239
  Children's Society, 205, 206, 263, 264, 278, 292
  Moral Welfare Associations. See Moral Welfare Associations
  Moral Welfare Council, 6, 115, 183, 200, 269, 273, 355
Church of Scotland, 87
Clinical studies, 274, 298-301
Code Napoleon, 314, 318
Cohabitation without marriage (unofficial families), 11, 36, 67-72, 74, 86, 91, 92, 97, 106, 126, 159, 185, 239-40, 244-5, 282, 288, 351
Colombia, 34

INDEX

Coloured children, 211-19, 273, 282
  fathers, 29, 147, 211, 273, 282
  mothers, 273
Columbia, U.S.A., 130
Conception. *See under* Mothers
Contraceptives, 36, 37, 39, 41, 59, 87, 96, 343, 347, 348-9
Cooper, Dr Christine, 251, 255, 259, 352
Copenhagen, 8, 45, 119, 203, 336, 338
Cornwall, 42, 43, 44
Costa Rica, 34
Courts, juvenile, 12, 130, 135, 277
  magistrates', 122, 126, 129-31, 134, 140-8, 254, 266, 267
'Cover-up' marriages. *See* Marriages
Crew, Prof. F. A. E., 23, 78, 347, 353
Crossroads Club, 193
Crusade of Rescue, 40
Cumberland, 40, 41, 42, 43, 44
Curtis report (1945), 282
Czechoslovakia, 34, 150, 151, 330

Dahl, Jørgen, 8
Daily minders, 113, 118, 172-3, 199
Danzig, 137, 139
Day nurseries. *See* Nurseries
Defectives, mental, 62-3, 100-2, 105, 189, 273-6, 279, 288, 289, 308
  moral, 104, 189, 192
Delinquency, juvenile, 12, 49, 64, 88, 260, 287, 289, 291-2, 296-8, 299, 302
Denmark, 8, 21, 42, 45, 118-20, 125, 129, 132, 136, 137, 139, 148, 151, 154, 160, 202-3, 284, 323, 335, 336-8
Deutsch, Helena, 238, 348, 353
Devon, 42, 43, 44, 273, 275-6, 278, 287-94
  Children's Committee, 8, 62, 273, 284-5, 287, 353
Divorce, 29-30, 42, 65, 68, 71, 79, 82, 101, 239-41, 247, 344, 346-7
Dr Barnardo's Homes. *See* Barnardo's Homes, Dr
Donnison, David, 285, 353

Dublin, 45
Durham, Co., 42, 43, 44, 80-1

Ecuador, 34
Edinburgh, 45
Education. *See under* CHILDREN; MOTHERS
Eire, 21, 37, 38-40, 41, 42, 43, 45, 287
Ellison, Mary, 266, 354

Fairfield, Dr Letitia, 8, 200
Family allowances. *See under* Allowances
  Planning Association, 77
  Service Units, 190, 202
FATHERS, 29-31, 34, 51-75, 79, 103-6, 108-9, 113, 115, 122-56, 165, 182, 188, 194, 211, 239-40, 247-8, 249-50, 253-4, 258, 271, 272, 274, 276, 282, 290, 291, 299, 301, 302, 305, 308, 313-32, 338, 339
  ages, 55
  from broken homes, 65
  child's claim on estate, 122, 151-2, 165, 314-23, 327, 330, 332
  coloured, 29, 147, 211, 273, 282
  earnings, 143-5; attachment of, 148, 153
  home environment, 61, 108, 188
  living abroad, 152-6, 182
  mental defectives, 105, 274
  paternity, acknowledgment of, 126-31, 321; establishment of, 314, 318-27, 331, 338, 339; proof of, 135-8
  psychology, 108-9
  servicemen, 29-31, 34, 61, 108, 144, 153, 154, 282, 291, 326
  social class, 60, 69-71, 72, 105
  status, civil, 65, 66; occupational, 60-2, 69-71, 276
  teen-agers, 55, 67, 272
Fenton, Dr John, 261
Fine, Benjamin, 88
Finland, 21, 43, 139, 154, 283, 284, 336, 338
Fisher, E. M., 87, 89, 355
  Lettice (Mrs H. A. L.), 183, 204, 354
Fitzgerald, Hilde, 24, 354
Flatlets, 201-2, 338

Follow-up surveys, 12-13, 51, 53, 243-309
Forced marriages. *See under* Marriages
Foster fees. *See* Allowances, boarding-out
  grants by voluntary societies, 205-7
  homes and parents, 106, 118, 139, 179, 186, 198-9, 204, 245, 259, 260-1, 262-4, 271, 286, 287, 288, 291, 292, 293
Fountain Hospital, Tooting, 274
France, 21, 42, 45, 155, 160, 313, 314-15
Frazer, W. M., 237, 354
Freeman, T. W., 42, 354

Gardiner, Dr Anna G., 259, 354
Germany, 24, 29, 103, 137, 153, 333
  Eastern, 138, 330-2, 335
  Western, 21, 22, 24, 29, 77, 124, 132, 155, 284, 331, 333-5
Glamorganshire, 280
Glass, Prof. D. V., 6
Glossop, 291
Gloucestershire, 280
Gorell, Lord, 207
Gorer, Geoffrey, 87, 354
Grandparents of illegitimate children, 82, 93, 94, 115, 116, 159, 164, 172, 178-9, 187-8, 192, 238, 245, 246, 254-8, 263-4, 270, 271, 285, 293, 296, 300, 305, 306,
Granger, Isabelle, 8, 211
Grants, home confinement, 158
  maternity, 158, 160
  by voluntary societies, 182, 198, 203-4, 205-7
Greece, 21, 24, 38
Greenland, Cyril, 8, 39, 61, 109, 174, 354
Guardianship, 98, 164-5, 253, 265, 293, 323, 331-2, 333-40
  allowance, 164-5, 293
Guatemala, 34
Guildford, 176

Hajnal, J., 82-3, 354
Harms, Irene, 276, 357
Hastings, 47, 282

Hawaii, 34
Herbert, Sir Alan P., 240
Herefordshire, 40, 42, 43, 44, 291
Hill, Matthew Davenport, 296
Holland. *See* Netherlands
Home Office, 182, 183, 190, 244, 354
Homes, Children's, 164, 264, 275, 278-9, 283-4, 290, 291, 292
  Mother and Baby, 6, 8, 52, 58-9, 92, 114, 159, 174, 176, 177, 180, 184, 186, 188, 190-7, 211-15, 217, 224-5, 241, 254, 260, 268, 273
Hopkin, W. A. B., 82-3, 354
Hopkirk, Mary, 22, 234, 354
Hostels for unmarried mothers, 8, 114-15, 116, 162, 176, 177, 179, 180, 184, 190, 197, 200-1, 214-18
Hughes, Valerie, 6, 51, 53, 114, 115, 128, 251
Hull, 47, 297
Hungary, 43, 45
Huntingdonshire, 44

Iceland, 21, 36, 38, 149, 154
ILLEGITIMACY
  Acts of Parliament, 359-60. *Reference in text as follows:* Affiliation Act (1952), 128, 140, 141; Affiliation Proceedings Act (1957) 133; Bastardy Act (1845), 180, 235; Bastardy Laws Amendment Acts (1872 and 1873), 11, 133, 180, 235; Bastardy Act (1923), 180; Births and Deaths Registration Act (1955), 181; Children Act (1948), 277; Legitimacy Act (1926), 31, 248; Legitimacy Act (1959), 129, 133, 134, 135, 248, 254, 271; Maintenance Orders Act (1958), 148; Nursery and Child-Minders Regulation Act (1948), 199; Poor Law (codified in the statute of 1601), 233-5; Visiting Services Act (1954), 153
  factors influencing, 22-4, 29, 30, 31, 37-50, 81, 343
  incidence, 21-50

INDEX

inheritance, 12, 122, 151-2, 165, 236, 248; in other countries, 313-23
legislation, 8, 11, 12, 122, 130, 180, 233-7, 240-1, 254; in other countries, 313-32
rates, 21-50, 343-52
social acceptance, 36, 95, 256, 285; customs, 36, 37-8, 49, 81, 103, 185, 239, 273; policies, 11, 169, 233-42, 260, 313, 344-5, 352; restraints, 23, 24, 88-90, 96, 239
in wartime, 22-4, 28, 29, 30-2, 34, 177, 273, 326, 348
Illsley, Dr R., 89
Infanticide. *See under* Children
Iowa, 276
Ireland. *See* Eire
  Northern, 21, 38-9, 287
Israel, 24
Italy, 21, 37, 38, 45, 155, 235, 315

Jamaica, 34, 37-8
Japan, 29, 34
Jordan, G. W., 87, 89, 355
Journal of Genetic Psychology, 276
Journal of Medical Science, 274
Joy, Celia M., 55, 355
Jugoslavia, 35, 161, 330
Juvenile delinquency. *See* Delinquency

Kent, 41, 259, 263
Kilmarnock, 69
King, Beatrice, 326, 359
Kinsey, Prof. A. C., 39, 356
Kornitzer, Margaret, 8, 266, 269, 355

Lancashire, 43, 44
Lancet, 39, 61, 99, 102, 174
Lavers, G. R., 81-2, 356
Law. *See* ILLEGITIMACY, legislation
League of Nations, 120-1, 139, 359
  Advisory Committee on Social Questions, 120, 359
  Child Welfare Committee, 334, 359
Leeds, 47, 297
Legislation. *See under* ILLEGITIMACY

Legitimacy Act (1926), 31, 248, 360
  Act (1959), 129, 133, 134, 135, 248, 254, 271, 360
Leicester, 48, 281, 283
Lincoln, 297
Listener, 88
Lithuania, 137
Liverpool, 39-40, 44, 46, 47, 184, 277-8, 281
Local Authorities, 176-210. *See also under such headings as:* Allowances; Case-work; Child Guidance Clinics; Children; Children's Departments; Clinical studies; Follow-up surveys; Grants; Guardianship; Homes; Hostels; Maternity and Child Welfare Departments; Nurseries; Part III accommodation; Welfare Services Department
London, 37, 39-40, 41, 44, 45, 46, 47, 48, 49, 75, 252, 273, 278, 281, 282, 284, 285-7, 296, 297
  County Council, 191, 228, 252, 284, 285-7

Macdonald, Dr E. K., 8, 355
MacDonald, James Ramsay, 11
Mackenzie, Prof. W. J. M., 7
Magistrates' Association, 130-1, 135, 138, 152, 253, 353
Maintenance Orders Act (1958), 148, 360
Manchester, 7, 44, 47, 51, 58, 68, 75, 243, 247, 255, 258, 264-5, 297
Manchester Guardian, 29, 77, 173
Manitoba, 130
Mann, Mrs J., M.P., 79
Mannheim, Hermann, 296, 297, 353, 355
Maps, 25, 26, 27, 31, 32, 33
Margaret Club and Day Nursery Fund, 207
Marriages, 'cover-up', 39, 67, 78, 82, 188, 239, 248, 343
  forced, 79, 106, 188, 235, 239, 345
Maternity and Child Welfare Departments, 52, 53, 180, 185, 188-9, 199, 204, 208

INDEX

Matrimonial Proceedings (Magistrates' Courts) Bill, 134
Means tests, 149, 152, 160, 161, 169, 173, 206
Medical Officer, 53, 244
Mental defectives. *See* Defectives
Mental Deficiency Committee. *See* Wood report
Merionethshire, 44
Merthyr Tydfil, 48, 281
Methodist Church, 83, 183, 193
Methven, Dr M. M., 260
Mexico, 34
'Midboro', 6, 51-75, 91, 117, 126, 128, 185, 243-5, 247, 249, 250, 252, 259, 262, 264, 271, 295, 345-6
Middlesex, 41
Mill, John Stuart, 235
MINISTRY OF
  Education, 227, 277
  Health, 177, 180, 191, 204, 209, 237, 255, 261, 277, 279, 354; Circular No. 2866, 177, 204, 237, 255
  Labour, 201
  Pensions and National Insurance, 124, 158
Minnesota, 284
Mitchell, George, 8
Mohammedans, 34, 37
Monmouthshire, 40
Montgomeryshire, 80
Moral Welfare Associations, 13, 52, 53, 54, 92, 115, 178, 179, 182, 183-8, 189, 190, 192-8, 205, 208, 212, 223, 237, 239, 247, 249, 264, 296, 351
Morlock, Maud, 129, 147, 356
Morris, Cherry, 188, 355
Moscow, 45
Mother and Baby Homes. *See* HOMES
MOTHERS
  ages, 41-3, 53-4, 77-9
  from broken homes, 64-5, 93, 94, 104, 238, 302
  coloured, 273
  conception, extra-marital, 11, 30-1, 35, 36, 39, 76, 81, 96-7, 236, 343; pre-marital, 11, 36, 49, 65, 76-84, 86, 196, 236
  domestic service, 58, 115, 116, 117-18, 162, 167, 199, 202-3, 205, 218-19, 225-7
  earnings and earning power, 30, 114-20, 143-5, 163-4, 201, 272, 283, 294
  education, 37, 40-1, 57, 72, 236
  employment, 57-60, 114-18, 123-4, 172, 186, 198, 201, 261, 263, 276; part-time work, 120, 166, 167-8, 173
  fertility, 36, 76, 82, 83
  foreign, 182-3
  health, 113, 119, 123, 157, 163-4, 246, 294, 298,
  home environment, 37, 39, 59, 64-5, 90-1, 93, 95, 101-2, 159, 174, 187-8, 256, 272, 287, 296, 351
  mental defectives, 62-3, 100-2, 189, 273-6, 279, 288, 289, 308
  mental level and stability, 62-4, 100-4, 105-8, 236, 273-6, 288, 291, 294, 302-3, 308
  moral defectives, 104, 189, 192
  neurosis. *See* Psychology
  occupation. *See* employment *above*
  parents of. *See* Grandparents of illegitimate children
  poverty, 37-8, 40, 100, 246, 293
  pregnancy, 11, 30, 40, 79-80, 81, 105-8, 113, 123, 124, 125, 165, 182-3, 184, 189, 193, 196, 298, 316
  promiscuity, 56, 102, 104, 108, 159, 171, 288, 290, 296
  prostitution, 45, 56, 92, 114, 120-1, 185-6
  rehabilitation, 190, 192, 202
  Roman Catholics, 38-40, 59, 185, 189, 191, 197, 271, 350
  social class, 56-7, 99, 100
  suicide, attempted, 105, 107
  teen-agers, 54, 67, 78-9, 106, 115-17, 272, 289
  vocational training, 119-20, 190, 194, 202-4, 338
Myrdal, Alva, 23, 42, 136, 150, 348, 358

National Assistance, 124, 128, 131, 133, 141, 157, 168-75, 186, 190, 198, 206, 212

INDEX

Children's Home and Orphanage, 206, 264
Council for the Unmarried Mother and Her Child (N.C.U.M.C.), 6, 7, 54, 130-1, 134, 138, 140, 147, 150, 154, 176, 180-3, 185, 195, 198, 201, 203-4, 206, 207, 209, 223, 237, 238, 253, 269, 273, 355
Insurance, 113, 124, 157-68, 180
Society for the Prevention of Cruelty to Children, 289, 290
Nelson, George R., 162, 357
Netherlands, 21, 37, 38, 43, 315, 343
Neue Justiz, 8, 331, 358
Newcastle-upon-Tyne, 47, 48, 69, 244, 245-6, 247, 250, 254, 258, 295, 296
Newport, Mon., 48, 281
New Zealand, 22, 34, 77
Nicaragua, 34
Nilsson, Nils, 77
Nisbet, Dr Bryce R., 69
Norfolk, 40, 41, 42, 43, 44
Norway, 8, 21, 125, 129, 132, 136, 137, 138, 139, 149, 154, 162-3, 313, 315-24, 339-40
Nottingham, 48, 281, 283, 297
Nottinghamshire, 40
Nurseries, day, 113, 114, 115, 157, 163, 167, 172-3, 179, 199, 200, 201, 259, 260
residential, 116, 117, 179, 199, 228, 259, 260, 292
Nursery and Child-Minders Regulation Act (1948), 199, 360

Odlum, Dr Doris, 261
Ontario, 124-5, 130, 140, 152
Oslo, 8, 339
Oxford, 48, 281

Panama, 35
Paraguay, 35, 37
Paris, 41, 45
Part III accommodation, 190, 191, 290, 291
Peebles, 89
Penrose, Prof. Lionel, 274
Peru, 35, 37
Peterborough, Soke of, 44, 280

Pinchbeck, Dr Ivy, 11, 236, 283, 355
Poland, 125, 330
Political and Economic Planning (P.E.P.), 195, 355
Poor Law. *See under* ILLEGITIMACY, Acts of Parliament
Population Investigation Committee, 39, 75, 160, 355
Portsmouth, 47, 297
Portugal, 21, 38, 315
Practitioner, 255
Problem families, 61, 62, 64, 174-5, 240, 285, 288, 290, 291, 293, 294
Prostitution, 45, 56, 92, 114, 120-1, 185-6
Psychology, 91-109, 238-9, 298-309
Puxley, Zöe, 8

Race, R. R., 138, 355
Radnorshire, 280
Rees, Alwyn D., 80-1, 355
Reeve, Barbara, 186, 237, 355
Religion, 11, 37-40, 81, 86, 87, 184, 188, 194-5, 196, 197, 212, 216, 235, 239, 343-4
Rhodes, E. C., 296, 353
Rodgers, Barbara, 7
Roman Catholic Church, 183, 185, 189, 193, 350
Roman Catholics, 38-40, 59, 183, 185, 189, 191, 194-5, 197, 271, 350
Rome, 45
Rotherham, 291
Rowntree, B. S., 81-2, 356
Royal College of Obstetricians and Gynaecologists, 75, 355
Commission on Population, 160, 162, 355
Rumania, 329
Russia. *See* U.S.S.R.
Ryerson, Rev. Egerton, 6

St. Vincent, Windward Is., 35
Salvador, 35
Salvation Army, 184, 193, 227
Sanger, R., 138, 355
Saskatchewan, 135
Saxony, 77

Scandinavia. *See* Denmark; Finland; Norway; Sweden
Schapiro, L., 8
Schlesinger, Rudolf, 8, 325, 328, 359
Scotland, 21, 38, 43, 45, 61-2, 76, 78, 81, 84, 131, 148, 235, 246, 265, 325
Scottish Daily Express, 273
Scottish Marriage Guidance Council, 89
Scottish N.C.U.M.C., 69, 353
Servicemen. *See under* Fathers
Shapiro, Sam, 54, 357
Sheffield, 47, 297
Shropshire, 40, 41, 42, 43, 44
Skeels, Harold M., 276, 357
Social customs and policies. *See under* ILLEGITIMACY
Somerset, 280
South Africa, Union of, 22, 34, 139
Spain, 21, 24, 38, 315
Spence, Sir James, 69, 244, 356
Staffordshire, 42
Stallybrass, C. O., 237, 354
Steel, Ena, 6, 186, 195, 206, 237, 355
Sterilization, 274, 291
   Departmental Committee on, 274, 356
Stevenson, A. C., 75, 356
Stockholm, 45, 201, 336
Stott, Dr D. H., 8, 93, 297-8, 356
Suffolk, 22, 43, 44
Sunday Times, 169
Surrey, 41
Sussex, 44
Sutherland, Dr Halliday, 40, 356
Sweden, 8, 21, 23, 36, 37, 38, 42, 45, 77, 125, 129, 132, 136, 137, 149, 151, 154, 160-2, 174, 201, 240-1, 283, 284, 323, 335-6, 347-8
Switzerland, 21, 22, 56, 93, 98-108, 124, 137, 284, 339

Tables, 21, 22, 34-5, 43, 44, 45, 46, 47, 48-9, 54, 55, 56, 57, 58, 60, 61, 65, 66, 68, 70, 73, 74, 78, 79, 100, 101, 106, 141, 144, 145, 186, 245, 246, 251, 280-1, 286, 289, 362-87

Taylor, Dr Dorothy, 237, 261
Teen-agers, 54-5, 58, 67, 77-9, 89-90, 106-7, 115-17, 170, 196, 213, 215, 219, 272, 288, 289
Thompson, Barbara, 62, 64-5, 83, 356
Titmuss, Prof. R. M., 7
Toronto, 120, 241, 257, 261, 301-9, 357
Trinidad and Tobago, 35
United Nations, 154-5, 359
   States of America, 22, 34, 39, 42-3, 54, 94-5, 129, 132, 147, 156, 205, 238, 308
Unofficial families. *See* Cohabitation without marriage
U.S.S.R., 29, 45, 136, 313, 324-9

Venereal Disease, 56, 108
Venezuela, 35
Vienna, 45
Visiting Services Act (1954), 153, 360
Voluntary societies, 51, 173, 176, 177, 178, 179, 180-8, 189, 190, 192-8, 200, 205-9, 263, 264-5. *See also under such headings as:* Barnardo's Homes, Dr; Buttle Trust; Church Army; Church of England Children's Society; Church of England Moral Welfare Council; Homes; Hostels; Moral Welfare Associations; National Council for the Unmarried Mother and Her Child; Salvation Army

Waifs and Strays. *See* Church of England Children's Society
Wales, 22, 40, 42, 44, 45, 80-1. *Other references, where included with England, are not indexed*
Walters, M., 8
War. *See* ILLEGITIMACY in wartime; World War I; World War II
Watson, Barbara, 6-7
Weinzierl, Egon, 103, 105, 358
Welfare Services Department, 190
West Indies, 37, 273, 345
Westmorland, 40, 42, 43, 44
Wigan, 45-6
Wilkinson, G. S., 7, 356

Willesden, 48, 263, 356
Wiltshire, 280
Windward Is., 35
Winner, Dr Albertine, 8, 201-2
Wittkower, E. D., 108, 356
Wollmer, Mrs Elsa, 8
Women's Group on Public Welfare, 291, 356
Wood report (1929) 62, 355
Woodforde, James, 235

World Health Organization, 13
World War I, 23, 24, 29, 313, 348
   II, 12, 22, 24, 29, 30, 31, 32, 177, 178, 273, 313, 326

Yorkshire, 80, 83
Young, Dr Leontine, 94-6, 102, 256, 308, 357
Yugoslavia. *See* Jugoslavia

For Product Safety Concerns and Information please contact our EU representative GPSR@taylorandfrancis.com
Taylor & Francis Verlag GmbH, Kaufingerstraße 24, 80331 München, Germany

www.ingramcontent.com/pod-product-compliance
Lightning Source LLC
Chambersburg PA
CBHW071231290426
44108CB00013B/1367